David Sang and Graham Jones

Cambridge International AS and A Level

Physics

Workbook

CAMBRIDGE
UNIVERSITY PRESS

University Printing House, Cambridge CB2 8BS, United Kingdom

One Liberty Plaza, 20th Floor, New York, NY 10006, USA

477 Williamstown Road, Port Melbourne, VIC 3207, Australia

4843/24, 2nd Floor, Ansari Road, Daryaganj, Delhi – 110002, India

79 Anson Road, #06–04/06, Singapore 079906

Cambridge University Press is part of the University of Cambridge.

It furthers the University's mission by disseminating knowledge in the pursuit of education, learning and research at the highest international levels of excellence.

Information on this title: www.cambridge.org/9781107589483

First published 2016

20 19 18 17 16 15 14 13 12 11 10 9 8 7 6 5 4 3 2 1

Printed in Spain by GraphyCems

A catalogue record for this publication is available from the British Library

ISBN 978-1-107-58948-3 Paperback

Additional resources for this publication at www.cambridge.org/education

How to use this book

A **Chapter outline** appears at the start of every chapter to set the scene and to help with navigation through the book

Chapter outline

- define and use distance, displacement, speed and velocity
- describe laboratory methods for determining speed
- draw and interpret displacement–time graphs
- distinguish between scalar and vector quantities, and give examples
- add and subtract vector quantities

A list of **Key terms** are defined and explained clearly at the start of each topic

KEY TERMS

resultant force: the single force acting on a body that has the same effect as the sum of all the forces acting on it

Equations: force = mass × acceleration; $F = ma$

weight = mass × gravitational field strength; $W = mg$

Each **Exercise** in every chapter helps students to practise the necessary skills for studying Chemistry at AS and A Level

Exercise 3.3 Force, mass and acceleration

Force, mass and acceleration are linked by the equation $F = ma$. In this equation, F represents the resultant force acting on mass m. This exercise gives you practice using and rearranging this equation.

1 a A truck of mass 40 000 kg accelerates at 1.20 m s^{-2}.

Calculate the resultant force acting on the truck. Give your answer in kilonewtons (kN).

b Calculate the acceleration of a ball of mass 2.8 kg when a force of 48 N acts on it.

c A spacecraft accelerates at 0.40 m s^{-2} when a force of 200 N acts on it. Calculate the mass of the spacecraft.

TIP

You may find it simplest to calculate the car's average speed.

Detailed **Learning support** is provided throughout to help students to tackle the different exercises and build confidence to answer questions independently.

Exam-style questions allow students to thoroughly prepare for examinations and check answers which are provided on the CD-ROM at the back of the book.

Exam-style questions

1 A bullet of mass 25 g is travelling at 450 m s^{-1} when it strikes the armour plating of a tank. It bounces back along the same path with a speed of 390 m s^{-1}.

a Calculate the change in momentum of the bullet.

b The time of impact of the bullet on the tank is 0.040 s. Calculate the average force that acts on the bullet in this time.

c State whether the impact is elastic or inelastic.

d Discuss how the principles of conservation of energy and momentum apply to this collision.

Contents

Chapter outline

- define and use distance, displacement, speed and velocity
- describe laboratory methods for determining speed
- draw and interpret displacement–time graphs
- distinguish between scalar and vector quantities, and give examples
- add and subtract vector quantities

KEY TERMS

displacement: the distance travelled in a particular direction

scalar: a quantity with magnitude only

vector: a quantity with both magnitude and direction

Equations: $\text{average speed} = \frac{\text{distance travelled}}{\text{time taken}}$

$\text{average speed} = \frac{\Delta d}{\Delta t}$

$\text{velocity} = \frac{\text{change in displacement}}{\text{time taken}}$

$\text{velocity} = \frac{\Delta s}{\Delta t}$

Exercise 1.1 Speed calculations

These questions will help you to revise calculations involving speed, distance and time. You will also practise converting units. The SI unit of time is the second (s). It is usually best to work in seconds and convert to minutes or hours as the last step in a calculation. The correct scientific notation for metres per second is m s^{-1}.

1 A train travels 4000 m in 125 s. Calculate its average speed.

2 A spacecraft is orbiting the Earth with a constant speed of 8100 m s^{-1}. The radius of its orbit is 6750 km.

- **a** Explain what is meant by the term *constant speed*.
- **b** Calculate how far it will travel in 1.0 hour.
- **c** Calculate how long it will take to complete one orbit of the Earth. Give your answer in minutes.

3 A police patrol driver sees a car that seems to be travelling too fast on a motorway (freeway). He times the car over a distance of 3.0 km. The car takes 96 s to travel this distance.

- **a** The speed limit on the motorway is 120 km h^{-1}. Calculate the distance a car would travel at 120 km h^{-1} in one minute.
- **b** Calculate the distance a car would travel at 120 km h^{-1} in 1 s.
- **c** Calculate the average speed of the car, in m s^{-1}.
- **d** Compare the car's actual speed with the speed limit. Was the car travelling above or below the speed limit?

4 It is useful to be able to compare the speeds of different objects. To do this, the speeds must all be given in the same units.

a Calculate the speed, in $m\ s^{-1}$, of the objects in each scenario, i-vi. Give your answers in standard form (also known as *scientific notation*), with one figure before the decimal point.

i Light travels at 300 000 000 $m\ s^{-1}$ in empty space.

ii A spacecraft travelling to the Moon moves at 11 $km\ s^{-1}$.

iii An athlete runs 100 m in 10.41 s.

iv An alpha-particle travels 5.0 cm in 0.043×10^{-6} s.

v The Earth's speed in its orbit around the Sun is 107 000 $km\ h^{-1}$.

vi A truck travels 150 km along a motorway in 1.75 h.

b List the objects in order, from slowest to fastest.

Exercise 1.2 Measuring speed in the laboratory

You can measure the speed of a moving trolley in the laboratory using a ruler and a stopwatch. However, you are likely to get better results using light gates and an electronic timer. In this exercise, you will compare data from these different methods and practise analysing it.

1 A student used a stopwatch to measure the time taken by a trolley to travel a measured distance of 1.0 m.

a Explain why it can be difficult to obtain an accurate measurement of time in this way.

b Explain why the problem is more likely to be greater if the trolley is moving more quickly.

2 This diagram shows how the speed of a trolley can be measured using two light gates connected to an electronic timer. An interrupt card is fixed to the trolley:

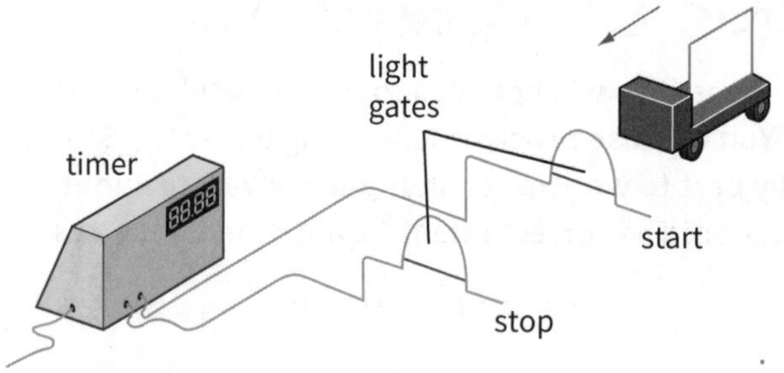

a Describe what happens as the trolley passes through the light gates.

b Name the quantity shown on the timer.

c What other measurement must be made to determine the trolley's speed? Describe how you would make this measurement.

d Explain how you would calculate the trolley's speed from these measurements.

e Explain why this method gives the trolley's *average* speed.

3 It is possible to determine the average speed of a trolley using a single light gate.

a Draw a diagram to show how you would do this.

b Describe what happens as the trolley passes through the light gate.

c Explain how you would find the trolley's average speed using this arrangement.

TIP

When using ticker-tape timers, think about whether to count the dots or the spaces between the dots.

4 A ticker-timer can also be used to record the movement of a trolley. The ticker-timer makes marks (dots) on paper tape at equal intervals of time.

a Sketch the pattern of dots you would expect to see for a trolley travelling at constant speed.

b A ticker-timer makes 50 dots each second on a paper tape. State the time interval between consecutive dots.

c A student measures a section of tape. The distance from the first dot to the sixth dot is 12 cm. Calculate the trolley's average speed in this time interval. Give your answer in m s^{-1}.

Exercise 1.3 Displacement–time graphs

A displacement–time graph is used to represent an object's motion. The gradient of the graph is the object's velocity. These questions provide practice in drawing, interpreting and using data from displacement–time graphs.

1 Velocity is defined by the equation:

$$\text{velocity} = \frac{\Delta s}{\Delta t}$$

a State what the symbols *s* and *t* stand for.

b State what the symbols Δs and Δt stand for.

c Sketch a straight-line displacement–time graph and indicate how you would find Δs and Δt from this graph. Remember to label your graph axes with the correct quantities.

2 This sketch graph represents the motion of a car:

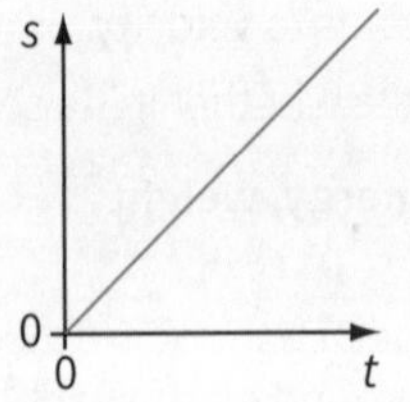

a Explain how you can tell that the car was moving with constant velocity.

b Copy the sketch graph and add a second line to the graph representing the motion of a car moving with a higher constant velocity. Label this 'faster'.

c On your graph, add a third line representing the motion of a car which is stationary. Label this 'stationary'.

3 This graph represents the motion of a runner in a race along a long, straight road:

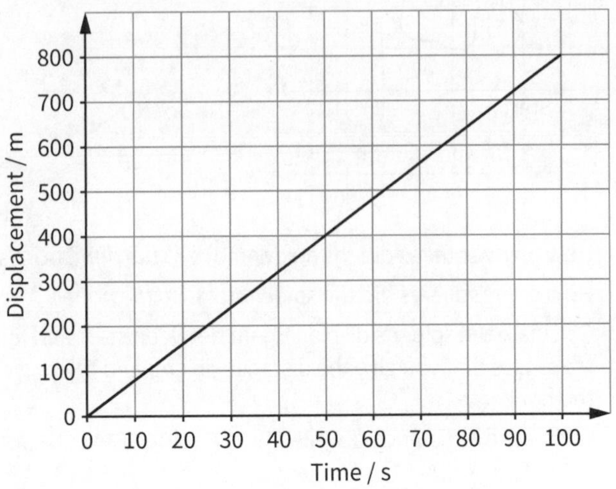

Use the graph to deduce:

- **a** the displacement of the runner after 75 s
- **b** the time taken by the runner to complete the first 200 m of the race
- **c** the runner's velocity.

4 This table gives values of displacement and time during a short cycle journey:

Displacement / m	0	80	240	400	560	680
Time / s	0	10	20	30	40	50

- **a** Draw a displacement–time graph for the journey.
- **b** From your graph, deduce the cyclist's greatest speed during the journey.

Exercise 1.4 Adding vectors

These questions involve thinking about displacement and velocity. These are vector quantities – they have direction as well as magnitude. Every quantity in physics can be classified as either a scalar or a vector quantity. A vector quantity can be represented by an arrow.

1 A scalar quantity has magnitude only.

- **a** Name the scalar quantity that corresponds to displacement.
- **b** Name the scalar quantity that corresponds to velocity.
- **c** For each of the following quantities, state whether it is a scalar or a vector quantity:

  mass, force, acceleration, density, energy, weight

2 This drawing shows a piece of squared paper. Each square measures 1 cm × 1 cm. The track shows the movement of a spider that ran around on the paper for a short while:

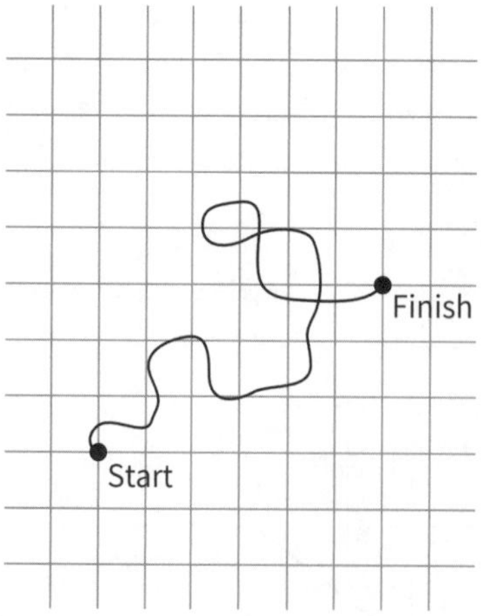

- **a** How many squares did the spider move *to the right*, from start to finish?
- **b** How many squares did the spider move *up the paper*?
- **c** Calculate the spider's displacement between start and finish.
  Make sure that you give the distance (in cm) and the angle of its displacement relative to the horizontal.
- **d** Estimate the distance travelled by the spider. Describe your method.

3 A yacht sails 20 km due north. It then turns 45° to the west and travels a further 12 km.

- **a** Calculate the distance, in km, travelled by the yacht.
- **b** Draw a scale diagram of the yacht's journey. Include a note of the scale you are using.
- **c** By measuring the diagram, determine the yacht's displacement relative to its starting point.

4 A passenger jet aircraft can fly at 950 km h^{-1} relative to the air it is flying through. In still air it will therefore fly at 950 km h^{-1} relative to the ground.

- **a** A wind of speed 100 km h^{-1} blows head-on to the aircraft, slowing it down. What will its speed relative to the ground be?
- **b** If the aircraft was flying in the opposite direction, what would its speed be relative to the ground?
- **c** The aircraft flies in a direction such that the wind is blowing at it sideways (in other words, at 90°).
  - **i** Draw a diagram to show how these two velocities add together to give the resultant velocity of the aircraft.
  - **ii** Calculate the aircraft's speed relative to the ground.

Exam-style questions

1 **a** Define 'speed'. [1]

This diagram shows a laboratory trolley with an interrupt card mounted on it. The trolley will pass through a single light gate:

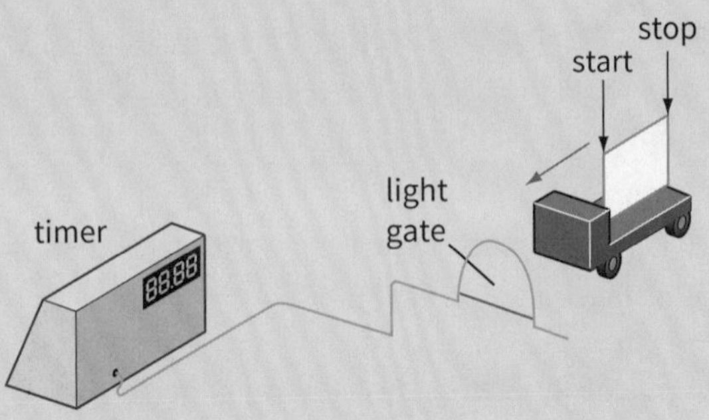

- **b** Explain how the card causes the timer to start and stop. [3]
- **c** The card is 10 cm wide. The timer indicates a time of 0.76 s. Calculate the average speed of the trolley. [2]
- **d** Explain why the speed you calculated in **c** is the trolley's *average* speed. [1]

2 A slow goods train is travelling at a speed of 50 km h^{-1} along a track. A passenger express train that travels at 120 km h^{-1} sets off along the same track two hours after the goods train.

- **a** Draw a displacement–time graph to represent the motion of the two trains. [4]
- **b** Use your graph to determine the time at which the express train will catch up with the goods train. [1]

3 This graph represents the motion of a car along a straight road:

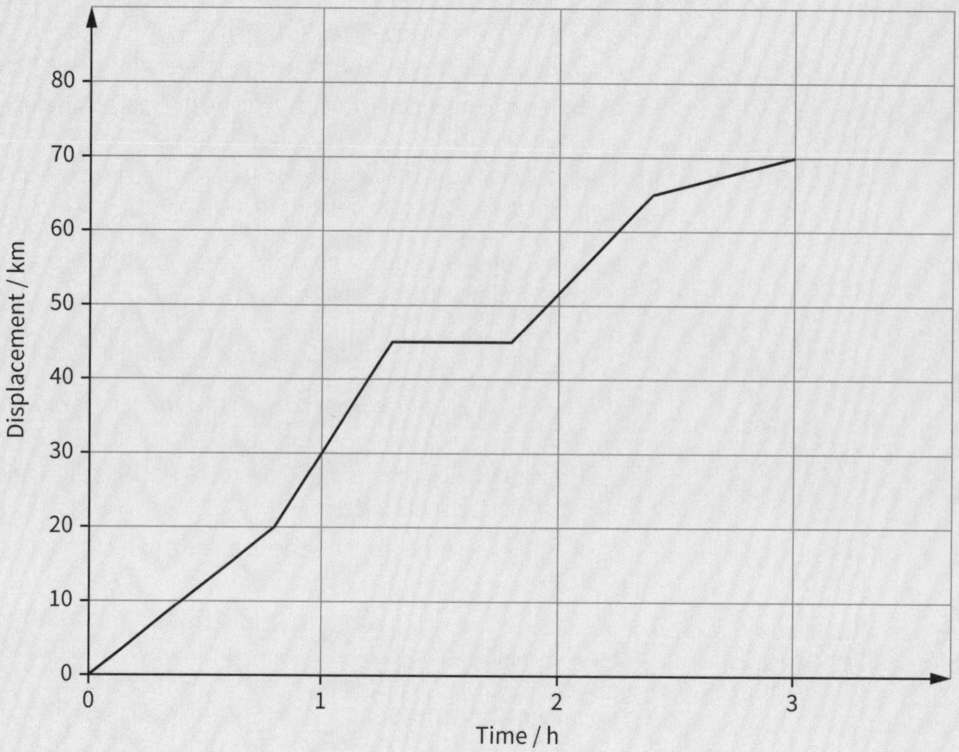

From the graph, deduce the following:

a the time taken for the car's journey [1]

b the distance travelled by the car during its journey [1]

c the car's average speed during its journey [1]

d the car's greatest speed during its journey [1]

e the amount of time the car spent travelling at the speed you calculated in **d** [1]

f the distance it travelled at this speed. [1]

4 A physical quantity can be described as either 'scalar' or 'vector'.

a State the difference between a *scalar quantity* and a *vector quantity.* [2]

b Define *displacement.* [1]

A light aircraft flies due east at 80 km h^{-1} for 1.5 h. It then flies due north at 90 km h^{-1} for 0.8 h.

c Calculate the distance travelled by the aircraft in each stage of its journey. [2]

d Draw a scale diagram to represent the aircraft's journey. [2]

e Use your diagram to determine the aircraft's final displacement relative to its starting point. [2]

Chapter 2:
Accelerated motion

Chapter outline

- define and use the term 'acceleration'
- draw velocity–time graphs and use them to determine acceleration and displacement
- derive and use the four equations of motion for uniformly accelerated motion in a straight line
- solve problems involving motion under gravity, including free fall and the motion of projectiles
- describe an experiment to determine the acceleration of free fall

KEY TERMS

acceleration: rate of change of velocity

Equations: $\text{acceleration} = \dfrac{\text{change in velocity}}{\text{time taken}}$

$$a = \frac{v-u}{t} = \frac{\Delta v}{\Delta t}$$

Equations of motion for constant acceleration: Equation 1: $v = u + at$

Equation 2: $s = \dfrac{(u+v)}{2} \times t$

Equation 3: $s = ut + \frac{1}{2}at^2$

Equation 4: $v^2 = u^2 + 2as$

Exercise 2.1 Velocity–time graphs

This exercise provides practice in drawing, using and interpreting velocity–time graphs. Remember that acceleration is the gradient of a velocity–time graph; displacement is the area under a velocity–time graph.

1 This graph represents the motion of a vehicle:

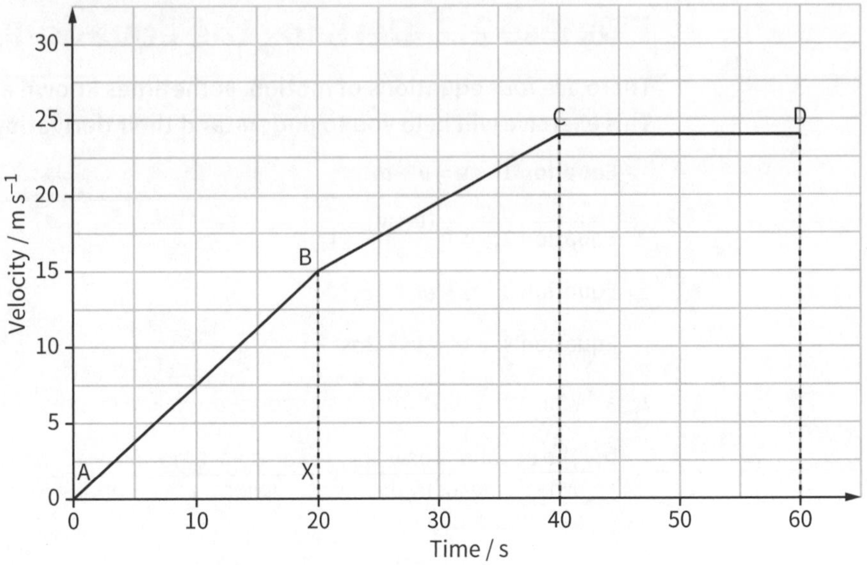

a How can you tell from the graph that the vehicle started from rest?

b After what time did the vehicle stop accelerating? Explain how you can tell.

c The vehicle is accelerating in the section AB. Use the triangle ABX to calculate the time for which the vehicle accelerated in this section.

d Deduce the increase in the vehicle's velocity in this time.

e Use your answers to **c** and **d** to calculate the vehicle's acceleration in the section AB.

f Now consider section BC of the graph. Follow the same steps as parts **c** to **e** to calculate the vehicle's acceleration in the section BC.

g Calculate the area of the triangle ABX. What does this area represent?

h Calculate the total distance travelled by the vehicle in its journey ABCD.

2 This table shows how the velocity of a car changed as it moved along a straight road:

Velocity / m s^{-1}	10	10	17	24	28	28	28
Time / s	0	20	40	60	80	100	120

a Draw a velocity–time graph to represent the car's journey.

b Between which two times was the car's acceleration greatest? Calculate its acceleration between these times.

c Calculate the distance travelled by the car during its journey. You will need to divide the area under the graph into rectangles and triangles.

3 A car is approaching traffic lights. The driver brakes so that the car's velocity decreases from 22 m s^{-1} to 7 m s^{-1} in a time of 10 s.

a Sketch a velocity–time graph to represent this section of the car's journey.

b Calculate the car's acceleration.

c State how the graph shows that the car is decelerating. Remember that 'decelerating' means that the car's velocity is decreasing; its acceleration is *negative*.

d On your graph, shade the area which represents the car's displacement as it is braking.

e Calculate the displacement of the car as it is braking.

4 A moving train decelerates at a rate of 0.2 m s^{-2} for a time of 50 s. In this time it travels a distance of 2000 m. Deduce the train's velocity just before it started to decelerate. Start by sketching a velocity–time graph and mark on it the information given in the question.

Exercise 2.2 Deriving the equations of motion

There are four equations of motion, sometimes known as the 'suvat equations'. This exercise will help you to understand their derivation.

Equation 1: $v = u + at$

Equation 2: $s = \frac{(u + v)}{2} \times t$

Equation 3: $s = ut + \frac{1}{2}at^2$

Equation 4: $v^2 = u^2 + 2as$

1 a Which quantities do the symbols *s*, *u*, *v*, *a* and *t* represent?

b The equations only apply to an object moving with *uniform acceleration* in a straight line. What is meant by the phrase 'uniform acceleration'? Remember that acceleration is a vector quantity.

2 Equation 1 can be deduced from the definition of acceleration.

a Acceleration can be defined as:

$$\frac{(\text{final velocity} - \text{initial velocity})}{\text{time}}$$

Write this equation in symbols.

b Rearrange the equation to give the first of the equations of motion.

c Which of the five quantities from question **1** is not involved in this equation?

3 Equation 2 can be found by imagining that an object moves at a constant velocity equal to its average velocity.

a Write an equation (in words and then in symbols) for the object's average velocity, in terms of its initial and final velocities.

b Use your answer to part **a** to write down the equation for displacement. To find the object's displacement, multiply the average velocity by the time taken.

c Which of the five quantities from question **1** is not involved in this equation?

4 To deduce the equations 3 and 4, we start from a simple velocity–time graph:

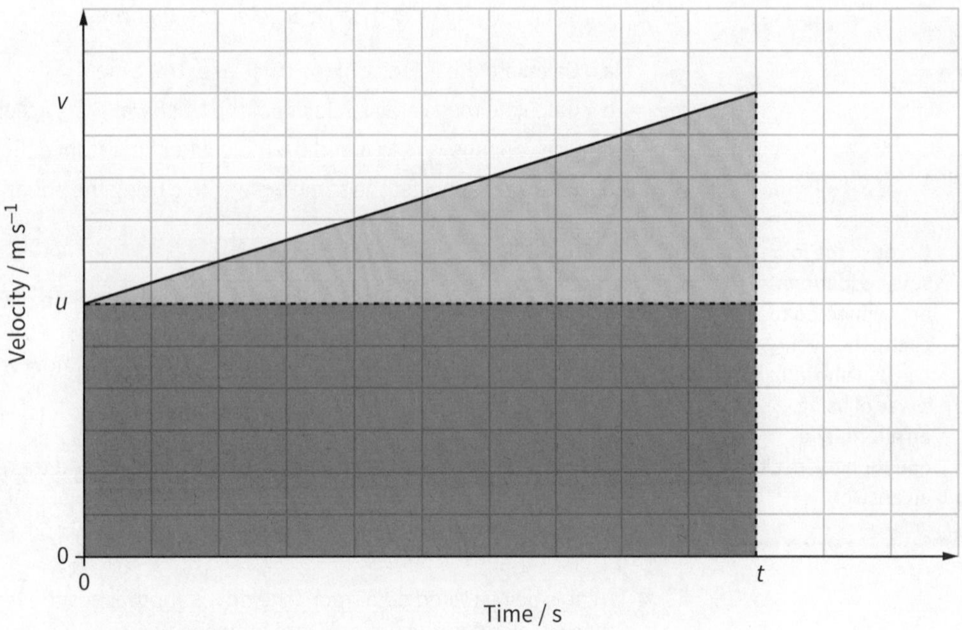

a Describe the motion represented by this graph.

We have to deduce an equation for displacement. This is represented by the area under the graph. We can divide this area into two parts:

displacement = area of rectangle + area of triangle

b The area of the rectangle represents the displacement if the object had moved at a steady speed u for time t. What is the value of this area?

c The area of the triangle represents the object's *additional* displacement resulting from its acceleration. The height of this triangle is $v - u$. Rearrange the equation that defines acceleration to find the height of the triangle in terms of a and t.

TIP

Equation 1 defines acceleration.

d The area of a triangle $= \frac{1}{2} \times$ base $\times$ height. Use your answer from **c** to write down the area of the triangle in terms of *a* and *t*.

e Write down the complete equation for displacement *s* in terms of the two areas.

f Which of the five quantities from question **1** is not involved in this equation?

5 Equation 4 has to be deduced from the equations 1 and 2, using algebra.

a Write out equation 1. Rearrange it so that time *t* is its subject.

b Write out equation 2. Substitute for *t* using your answer to part **a**.

c Rearrange the equation to give an expression which has the form of 'the difference of two squares'.

d Make v^2 the subject of the equation.

e Which of the five quantities from question **1** is not involved in this equation?

Exercise 2.3 Using the equations of motion

When using the equations of motion, you need to identify the 'suvat' quantities involved and the equation that links them.

1 A truck is moving at 12 m s^{-1}. It accelerates uniformly at 0.75 m s^{-2} for 20 s.

a Calculate the velocity of the truck after this time.

b Calculate the average velocity of the truck while it is accelerating.

c Use your answers to **a** and **b** to calculate the distance the lorry travels while it is accelerating.

d Check that you get the same answer to **c** using the equation:

$s = ut\frac{1}{2} + at^2$

TIP

Because the four suvat equations are connected to each other, you can usually find a way of using an alternative equation to check an answer.

2 A moving train decelerates at a rate of 0.2 m s^{-2} for a time of 50 s. In this time it travels a distance of 2000 m. Use one of the equations of motion to deduce the train's velocity just before it started to accelerate. (This is question 4 from Exercise 2.1 but now you can solve it more directly using one of the equations of motion.)

3 A car is stationary. It accelerates at 0.8 m s^{-2} for 10 s and then at 0.4 m s^{-2} for a further 10 s. Use the equations of motion to deduce the car's final displacement. You will have to split the journey into two parts, since the acceleration changes after 10 s.

4 A car is being tested on a track. The driver approaches the test section at a speed of 28 m s^{-1}. He then accelerates at a uniform rate between two markers separated by 100 m. The car reaches a speed of 41 m s^{-1}.

a Calculate the car's acceleration.

b Calculate the time during which the car is accelerating.

Exercise 2.4 Motion under gravity

When an object moves in free fall under gravity, the only force acting on it is its weight, which acts vertically downwards. Near the surface of the Earth, the acceleration due to gravity is $g = 9.81$ m s^{-2} (approximately) vertically downwards. You can use the equations of motion to solve problems involving motion under gravity.

> **TIP**
> When considering motion under gravity, we need to use vector quantities. We have to be careful to take into account the directions of forces and velocities. A useful sign convention is to regard upwards as positive, downwards as negative.

1 Give the sign, positive or negative, of the force due to gravity near the surface of the Earth.

2 A stone is thrown vertically upwards. Eventually it falls to the ground.

a Copy and complete this table to show the signs, positive or negative, of the quantities shown.

Quantity	Displacement	Velocity	Acceleration
stone moving upwards			
stone at highest position			
stone falling downwards			

b Which of these velocity–time graphs represents the motion of the stone? Explain your choice.

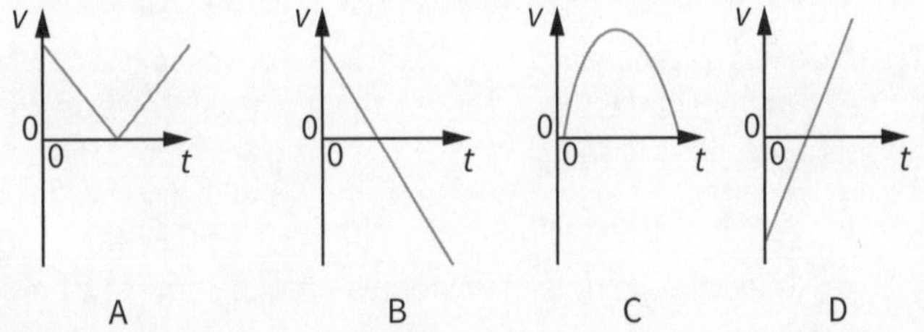

3 A child throws a ball vertically upwards and catches it when it returns to the ground. The ball's initial upward velocity is 6.5 m s^{-1}.

a Calculate the height to which the ball rises. Think about the ball's velocity at its highest point.

b Calculate the time the ball spends in the air. Think about the ball's final velocity.

The child is standing on the edge of a cliff 55 m high when she throws the ball. She allows the ball to fall to the bottom of the cliff.

c Calculate the speed with which the ball reaches the ground at the foot of the cliff.

d Calculate the time the ball spends in the air. Remember to consider both the upward and downward parts of the ball's movement.

4 An object that is fired or thrown upwards at an angle is called a *projectile*. This diagram shows the path of a projectile – in this case, an arrow – fired at 45° to the horizontal with an initial velocity of 24 m s^{-1}. It then moves freely through the air, so that the only force acting on it is gravity. It lands some distance away on the level ground:

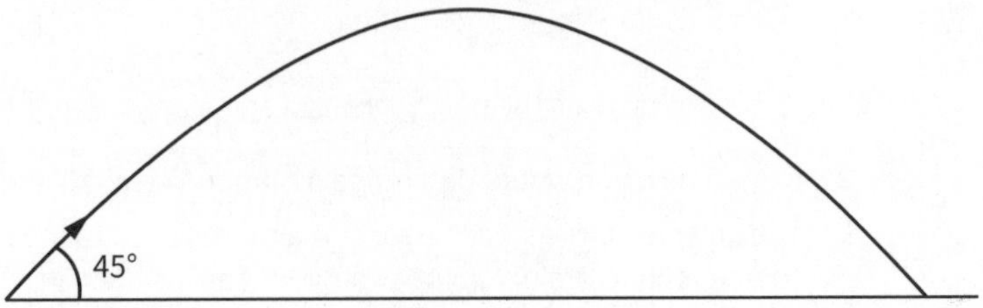

To calculate the distance travelled by the arrow, we must first calculate the time it spends in the air. To do this, we consider its vertical motion.

a Calculate the vertical (upward) component of the arrow's initial velocity.

b What is the arrow's vertical displacement when it lands on the ground?

c Calculate the time the arrow spends in the air.

Now we can consider the arrow's horizontal motion.

d No horizontal forces act on the arrow. What is its horizontal acceleration?

e Calculate the horizontal component of the arrow's initial velocity.

f Calculate the distance travelled horizontally by the arrow. (You have calculated the time taken in part **c** and the arrow's horizontal velocity in part **e**.)

5 A projectile travels the greatest horizontal distance on level ground if it is initially fired at 45° to the horizontal. Calculate the distance travelled by the arrow in question **4** if it was fired at 50° to the horizontal, at the same initial velocity as before. You can follow the same logical approach as in question **4**.

Exam-style questions

1 **a** Define *acceleration*. [1]

A train is travelling at 40 m s^{-1} when the driver sees a red signal at a distance of 2.2 km ahead. The driver applies the brakes so that the train slows down with uniform acceleration and stops as it reaches the signal.

b Calculate the train's acceleration as it is braking. [3]

c Calculate the time taken for the train to come to a halt. [2]

d Sketch a velocity–time graph for this part of the train's journey. State how your graph shows that the train's acceleration is *uniform*. [2]

e Indicate on your graph the area that represents the distance travelled by the train. [1]

2 In an experiment to determine *g*, the acceleration of free fall, a ball-bearing is released so that it falls through a trapdoor, as shown in this diagram:

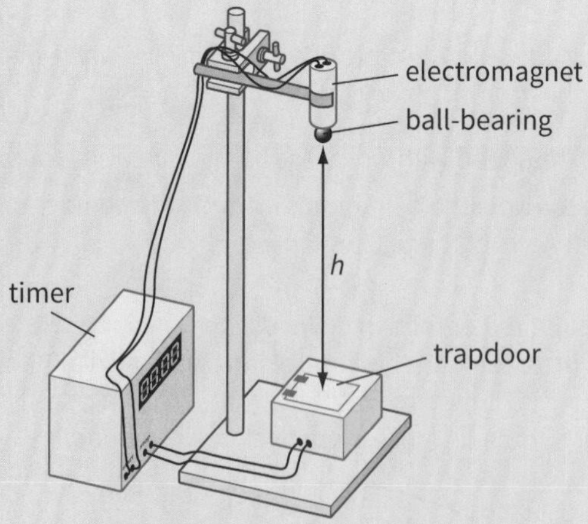

The timer starts when the ball is released and stops when the ball reaches the trapdoor.

a Explain how you would determine *g* from the height *h* and the time taken *t*. [3]

b The timer used is very accurate and a ruler is used to measure *h*. Suggest two sources of uncertainty in the experiment and explain in each case how they affect the calculated value for *g*. [4]

c In an attempt to determine g using projectile motion, a student fires a metal ball with an initial velocity of 12.0 m s^{-1} and at an angle of 45° to the horizontal, as shown below. The ball lands at a distance of 14.7 m on level ground. (You may assume air resistance is negligible.)

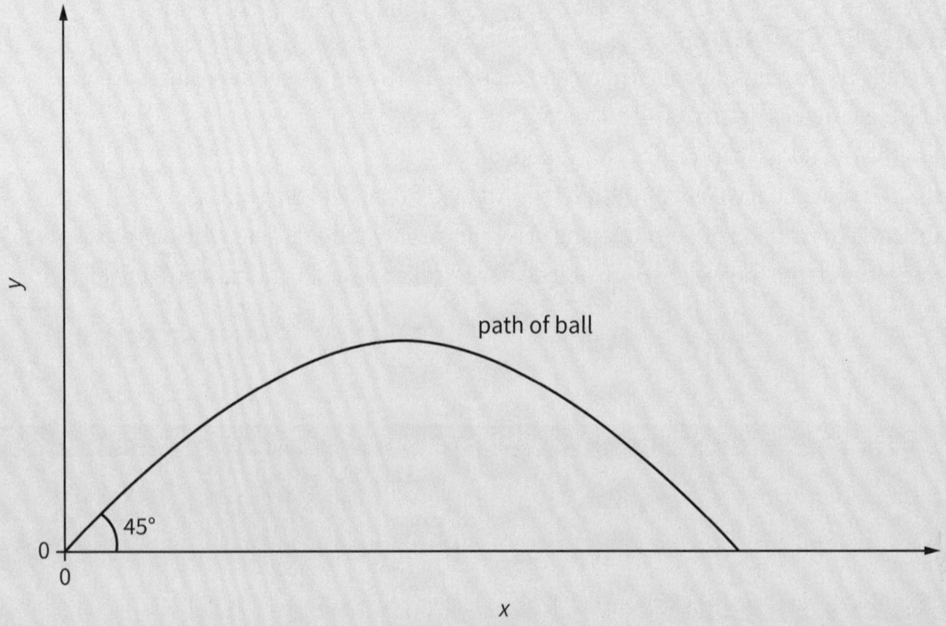

By considering the ball's horizontal motion, calculate the time taken for the ball to travel this distance. [2]

d By considering the ball's vertical motion, calculate a value for the acceleration of free fall. [2]

Chapter 3:
Dynamics – explaining motion

Chapter outline

- identify the forces acting on a body and represent them on a free body diagram
- calculate the resultant of several forces
- use the relationship force = mass × acceleration
- use the concept of weight as the effect of a gravitational field on a mass
- describe the motion of objects falling in a uniform gravitational field with air resistance
- understand that the weight of an object may be taken as acting at its centre of gravity

KEY TERMS

resultant force: the single force acting on a body that has the same effect as the sum of all the forces acting on it

Equations: force = mass × acceleration; $F = ma$

weight = mass × gravitational field strength; $W = mg$

Exercise 3.1 Identifying forces

You can determine how an object will move by considering all the forces acting on it. But first you must be able to identify the forces acting on an object and represent them on a free body diagram.

1 This diagram shows a man pushing a car to start it moving:

a To represent the car as a free body diagram, draw a rectangle. Add arrows to represent each of these forces:

- the pushing force provided by the man
- the weight of the car
- the upward contact force of the ground on the car.

Note that, although there will be an upward force on each of the car's wheels, we can represent this as a single upward force.

b Now imagine that the car is travelling at a steady speed. The forward force on the car is provided by the engine; a backward force is provided by friction with the air. Draw a second free body diagram to represent this situation.

c The car presses down on the road. Explain why this force is not included on the free body diagram.

2 This diagram shows a skier moving quickly down a slope:

a Copy the rectangle which represents the skier. Add arrows to represent each of these forces acting on the skier:
- her weight; remember that weight acts vertically downwards
- the contact force of the ground; remember that the contact force acts at right angles to the surface
- air resistance and friction with the ground (these can be represented by a single arrow); remember that these forces act in the opposite direction to an object's motion.

b Now imagine that the skier reaches level ground. Draw a free body diagram to show the forces acting on her.

3 When a fish moves through water, four forces act on it:
- its weight
- the upthrust of the water
- the forward force produced by the movement of its body and fins
- the resistance of the water.

a Draw a free body diagram to represent these forces acting on a fish as it moves horizontally through water.

b Some fish leap out of the water to avoid predators. Think about the forces acting on the fish as it moves horizontally through the air. Draw a free body diagram for the fish in this situation. (Air resistance is negligible.)

Exercise 3.2 How forces affect motion

If the forces acting on a body are unbalanced, it will accelerate. Otherwise it will remain at rest or moving with constant velocity. This exercise gives you practice identifying resultant forces and the resultant accelerations.

1 These diagrams represent the forces acting on each of three objects, A, B and C:

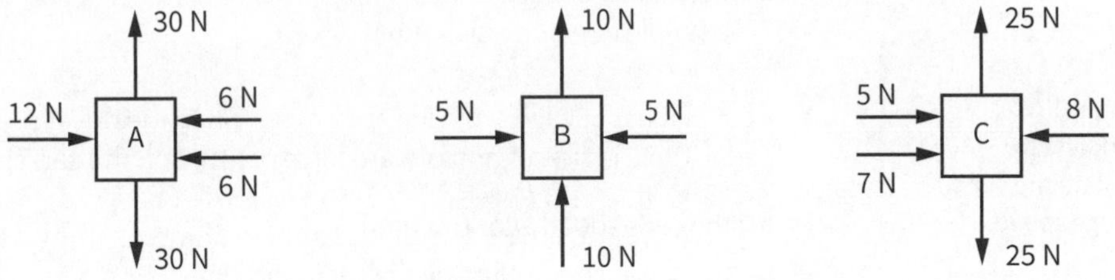

a Determine the resultant force acting on each object. Which object has balanced forces acting on it?

b For each of the other two objects, draw a diagram and add an arrow to represent the resultant force.

c Describe how each of the objects will move as a result of the forces acting on it.

2 These free body diagrams represent the forces acting on two cars:

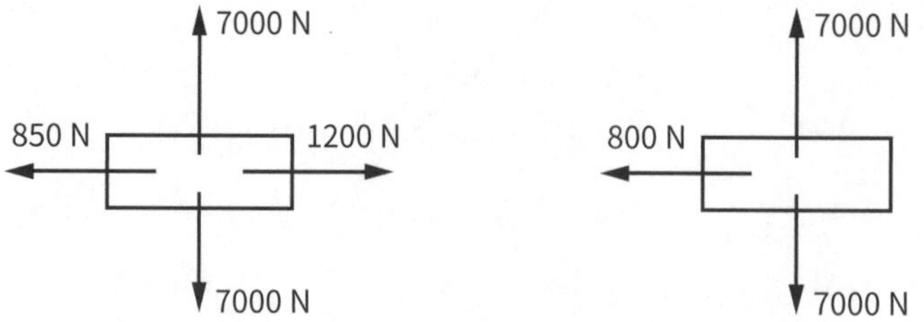

Diagram 1 Diagram 2

a Which diagram represents the forces acting on a car that is accelerating to the right?

b Calculate the resultant force acting on this car.

The other diagram represents the forces on a car that is braking.

c Name the forces acting on this car.

d Calculate the resultant force acting on this car.

Exercise 3.3 Force, mass and acceleration

Force, mass and acceleration are linked by the equation $F = ma$. In this equation, F represents the resultant force acting on mass m. This exercise gives you practice using and rearranging this equation.

1 a A truck of mass 40 000 kg accelerates at 1.20 m s^{-2}.

Calculate the resultant force acting on the truck. Give your answer in kilonewtons (kN).

b Calculate the acceleration of a ball of mass 2.8 kg when a force of 48 N acts on it.

c A spacecraft accelerates at 0.40 m s^{-2} when a force of 200 N acts on it. Calculate the mass of the spacecraft.

2 A parachutist has a mass of 95 kg. She is acted on by an upward force of 1200 N caused by her parachute. (Acceleration due to gravity $g = 9.81$ m s^{-2}.)

a Calculate the parachutist's weight.

b Calculate the resultant force acting on her and give its direction.

c Calculate her acceleration and give its direction. (To find the direction, it can help to draw a simple free body diagram.)

TIP

You may find it simplest to calculate the car's average speed.

3 A car of mass 680 kg is moving at 12 m s^{-1}. When the driver presses harder on the accelerator pedal, there is a resultant forward force of 510 N on the car. This force acts for 20 s. Calculate:

a the car's speed after this time

b the distance travelled by the car in this time.

4 An astronaut is on the Moon. He picks up a small rock. He carries out two simple experiments to determine its mass.

a He drops the rock from a height of 2.0 m and finds that it takes 1.6 s to reach the ground. Use this result to estimate the acceleration due to gravity on the Moon's surface.

b He hangs the rock from a newtonmeter and finds that its weight is 3.9 N. Use your answer to part **a** to estimate the mass of the rock.

c Calculate the weight of the rock on the surface of the Earth. Remember, the equation $W = mg$ is true everywhere, but g varies from place to place.

Exercise 3.4 Terminal velocity

When an object moves through a fluid, such as air or water, it experiences an additional drag force. These questions are about how this force affects the body's motion.

1 This diagram shows a ship moving through water:

Two horizontal forces act on the ship: the forward thrust provided by its engines and the backward drag force of the water.

a Determine the resultant force acting on the ship. Remember to give both magnitude and direction.

b The ship has a mass of 200 tonnes. Calculate its acceleration. (1 tonne = 10^3 kg)

The drag force on the ship increases as it moves faster. Eventually the ship's velocity is constant.

c The ship has reached terminal velocity. Calculate the ship's acceleration at this point.

d What can you say about the two horizontal forces acting on the ship?

e Suggest two ways in which the ship's terminal velocity might be increased.

The ship leaves port and its engines are set to deliver constant maximum thrust.

f Look at these graphs:

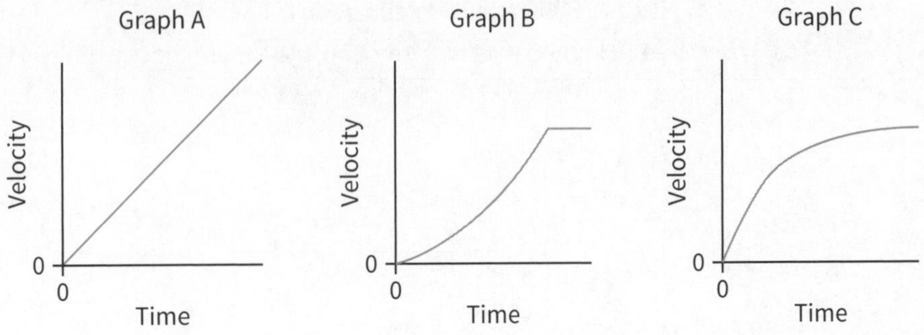

Which of the graphs might represent how the ship's velocity changes? Explain your choice. Think about the gradient of the graphs.

g Sketch a graph to show how the ship's acceleration changes up to the time when it reaches terminal velocity.

2 These two diagrams show the forces acting on a parachutist at different points as he falls towards the ground:

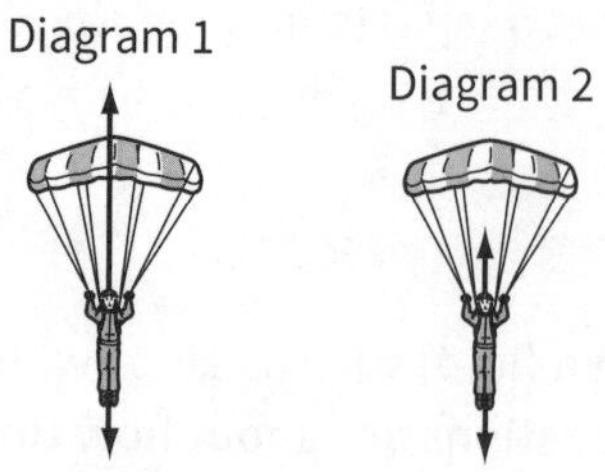

The lengths of the arrows represent the relative sizes of the forces.

a Name the two forces acting upwards and downwards on the parachutist.

b Which of the two diagrams represents the forces acting when the parachutist is moving more quickly through the air? Explain how you know.

c Which of the diagrams represents the forces acting as the parachutist falls at a slow, steady speed? Explain how you know.

d A parachutist falls freely through the air before opening his parachute. Explain why he decelerates when his parachute opens.

Exam-style questions

1 A spherical ball of mass 12 g is dropped from rest near the Earth's surface. It accelerates but eventually reaches a constant velocity downwards, known as the terminal velocity.

Two forces act on the ball, its weight, 0.12 N and air resistance *F* which acts upwards.

a Explain, using ideas about these forces why the initial downwards acceleration of the ball is 10 m s^{-2}. [2]

b Explain, using ideas about the forces, why the ball eventually reaches a constant speed. [2]

c The ball falls through a vertical height of 4.0 m.

i Assuming that there is no air resistance, calculate the final speed of the ball. [2]

ii At low speeds, the air resistance force *F* is given by the expression $F = 3.6 \times 10^{-6}\,v$, where *v* is the speed of the ball measured in m s^{-1} and *F* is measured in N. Show that the assumption in **i** is justified.

d At one instant in the motion, the air resistance acting on the ball is 0.050 N. Calculate the acceleration of the ball. [2]

2 A box of mass 12 kg is pulled along a rough floor by a force *F*. As it moves along the floor, a resultant force of 40 N acts on the box.

a Draw a labelled free body diagram to represent all the forces acting on the box and explain how a resultant force acts on the box. [3]

b The box accelerates from rest to a speed of 6.0 m s^{-1} in a time *t* and travels a distance *d*.

i Calculate the value of *t*. [2]

ii The same resultant force continues to act in the box and the speed changes from 6.0 m s^{-1} to 12 m s^{-1}. Explain why the time taken is the same as *t* **but** the distance travelled is not the same as *d*. [2]

c The box passes over a rough patch in the floor and the box slides in a straight line with a constant velocity. Explain what has happened to the forces on the box. [2]

3 A table tennis ball is thrown upwards. It rises through the air and then falls back to the ground, as shown in this diagram:

For such a light-weight ball, air resistance is a significant force. Air resistance acts in the opposite direction to the ball's velocity and increases as its velocity increases.

a Draw a free body diagram to show the forces acting on the ball when it is moving upwards at point A. [2]

b State the direction of the ball's resultant acceleration when it is moving upwards at point A. [1]

c As the ball falls downwards, it passes again through point A. State whether its acceleration will be greater than, less than, or the same as when it was at point A, moving upwards. Explain your answer. [2]

d State the ball's acceleration when it is at its highest point. Explain your answer. [2]

Chapter 4:
Forces – vectors and moments

Chapter outline

- add two or more coplanar forces
- resolve a force into perpendicular components
- define and calculate the moment of a force
- state the conditions for a body to be in equilibrium
- use a vector triangle to represent coplanar forces in equilibrium
- state and apply the principle of moments
- define and use the concept of a 'couple' and calculate the torque of a couple

KEY TERMS

component of a force: the resolved part of a force in a particular direction

equilibrium: when the resultant force and the resultant moment on a body are both zero

Equations: moment = force × perpendicular distance from pivot

moment of a couple (torque) = one of the forces × perpendicular distance between the forces

Exercise 4.1 Adding forces

Chapter 3 included some problems in which a body was acted on by more than one force. This exercise includes situations where you need to use vector addition to find a resultant force.

1 This diagram shows an object with two forces acting on it. The forces are at 90° to each other:

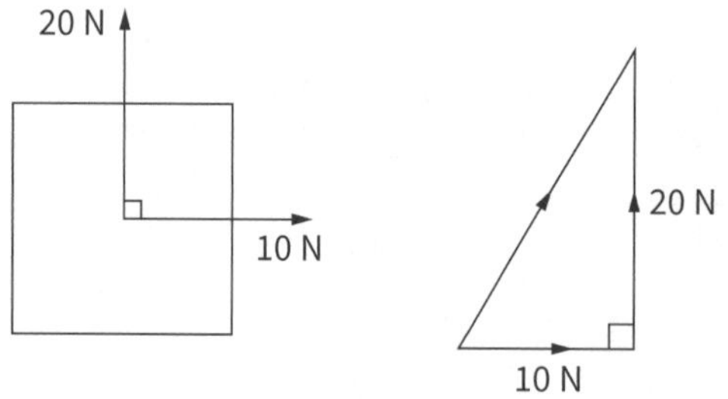

The diagram also shows the triangle we use to add these forces. In this case, it is sufficient to sketch the triangle.

a Which side of the triangle represents the resultant force acting on the object?

b Calculate the magnitude of the resultant force.

c Use trigonometry to calculate the angle of the resultant force to the horizontal.

TIP

If you see an angle of 90° in a question, you will probably have to use Pythagoras' theorem.

2 A falling stone is acted on by two forces:

- its weight, acting vertically downwards, of magnitude 15 N
- a force due to the wind, acting horizontally, of magnitude 3 N.

a Draw a free body diagram to show the forces acting on the stone.

b Sketch a triangle that will allow you to determine the resultant of the two forces.

c In your triangle, the forces will have the same directions as in the free body diagram but they will be shown head-to-tail. Use Pythagoras' theorem to determine the magnitude of the resultant force on the stone.

d Use trigonometry to calculate the angle of the resultant force to the horizontal.

3 This diagram shows an object with two forces acting on it. In this case the two forces are not at 90° to each other:

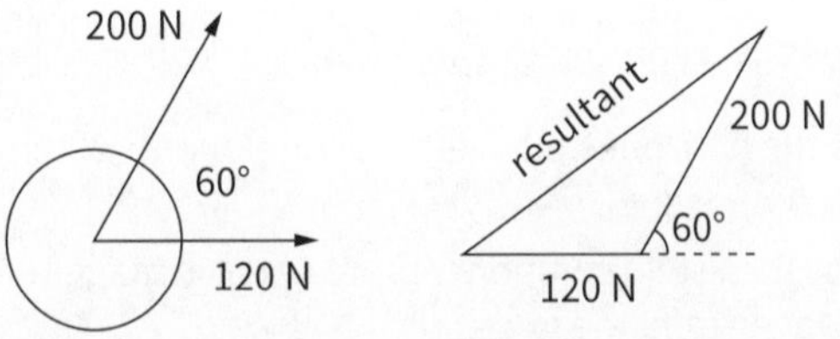

The diagram also shows the triangle we use to add these forces. Note that the lines representing the two forces are joined head-to-tail.

a Draw a scale diagram of the triangle. Use a scale of 20 N cm^{-1} so that the 200 N force is represented by a line of length 10 cm.

b Measure the length of the side of the triangle that represents the resultant force. State the value of the resultant force.

c Measure the angle between the resultant force and the horizontal. State its value.

4 This free body diagram shows the two forces acting on a ship as its engine causes it to change direction:

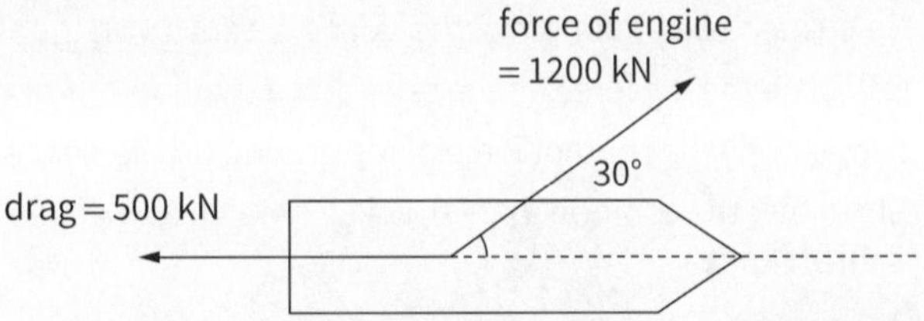

a Sketch a triangle that will allow you to determine the resultant force on the ship.

b Now, following the same procedure as in question 3, make a scale drawing and use it to deduce the magnitude and direction of the resultant force on the ship. Choose a scale that will give a large triangle covering, perhaps, half a page.

Exercise 4.2 Resolving forces

A single force can be broken down (resolved) into two components at right angles to each other.

1 Look at these diagrams:

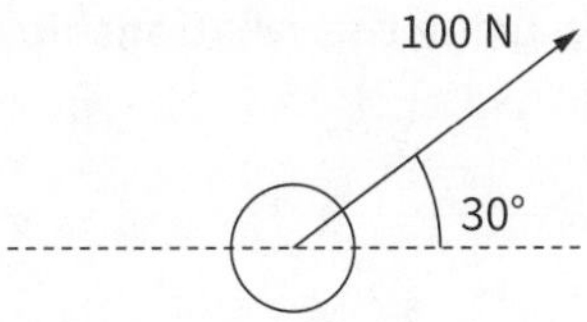

Diagram 1

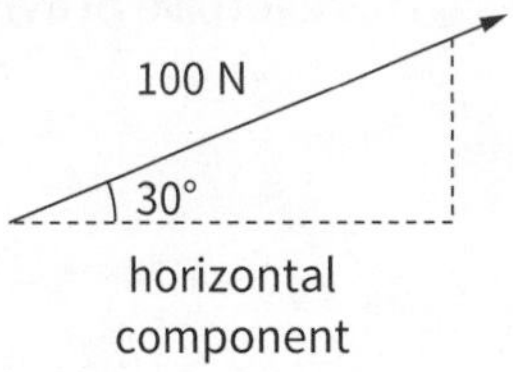

Diagram 2

Diagram 1 represents a force of 100 N acting at 30° to the horizontal.

Diagram 2 indicates how we would find the horizontal component of this force. We draw a right-angled triangle with the force vector as its hypotenuse. The horizontal component is then represented by the horizontal side of the triangle.

a Use trigonometry to determine the horizontal component of the force.

b Use a similar method to calculate the vertical component of the force. (You could draw a new triangle or use the one (shown) above.)

c Check your answers by using Pythagoras' theorem to show that the resultant of the two components is equal to the original force (100 N).

2 A force of 250 N acts at an angle of 45° to the vertical.

a Determine the horizontal and vertical components of this force. Include a sketch to show these two components.

b Explain why these two components are equal in magnitude. (Think about the angle between each component and the force.)

3 This diagram represents the forces acting on a skier moving down a slope. The skier is accelerating down the slope:

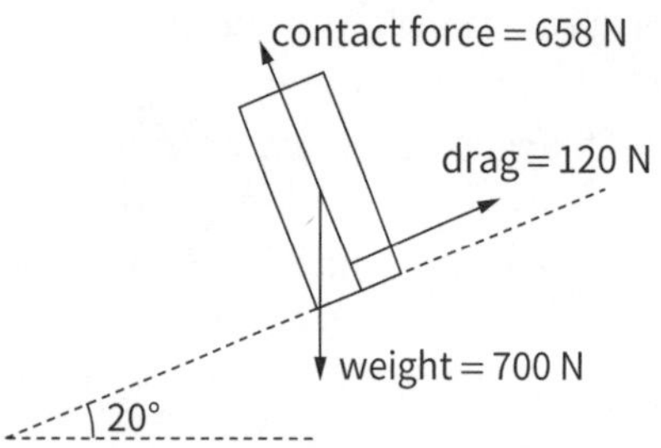

a Calculate the component of the skier's weight down the slope.

b Calculate the net force on the skier down the slope.

c Explain why the contact force of the ground on the skier does not cause him to accelerate.

d Show that the component of the skier's weight at right angles to the slope is equal to the contact force.

4 The idea of resolving a force to find its component in a particular direction can be extended to any other vector quantity. For example: if an aircraft is flying NE at 300 m s^{-1}, calculate the component of its velocity in the direction due east.

Exercise 4.3 Moment of a force

There are two ways to increase the turning effect of a force (its moment):

- **increase the force**
- **increase the distance of the force from the pivot.**

This exercise provides practice in using this relationship.

1 This diagram shows a beam that is acted on by four forces:

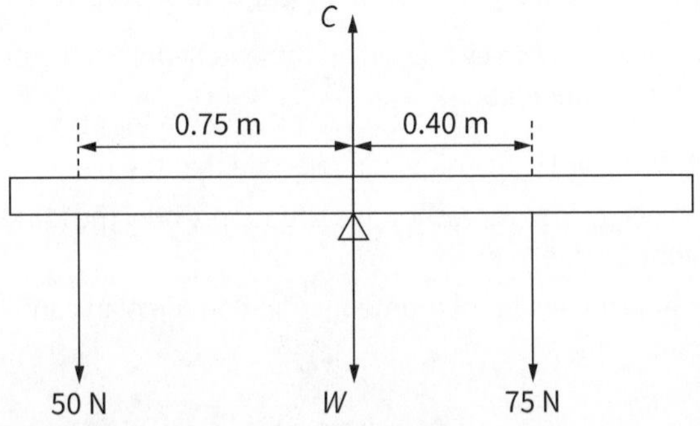

The beam is balanced at its centre of gravity. This means that we can ignore two forces (the weight of the beam *W* and the upward contact force *C* of the pivot on the beam) because they pass through the pivot (distance = 0).

You have to decide whether the beam is in equilibrium.

a Calculate the moment of the 50 N force about the pivot. State whether the moment acts clockwise or anticlockwise.

b Repeat for the 75 N force.

c Is the beam in equilibrium? Explain your answer.

2 This diagram shows a beam that is acted on by four forces. It is in equilibrium:

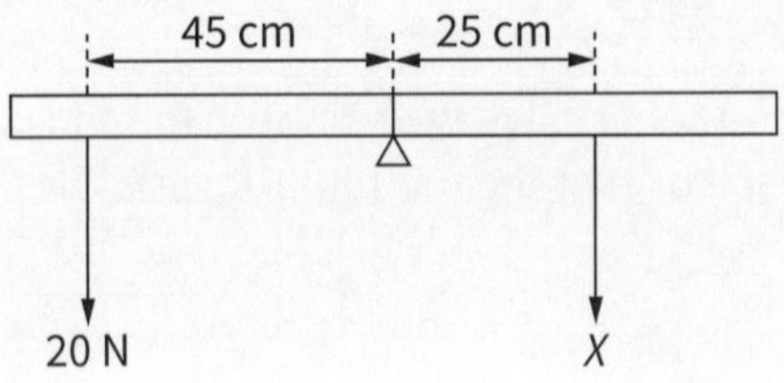

You have to find the unknown force *X*.

a Calculate the moment of the 20 N force about the pivot. State whether the moment acts clockwise or anticlockwise.

b The beam is balanced so the unknown force *X* has an equal but opposite moment about the pivot. Use this fact to calculate the value of *X*.

3 This diagram shows a beam that is acted on by four forces. It is in equilibrium:

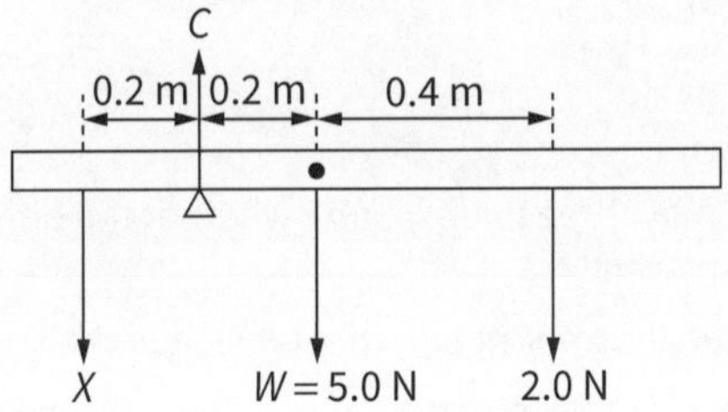

The beam's weight does not act through the pivot and so it will have a turning effect that must be taken into account.

a Two forces act clockwise about the pivot. Calculate the moment of each of these forces. Add the moments to find the total clockwise moment.

b Calculate the unknown force *X*.

c Knowing that the beam is balanced (in equilibrium), we can say that there is no resultant force acting on it. Use this idea to calculate the contact force *C* that acts on the beam at the pivot.

> **TIP**
> In calculating *X*, you can ignore the contact force *C* because it acts at the pivot, the point about which we are taking moments.

4 Two children are using a long, uniform plank balanced on a cylindrical oil drum as a seesaw. The plank has a mass of 40 kg. It is 5.0 m in length and it is pivoted at a point 2.0 m from one end.

Child A has a mass of 45 kg and sits at the end nearer to the pivot. Child B has a mass of 25 kg and sits at the other end.

a Which one word in the question tells you that the plank's centre of gravity is at its midpoint?

b Draw a diagram to represent this situation. Show the forces acting as multiples of g, the acceleration due to gravity.

c Determine the resultant moment acting on the plank and indicate its direction on your diagram.

5 This diagram shows a box of length 25 cm acted on by four forces:

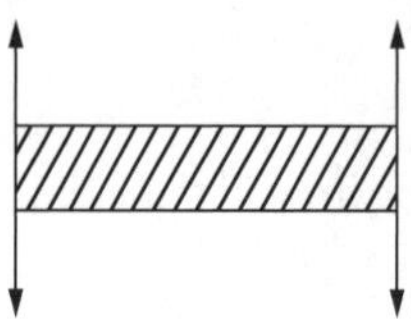

a Which two forces constitute a couple acting on the box? Explain your choice.

b Calculate the torque of the couple.

Exam-style questions

1 A pendulum consists of a spherical mass (a bob) on the end of a light string. In this diagram, the bob is stationary. It is acted on by the horizontal force *F*. The bob has a weight of 1.8 N.

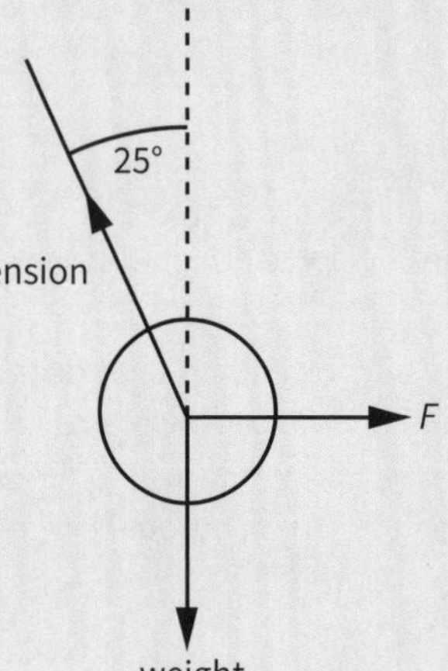

a The bob is acted on by three forces. State whether the bob is in equilibrium, and explain your answer. [2]

b Determine the vertical component of the tension in the string. [2]

c Determine the tension in the string. [2]

d Determine the value of the force *F*. [2]

e The bob is released by removing the force *F*. What will be the resultant force acting on the bob at this instant? Give its magnitude and direction. [2]

2 This diagram represents a uniform rectangular block of weight 40 N. The block is stationary; it has been raised at one corner by a vertical force X:

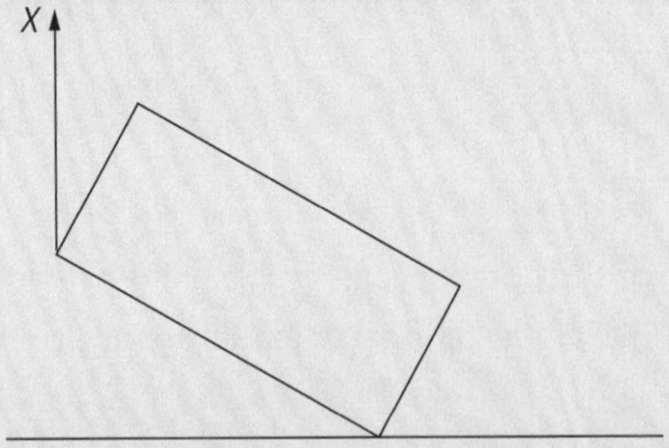

a State the two conditions required for a body to be in equilibrium. [2]

b Calculate the value of the force X. [2]

c Calculate the value of the contact force that acts on the box at the point where the box touches the ground. Give the direction of this force. [2]

3 A flower basket is hung from the end of a uniform horizontal pole which projects from a wall, as shown. The pole is supported by a cable attached to a higher point on the wall:

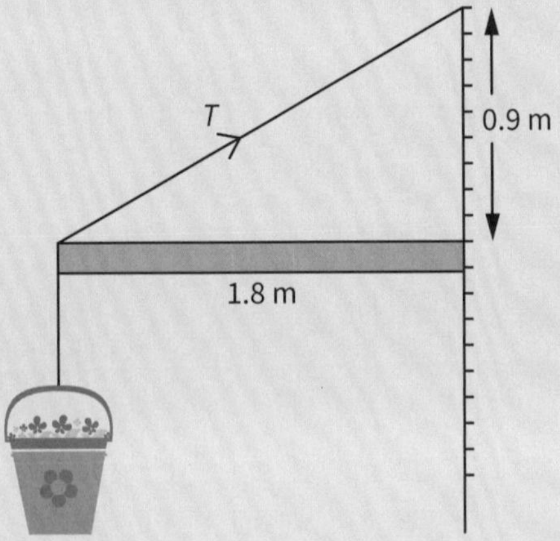

The pole has a mass of 10.0 kg; the flower basket has a mass of 14.0 kg.

a By taking moments about the right hand end of the pole, determine the value of the tension in the cable T. [5]

b The wall exerts a force R on the pole. Deduce the horizontal component of R. [3]

Chapter 5: Work, energy and power

Chapter outline

- understand and use the concept of work
- apply the principle of conservation of energy
- understand and use the relationship between force and potential energy in a uniform field
- derive and use the formulae for kinetic energy (KE) and gravitational potential energy (GPE)
- use the equation for power
- understand what is meant by the *efficiency* of a system, and use this to solve problems
- describe how energy losses arise in practical devices

KEY TERMS

kinetic energy (KE): the energy of an object due to its motion

gravitational potential energy (GPE): the energy of an object due to its position in a gravitational field

joule: the work done (or energy transferred) when a force of 1 N moves a distance of 1 m in the direction of the force

power: the rate at which work is done (or energy is transferred)

Equations: work done = force × displacement $W = Fs$

work done by a gas expanding, $W = p\Delta V$

change in gravitational potential energy, $\Delta E_p = mg\,\Delta h$

kinetic energy, $E_k = \frac{1}{2}mv^2$

$$\text{efficiency} = \frac{\text{useful output energy}}{\text{total input energy}} \times 100\%$$

power, $P = \frac{W}{t}$

Exercise 5.1 The concept of work

When a force *F* acts on a body, the force may do work on the body. This exercise provides practice in calculating the work done in a number of different situations.

TIP

You can calculate the work done W using $W = Fs$. Take care! The displacements must be in the direction of the force.

1 The joule is defined as the work done (or energy transferred) when a force of 1 N moves a distance of 1 m in the direction of the force. You should be able to answer the following questions using mental arithmetic.

Calculate the work done when:

a a force of 1 N moves a distance of 5 m in the direction of the force

b a force of 30 N moves a distance of 1 m in the direction of the force

c a force of 30 N moves a distance of 5 m in the direction of the force.

2 Imagine that you are trying to push a broken-down car along the road. You are not strong enough to make the car move.

a Four forces are acting on the car (its weight, the upward reaction of the road, your push and friction). Explain how you know that none of these forces does work on the car.

b A crane is used to lift the car upwards, off the road. Draw a free body diagram showing the forces that act on the car when it is above the ground.

c Which force has done work on the car when it has been lifted like this?

d The lifting force of the crane is 7500 N. Calculate the work done on the car when it has been raised 2.4 m above the road.

3 A child sits at the top of a long, smooth slide, as shown below. Her mass is 50 kg.

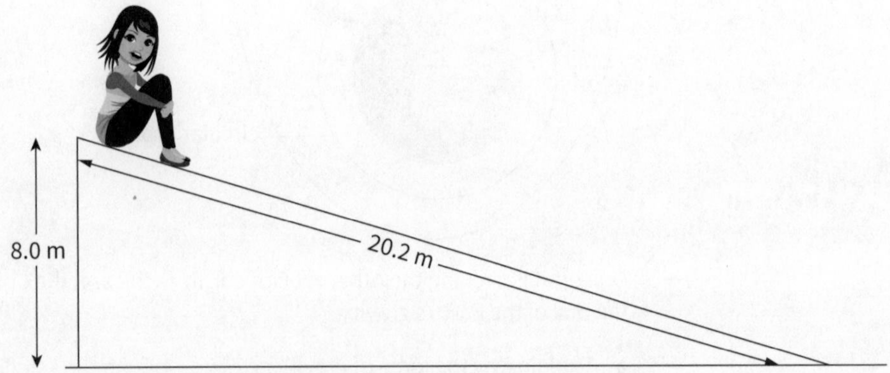

a Calculate the child's weight.

b What does the word 'smooth' suggest to you about the frictional force on the child when she goes down the slide?

c Which force does work on the child as she goes down the slide?

d Calculate the work done on the child by this force as she moves from the top of the slide to the bottom. Remember that the distance moved must be in the direction of the force.

e Describe how the child's speed changes as she slides down.

TIP

Look out for the 'code' word *smooth* in future questions during your course.

4 When a force does work on a body, it transfers energy to the body. The amount of energy transferred to the body is equal to the work done on it by the force.

Look back at question 2 to answer parts **a** and **b**.

a By how much does the energy of the car increase when the crane lifts it to a height of 2.4 m above the ground?

b What form does this increase in energy take?

Look back at question 3 to answer part **c**.

c The child's KE increases as she moves down the slide. Determine the increase in her KE as she moves down the full length of the slide.

Use the principle of conservation of energy to answer part **d**.

d In practice, no slide is perfectly smooth. Suppose that a frictional force of 80 N acts up the slide. Calculate the work done against this force as the girl moves down the slide.

e Calculate the increase in the girl's KE in this situation.

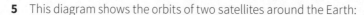

5 This diagram shows the orbits of two satellites around the Earth:

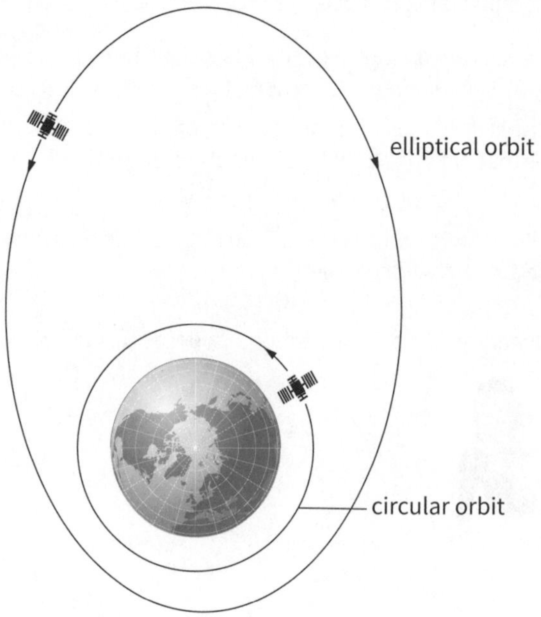

One orbit is circular; the other is elliptical. In each case, the only force acting on the satellite is the pull of the Earth's gravity.

a Explain why the force of gravity does no work on the satellite that is in a circular orbit.

For the satellite in an elliptical orbit, its distance from the Earth changes. Some of the time it is closer to the Earth, and some of the time it is further away.

b At which point in its orbit does the satellite have its maximum GPE?
Think about how GPE depends on height above the Earth's surface.

c Use the idea of 'work done by a force' to explain why the satellite's speed increases as it moves closer to the Earth.

d At which point in its orbit does the satellite have its maximum KE?

e Describe how the satellite's speed changes as it travels around its orbit.

6 This diagram shows a mass of gas trapped in a cylinder by a piston:

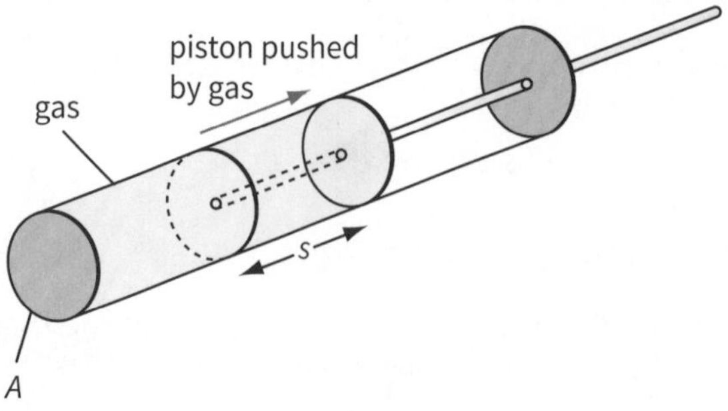

The gas exerts pressure on the circular end of the piston. The gas is heated and it expands. It must do work pushing the piston outwards.

In parts **a** and **b** of this question you will calculate, from first principles, the work done on the piston by the gas as it expands.

a The pressure of the gas is 100 kPa. It presses on the piston whose area A is 50 cm^2. Calculate the force on the piston.
Remember:

$$p = \frac{F}{A}$$

where p = pressure; F = force; A = area.

b As the gas expands, the piston is pushed through a distance s = 80 cm. Calculate the work done on the piston by the gas.

An alternative way to calculate the work done by the gas is to use the equation:

$$W = p\Delta V$$

where W = work done; p = pressure; ΔV = increase in volume of the gas.

Look at the diagram again. The increase in volume ΔV is the cylindrical section of length s and area A.

c Calculate ΔV using the values of s and A given above. Give your answer in m^3.

d Calculate W using $W = p\Delta V$. Do you get the same answer as in part b before?

e You can only use the equation $W = p\Delta V$ in situations where the pressure p is constant. Explain why this is so. Think about the force exerted by the gas on the piston.

Exercise 5.2 Gravitational potential energy and kinetic energy

You can calculate the GPE and the KE of an object using these equations:

$$E_p = mgh$$

$$E_k = \frac{1}{2}mv^2$$

In this exercise you will look at the derivations of these equations. (The acceleration due to gravity at the surface of the Earth is 9.81 m s^{-2}.)

1 A ball of mass 0.35 kg was thrown upwards. It reached a height of 5.3 m above its starting position.

a Calculate the weight of the ball.

b Calculate the increase in its GPE when it is at its highest point.

c Determine the decrease in the ball's GPE as it falls back down to its starting position.

2 The equation for GPE is $E_p = mgh$.

a State the quantities represented by the symbols m, g and h.

A body of mass m was raised at a steady speed in a gravitational field by a force F.

b Explain how you know that the forces on the body were balanced.

c Explain why it follows that $F = mg$.

d The body was raised through a height h. Calculate the work done by the force F.

e Determine the increase in the body's GPE.

3 The equation for KE is:

$E_k = \frac{1}{2}mv^2$

a State the quantities represented by the symbols m and v.

You can derive the KE equation starting from one of the equations of motion:

$v^2 = u^2 + 2as$.

Imagine a body that is initially at rest. A force F acts on it to accelerate it to speed v.

b Write down the body's initial velocity u.

c Write down a modified equation of motion that takes your answer to part **a** into account.

d Multiply both sides of the equation by $\frac{1}{2}m$.

e On the right-hand side you now have the quantity *mas*. What is the quantity *ma* equal to? What is the quantity *mas* equal to?

4 This question involves calculating a *change* in KE. Take care when calculating a change in KE. You need to calculate the KE before and the KE after the change; do not be tempted to calculate using the change in *speed*.

a A boy of mass 54 kg is running at a speed of 5.0 m s^{-1}. Calculate his KE.

b The boy accelerates to a speed of 6.3 m s^{-1}. Calculate the change in his KE.

5 This diagram shows a simple pendulum:

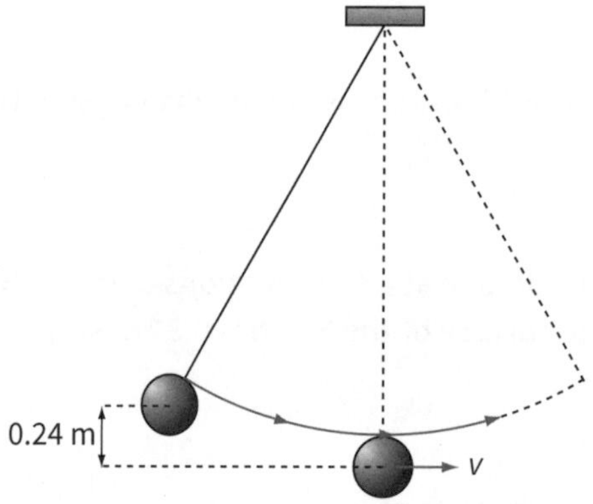

The pendulum bob has a mass of 25 g. When pulled to the left, it is 0.24 m above the lowest point in its swing.

a Determine the change in the bob's GPE when it swings from its starting point to the lowest point.

b Determine the speed v of the bob at its lowest point.

c Explain why the speed of the bob is greatest at the lowest point in its swing.

Exercise 5.3 Energy efficiency

Everything we do involves energy changes. We want to make the best use of our energy resources; we want to waste as little energy as possible – That's why it is important to understand the idea of energy efficiency.

1 An electric lamp is supplied with 60 J of energy each second. It produces 2.4 J of light energy per second.

a Determine the amount of energy wasted as heat each second.

b Calculate the lamp's efficiency. Give your answer as a percentage. Remember that efficiency is the amount of useful energy as a fraction of the total energy.

2 This Sankey diagram represents the energy changes each second in a combined heat and power (CHP) station. CHP stations burn fuel to generate hot water and electricity:

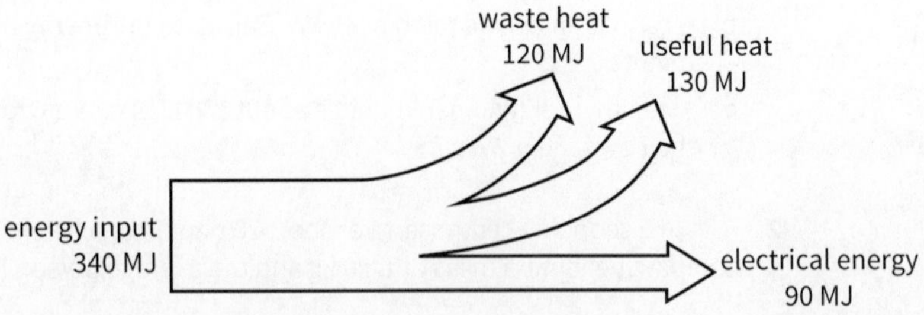

a How much energy is supplied to the power station, by its fuel, each second?

b How much useful energy does the power station supply each second?

To calculate efficiency you need to identify all *useful* energy transfers. Wasted energy is usually heat, but not all heat is wasted energy.

c How much energy is wasted by the power station each second?

d Calculate the efficiency of the power station.

3 Imagine that you are lifting some heavy boxes on to a conveyor belt. Each box weighs 175 N and you have to lift it to a height of 1.2 m.

a Calculate the work done in lifting each box.

b After ten minutes, you have lifted 40 boxes. Calculate the work you have done.

c In this time, your body has used 95 kJ of energy. How much of this energy is wasted?

d Suggest the form taken by most of this wasted energy.

e Calculate the efficiency of your body in this task. State whether you think the human body is efficient as a lifting machine.

4 A car of mass 650 kg accelerates from rest to a speed of 22 m s^{-1}.

a Calculate the car's kinetic energy.

To achieve this acceleration, the car's engine burns 0.023 litre of petrol. Each litre of fuel stores 40 MJ of chemical energy.

b Calculate the energy in the burned fuel.

c Calculate the efficiency of the engine in accelerating the car.

Exercise 5.4 Power

Power is the rate at which work is done, or the rate at which energy is transferred. Its unit is the watt, W (1 W = 1 J s^{-1}).

1 You can apply the idea of power to any situation where energy is transferred. In these examples, divide energy by time to find power, or multiply power by time to find energy.

a Calculate the power of an electric motor which transfers 180 000 J of energy in one minute. Give your answer in kW.

b A car has an engine rated at 45 kW. Calculate the energy transferred by the engine in one minute.

c A healthy, adult human requires about 10 MJ of energy from their food each day. Estimate their average power.

2 A lift in a shopping centre can transport 20 people to a height of 54 m in a time of 14 s. The lift compartment has a mass of 1420 kg and the average person has a mass of 60 kg.

a Calculate the combined mass of the compartment and the 20 people in it.

b Calculate the energy gained as the lift travels upwards.

Think about the lift as it rises. Which form of energy is increasing?

c Calculate the rate at which energy is transferred by the lift motor to the compartment.

3 The power rating of an electric lamp tells you the rate at which it uses electrical energy.

Lamp A has a power rating of 24 W, and a light output of 2.3 W

Lamp B has a power rating of 100 W, and a light output of 3.2 W

Which lamp is the more efficient? Show your calculation for each lamp. Note that efficiency can be calculated using values of power instead of energy.

Exam-style questions

1 **a** A steel ball of mass 20.0 g is placed on a smooth, curved track as shown:

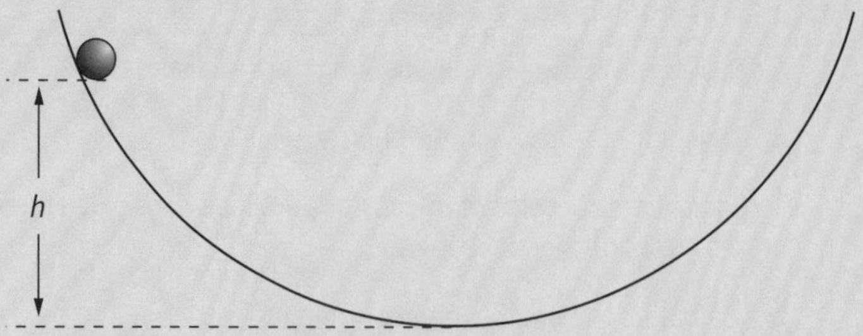

When released, the ball rolls back and forth along the track. At its lowest point, its speed is 0.47 m s^{-1}. Calculate its KE at this point. [3]

b Deduce the height h above the bottom of the track from which it was released. [2]

2 This diagram shows a wooden block on a rough, 1.7 m long slope. It shows the four forces acting on the block as it is pulled, by a length of string, directly up the slope at a constant speed of 0.60 m s^{-1}:

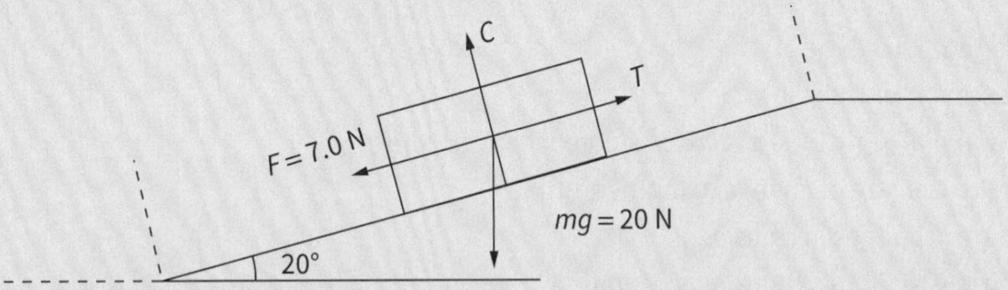

a Explain what is meant by *work done*. [1]

b With reference to Newton's first law of motion, discuss whether the box is in equilibrium. [2]

c Explain why the contact force *C* does no work as the block moves. [2]

d Write down a word equation that relates the work done by the force *T* that pulls the block up the slope, the gravitational potential energy of the box and the work done by force *F*. [1]

e Use your equation in **d** to calculate a value for the force *T*. [3]

f Calculate the power needed to pull the box up the slope at the constant speed. [2]

3 **a** Define *power*. [1]

b Use your definition of power to show that the SI base units of power are kg m^2 s^{-3}. [2]

c A car of mass 1000 kg travels at a constant speed of 7.4 m s^{-1} up a road that is inclined at 6.0° to the horizontal. The effect of air resistance on the car is negligible.

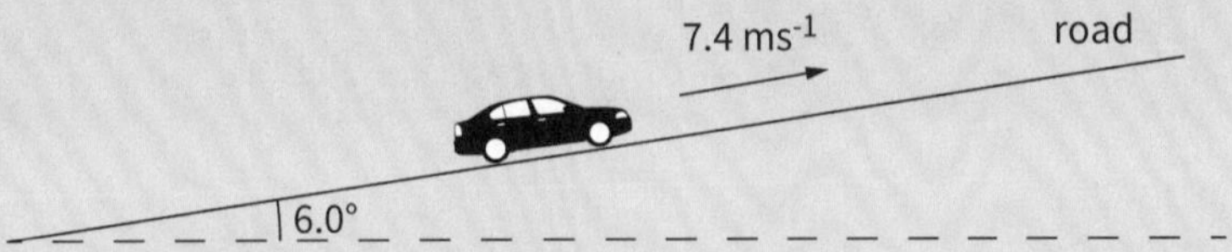

i Calculate the useful power needed to move the car up the road at a constant speed. [3]

ii Explain why the value you have calculated in **i** is equal to the increase in gravitational energy of the car per second. [1]

Chapter outline

- define linear momentum
- state and apply the principle of conservation of momentum
- relate force to the rate of change of momentum
- discuss energy changes in collisions
- state and apply Newton's three laws of motion

KEY TERMS

linear momentum: the product of mass and velocity

principle of conservation of momentum: within a closed system the total momentum in any direction is constant

Newton's first law of motion: an object will remain at rest or keep travelling at constant velocity unless it is acted on by a resultant external force

Newton's second law of motion: the net force acting on an object is equal to the rate of change of its momentum. The net force and the change in momentum are in the same direction

Newton's third law of motion: when two bodies interact, the forces they exert on each other are equal and opposite

Equations: momentum = mass × velocity; $p = mv$

force = rate of change of momentum; $F = \frac{\Delta p}{\Delta t}$

Exercise 6.1 Momentum calculations

The following exercise provides practice in rearranging and using the equation for momentum. Calculating the momentum of an object is not difficult, but remember that momentum is a vector quantity.

Always remember to check units and convert to scientific notation as needed.

1 Calculate the momentum of:

a a lab trolley of mass 1.0 kg moving at 20 cm s^{-1}

b a car of mass 650 kg moving at 24 m s^{-1}

c the Earth, mass 6.0×10^{24} kg, moving at 29.8 km s^{-1} in its orbit around the Sun.

2 A runner of mass 74 kg is moving at 7.5 m s^{-1}. She accelerates to a speed of 8.8 m s^{-1}.

a By how much has her momentum increased?

You can use the change in velocity to calculate change in momentum.

b By how much has her kinetic energy increased?

Take care! You cannot use the change in velocity to calculate change in kinetic energy.

3 A spacecraft of mass 40 kg is in a circular orbit around the Earth. It moves at a constant speed of 8.1 km s^{-1}. It completes exactly half an orbit in a time of 46 minutes.

a By how much does its momentum change in this time? Remember that momentum is a vector quantity.

b By how much does its kinetic energy change in this time? Explain your answer.

c The force of gravity holds the spacecraft in its orbit. Calculate the work done by this force during one half-orbit.

Exercise 6.2 Getting a feel for momentum changes

You can use the idea of conservation of momentum to picture what happens when two objects collide head-on, or when two objects explode apart.

1 Picture a collision in which a moving object collides with a stationary object; they stick together. They must move after the collision if momentum is to be conserved, and their velocity must be less than that of the original moving object.

a A 1 kg mass moving at 6 m s^{-1} collides with a stationary 2 kg mass. They stick together. Determine their speed after the collision.

b A 4 kg mass moving at 5 m s^{-1} collides with a stationary 1 kg mass. They stick together. Determine their speed after the collision.

2 Now picture a collision in which the two objects do not stick together.

a A 1 kg mass moving at 6 m s^{-1} collides with a stationary 1 kg mass. They do not stick together. After the collision, the first mass is stationary. What is the speed of the second mass?

b State whether kinetic energy is conserved in this collision.

3 Now picture an explosion in which a stationary object splits into two parts that move away from each other in opposite directions.

a An object explodes into two parts of equal mass. What can you say about their velocities?

b An object explodes into two parts, of masses 2 kg and 5 kg. The 2 kg mass moves at 30 cm s^{-1}. Calculate the speed of the 5 kg mass.

4 Trolley A has a mass of 5 kg and is moving at 2.0 m s^{-1}. Trolley B has a mass of 2.5 kg and is moving at 4.0 m s^{-1} in the opposite direction. They collide and they stick together.

a Calculate the momentum of each trolley.

b What will be their velocity after the collision? Explain your answer.

c Explain why this is like an explosion in reverse.

Exercise 6.3 Momentum conservation calculations

Because momentum is always conserved when two or more objects interact, we can calculate unknown values of velocity. For two objects, we can represent the conservation of momentum as an equation:

$$m_1u_1 + m_2u_2 = m_1v_1 + m_2v_2$$

This exercise provides practice in using this equation.

1 A stationary mass explodes into two parts with masses 3.0 kg and 4.5 kg. The smaller mass flies off with a speed of 12 m s^{-1}.

a Determine the values of m_1u_1 and m_2u_2.

b Calculate the speed of the larger mass after the explosion.

c What can you say about the directions in which the two masses move?

2 A ball of mass 0.35 kg rolls along the ground at 0.60 m s^{-1}. It collides with a second, stationary ball of mass 0.70 kg and bounces back with a speed of 0.40 m s^{-1}. The second ball moves off with speed 0.10 m s^{-1}.

a Calculate the momentum of the moving ball before the collision.

b Calculate the momentum of each ball after the collision.

c Show that momentum is conserved in this collision.

d In a perfectly elastic collision, kinetic energy is conserved. Calculate the kinetic energy of each mass before and after the collision. Is this a perfectly elastic collision?

3 A child throws a ball of mass 0.30 kg at a wall. It strikes the wall with a speed of 5.0 m s^{-1} and bounces off with the same speed in the opposite direction.

a Calculate the change in the ball's momentum.

b The ball collides with the wall, but the wall is attached to the Earth. This means that the momentum of the Earth has been changed by the collision. The mass of the Earth is 6.0×10^{24} kg. Estimate the change in the Earth's velocity caused by the collision with the ball.

Exercise 6.4 Force and momentum

When a force acts on a body and there is a displacement, work is done by the force on the body. The body accelerates, so its momentum changes. The force and the rate of change of momentum it produces are related by force = rate of change of momentum. For a constant force, we can write this as:

$$\text{force} = \frac{\text{change of momentum}}{\text{time taken}}$$

1 A car of mass 750 kg accelerates from 10 m s^{-1} to 25 m s^{-1} in a time of 22.5 s.

a Calculate the change in momentum of the car.

b Use your answer to part **a** to calculate the force causing the car to accelerate.

You can calculate the force in another way:

c Calculate the car's acceleration.

d Calculate the force using $F = ma$. Do you get the same answer as in part **b**?

2 A spacecraft is orbiting the Earth, as shown. Its velocity is shown at opposite points in its circular orbit:

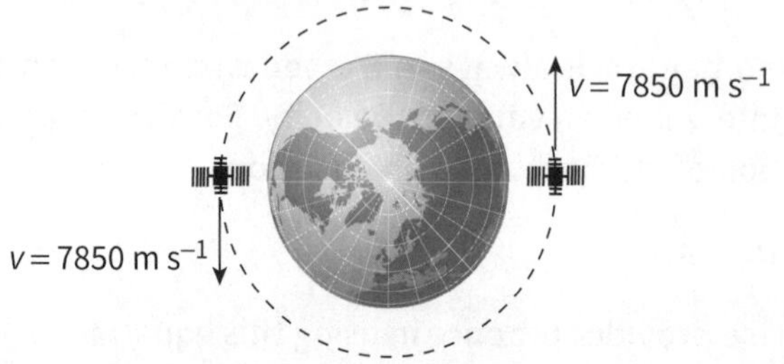

a The spacecraft has a mass of 420 kg. Calculate the change in its momentum as it travels half-way around its orbit.

b The force on the spacecraft keeping it in orbit is its weight. Calculate its weight, if the gravitational field strength is 8.9 N kg^{-1}.

c Use your answers to parts **a** and **b** to calculate the time taken for the spacecraft to complete half an orbit, and hence find its orbital period.

3 Your friend is running down the street and bumps into someone, who falls to the ground. The person complains, "You really hurt me!" Your friend replies, "But you hit me with exactly the same force as I hit you!"

Is your friend correct? Explain your answer.

Exercise 6.5 Newton's laws of motion

Newton's laws summarise much of the material covered in the first six chapters of this book. This exercise is designed to check your understanding of these important laws.

1 This question is about Newton's first law of motion.

a An object is stationary. No force acts on it. What does Newton's first law say about its motion?

b An object is moving. No force acts on it. What does Newton's first law say about its motion?

c An object is moving. It is acted on by four forces whose resultant force is zero. What does Newton's first law say about its motion?

d An object is moving with constant velocity. What does Newton's first law say about the forces acting on it?

e An object is moving at a steady speed along a curved path. What does Newton's first law say about the forces acting on it?

2 This question is about Newton's second law of motion.

a An object is moving in a straight line with constant acceleration.

i What can you say about the rate of change of the object's momentum?

ii What does Newton's second law say about the forces acting on the object?

b A skydiver is falling towards the Earth. Her velocity is increasing but her acceleration is decreasing.

i What does Newton's second law say about the forces acting on the skydiver? Think about the skydiver's momentum and the rate at which it is changing.

ii Two forces act on the skydiver as she falls. Referring to these forces, explain how her velocity can be increasing while her acceleration is decreasing.

3 We can write Newton's second law using SI units:

resultant force = rate of change of momentum

a Explain why we have to say 'in SI units'.

b Use the equation to express the newton (N) in terms of SI base units.

4 This question is about Newton's third law of motion.

a Two bar magnets are placed close to one another with their north poles facing each other.

i State whether the magnets attract or repel each other.

ii What does Newton's third law tell you about the force each magnet exerts on the other?

b If you stand on the floor, two forces act on you: your weight and the upward contact force of the floor.

i Explain why these two forces are not an 'equal and opposite pair' in the sense of Newton's third law.

ii For each of the two forces, state the force that is equal and opposite to it, as described by Newton's third law. Remember that 'weight' is the Earth's gravitational pull on an object.

Exam-style questions

1 A bullet of mass 25 g is travelling at 450 m s^{-1} when it strikes the armour plating of a tank. It bounces back along the same path with a speed of 390 m s^{-1}.

a Calculate the change in momentum of the bullet. [3]

b The time of impact of the bullet on the tank is 0.040 s. Calculate the average force that acts on the bullet in this time. [2]

c State whether the impact is elastic or inelastic. Explain your answer. [2]

d Discuss how the principles of conservation of energy and momentum apply to this collision. [3]

2 In an experiment to measure the speed of a bee as it flies, a small ball is hung by a thread. When the bee lands on the ball, the ball swings upwards. Scientists record a video of the bee as it lands and analyse the video to determine the height to which the ball swings.

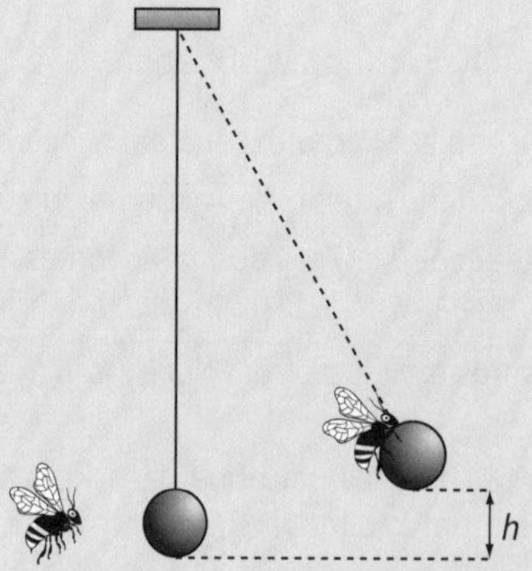

mass of bee = 0.25 g; mass of ball = 0.45 g

a The ball with the bee attached to it is found to rise to a vertical height *h* of 6.0 cm. Calculate its increase in gravitational potential energy. [2]

b Determine the speed of the ball+bee when it starts to swing upwards. [2]

c Determine the momentum of the ball+bee. [1]

d Determine the speed with which the bee lands on the ball. [2]

e Suggest the optimum horizontal point of the swing for the bee to take off from the ball. State your criteria for choosing this point and explain your answer. [2]

Chapter outline

- define density and pressure
- derive and use the equation $\Delta p = \rho g \Delta h$
- understand how upthrust arises on a body in a fluid
- understand the effects of tensile and compressive forces, including Hooke's law
- define and use stress, strain and the Young modulus
- describe an experiment to determine the Young modulus
- distinguish between elastic and plastic deformation of a material
- understand and use force–extension graphs, including calculating work done and strain energy from the area under the graph

KEY TERMS

density: the mass per unit volume of a material

pressure: the force acting normally in a fluid per unit area of a surface

strain: the extension per unit length produced by tensile or compressive forces

stress: the force per unit cross-sectional area

Young modulus: the ratio of stress to strain for a given material, provided Hooke's law is obeyed

Equations: $\text{density} = \frac{\text{mass}}{\text{volume}}$; $\rho = \frac{M}{V}$

$\text{pressure} = \frac{\text{force}}{\text{area}}$; $P = \frac{F}{A}$

pressure in a fluid = density × acceleration due to gravity × depth; $p = \rho g h$

$\text{stress} = \frac{\text{force}}{\text{cross-sectional area}}$; $\sigma = \frac{F}{A}$

$\text{strain} = \frac{\text{extension}}{\text{original length}}$; $\varepsilon = \frac{x}{L}$

$\text{Young modulus} = \frac{\text{stress}}{\text{strain}}$; $E = \frac{\sigma}{\varepsilon}$

elastic potential energy, $E = \frac{1}{2}Fx = \frac{1}{2}kx^2$

Exercise 7.1 Density and pressure

A fluid exerts pressure on any surface with which it comes into contact. Pressure is the cause of the upthrust on any object immersed in a fluid. This exercise provides practice in calculations involving density and pressure.

Density calculations are not complicated but, in these examples, you will have to calculate the volume of a sphere and work with numbers in standard form (scientific notation).

1 Saturn is a gas giant planet – it consists mostly of a sphere of solidified hydrogen and helium.

Saturn: mass = 5.7×10^{26} kg; mean radius = 58 200 km

a Calculate the mean density of Saturn. Note: volume of a sphere = $\frac{4}{3}\pi r^3$

b The mean density of the Earth is 5510 kg m^{-3}; its mean radius is 6371 km. Calculate the Earth's mass.

c What does this suggest about the composition of the Earth, compared with Saturn?

2 The pressure at a point in a fluid is caused by the weight of fluid above, pressing downwards. The pressure is given by $p = \rho gh$.

a State the quantity represented by each symbol in this equation and give its unit (name and symbol).

b Use the equation to find an expression for the pascal in terms of SI base units.

This diagram shows a tank containing a liquid of density 850 kg m^{-3}:

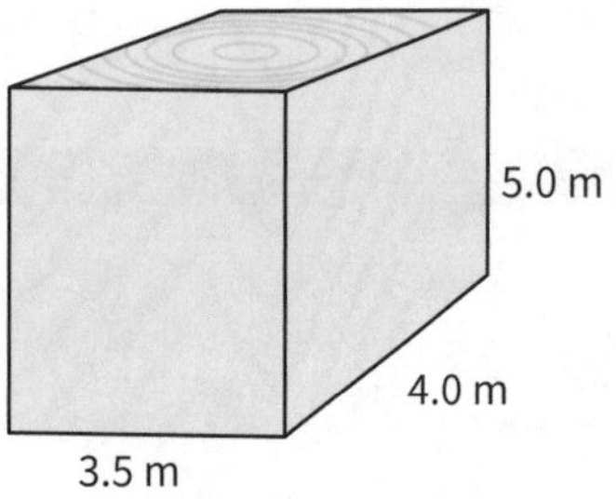

You can calculate the pressure on the base of the tank in steps which follow the derivation of the equation for pressure $p = \rho gh$.

c Calculate the volume, mass and weight of the liquid in the tank.

d Calculate the area of the base of the tank.

e Calculate the pressure on the base of the tank using pressure = force / area.

f Check your answer, using $p = \rho gh$.

In fact, the pressure at the surface of the liquid is atmospheric pressure, due to the atmosphere above.

TIP
You can simply add the pressures.

g Atmospheric pressure is approximately 101 kPa. Calculate the total pressure on the base of the tank.

The *change* in pressure Δp if you move up or down in a fluid is given by:

$\Delta p = \rho g \Delta h$

where Δh is the change in depth.

h If you move upwards through the atmosphere, does atmospheric pressure increase or decrease?

i Calculate the change in pressure when a diver descends through a 5.0 m depth of water. (Assume the density of water = 1000 kg m^{-3} is constant over this depth.)

3 This diagram shows two identical wooden blocks A and B immersed in a tank of water:

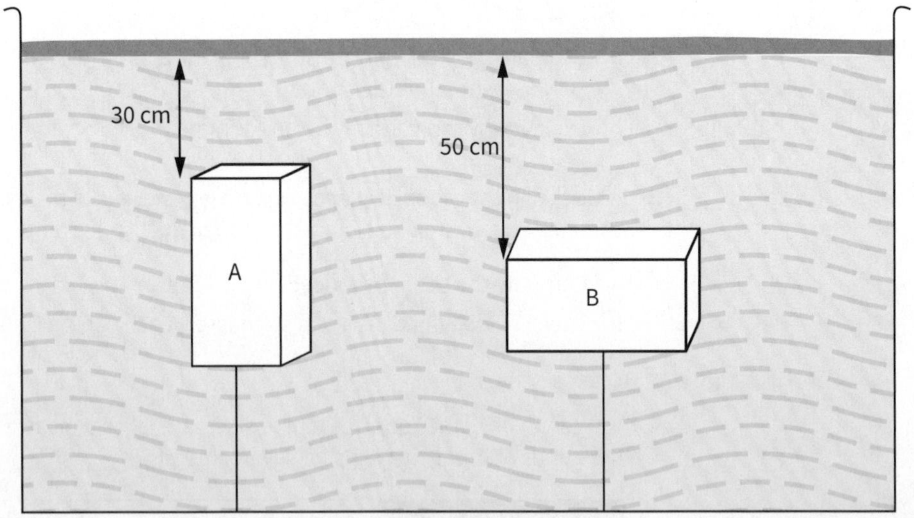

Each block is held in position by a length of string attached to the bottom of the tank. Each block measures 20 cm × 20 cm × 50 cm. The density of the wood is 950 kg m^{-3}. The density of water is 1000 kg m^{-3}.

a Use the idea of density to explain why the blocks tend to float upwards in the water.

b Calculate the weight of a block.

c Draw a free body diagram to show the forces acting on block A.

The upthrust of the water on the block arises because the pressure of the water produces a greater force on the lower surface of the block than on the upper surface.

d Calculate the pressure of the water on the upper surface of block A.

e Calculate the force exerted by the water on the upper surface of block A. State its direction.

f Calculate the force exerted by the water on the lower surface of block A. State its direction.

g Deduce the upthrust of the water on block A.

h Calculate the tension in the string which holds block A in place.

i Show that the upthrust of the water on block B is the same as on block A.

With more advanced maths, it can be shown that the upthrust on an object immersed in water is the same no matter how it is orientated.

Exercise 7.2 Stretching things

When considering the effect of tensile forces on a spring, we need only consider the load and extension. For a metal wire, we must take into account its physical dimensions by considering stress and strain.

1 The extension x of a spring is related to the load F by $F = kx$, where k is the force constant (provided Hooke's law is obeyed).

a Sketch a load–extension graph for a spring, indicating the region in which it obeys Hooke's law.

b A spring has a force constant $k = 150$ N m^{-1}. Its un-stretched length is 30.0 cm.

i Estimate the load required to increase its length to 35.0 cm.

ii Explain why your answer to part i can only be an estimate.

2 A spring is stretched so that its length increases from 24.5 cm to 30.2 cm. The load producing this extension is 20.0 N.

a Estimate the work done in stretching the spring. Remember that the load increases from 0 to 20 N as it stretches the spring.

b Explain why this can only be an estimate.

3 A block of plastic foam is placed on firm ground. It is in the shape of a cube with sides of length 20.0 cm. A heavy weight is placed on top of the block, compressing it to a thickness of 17.4 cm.

a Calculate the strain produced by the load.

b The heavy weight consists of six masses, each of 5 kg. Determine the stress in the block. Give your answer in kPa.

4 You can think of the Young modulus of a material as a measure of its stiffness. This table shows the values of Young modulus for several metals:

Metal	copper	steel	aluminium	tin
Young modulus / GPa	130	210	70	50

a Which of the metals shown in the table is the stiffest?

Wires of copper, steel and aluminium are compared in a test. Each wire is 1.0 m in length and has a cross-sectional area of 1.0 mm^2.

b A tensile load of 100 N is applied to each wire. Which wire will extend the most? Explain your answer. There is no need for calculations here.

c The Young modulus of steel is three times that of aluminium. If a particular load produces an extension of 0.20 mm in the steel wire, what extension will be produced in the aluminium wire? You can answer this by thinking in proportions.

d Calculate the extension in the tin wire when a load of 200 N is applied. You may need to calculate this in steps, starting by calculating the stress in the wire.

5 This diagram shows a method for determining the Young modulus of a metal:

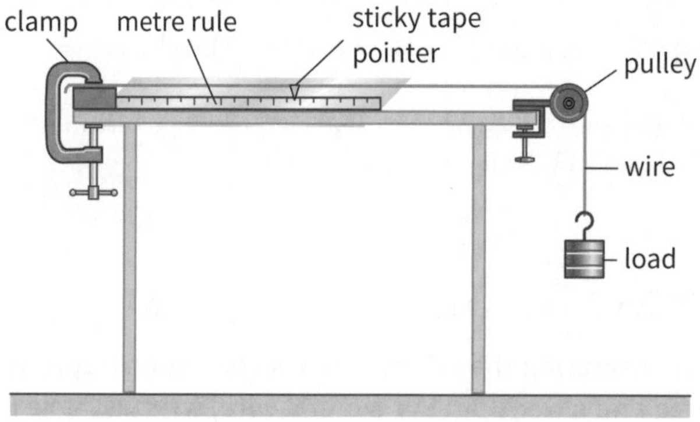

The length of the wire can be measured to the nearest 0.5 mm. To obtain satisfactory measurements of the extension of the wire, it should be several metres in length.

a A thin steel wire is stretched so that its length increases from 4.539 m to 4.543 m. Calculate the strain in the wire.

b The diameter of the wire is 1.20 mm. What instrument could be used to determine this?

c Calculate the cross-sectional area of the wire.

d The load on the wire is 200 N. Calculate the stress in the wire. Give your answer in MPa.

e Deduce a value for the Young modulus of steel. Give your answer in GPa. Make sure you are familiar with the SI prefixes M and G.

f In practice, several measurements of load and extension would be made and a graph drawn of stress against strain. Sketch the graph you would expect to obtain and indicate how you would deduce the Young modulus from the graph.

Exam-style questions

1 **a** Define pressure. [1]

b Use your definition of pressure to show that the pressure p at depth h in a liquid of density ρ is given by the expression $p = \rho gh$, where g is the acceleration of free fall. [3]

c Show that the SI base units of pressure are kg m^{-1} s^{-2} [3]

d A stone slab has a mass of 50 kg and dimensions 40 mm × 600 mm × 800 mm. Calculate the maximum pressure the slab exerts when resting on the ground on one of its surfaces. [3]

2 The diagram shows the load-extension graph for wire that extends elastically until it breaks.

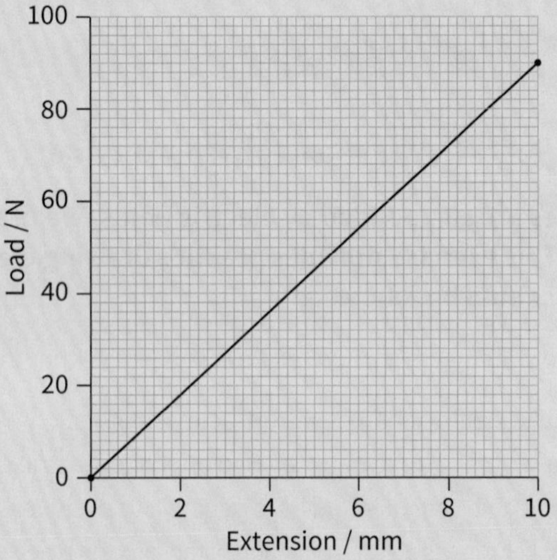

a Explain what is meant by an *elastic extension.* [2]

b The wire is of length 2.00 m and cross-sectional area 2.5×10^{-7} m^2. Use the diagram to determine, for this wire,

i the maximum stress in the wire, [2]

ii the Young modulus, [3]

iii the maximum strain energy stored in the wire before it breaks. [2]

c A load of 90 N is hung from a second wire made of the same material. The second wire has the same volume as the original wire but has twice the length. Compare the extensions of the two wires, explaining your reasoning. [3]

Chapter outline

- represent an electric field using field lines
- define and calculate field strength and force
- describe the motion of charged particles in an electric field

KEY TERMS

electric field: a region in which a charged body experiences a force

electric field strength: the force per unit positive charge

Equations: electric field strength $= \frac{\text{force}}{\text{charge}}$; $E = \frac{F}{Q}$

acceleration of a charged particle, $a = \frac{QE}{m}$

electric field strength in a uniform field, $E = \frac{V}{d}$

Exercise 8.1 Representing an electric field

Electric charges are surrounded by electric fields. We draw field lines to represent an electric field. This exercise provides practice drawing electric fields and understanding the rules that should be followed.

1 Each of these statements is *incorrect*. Rewrite them so that they are correct:

- **a** Two positive electric charges will attract each other.
- **b** There is a repulsive force between two opposite electric charges.
- **c** Electric field lines are directed from negative to positive.
- **d** An electric field line shows the direction of the force on a negative charge placed at a point in a field.

2 Draw diagrams to represent these electric fields:

- **a** the uniform field between two parallel plates with opposite charges
- **b** the field around a positively charged sphere
- **c** the field around a pair of charges, one positive and one negative.

Remember that field lines always enter a charged surface at right angles; also, remember the direction of the arrows on field lines.

3 Each of these diagrams, **a**, **b** and **c**, shows a positive charge Q placed in an electric field produced by other charges:

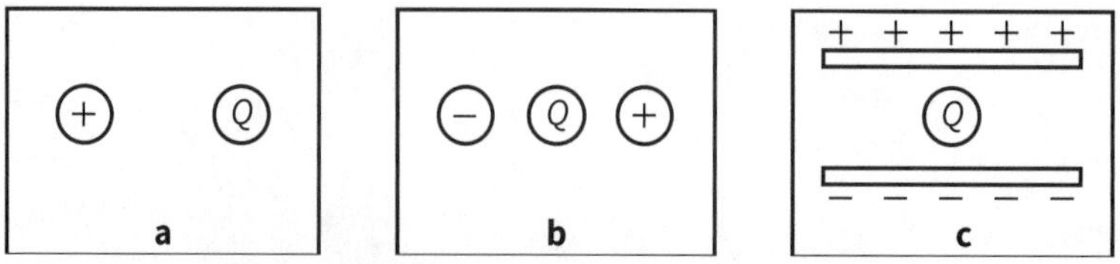

Copy each diagram and add an arrow to show the direction of the force on Q.

Exercise 8.2 Calculating force and field strength

We define electric field strength at a point in a field in terms of the force on a positive charge placed at that point. This exercise tests your understanding of the equations that define electric field strength and how to apply them.

Note: elementary charge, $e = 1.6 \times 10^{-19}$ C.

1 Electric field strength is defined by the equation:

$$E = \frac{F}{Q}$$

a State the quantities represented by E, F and Q, and give the units of each.

b Rearrange the equation to make F its subject.

c Deduce an equation for the acceleration a of a charged particle of mass m in an electric field. Note: use the equation that relates F, m and a.

2 a Calculate the electric field strength when a force of 2.0×10^{-9} N acts on a charge of 4.5×10^{-6} C.

b Calculate the force on an electron placed in a field of strength 2.0×10^{4} N C^{-1}.

3 The field strength is the same at all points in a uniform electric field.

A uniform electric field can be produced by applying a potential difference between two parallel plates. The field strength is given by $E = V/d$.

a State the quantity represented by each of the symbols E, V and d, and give the units of each.

b Calculate the field strength between two parallel metal plates separated by a distance of 20.0 cm when there is a p.d. of 5.0 kV between them. Your answer can be in V m^{-1} or N C^{-1} as they are the same.

c What p.d. is needed to produce a field strength of 500 V m^{-1} between two parallel metal plates separated by 1.0 cm?

d What force will be exerted on a particle of charge +2e placed between two parallel plates separated by a distance of 140 mm when there is a p.d. of 400 V between them? You can do this in two steps: first calculate the field strength.

e Calculate the force on the charge shown in this diagram:

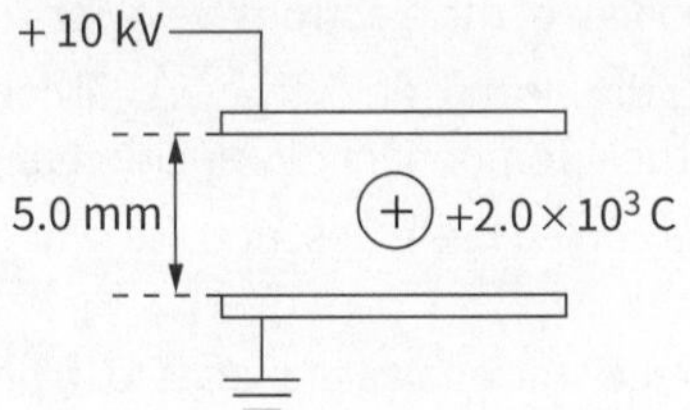

State the direction of the force.

Exercise 8.3 Moving in an electric field

This exercise considers charges moving in an electric field. A charged particle moving in a uniform electric field is like a mass moving in a uniform gravitational field (in other words, like a projectile). Remember that the usual laws of motion apply to a charged particle moving in an electric field.

1 This diagram shows a proton placed in a uniform electric field between two metal plates. The reading on the voltmeter is 240 V.

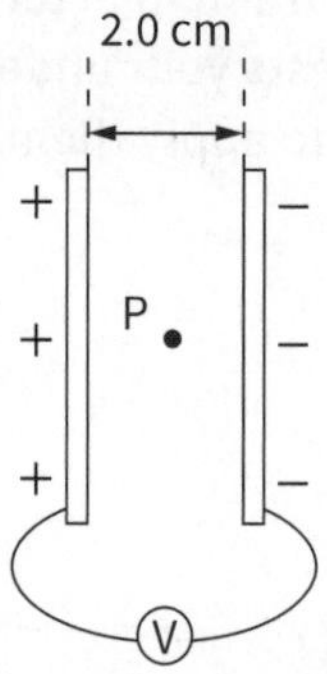

Proton mass = 1.67×10^{-27} kg; proton charge = $+1.60 \times 10^{-19}$ C.

a Calculate the electric field strength.

b Calculate the force on the proton.

c Calculate the acceleration of the proton.

d The proton is initially stationary. Describe how it will move in the electric field.

2 This diagram shows the path of a beam of electrons which is moving horizontally as it enters a uniform electric field:

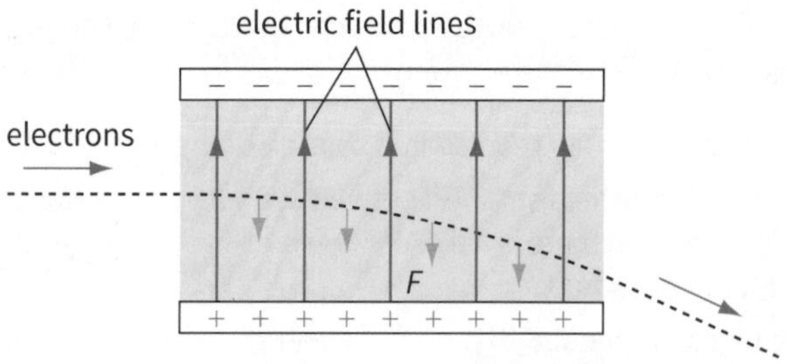

a Explain how you can tell from the pattern of the field lines that this is a uniform electric field.

b Explain why the arrows on the field lines are directed upwards.

c Explain why the force arrows on the electrons are directed downwards. Think about the electron charge.

d The horizontal component of the electrons' velocity is constant. Explain why this is so.

e As the electrons enter the electric field, the vertical component of their velocity is zero. Describe how this vertical component of velocity changes in the field.

f The electrons follow a curved path. Describe the shape of this path.

In parts **d–f**, you should recall the equivalent ideas for a projectile moving in a uniform gravitational field (Chapter 2).

Exam-style questions

Gravitational field strength $g = 9.81$ N kg^{-1}; elementary charge $e = 1.60 \times 10^{-19}$ C

1 **a** Explain what is meant by an *electric field*. [2]

b Define *electric field strength*. [2]

This diagram shows a charged particle of mass 1.0×10^{-6} kg placed in an electric field directed from left to right:

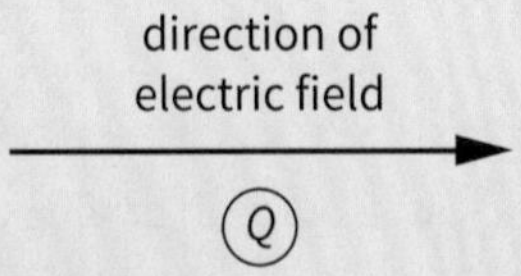

The field has a strength of 2500 N C^{-1} and the particle has a charge of -4.5×10^{-9} C.

c Calculate the electrical force on the particle. [2]

d Calculate the gravitational force on the particle. [2]

e Draw a diagram to represent the forces on the particle. Add an arrow to your diagram to show the approximate direction of the resultant force on the particle. [3]

2 The diagram shows two vertical metal plates AB and CD in a vacuum. There is a potential difference between them, as shown:

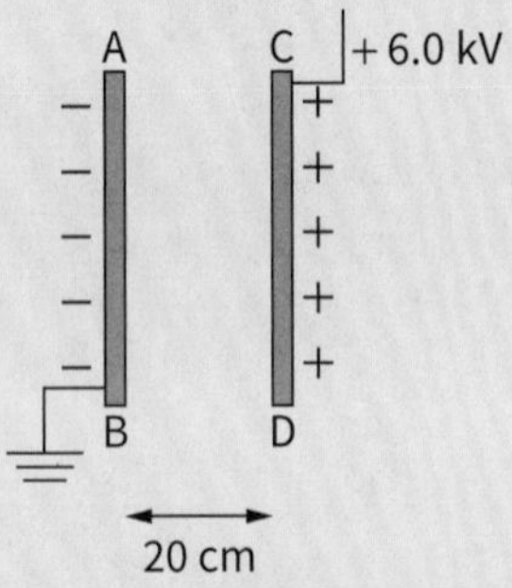

The potential difference between the two plates is 6.0 kV and they are separated by 20 cm. There is a uniform electric field between the plates.

An electron is released from rest at the surface of plate AB and moves to plate CD.

a Calculate the electric field strength between the plates. [2]

b **i** State the direction of the force on the electron and the direction of the electric field. [2]

ii Explain why the force on the electron is constant as it moves from AB to CD. [1]

c Calculate

i the work done by the electric field on the electron as the electron moves from AB to CD. [2]

ii the speed of the electron just before it reaches plate CD. [2]

d In a separate experiment, an α-particle moves between the plates.

Calculate the ratio $\frac{\text{force on the } \alpha\text{-particle as it moves between the plates}}{\text{force on the electron as it moves between the plates}}$.

Explain your reasoning. [2]

Chapter 9: Current, p.d. and resistance

Chapter outline

- understand that electric current is a flow of charge carriers, with quantised charge
- define the coulomb and use the equation $Q = It$
- derive and use, for a current-carrying conductor, the expression $I = Anvq$
- define potential difference, resistance, the volt, and the ohm
- recall and use $W = QV$, $V = IR$, $P = VI$ and $P = I^2R$
- draw and interpret circuit diagrams
- define electromotive force (e.m.f.) in terms of the energy transferred by a source in driving unit charge around a complete circuit
- distinguish between e.m.f. and potential difference (p.d.)

KEY TERMS

electromotive force (e.m.f.): the amount of energy changed from other forms into electrical energy per unit charge produced by an electrical supply

potential difference (p.d.): the energy lost per unit charge as charge passes between two points

the volt: the p.d. across a component when 1 J of electrical energy is changed into other forms when 1 C passes through the component

the coulomb: the charge that passes a point in a circuit when a current of 1 A flows for 1 s

resistance: ratio of the potential difference across component to the current in the component

the ohm: the resistance of a resistor when a p.d. of 1 V produces a current of 1 A in the resistor

mean drift velocity: the average speed of charge carriers when a current flows

Equations: $Q = It$

$V = IR$

$P = VI \qquad P = I^2R$

$E \text{ (or } W) = QV = VIt$

$I = Anvq$

Exercise 9.1 Basic definitions and units, resistance, p.d. and e.m.f.

This exercise will help you understand and use basic definitions and their units. Rearranging units can be a challenge. If you are unsure, look up the definitions of the quantities first.

1 **a** State one similarity between potential difference and electromotive force.

b State one difference between potential difference and electromotive force.

2 Match each quantity in the left column with a suitable unit from the right column:

electromotive force	A s
charge	$V\,A^{-1}$
resistance	$J\,C^{-1}$
power	$J\,s^{-1}$

3 State the quantity that can be described as:

- **a** 'the amount of energy transferred from a source to electrical energy per unit charge'
- **b** 'the amount of energy transferred from electrical energy to thermal energy per unit charge'
- **c** 'the rate of flow of electric charge'
- **d** 'one joule of energy per coulomb of charge'
- **e** 'one volt per amp'.

4 Four electrical quantities are:

charge, current, potential difference, resistance

State which quantity in the list:

- **a** can be measured in joules per coulomb
- **b** equals the product of two other quantities in the list
- **c** equals the rate of change of another quantity in the list
- **d** is a base quantity in the S.I. system
- **e** is quantised (in other words, only occurs in multiples of a certain value).

5 Show that it is possible to express the Ω as J s C^{-2}.

6 Four cells each of e.m.f. 1.5 V are connected together to make a 3.0 V battery connected to a filament lamp and a switch. Draw the circuit diagram. Make sure you use all four cells but that there is only a total e.m.f. of 3 V.

7 You are provided with a resistor, a power supply, an ammeter and a voltmeter.

- **a** State what measurements must be made to find the resistance of the resistor.
- **b** Draw a circuit diagram of the apparatus.
- **c** State whether the voltmeter and the ammeter used in your circuit should have a low or a high resistance. The resistance of the resistor is a few ohms.
- **d** Explain why the voltmeter and ammeter should have the values of resistance you have chosen.

8 The current in a resistor is 0.80 A when the p.d. across it is 12 V.

- **a** Calculate the resistance of the resistor.
- **b** Calculate the p.d. which would be needed to produce a current of 1.2 A.

Exercise 9.2 Current and charge

This exercise offers practice in calculating current and the amount of charge.

Electrical current is often measured in mA (10^{-3}A) and μA (10^{-6}A). You need to use the correct power of ten with the prefix given in the question. Some equations may include time, which should be measured in seconds. You will need to use the elementary charge $e = 1.6 \times 10^{-19}$ C. The charge on an electron is $-e$.

1 State the difference between the direction of electron flow in a circuit and the direction of the conventional current.

2 **a** Explain what is meant by *the electric current* in a conductor.

- **b** The charge passing through an electric drill in each minute is 360 C. Calculate the current.
- **c** A current of 250 μA passes through a lamp for three minutes. Calculate the charge that flows though the lamp in this time.

3 A current of 5.0 mA flows through a resistor for 12 minutes.

- **a** Calculate the amount of charge which passes through the resistor in this time.
- **b** Calculate the number of electrons which pass through the resistor in this time.
- **c** Calculate the time needed for a charge of 2.0 C to pass through the resistor.

4 In a time of 5.0×10^{-9} s, one hundred electrons pass a point in a wire.

- **a** Calculate the charge that passes the point in this time.
- **b** Calculate the current in the wire.
- **c** Explain why the charge that passes the point is a multiple of 1.6×10^{-19} C.

5 Calculate the number of electrons in a beam hitting the screen of a TV tube each second when the beam current is 1.0 mA.

Exercise 9.3 Electrical power and energy

This exercise provides practice in using several electrical formulae for power.

Remember also that power is $\frac{\text{work}}{\text{time}}$ or $\frac{\text{energy}}{\text{time}}$. Power is sometimes measured in kW (10^3 W) or MW (10^6 W).

1 A lamp operates at a voltage of 8.0 V and has a power rating of 2.0 W.

- **a** Calculate the current.
- **b** Calculate the resistance of the lamp.

2 A 20 Ω resistor has a maximum power rating of 1.0 W. Calculate the maximum current in the resistor.

3 The battery in an electric car provides a steady power of 3.6 kW to the motor for a time of 2.0 hours. The e.m.f. of the battery is 180 V.

- **a** Calculate the current in the motor.
- **b** Calculate the charge the battery delivers.
- **c** Calculate the energy delivered to the motor. Give your answer in MJ.

4 A battery provides a steady current of 0.25 A for 20 hours. In this time, the electrical energy produced by the battery is 9.6×10^4 J.

- **a** Calculate the e.m.f. of the battery.
- **b** Calculate the electrical power produced by the battery.

5 The generator in a power station has a power of 2.4 MW. The cable from the power station has a resistance of 4.0 Ω and carries a current of 20 A.

- **a** Calculate the e.m.f. of the generator.
- **b** Calculate the power wasted in the cable.

6 A student wants to obtain a large heating effect in a resistor connected to a laboratory power supply. He uses the formula $P = I^2R$, and decides to use a high resistance. Another student uses the formula $P = \frac{V^2}{R}$ and decides to use a low resistance. Explain which student is correct and why the other student is incorrect.

7 Discuss the energy transfer taking place within the battery of a mobile phone:

a when it is being used to make a call

b when it is being charged.

Exercise 9.4 Charge carriers

In this exercise, you will have to think about and use the equation $I = nAvq$. The elementary charge $e = 1.6 \times 10^{-19}$ C is usually the value for q.

1 The current I in a metal conductor of cross-sectional area A is given by the formula $I = nAvq$.

a Define the terms n, q and v.

b Show how the equation is derived.

c A piece of metal and a piece of plastic insulator each have the same dimensions and the same potential difference across them. Explain how the relative values of n for the metal and the plastic affect the current in each.

2 Name the charge carriers responsible for the current in a:

a metal

b salt solution that conducts electricity.

3 When a current of 2.0 A flows through a piece of wire that has a cross-sectional area of 1.0×10^{-6} m^2, the average drift velocity of the electrons is 2.5×10^{-4} m s^{-1}.

a Calculate the number of free electrons per unit volume of the material. Be careful to give the unit of n correctly.

b State what happens to the drift velocity if the current is halved.

c State what happens to the drift velocity if the diameter of the wire is doubled and the current is unchanged. Think about what happens to the area if diameter is doubled. Then look at the equation.

4 An aluminium wire, with cross-sectional area 1.2×10^{-6} m^2 and length 5.0 m, contains 3.6×10^{23} atoms. Each atom contributes 3 free electrons to the wire.

a Calculate the number of free electrons per unit volume in aluminium.

b The wire carries a current of 5.0 A. Calculate the mean drift velocity of the electrons.

5 A wire has a cross-sectional area of 1.8×10^{-7} m^2 and contains 8.0×10^{28} free electrons per m^3. The mean drift velocity of electrons in the wire is 8.7×10^{-4} m s^{-1}.

a Calculate the current in the wire.

b The wire is 5.0 m long. Calculate the time it takes a free electron in the wire to travel from one end to the other.

c Calculate the number of free electrons in the wire.

d The wire carries current to a motor. Explain why there is no time delay in the motor starting when the current is switched on.

6 Two pieces of wire P and Q are made of the same material but have different diameters. They are connected in series with each other and a power supply.

a State which terms in the equation $I = Anvq$ are the same for both wires.

b The cross-sectional area of P is twice that of Q. Calculate the ratio v_P:v_Q.

Exam-style questions

1 **a** Define the *e.m.f.* of a cell. [2]

b The current in a power cable from a power station is 300 A. Calculate the number of electrons passing through the cross-section of the wire in one second. $e = 1.6 \times 10^{-19}$ C. [1]

c The cross-sectional area of the wire is 9.0×10^{-4} m^2 and the density of the free electrons is 1.6×10^{29} m^{-3}.

i Calculate the mean drift velocity of the free electrons in the wire. [1]

ii Explain the difference between the mean drift velocity and the mean speed. [1]

iii One part of the wire has a smaller diameter than the rest. Explain why the mean drift velocity is different in this part of the wire. [2]

2 **a** Define the *resistance* of a resistor. [2]

b An electric heater contains three identical heating elements, shown as resistors P, Q and R, in this diagram:

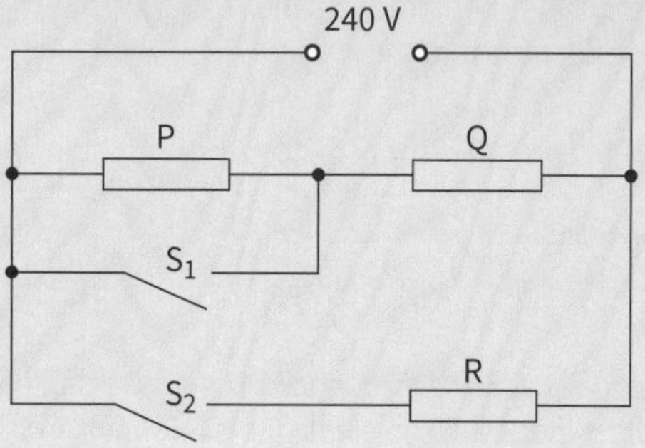

Each heating element has a constant resistance and is designed to operate at a voltage of 240 V and a power of 1.2 kW.

i Calculate the resistance of one of the elements. [3]

ii Calculate the power developed in an element that operates on a voltage of 120 V. [2]

iii The switches shown in the diagram are open. Complete the table to show the total power output of the heater when the switches are closed as shown. [4]

S_1	S_2	Total power / kW
closed	closed	
closed	open	
open	closed	
open	open	

Chapter 10: Kirchhoff's laws

Chapter outline

- recall Kirchhoff's first and second laws and their links to conservation of charge and energy
- use Kirchhoff's laws to derive and apply a formula for the combined resistance of two or more resistors in series
- use Kirchhoff's laws to derive and apply a formula for the combined resistance of two or more resistors in parallel
- apply Kirchhoff's laws to solve simple circuit problems

KEY TERMS

Kirchhoff's first law: the sum of currents entering any point is equal to the sum of the currents leaving that same point. This law represents the conservation of charge

Kirchhoff's second law: the sum of the e.m.f.s around a closed loop is equal to the sum of the p.d.s in that same loop. This law represents the conservation of energy

Equations: Kirchhoff's first law, $\Sigma I_{in} = \Sigma I_{out}$

Kirchhoff's second law, $\Sigma E = \Sigma IR$

(where Σ means 'sum of')

series resistors, $R = R_1 + R_2 + R_3 + \ldots$

parallel resistors, $\frac{1}{R} = \frac{1}{R_1} + \frac{1}{R_2} + \frac{1}{R_3} + \ldots$

$Q = It$

$V = IR$

$P = VI$

$E = QV$

Exercise 10.1 Kirchhoff's laws and conservation

This exercise tests your understanding of Kirchhoff's laws and how they relate to conservation of charge and energy.

1 Write, in your own words, Kirchhoff's first and second laws. You may have to remind yourself of the laws from a book – do not just copy them out.

2 Look at these quantities:

charge, e.m.f., energy, p.d., time

State the quantity from the list that is conserved in:

a Kirchhoff's first law

b Kirchhoff's second law.

3 Look at this circuit:

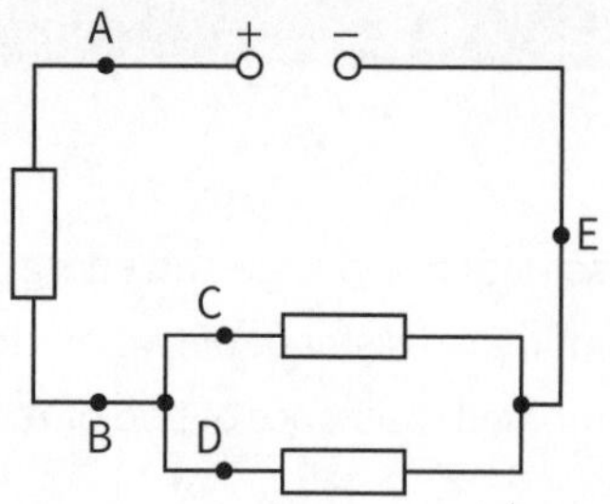

The current at **A** is 6.0 A. The current at **C** is 1.0 A.

a Calculate the charge that flows through **A** in 10 s.

b Explain why the current at **B** is the same as at **A**.

c Using Kirchhoff's first law, calculate the current at **D**.

d Using Kirchhoff's first law, calculate the current at **E**.

e Explain why the current at **C** is different from the current at **D**.

4 In this circuit, the potential difference (p.d.) across the 40 Ω resistor is 8.0 V:

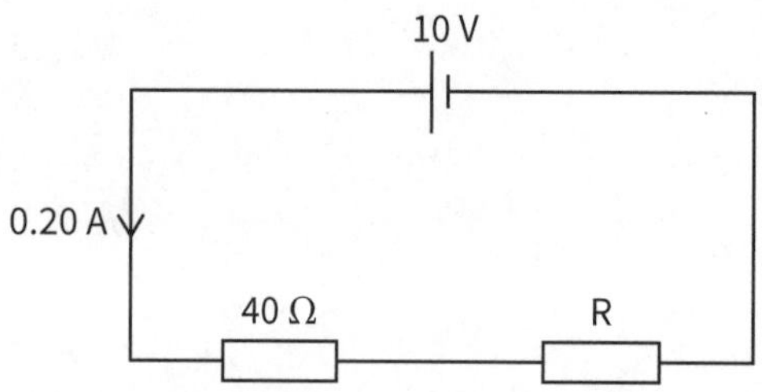

The circuit operates for a time of 10 s.

a Calculate the charge that passes through the cell in this time.

b Calculate the energy produced by the cell.

c Calculate the thermal energy (heat) produced in the 40 Ω resistor.

d Using the idea of conservation of energy, calculate the thermal energy produced in the resistor R in 10 s.

e Using your answers to **a** and **d**, calculate the p.d. across the resistor R.

f Explain how Kirchhoff's second law is a consequence of the conservation of energy in this circuit. Use values for energy that you have calculated.

5 **a** Look at this diagram:

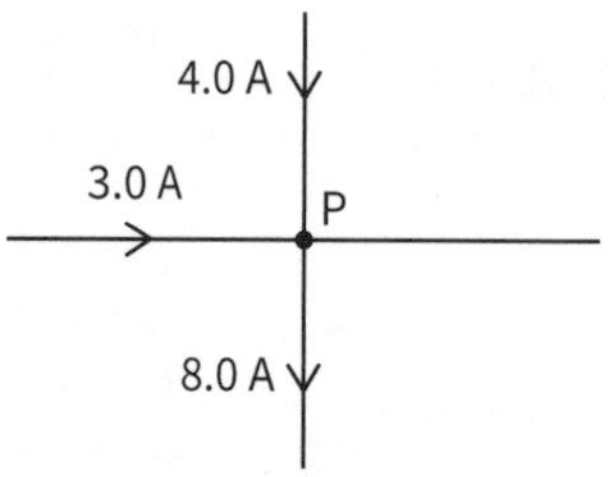

Find the current and the direction of the current at P.

b Explain your answer to **a** in terms of the charges that flow in 1.0 s.

6 In this circuit, two batteries are connected as shown. They have negligible internal resistance:

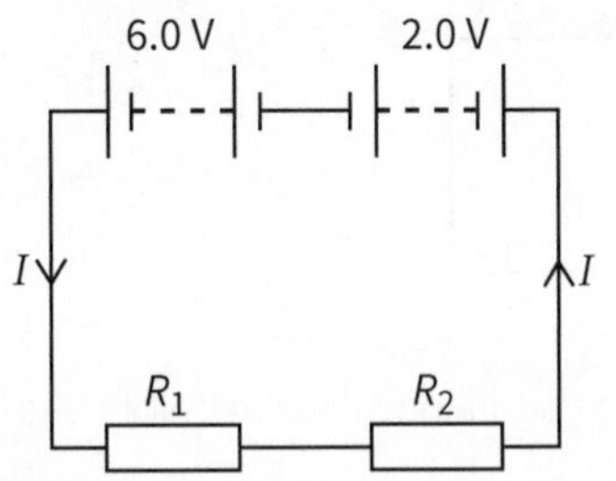

Notice that the batteries are connected the opposite way around to each other as one moves around the circuit.

a State the sum of the e.m.f.s in the circuit.

b The p.d. across R_1 is 1.0 V. Calculate the p.d. across R_2.

c Explain why the current is in the direction shown.

d 1.0 C of charge passes around the circuit. State the energy change that occurs in:

i the 6.0 V battery

ii the 2.0 V battery

iii R_1.

Exercise 10.2 Series and parallel circuits

In this exercise you will make calculations on circuits, where resistors are connected in series and in parallel.

1 Four resistors of resistance R are connected as shown. There are no other connections:

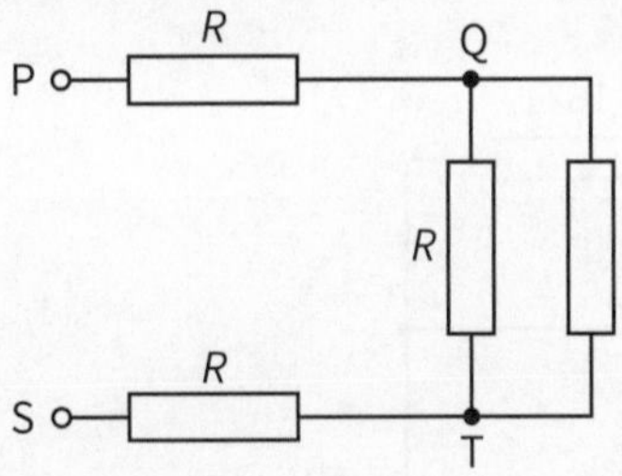

Calculate the total resistance, in terms of R, between:

a P and Q

b Q and T

c P and T

d P and S.

2 Three resistors are connected to terminals A and B, as shown:

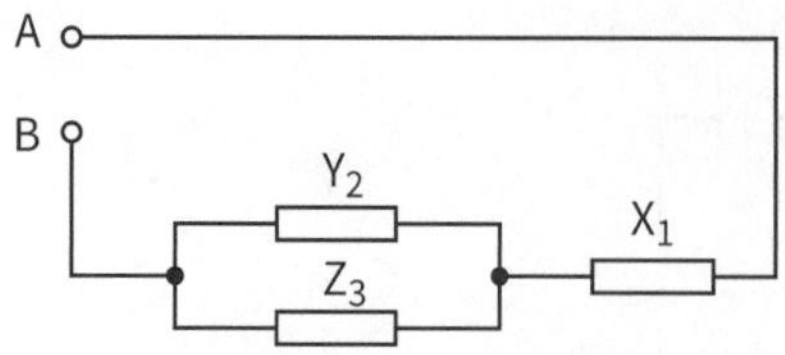

a Complete this table to find the unknown values. Note: R_{AB} is the resistance of the circuit between terminals A and B.

X_1 / Ω	Y_2 / Ω	Z_3 / Ω	R_{AB} / Ω
400	400	400	
20	400	400	
200	300		400
400		500	500

b When X_1, Y_2 and Z_3 are each 400 Ω, a p.d. of 12 V is applied between A and B:

i Calculate the current in X_1 (12 V is not the voltage across X_1 so $I \neq \frac{12}{400}$).

ii Calculate the p.d. across X_1 (You can use $V = IR$ with the current from **i**).

iii Calculate the p.d. across Y_2 (You can use Kirchhoff's second law).

3 A student has three 6.0 Ω resistors. He uses two or three of the resistors in an electric circuit. Calculate the six possible values for the total resistance of the circuit and describe each combination of the resistors. The resistances may be connected in series, in parallel or both in series and in parallel. Draw a circuit with two or three of the resistors before you start each calculation.

4 A battery of e.m.f. 6.0 V and no internal resistance is connected as shown:

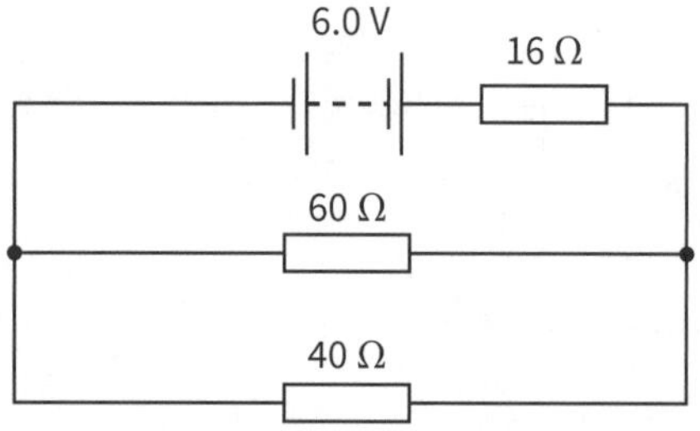

a Calculate the total resistance of the circuit.

b Calculate the current in the 16 Ω resistor.

5 A student writes a proof that the total resistance of two resistors in series is $R_1 + R_2$.

She uses the idea of two resistors connected to an e.m.f. V_t.

Her proof is:

$V_t = V_1 + V_2$

$IR_t = IR_1 + IR_2$

So, $R_t = R_1 + R_2$

a State where Kirchhoff's first law is used in the proof.

b State where Kirchhoff's second law is used in the proof.

c Write out a proof that the total resistance of two resistors in parallel is $\frac{1}{R_t} = \frac{1}{R_1} + \frac{1}{R_2}$. Indicate where Kirchhoff's laws are used in your proof.

Exercise 10.3 Applying Kirchhoff's second law to more complex circuits

In this exercise, you will need to apply Kirchhoff's second law to more complex circuits. Make sure that you understand what is meant by the total e.m.f. in a closed loop. Sometimes you have to add and sometimes subtract e.m.f.s.

1 In this circuit there are three loops that can be drawn to apply Kirchhoff's second law. The cells have negligible internal resistance:

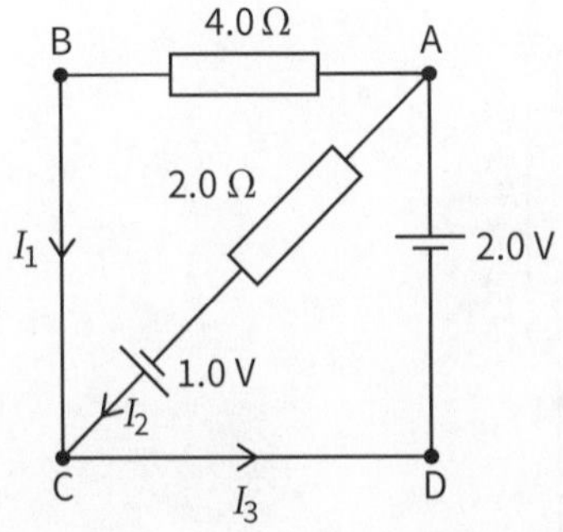

a One of the closed loops is ABCDA. State the other two closed loops.

b State the total e.m.f. in each of the three closed loops:

Choose a direction to follow around a loop, in the direction of the current. If there are two cells in the loop, you either need to add or subtract their e.m.f.s. You should add the e.m.f.s if both cells on their own produce a current in the direction of the loop. You should subtract an e.m.f. if a cell produces a current in the *opposite* direction to the current you have drawn around the loop.

Kirchhoff's second law for loop ABCDA gives the equation $2.0 = 4.0\ I_1$, where I_1 is the current in A.

c Write similar equations using Kirchhoff's second law for each of the other two loops.

d Solve the equations for I_1 and I_2.

e Write the formula that relates I_1, I_2 and I_3.

2 In this circuit, the cells have negligible internal resistance:

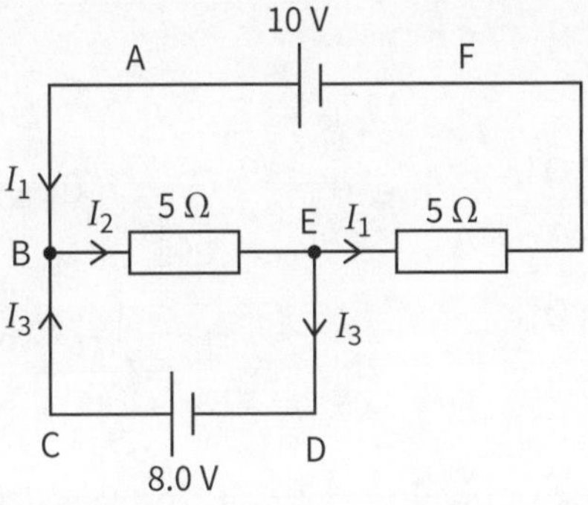

a Write the formula that relates I_1, I_2 and I_3.

b Write an equation that uses Kirchhoff's second law in the closed loop CBEDC.

c Write an equation that uses Kirchhoff's second law in the closed loop ABEFA.

d Calculate I_1, I_2 and I_3.

e Write an equation that uses Kirchhoff's second law in the loop ABCDEFA.

3 A battery of e.m.f. 8.0 V and resistance 3.0 Ω is connected with a battery of e.m.f. 4.0 V and resistance 1.0 Ω. All the components are in series. One of the batteries can be reversed in direction.

a Calculate the maximum and minimum total e.m.f. in the circuit.

b Calculate the maximum and minimum current in the circuit.

4 Four resistors of resistance R are connected as shown. There are three closed loops. The top loop includes E_1 and three resistors, the bottom loop contains E_2 and two resistors.

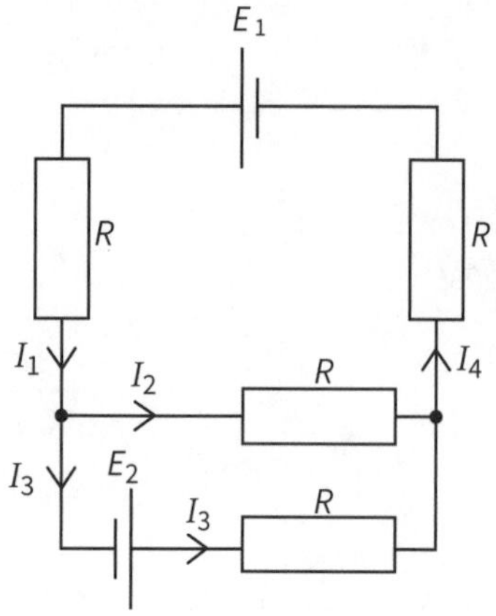

a Write the formula that relates I_1, I_2 and I_3.

b Explain why $I_4 = I_1$.

c Write the formula that relates E_1, R, I_1, I_2 and I_4 using the top loop.

d Write the formula that relates E_2, R, I_2 and I_3 using the bottom loop. The positive direction for the e.m.f. is anticlockwise (the 'direction' of E_2) so, for a resistor where the current is clockwise, the 'IR' term will be negative.

e Write the formula that relates E_1, E_2, R, I_1 and I_3 using the outside loop. Take the positive direction as anticlockwise so that both E_1 and E_2 are positive in this direction.

Exam-style questions

1 This diagram shows a 12 V power supply with negligible internal resistance connected to three resistors:

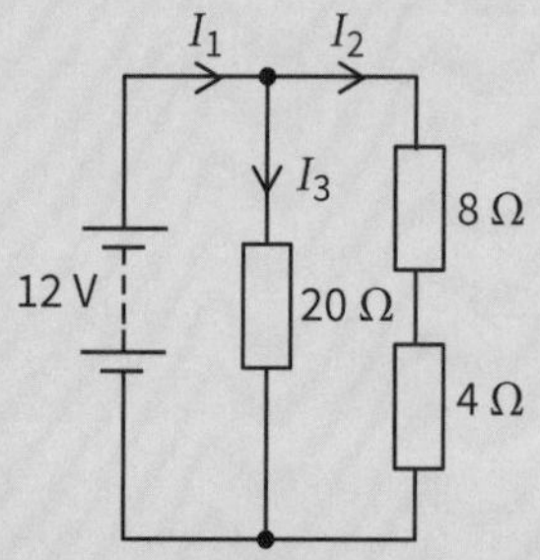

a Use Kirchhoff's first law to state the relationship between I_1, I_2 and I_3. [1]

b Use Kirchhoff's second law to calculate I_2. [2]

c Calculate I_3. [1]

d Explain how Kirchhoff's second law can be applied to the closed loop that contains just the three resistors. [2]

e Calculate the total resistance of the circuit. [2]

f Calculate the ratio: $\frac{\text{power provided by battery}}{\text{power in 20 Ω resistor}}$ [3]

2 **a** State Kirchhoff's first law. [1]

b State the quantity that is conserved in the first law. [1]

c Kirchhoff's second law shows that when a cell of e.m.f. E is connected to two resistors in series, the e.m.f. is equal to the sum of the p.d.s across the two resistors. Explain how this is a consequence of conservation of energy. [2]

d A car battery is charged using a battery charger with an e.m.f. of 16 V. The e.m.f. of the car battery at the start of the charging process is 8.0 V. The connections of the charger to the battery and the resistances in the circuit are shown in this diagram:

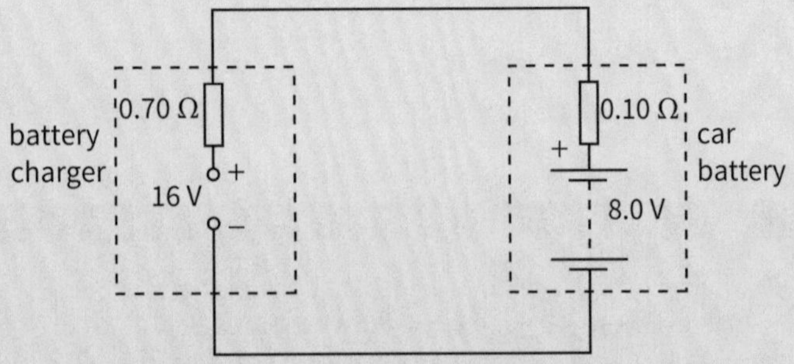

i Calculate the total resistance of the circuit. [1]

ii Calculate the current in the circuit. [2]

iii To reduce the current in the battery to 2.0 A, a resistor is placed in series in the circuit. Determine the resistance of this resistor. [2]

iv State two reasons why the positive terminal of the battery charger must **not** be connected to the negative terminal of the car battery. [2]

3 A current I enters a network of sixteen identical resistors, as shown:

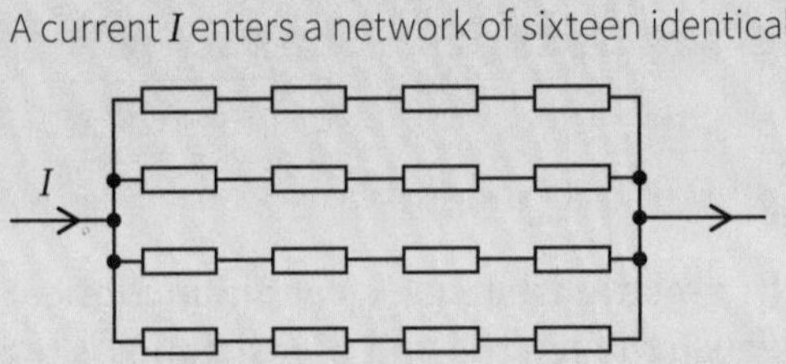

Each resistor has a resistance of 20 Ω.

a Calculate the total resistance of the network. [2]

b Describe how all sixteen resistors can be connected together to have a total resistance of 80 Ω. [2]

c Explain one advantage of using many resistors in a network, rather than using a single resistor. [1]

4 A p.d. of 12 V is applied to the resistor network shown in this diagram:

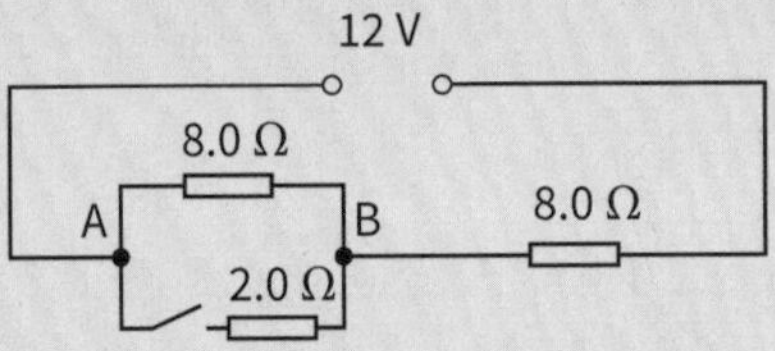

a Calculate the resistance of the circuit when the switch is closed. [2]

b Calculate the current at A when the switch is closed. [2]

c Calculate the p.d. between A and B when the switch is closed. [2]

d Describe what happens to the p.d. between A and B when the switch is opened. Explain your ideas. [2]

Chapter 11: Resistance and resistivity

Chapter outline

- sketch and discuss the I–V characteristics of a metallic conductor at constant temperature, a semiconductor diode and a filament lamp
- state Ohm's law
- recall and use $R = \frac{\rho l}{A}$

KEY TERMS

Ohm's law: the current in a metallic conductor is directly proportional to the potential difference across its ends provided physical conditions, such as temperature, remain constant

resistivity: the resistance of a sample of a material of unit cross-sectional area and unit length

semiconductor diode: an electrical component made from a semiconductor material that only conducts in one direction

Equations: $V = IR$

$$R = \frac{\rho l}{A}$$

$$P = VI = I^2R = \frac{V^2}{R}$$

Exercise 11.1 Ohm's law

Ohm's law is both a relationship *and* a condition. Notice it does not mention the word resistance at all, even though the unit of resistance is the ohm. This exercise allows you to learn and think about the law.

1 **a** Explain why each of these statements is *not* a correct statement of Ohm's law:

- **i** The potential difference across a component is proportional to its resistance.
- **ii** The potential difference across a component is proportional to the current.
- **iii** The potential difference across a component equals the current multiplied by the resistance.
- **iv** The resistance of a wire is constant, provided the temperature is constant.

b Suggest which statement is the best and rewrite it correctly.

2 This graph shows the variation with current of the p.d. across three components, A, B and C:

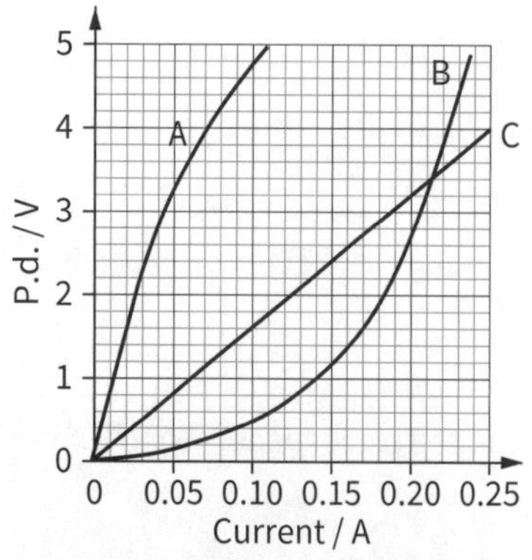

a State which component obeys Ohm's law. Explain how you know.

b State which line shows an increasing resistance at higher currents. Explain your ideas.

c State, for each component, any range of voltages where the resistance is constant.

3 This table shows values of current and p.d. obtained for a metal wire:

Current / A	0	0.10	0.20	0.30	0.40	0.50
P.d. / V	0	0.20	0.40	0.60	1.00	1.80

a Explain whether Ohm's law applies over the whole range of currents.

b State the range of currents where the resistance is constant.

Exercise 11.2 Other components

For this exercise, you need to know the *I–V* characteristic graphs for a diode and for a filament lamp, and some reasons why these graphs are not straight lines. This exercise also contains practice in writing out an experiment and describing precautions for an electrical experiment.

1 You plan to carry out an experiment to obtain the (*I–V*) characteristic of a lamp.

a Draw a suitable circuit diagram for your experiment.

b Describe how to carry out the experiment.

c Suggest one precaution that would enable accurate results to be obtained.

Your experiment needs to vary the voltage. Check that your experiment can do this. A simple series variable resistor may be used, but is not ideal as it cannot reduce the voltage down to 0 V. If you know about a potential divider, draw a circuit that can reduce the voltage down to 0 V.

2 This graph shows the (*I–V*) characteristic of a light-emitting diode in the forward direction:

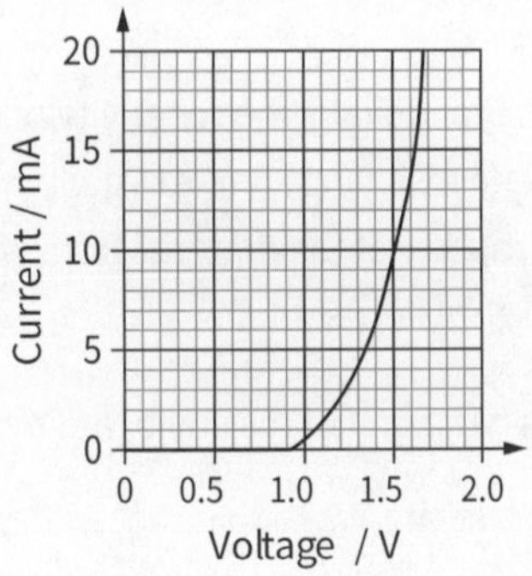

a Explain how the graph shows that the diode does not obey Ohm's law.

b Name one other device that does not obey Ohm's law.

c Calculate the resistance of the diode when the voltage is 1.5 V.

d Describe how the resistance of the diode changes as the voltage increases from 0 to 1.6 V.

e The voltage applied to the diode is reversed. State the resistance of the diode.

f Describe the new current–voltage graph.

3 The light-emitting diode from question 2 operates with a current of 15 mA and a p.d. of 1.6 V. When a voltage larger than 1.6 V is applied to the diode it becomes too hot. A protective resistance R is placed in series with the diode and a 16 V supply, as shown:

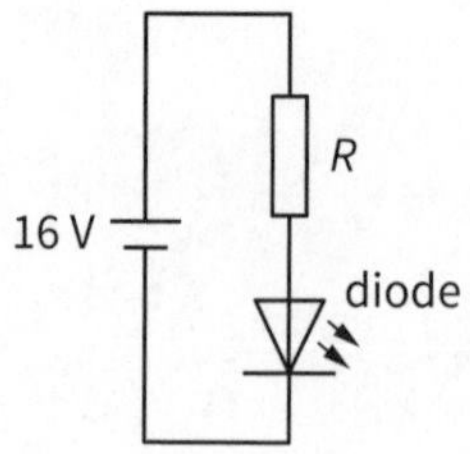

Determine the value of R that allows the diode to operate at 15 mA. (Use the p.d. across the diode to find the p.d. across the protective resistor and then find the value of R.)

4 A lamp is rated as 12 V, 48 W. The resistance of the lamp has a constant value of 0.50 Ω when the p.d. is between 0 and 1 V.

a Calculate the current in the lamp at its working temperature. The working temperature is when the lamp is at the rated voltage. Use the formula for power, voltage and current.

b Sketch a graph to show the current-voltage (I–V) characteristic of the lamp. Draw an appropriate scale for current on the y-axis and a scale for voltage on the x-axis. Mark points on your graph where you can. You can find the current at 1 V and plot points at 0, 1 V and 12 V and then make the shape correct.

c On your graph from part **b**, draw the current-voltage (I–V) characteristic of a resistor of constant resistance 3.0 Ω.

d State why the lamp does not have a constant resistance.

11.3 Resistivity and resistance: the basics

This exercise helps you think about the relationship between resistance, length and area, and the difference between resistance and resistivity. Some simple calculations can be done just by recognising that resistance is proportional to length and inversely proportional to area. To help you use the correct unit for resistivity and other electrical units, you will gain practice in changing electrical and other units into the base SI units.

1 **a** Write down a word equation that defines the resistivity of a material.

b Explain the difference between resistance and resistivity.

c Explain why resistivity is a property of the material from which a wire is made but the resistance per unit length of a wire is not.

2 A student incorrectly writes down the unit of resistivity as Ω/m.

a State the correct SI unit of resistivity.

b Express the unit of resistivity in terms of the SI units V, A and m. (You need to change Ω into a combination of V and A.)

c Express the unit of resistivity in terms of the SI base units kg, m, s and A. (First change V into J C^{-1}, then use C = A s, and finally use J = N m and N = kg m s^{-2}.)

3 Describe a method to determine, accurately, the resistivity of a metal wire. The available apparatus includes a battery, a switch, a variable resistor, an ammeter and a voltmeter.

Your method should involve readings of different lengths, plotting a graph and using its gradient.

Your description should include:

- a circuit diagram
- a statement of the quantities to be measured and the instruments used
- the graph to plot

- how the gradient is used.
- a statement of which measurement is likely to have the largest percentage uncertainty if ordinary school apparatus and a thin wire is used
- one precaution to enable the temperature of the wire to be constant for all readings and one other precaution to increase the accuracy of the result.

4 A wire is 20 m long, has a cross-sectional area of 10^{-8} m^2 and a resistance of 200 Ω. Several other wires are made from the same material but with different dimensions. In each case, calculate the resistance of the wire.

These calculations can be performed simply using the idea that resistance is proportional to length and inversely proportional to area. You do not need to actually calculate the resistivity but you can if you want to.

a length = 40 m; cross-sectional area = 10^{-8} m^2

b length = 20 m; cross-sectional area = 2×10^{-8} m^2

c length = 100 m; cross-sectional area = 5×10^{-8} m^2

5 Calculate the resistivity of a length of wire which has a resistance of 60 Ω, cross-sectional area of 2.0×10^{-8} m^2 and length of 20 m.

Rewrite the formula, making ρ the subject, and then insert the numbers.

6 Calculate the length of wire required to make a resistance of 1000 Ω if the wire has cross-sectional area of 1.0×10^{-8} m^2 and the material has resistivity of 1.0×10^{-6} Ω m.

7 A wire is 2.0 m long and has a resistance of 50 Ω.

a Calculate the cross-sectional area of the wire if it is made of a material of resistivity 5×10^{-7} Ω m.

b Calculate the radius of the wire.

Exercise 11.4 Resistivity and resistance: harder problems

This exercise gives you practice in some harder examples where you have to use $R = \frac{\rho l}{A}$. The units are mixed – for example, resistivity in Ω m and length in cm – so make sure you convert them so they are consistent.

1 The cylindrical core of a pencil is made of material of resistivity 5.0×10^{-3} Ω m. The core has a length of 15 cm and a diameter of 0.20 cm.

a Calculate the resistance of the core. (As resistivity is given in Ω m, work throughout with metres. Convert the length and diameter to metres before using the equation.)

b Outline how to use the resistivity of the core to find the thickness *t* of a line of width *w* and length *l* drawn by the pencil on a piece of paper. (Think about a thin pencil line. Write down the formula using *w* and *t* instead of *A* and rearrange the formula to find *t*.)

2 A sample of conducting putty is rolled into a cylinder which is 8 cm long and has a radius of 1.5 cm. The resistivity of the putty = 4.0×10^{-3} Ω m.

a Calculate the resistance between the ends of the cylinder.

b The putty is rolled into a cylinder with half the radius and a length which is four times longer. Determine the new resistance.

3 A wire made from tin has a cross-sectional area of 7.8×10^{-8} m². The resistivity of tin is 1.2×10^{-7} Ω m.

a Calculate the minimum length of wire needed so that the current in the wire is smaller than 3.0 A when there is a p.d. of 2.0 V across the wire.

b A second wire made from tin has the same volume as the first wire but is longer. The second wire also has a p.d. of 2.0 V across it. Complete this table, stating whether the given quantity is **smaller**, **bigger** or **the same** for this second wire:

Quantity	For the second wire the quantity is:
cross-sectional area	
resistance	
resistivity	
current	
power produced	

4 This diagram shows a thin film of carbon used as a resistor:

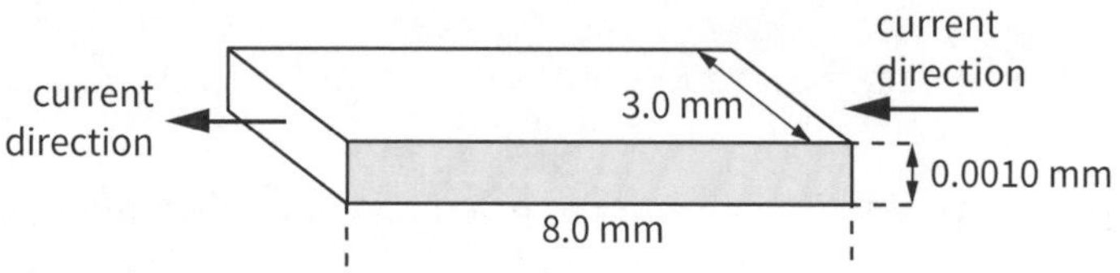

a The resistivity of carbon = 5.0×10^{-6} Ω m. Calculate the resistance of the thin film.

b The current direction is changed so that current enters the top face of the film and leaves by the lower face. Calculate the resistance of this film.

5 The fuse fitted to a three-pin plug contains a piece of fuse wire with a resistance of 0.20 Ω. The wire is 15 mm long and has a resistivity of 1.45×10^{-6} Ω m.

a Calculate the diameter of the fuse wire.

b Another fuse wire is required to produce the same power with a smaller current. Explain how. (This is possible using a wire of the same length and of the same material.)

6 Wire A and wire B are connected in parallel. There is the same p.d. across each wire.

This table gives data about the two wires:

	Wire A	Wire B
resistivity of metal	ρ	2ρ
length	l	$\frac{1}{2}l$
radius	r	$2r$

a Using the formula area = πr^2, calculate this ratio:

cross-sectional area of wire A : cross-sectional area of wire B

b Using the formula $R = \frac{\rho l}{A}$, calculate this ratio:

resistance of wire A : resistance of wire B.

c Calculate this ratio:

current in wire A : current in wire B

d Calculate this ratio:

power dissipated in wire A : power dissipated in wire B

Exam-style questions

1 This graph shows the (I–V) characteristic of a 350 mA, 6.0 V filament lamp:

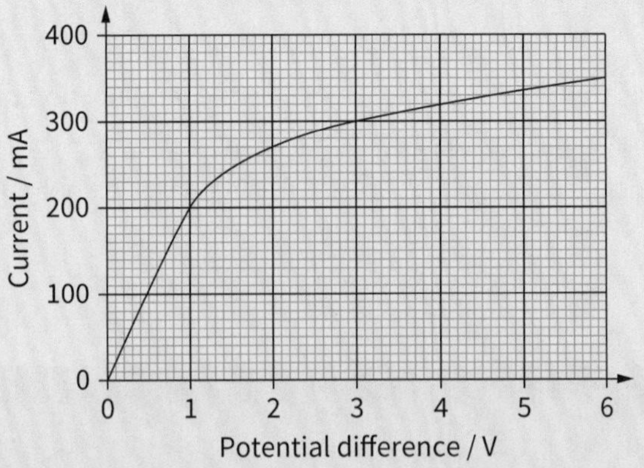

a State how the graph shows that the filament lamp does not obey Ohm's law. [1]

b Calculate the resistance of the lamp for currents between 0 and 200 mA. [2]

c State and explain what happens to the resistance of the lamp as the current increases. [2]

d Draw a sketch graph to show how the resistance of the filament lamp varies with current. [2]

e The filament of the lamp is a wire of constant radius 8.0×10^{-6} m, made from tungsten. The resistivity of tungsten is 3.5×10^{-7} Ω m. The current in the lamp is 350 mA. Calculate the length of the filament in the lamp. [2]

2 A semiconducting diode is an example of a non-ohmic component.

a State what is meant by a *non-ohmic component* and give one other example of such a component. [2]

b Sketch the (I–V) characteristic of a semiconductor diode in both forward bias (positive values of V) and negative bias (negative values of V). [3]

c Describe the significant features of the graph in terms of potential difference, current and resistance. [3]

3 **a** State Ohm's law. [2]

b A cable consists of twelve strands of copper wire, each of diameter 1.2 mm, connected in parallel. The resistivity of copper is 1.7×10^{-8} Ω m.

i Calculate the cross-sectional area of one strand of the copper wire. [2]

ii Calculate the resistance of one strand of copper wire of length 10 m. [2]

iii Determine the combined resistance of all the twelve strands in the cable. [2]

4 The table shows data for a filament lamp operated at a low voltage, when the temperature of the filament is only 20 °C and at a high voltage when the temperature of the filament is 2500 °C.

p.d. /V	current / mA
0.10	30
6.00	250

a State and explain how the data in the table shows that the lamp does not obey Ohm's law. [2]

b The filament in the lamp is a 0.018 m length of tungsten wire. The resistivity of tungsten at 20 °C is 5.6×10^{-8} Ω m.

i Calculate the cross-sectional area of the wire. [2]

ii Estimate the value of the ratio $\frac{\text{resistivity of tungsten at 2500 °C}}{\text{resistivity of tungsten at 20 °C}}$. State any assumption that you make. [2]

Chapter outline

- understand the effects of the internal resistance of a source of e.m.f. on the terminal potential difference (p.d.)
- understand the principle of a potential divider circuit as a source of variable p.d.
- recall and solve problems using the principle of the potentiometer as a means of comparing potential differences

KEY TERMS

internal resistance: the resistance of a source of e.m.f which decreases the terminal p.d. across the source when there is a current; numerically equal to the lost volts divided by the current

terminal potential difference: the p.d. across an external resistor connected across a source of e.m.f.

lost volts: the difference between the e.m.f. and the terminal p.d. across a source. It is equal to the voltage lost across the source due to internal resistance

potential divider: a circuit in which two or more components are connected in series to a supply; the output voltage is taken across one of the components

potentiometer: a device used to compare potential difference or e.m.f.

Equations: $r = \frac{(E - V)}{I}$

$V = IR$

$E = \frac{I}{(R + r)}$

$P = VI$ for the external resistor

$P = EI$ for the source

$P = I^2r$ for the internal resistance

$V_{out} = V_{in} \frac{R_2}{R_1 + R_2}$

Exercise 12.1 One cell, three voltages

This exercise develops your understanding of the differences and relationships between e.m.f., potential difference and internal resistance.

1 The equation $E = V + Ir$ applies to a cell of e.m.f. E and internal resistance r.

a Describe each quantity as a potential difference. One has been done for you.

E	The e.m.f. of a cell – the p.d. across the cell when there is no current
V	
Ir	

b Describe each quantity using ideas about energy. One has been done for you.

E	The electrical energy per unit charge produced in the cell
V	
Ir	

2 Real cells have internal resistance.

a State a situation where the e.m.f. E of a cell is equal to V, the terminal p.d.

b In use, E is normally greater than V. Explain why.

c It is possible that $E = Ir$ and that $V = 0$. Explain how this is done.

3 A high resistance voltmeter placed alone across the terminal of a battery reads 6.0 V. When a 12 Ω resistor is also placed across the terminals, the p.d. falls to 4.0 V.

a State the value of the e.m.f. of the battery.

b Explain why there are no 'lost volts' across the internal resistance of the battery when the reading is 6.0 V.

c State the value of the 'lost volts' when the resistor is connected.

d A student finds the current using the formula $I = \frac{V}{R}$. The value of the resistance she uses is 12 Ω. State which value of voltage she should use. (Look to see the voltage across the resistor that you use in the equation).

e A student finds the internal resistance of the cell current using the formula $R = \frac{V}{I}$. State which value of voltage he should use.

4 This graph shows the variation of the potential difference across a cell with the current in it:

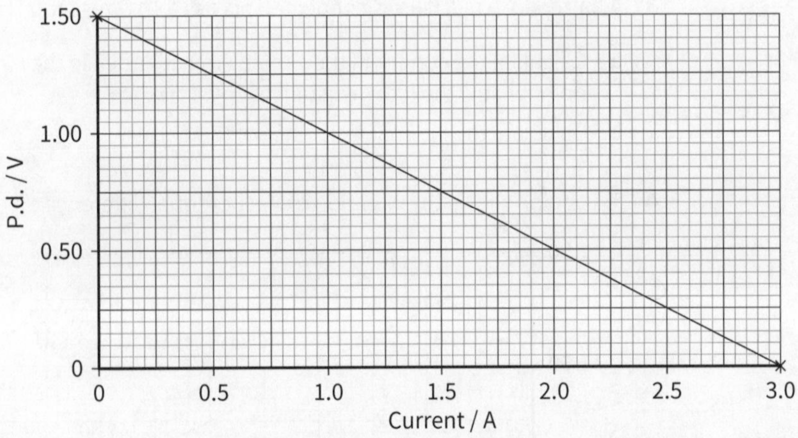

a The formula for the cell is $E = V + Ir$

Using the graph, copy and complete this table to show the values of the three terms. One has been done for you:

Current / A	E / V	V / V	Ir / V
0			
0.5	1.50	1.25	0.25
1.0			
2.0			
3.0			

b When the current is 0.50 A, the voltage across the cell is measured as 1.25 V. The label on the cell is marked as 1.5 V. Explain what has happened to the e.m.f. of the cell.

c Explain, in terms of the external resistance, how different points on the graph are obtained.

5 When used to start the engine of a car, the p.d. across the motor at this time is only 2.0 V. However the battery has e.m.f. 12 V. Explain why the p.d. across the motor is less than the e.m.f. of the battery.

Exercise 12.2 Using the internal resistance equations

This exercise will give you practice using, rearranging and performing calculations involving internal resistance. You will use equations such as $V = IR$ but must choose the right voltage and resistance.

1 The e.m.f. of a battery is 9.0 V. When a resistor is connected to the battery, the voltmeter reading drops to 8.0 V and the current is 0.40 A.

a Calculate the resistance of the external resistor.

b Calculate the internal resistance of the battery.

2 A 9.0 Ω resistor is connected to a battery of e.m.f. 4.0 V and internal resistance 1.0 Ω.

a Calculate the current in the circuit. (Only the e.m.f. is given, so choose as *R* the total resistance of the circuit.)

b Calculate the p.d. across the 9.0 Ω resistor.

c State the p.d. across the battery terminals.

d State the p.d. across the battery terminal when the resistor is removed. (Without any resistor, the battery is said to be in an open circuit.)

3 A battery of e.m.f. 6.0 V is connected across a 10 Ω resistor. The p.d. across the resistor is 4.0 V.

a Calculate the current in the circuit. (You cannot use the e.m.f. directly in $V = IR$ because you do not know the total resistance.)

b Calculate the internal resistance of the battery.

4 This graph shows the variation of the potential difference across a cell with the current in it:

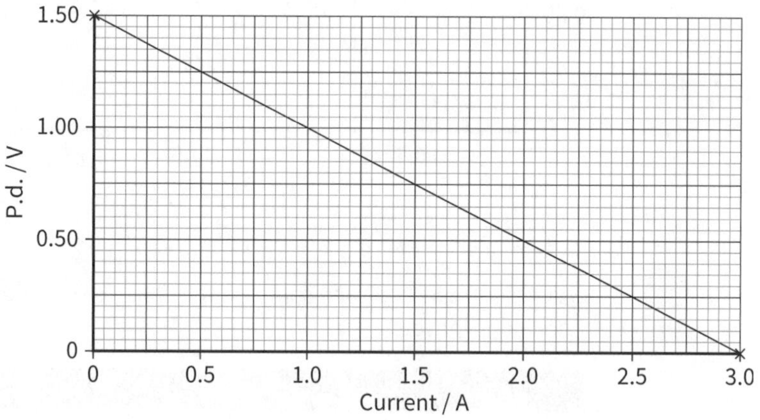

a Rearrange the formula $E = V + Ir$ to find expressions for the gradient of the graph and for the *y*-intercept of the graph in terms of *E* and *r*.

b Use the graph to find the internal resistance of the cell.

c Draw a circuit diagram of all the apparatus needed to be able to take the measurements shown in the graph. Your apparatus should enable the current to be adjusted.

5 A torch is powered by a 4.5 V battery. The p.d. across the filament lamp in the torch is 3.8 V and the power produced in the lamp is 0.80 W.

a Calculate the current in the lamp. (There are many equations to choose from, but without knowing a resistance you must use an equation for power.)

b Calculate the internal resistance of the battery.

c Calculate the energy lost per second as heat in the internal resistance of the battery.

6 A 1.2 Ω resistor is connected across a battery which has an internal resistance of 0.30 Ω. The current is 3.0 A.

a Calculate the e.m.f. of the battery.

b Calculate the potential difference across the terminals of the battery.

c The 1.2 Ω resistor is replaced with another resistor. The current is 1.5 A. Calculate the resistance of the new resistor.

7 A battery of internal resistance 2.0 Ω and e.m.f. 6.0 V is connected to a variable resistor R:

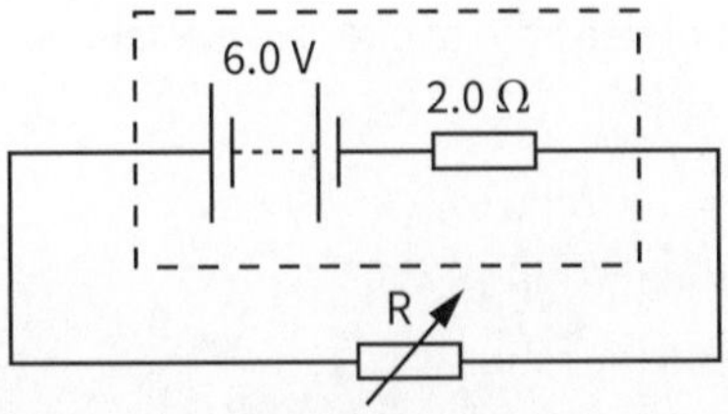

a Copy and complete this table, which gives some values of *R*, the current *I* and the power *P* dissipated in *R*:

R / Ω	I / A	P / W
0	3.0	0
1.0	2.0	
2.0		
3.0		4.3
4.0		

When $R = 1.0$ Ω:

b Calculate the power dissipated in the internal resistance.

c Calculate the total power produced by the e.m.f. of the battery.

d Compare *P* and the values obtained in **b** and **c**.

8 A battery with e.m.f. of 6.0 V and internal resistance of 12 Ω is connected to two resistors in parallel, as shown:

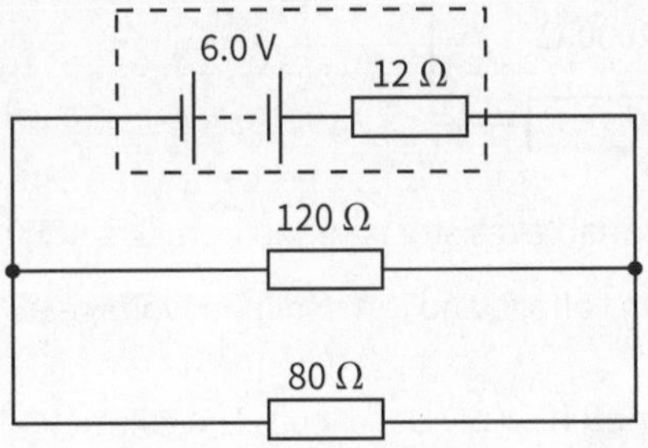

a Calculate the total resistance of the circuit.

b Calculate the current in the battery.

c Calculate the potential difference across the terminals of the battery.

Exercise 12.3 The potential divider

Sometimes it is useful to calculate voltage by using the principle of a potential divider. You may then not have to calculate a current at all. This exercise gives practice with the equation for a potential divider.

1 Two resistors with resistance R_1 and R_2 are connected in a potential divider arrangement, as shown:

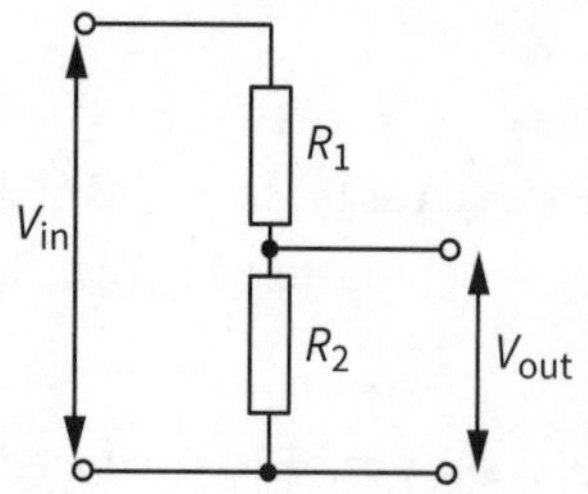

The voltage V_{in} is divided between the two resistors R_1 and R_2 in the ratio R_1:R_2. One of the parts is the output voltage V_{out}.

a Divide the number 30 in the ratio 6:4.

b Divide the voltage 80 V in the ratio 6:4.

c Divide the voltage 60 V in the ratio 12:3.

d In terms of V_{in}, R_1 and R_2 find an expression for the current in the potential divider.

e In terms of V_{out} and R_2 find an expression for the current in the potential divider.

f The current in **d** and **e** is the same. Use this fact to show that:

$$V_{out} = V_{in}\frac{R_2}{R_1 + R_2}$$

g Copy and complete this table. You may use the formula or simple ideas of splitting a voltage into parts:

V_{out} / V	V_{in} / V	R_1 / Ω	R_2 / Ω
	6.0	50	250
2.0	10.0	100	
4.0	24.0		200
5.1	16.2	400	

2 A variable resistor is connected to a 2000 Ω fixed resistor and a battery of e.m.f. 6.0 V and zero internal resistance, as shown:

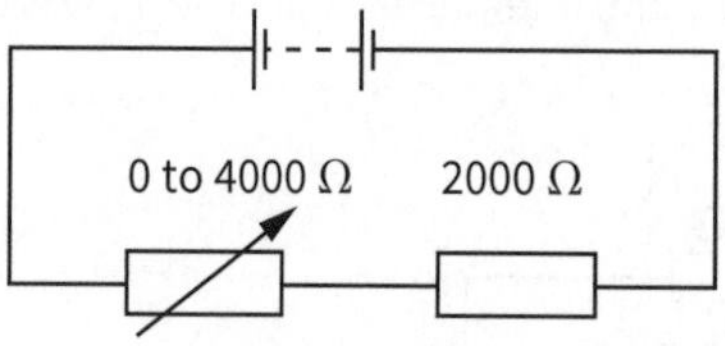

The resistance of the variable resistor is varied from 0 to 4000 Ω.

Calculate the maximum voltage and the minimum voltage across the 2000 Ω resistor.

3 This diagram shows a potential divider circuit. The voltmeter has a very high resistance:

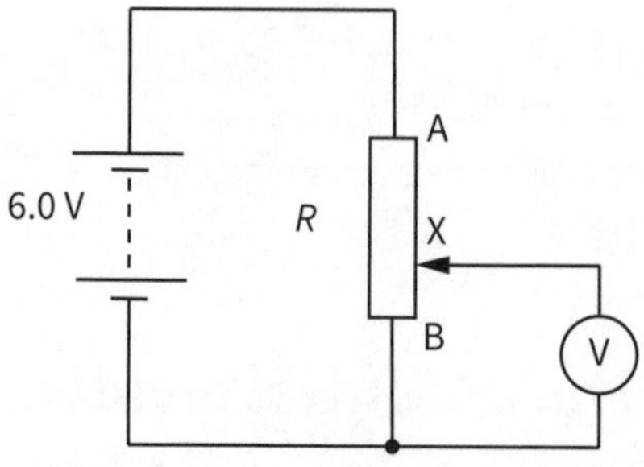

The resistor R is divided into two sections, AX and AB, by the slider X.

a State the reading on the voltmeter when the slider is at A.

b State the reading on the voltmeter when the slider is at B.

c Calculate the reading on the voltmeter when the resistance of AX is 4.0 Ω and the resistance of XB is 8.0 Ω.

4 A potential difference of 6.0 V is applied to a combination of resistors, as shown:

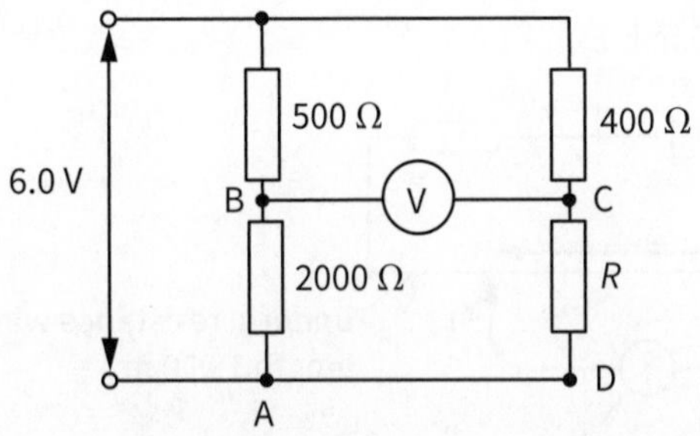

a Calculate the p.d. between points A and B.

b Calculate the p.d. between C and D when the resistor R has resistance:

i 200 Ω

ii 400 Ω

iii 1600 Ω.

c Calculate the p.d. between B and C when the resistor R has resistance:

i 200 Ω

ii 400 Ω

iii 1600 Ω.

TIP

Think of the line AD as being at 0 V. Find the voltage at B and at C and subtract them.

Exercise 12.4 The potentiometer

A potentiometer can be used to compare voltages quickly and accurately. This exercise gives you practice in using the readings from a potentiometer.

1 A uniform resistance wire PQ of length 100 cm is connected in parallel with a supply of e.m.f. 10 V and zero internal resistance. A cell of e.m.f. 2.0 V is connected across part of the wire, as shown:

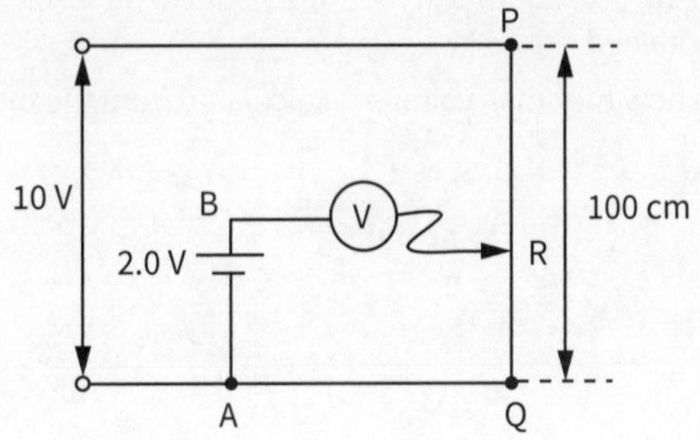

a Calculate the potential difference across 1.0 cm of the resistance wire.

b Calculate the p.d. across points R and Q when the distance RQ is:

i 20 cm

ii 25 cm

iii 40 cm.

c Calculate the reading of the voltmeter when the distance RQ is:

i 20 cm

ii 25 cm

iii 40 cm.

2 This circuit is a potentiometer used to measure a potential difference V_B:

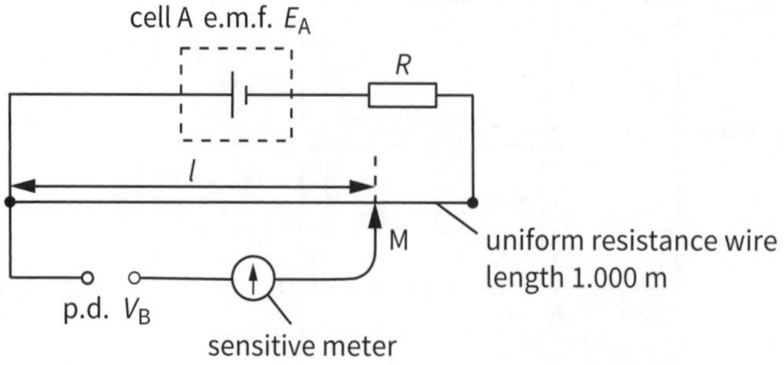

The movable contact M is always adjusted until the sensitive meter records zero current. The resistance of the 1.000 m length of resistance wire is 10 Ω.

a Assume $R = 0$. Copy and complete this table:

E_A / V	V_B / V	l / m
2.0	0.60	0.30
2.0	0.44	
	0.60	0.40
6.0		0.80

b Assume $E_A = 2.00$ V; $R = 90$ Ω.

i Calculate the p.d. across the resistance wire.

ii Calculate V_B if $l = 0.245$ m.

iii Having a large resistance R allows small voltages to be measured. Explain why.

c The circuit can be used to measure a small voltage of 2.0 mV. Cell A is a power supply of known voltage 6.00 V.

i Calculate the value of R which produces a p.d. of 3.0 mV across the wire.

ii Outline the procedure and measurements to be taken that allow the small voltage to be obtained.

iii Explain how the small voltage is calculated from the measurements.

Exam-style questions

1 A battery has e.m.f. E and internal resistance r. It is connected to six lamps, as shown:

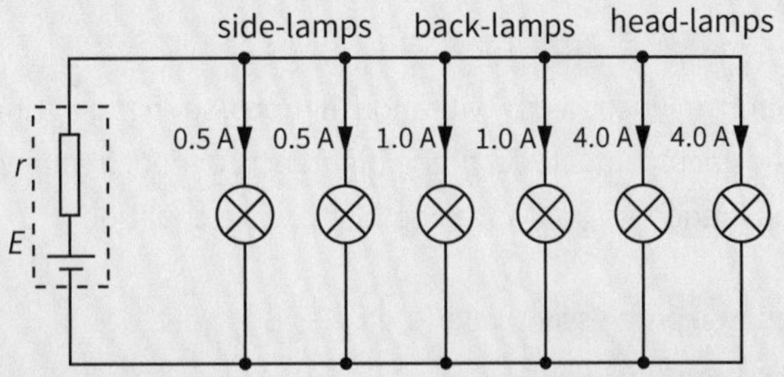

The switches to the individual lamps are not shown. The currents in the lamps, when they are all switched on, are shown. The e.m.f. E of the battery is 12.0 V and the internal resistance r is 0.150 Ω.

a Explain what is meant by the *internal resistance* of the battery. [1]

b Use energy considerations to explain why the e.m.f. of the battery is not equal to the p.d. across the battery. [2]

c Calculate the p.d. across the terminals of the battery when all the lamps are switched on. [3]

d Calculate the resistance of a single head-lamp bulb. [2]

e Calculate the current in the battery when only the two head-lamp bulbs are switched on. [1]

f The car driver notices that the side-lamps are slightly dimmer when the head-lamps are on. Explain why. [2]

2 A battery of e.m.f. 6.0 V is connected to two resistors in series. One resistor has resistance 1600 Ω and the other 1200 Ω. The two resistors in series are a potential divider.

a Explain what is meant by a *potential divider*. [1]

b Explain why the p.d. across the 1600 Ω resistor is larger than the p.d. across the 1200 Ω resistor. [2]

c The internal resistance of the battery is very small. Calculate the p.d. across the 1600 Ω resistor. [2]

d A resistor of resistance R is connected in parallel across the 1600 Ω resistor. The p.d. across this resistor falls to 2.0 V. Calculate the value of R. [2]

e A potentiometer is a device for comparing voltages. Draw a circuit diagram of a potentiometer used to compare the e.m.f. of two cells. You will need another cell, a resistance wire and a sensitive ammeter. Explain the procedure used to find the ratio of the e.m.f.s of the two cells. [3]

Chapter outline

- describe what is meant by wave motion as illustrated by vibration in ropes, springs and ripple tanks
- understand and use the terms displacement, amplitude, phase difference, period, frequency, wavelength and speed
- deduce, from the definitions of speed, frequency and wavelength, the wave equation $v = f\lambda$, recall and use the equation $v = f\lambda$
- understand that energy is transferred by a progressive wave
- recall and use the relationship *intensity* $\propto$ (*amplitude*)^2
- compare transverse and longitudinal waves and analyse and interpret graphical representations of these waves
- determine the frequency of sound using a calibrated cathode-ray oscilloscope (c.r.o.)
- understand that a Doppler shift is observed with all waves, including sound and light and use the equation $f_o = \frac{f_s v}{(v \pm v_s)}$ for the observed frequency when a source of sound waves moves relative to a stationary observer
- state that all electromagnetic waves travel with the same speed in free space and recall the orders of magnitude of the wavelengths of the principal radiations

KEY TERMS

displacement: the distance moved by an object in a particular direction (measured from a fixed starting point)

amplitude: the maximum displacement of a particle from its equilibrium position

phase difference: the difference in the phases of two oscillating particles; the amount by which one oscillation leads or lags another, expressed as 360° if they are one whole oscillation out of step

period: the time taken by an object to complete one cycle of an oscillation

frequency: the number of oscillations or waves that pass a point in unit time

wavelength: the distance between two adjacent peaks or troughs in a wave or the distance between adjacent points having the same phase

intensity: the power transmitted normally per unit area of a surface (the brightness of light striking a surface)

Doppler shift: the change in frequency or wavelength of a wave when the source of the wave is moving towards or away from the observer (or when the observer is moving relative to the source)

Equations: $v = f\lambda$

intensity $\propto$ (amplitude)^2

$$\text{period} = \frac{1}{\text{frequency}}$$

$$f_o = \frac{f_s v}{(v \pm v_s)}$$

Exercise 13.1 Basic terms and wave diagrams

In this exercise you use wave terms and practise with phase differences and wave diagrams.

1 These two diagrams represent a transverse wave. The one on the left shows how the displacement varies with distance at one instant in time. The one on the right shows how the displacement varies with time at one distance from the source:

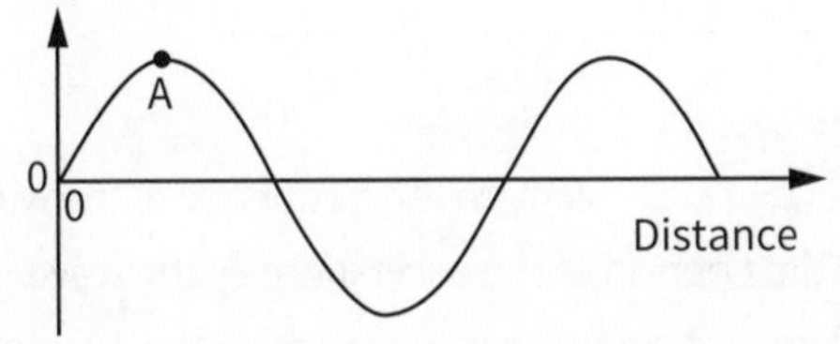

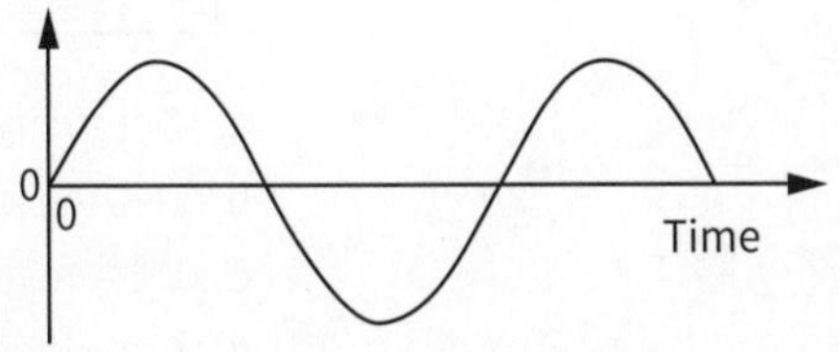

a Copy both diagrams and, on either one or both of them, label the quantities: amplitude, wavelength, period, $\frac{1}{\text{frequency}}$

Use your displacement–distance diagram to answer parts **b**-**d**:

b Mark a point that is in phase with A. Label this B.

c Mark a point that has a phase difference of 180° compared with A. Label this C.

d Mark a point that has a phase difference of 90° compared with A. Label this D.

Remember: 360° is one whole circle and one whole wavelength further along the wave.

2 **a** Complete these statements about progressive waves:

In longitudinal waves the vibrations are ________________ to the direction of the energy transfer.

In transverse waves the vibrations are ________________ to the direction of the energy transfer.

b State whether these waves are longitudinal or transverse:

Type of wave	Longitudinal or transverse
radio waves	
ultrasound waves	
microwaves	
ultra-violet waves	
waves on a rope	

c Describe how to use a long spring to produce a longitudinal wave that travels along the spring.

d Describe how the same spring can be used to produce a transverse wave.

3 A spring is vibrating longitudinally at a frequency of 2.0 Hz. At one instant the distance between a compression and the adjacent rarefaction is 16 cm. Calculate the speed of the wave.

Remember: a compression is where the coils are close together; it is half a wavelength from the nearest rarefaction, where the coils are far apart.

4 This diagram shows a transverse wave travelling to the right at $6.0\ \text{cm s}^{-1}$:

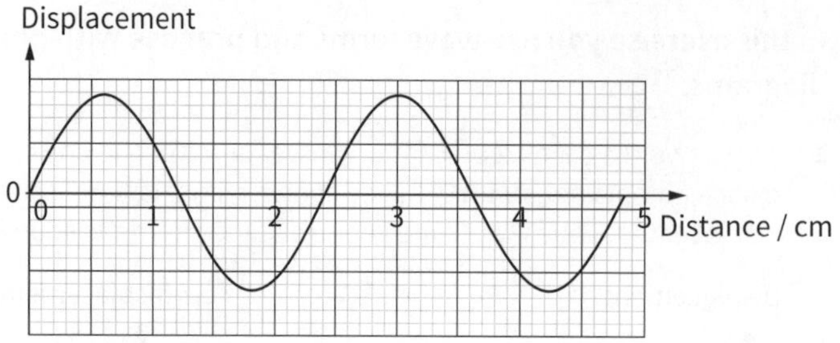

a Determine the wavelength of the wave.

b Use the formula $v = f\lambda$ to calculate the frequency of the wave.

c Determine the time period of the oscillations of the wave.

d Copy the diagram and, on the same axes, draw the position of the wave 0.20 s later. You might find how far the wave has moved using speed = distance × time

5 This diagram shows how the displacement of a particle in a wave varies with time:

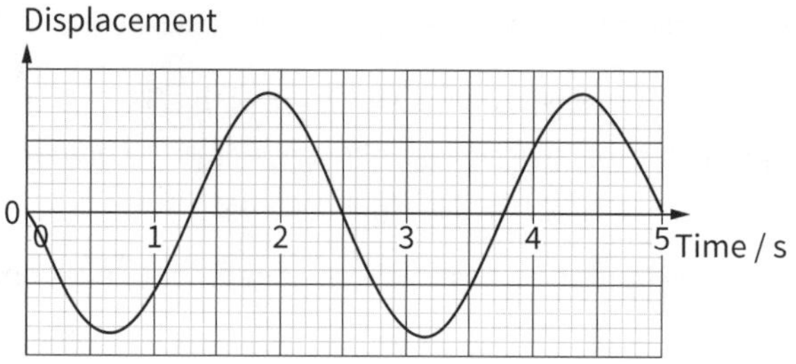

a Determine the time period of the wave.

b Determine the frequency of the wave.

c The speed of the wave is $16\ \text{cm s}^{-1}$. Calculate the wavelength of the wave.

d Copy the diagram and, on the same axes, draw the displacement–time graph for a point that has a phase difference of 90° to the oscillation of the particle shown.

Remember: as 360° is one whole circle, your new graph should move along $\frac{90}{360}$ of a time period.

Exercise 13.2 More about phase difference

This exercise focuses on phase difference and how it can be shown in wave diagrams.

1 This diagram shows five points on a wave:

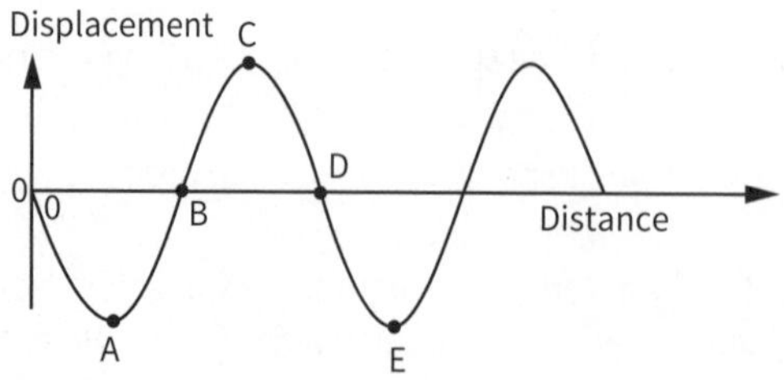

a State which two points have a phase difference of zero.

b State which two pairs of points have a phase difference of 270°.

c The wave moves to the right. At the instant shown in the diagram:

i State the direction in which a particle at A moves.

ii State the direction in which a particle at B moves.

2 Two points on a progressive wave are 25 cm apart and differ in phase by 90°.

a Explain how this information shows that the wavelength of the wave is 100 cm.

b Determine the distance between two points on the wave that have a phase difference of 270°.

c Two points on the wave are separated by a distance of 15 cm. Calculate the phase difference between the two points.

3 Explain in your own words what is meant by *a phase difference*.

4 This diagram shows the variation of displacement with time of two points A and B on the same rope:

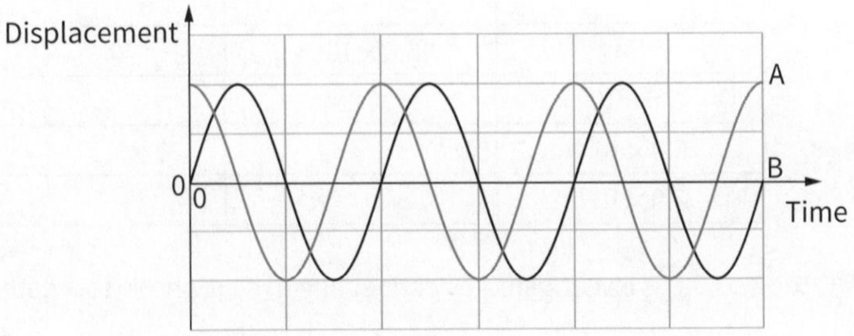

a Compare the amplitude of the motions of A and B.

b Compare the frequency of the motions of A and B.

c Compare the phases of the motions of A and B.

Exercise 13.3 Wave intensity, measuring time and the electromagnetic spectrum

This exercise involves some more complex ideas, such as intensity, the electromagnetic spectrum and using the time base on an oscilloscope to measure a time.

1 Two waves of the same frequency have amplitudes of 1.5 cm and 3.0 cm.

Calculate the ratio $\frac{\text{intensity of wave of amplitude 1.5 cm}}{\text{intensity of wave of amplitude 3.0 cm}}$

Remember: intensity $\propto$ (amplitude)^2.

2 A wave has amplitude A_0 and intensity I_0. The other waves in this table have the same frequency but different intensities and amplitudes:

	Amplitude	Intensity
initial wave	A_0	I_0
wave A	$\frac{1}{2}A_0$	
wave B		$\frac{1}{2}I_0$
wave C	$3A_0$	
wave D		$16\,I_0$

Copy and complete the table, determining the missing amplitudes and intensities, in terms of A_0 and I_0.

3 A wave has amplitude of 0.5 m and intensity 2000 W m^{-2}.

a Calculate the intensity of a wave of the same frequency with an amplitude of 1.0 m.

b Calculate the amplitude of a wave of the same frequency that has an intensity of 5000 W m^{-2}.

4 Copy and complete this table. It shows the wavelengths and frequencies of some electromagnetic waves. The speed of all the waves is 3.0×10^8 m s^{-1}:

Frequency / Hz	Wavelength /m	Region of the spectrum
	3.0×10^{-2}	
	5.0×10^{-7}	visible
	6.0×10^{-10}	
5.0×10^{7}		
6.0×10^{22}		
3.0×10^{13}		

5 A sound is investigated by connecting a microphone to a cathode-ray oscilloscope (c.r.o.).

This diagram shows the trace of the sound wave on the c.r.o. One division on the *x*-axis of the c.r.o. represents 0.5 ms:

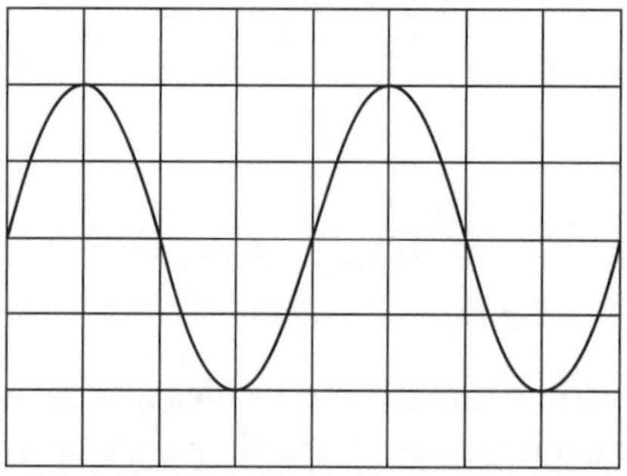

a Determine the time period of the sound. (The *x*-axis measures time so find the number of divisions or squares for one cycle and then use the 'timebase' of 0.5 ms per division.)

b Use the equation period $= \frac{1}{\text{frequency}}$ to determine the frequency of the sound.

c Another sound is connected to a different c.r.o. and the same trace is produced. Determine the frequency of the sound if one division on the *x*-axis of the new c.r.o. represents 2.0 ms.

Exercise 13.4 The Doppler effect

This exercise tests your understanding of what causes the Doppler effect, particularly with sound and light. You will also practice using the equation for the Doppler effect when a source is moving.

1 A stationary observer notices an increase in frequency when a source of sound moves towards him.

Three students suggest that the increase in frequency is caused because:

- the velocity of the sound in the air is larger because the source is moving
- the waves are squashed together because the source is moving towards him
- the sound is louder as the source comes nearer.

a State which of the suggestions is the best description.

b Explain why the sound has a higher frequency as the source approaches.

2 A train sounding a whistle of frequency 400 Hz travels at 40 m s^{-1}. The sound heard by an observer standing very close to the track has a frequency greater than 400 Hz as the train approaches. The speed of sound in air is 340 m s^{-1}.

a Calculate the frequency heard by the observer as the train approaches.

b Calculate the frequency heard by the observer as the train travels away from her.

3 A police car drives at 30 m s^{-1} with its siren blaring at a frequency of 2500 Hz. Calculate the frequency heard as the car approaches directly towards some observers. The speed of sound in the air is 340 m s^{-1}.

4 A loudspeaker which emits a note of frequency 300 Hz is whirled in a horizontal circle at a speed of 20 m s^{-1}. Calculate the maximum and minimum frequencies heard by a stationary observer. The speed of sound is 340 m s^{-1}.

5 An aircraft flies directly over a stationary observer on a windless day. The engine note heard on the ground before take-off is 250 Hz. As the plane approaches the observer, the frequency heard by the observer is 300 Hz. The speed of sound in air is 340 m s^{-1}.

a Calculate the speed of the aircraft.

b Calculate the frequency heard by the observer as the aircraft moves away from him at the same speed.

6 A line in the spectrum of calcium has a frequency 7.557×10^{14} Hz when measured in the laboratory. When the same spectral line is observed in the spectrum from a star, the frequency observed is 7.449×10^{14} Hz.

The speed of light is 3.00×10^{8} m s^{-1}.

Calculate the speed with which the galaxy is moving away from the Earth.

7 A very hot distant galaxy emits violet light of wavelength 4.0×10^{-7} m. This light cannot be detected by the human eye on Earth as the violet light is shifted into the infra red part of the spectrum. The smallest wavelength of infra red is 7.0×10^{-7} m.

Estimate the minimum velocity of the galaxy away from Earth.

The speed of light is 3.00×10^{8} m s^{-1}. You do not need to take relativistic effects into account.

Exam-style questions

1 These diagrams show the same progressive wave on a string. Diagram 1 shows the wave at time $t = 0$, and diagram 2 shows the wave at $t = 0.10$ s. The wave is moving from left to right.

Diagram 1

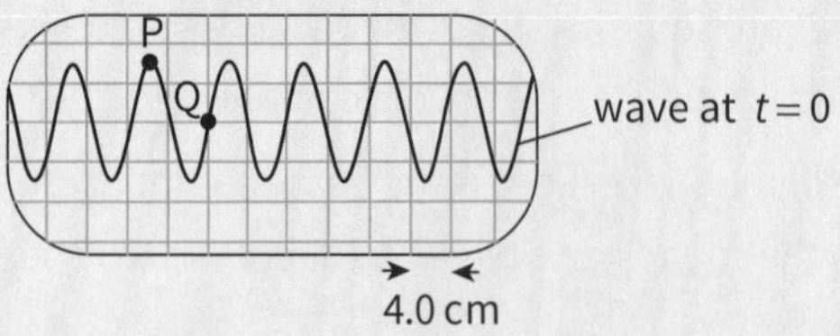

Diagram 2

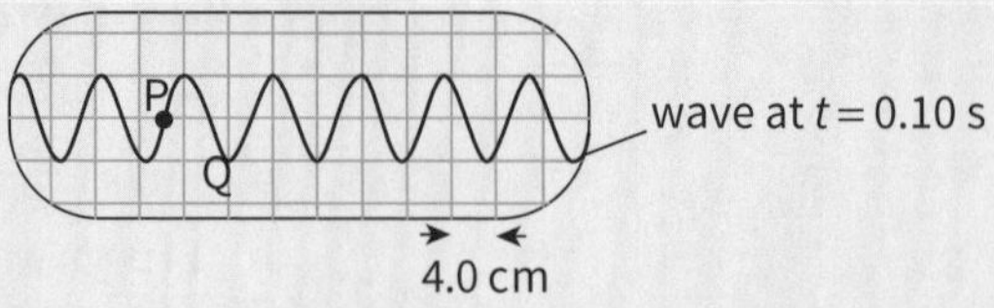

Two points P and Q are marked on the string and appear in both diagrams.

a Determine the wavelength of the wave. [1]

b Calculate the speed of the wave, stating any assumption that you make. (Look at the peak of one line in the diagram at $t = 0$ and see how far it has moved along horizontally by the time $t = 0.10$ s. The vertical lines on the diagrams are 4.0 cm apart). [3]

c Calculate the frequency of the wave. [2]

d Compare the amplitude of the wave at P and Q. [1]

e Calculate the phase difference between the oscillations of P and Q. [2]

f At time t_1, the amplitude of the oscillation of P is 6.0 cm and at time t_2 the amplitude is 4.0 cm. Calculate this ratio: [2]

intensity of the wave at t_1 : intensity of the wave at t_2

2 **a** Waves can be longitudinal or transverse.

i State one difference and one similarity between longitudinal and transverse waves. [2]

ii Give one example of each type of wave. [2]

b This diagram shows a longitudinal wave of frequency 3.0 Hz:

A, B, C, D and E are points through which the wave travels.

i Explain what is meant by *frequency*. [1]

ii State which two points are one wavelength apart. [1]

iii The distance between points A and B is 14.0 cm. Calculate the speed of the wave. [2]

iv Determine the phase difference between the oscillation of the wave at point A and B. (First work out the fraction of one wavelength that exists between A and B.) [2]

c Electromagnetic radiation at a frequency of 1.4286×10^9 Hz and a wavelength of 21.000 cm is emitted by hydrogen in the laboratory. The same radiation received on Earth from a hydrogen cloud in a distant galaxy has a frequency of 1.4194×10^9 Hz.

i State the part of electromagnetic spectrum in which this radiation is found. [1]

ii Explain why the two frequencies are different. [2]

iii Calculate the velocity of the hydrogen cloud relative to the Earth. [2]

Chapter outline

- explain the meaning of the term *diffraction*
- show an understanding of experiments that demonstrate diffraction
- understand the terms *interference* and *coherence*
- understand the conditions required if two-source interference fringes are to be observed and understand experiments that demonstrate two-source interference using water ripples, light and microwaves
- recall and solve problems using the equation $\lambda = \frac{ax}{D}$ or double-slit interference using light
- recall and solve problems using the formula $d \sin \theta = n\lambda$
- describe the use of a diffraction grating to determine the wavelength of light

KEY TERMS

interference: the cancellation and reinforcement when two waves pass through each other

diffraction: the spreading of a wave at an edge or slit

superposition: when two waves pass meet at a point and the resultant displacement is the algebraic sum of the displacement of each wave

constructive interference: when two waves arrive in phase and the resultant amplitude is the sum of the amplitudes of the two waves

destructive interference: when two waves arrive out of phase and the resultant amplitude is the difference in the amplitude of the two waves

coherent: two waves are coherent if they have a constant phase relationship

conditions for fringes to be observed: in two-source interference the waves must:

- have the same wavelength (frequency and speed)
- be coherent

Equations: $\lambda = \frac{ax}{D}$ for double-slit interference

$d \sin \boldsymbol{\theta} = n\boldsymbol{\lambda}$ for the diffraction grating

Exercise 14.1 Superposition and interference

This exercise helps you to think about interference and path difference. Remember that path difference is an actual distance and it is not the same as phase difference, although the two are related.

1 This diagram shows how the displacement of a particle at a point on the surface of water varies with time:

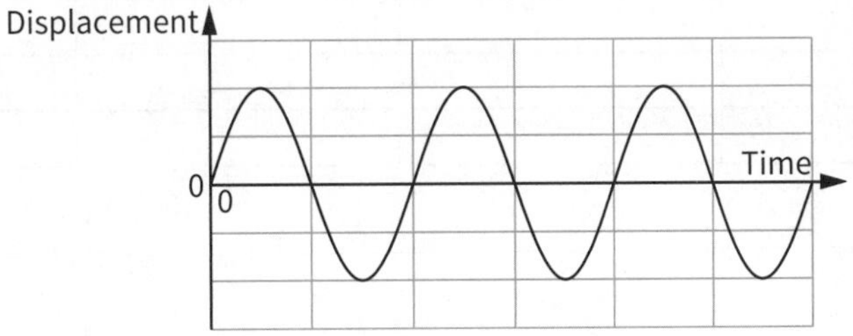

Copy the diagram and, using the same axes:

a Sketch the variation with time of a wave with twice the amplitude; your wave should be in phase with the wave in the diagram.

b Show the resultant displacement if both waves pass through the same point.

c Draw a wave that has the same amplitude as the original wave but is out of phase with it.

d Show the resultant displacement if the original and the wave in part **c** pass through the same point.

2 Circular waves are produced at points P and Q. This diagram shows the wavefronts produced that are one wavelength apart:

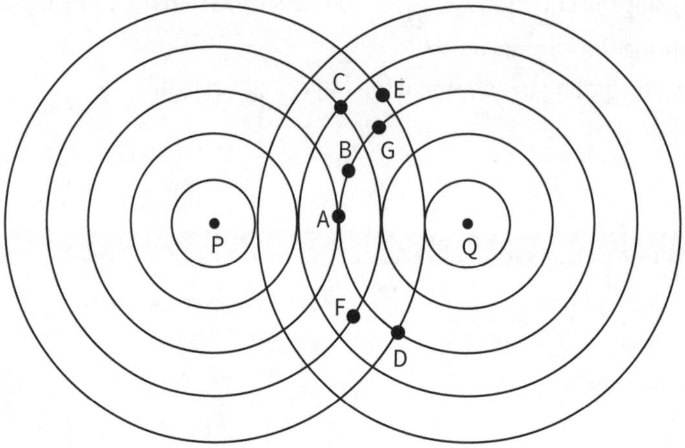

Look at point A. Two sets of waves arrive at A, one from source P and the other from source Q. There are three whole wavelengths between A and P (i.e. $AP = 3\lambda$). There are also three whole wavelengths between A and Q, so $AQ = 3\lambda$. The path difference between the two sets of waves $AP - AQ = 0$.

Look at point B. There are $3\frac{1}{2}$ whole wavelengths between B and P (i.e. $BP = 3\frac{1}{2}\lambda$). There are also three whole wavelengths between B and Q, so $BQ = 3\lambda$. The path difference between the two sets of waves $BP - BQ = \frac{1}{2}\lambda$.

a Explain why there is constructive interference at point A.

b Explain why there is destructive interference at point B.

c Copy and complete this table to find the path difference for each of the points C to G. For each, decide whether the interference is constructive or destructive.

Point X	Distance from X to P	Distance from X to Q	Path difference	Interference at the point
A	3λ	3λ	0	constructive
B	$3\frac{1}{2}\lambda$	3λ	$\frac{1}{2}\lambda$	destructive
C				
D				
E				
F				
G				

d Copy and complete these sentences:

i At points A, C and D, the path difference from the point to the two sources is ________________

ii The two waves arrive ________________ phase and they ________________ interfere.

iii At points B, E, F and G, the path difference from the point to the two sources is ________________

iv The two waves arrive ________________ phase and they ________________ interfere.

e Copy or trace the two sets of wavefronts in the diagram. On your diagram, join up all the points where the path difference from the point to P and Q is 0. You will find these points where a circle from P crosses the 'same' circle from Q.

f Using your diagram, join up all the points on one side of the point A where the path difference is λ. To do this: Starting at source Q, count three circles outwards from Q and four circles outwards from P. Where these two circles cross there are two points where the path difference is λ. Now repeat with four circles out from Q and five from P and also $3\frac{1}{2}$ circles out from Q and $4\frac{1}{2}$ circles out from P, and so on. You can also find points on the left-hand side where the path difference is such that Q is further than P from the point chosen.

Exercise 14.2 Two-source interference experiments

This exercise help you to think about the apparatus used and results found in two-source interference experiments.

1 This diagram shows light from a laser that passes through two slits:

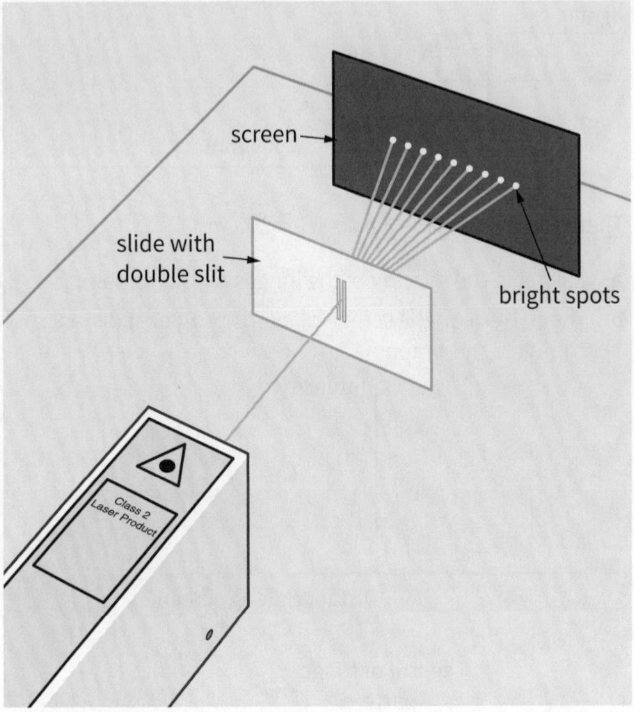

The equation $\lambda = \frac{ax}{D}$ is used to determine the wavelength λ of the laser light.

a State what is meant by the other quantities in the formula and, on a copy of the diagram, mark the distances *a*, *x* and *D*.

b State how you would measure each distance used in finding the wavelength. Indicate the instrument used in each case and include one precaution that you would take to ensure an accurate result.

c The wavelength of red light is about 7×10^{-7} m. Use this value to suggest suitable values for all of the other distances in the formula.

d The bright spots are found to be too close together on the screen for accurate measurement. Suggest two changes that can be made to the experiment to increase the separation of the spots.

e A laser is used in the experiment. Give two reasons why a laser is preferred to an ordinary white lamp. Think about brightness and the effect of the different colours in white light.

2 Two-source interference can be shown with water waves and microwaves as well as light.

a Draw the apparatus that is used to show two-source interference of water waves.

b Draw the apparatus that is used to show two-source interference of microwaves.

c The wavelengths of light and microwaves are different. For a double-slit experiment, suggest how the wavelength of the microwaves leads to differences in the quantities a, x and D as compared with those used in light experiments.

Exercise 14.3 Calculations and descriptions with the double-slit experiment

This exercise helps you practise using the double-slit interference formula and applying it to experiments.

1 This diagram shows a double-slit experiment using coherent light:

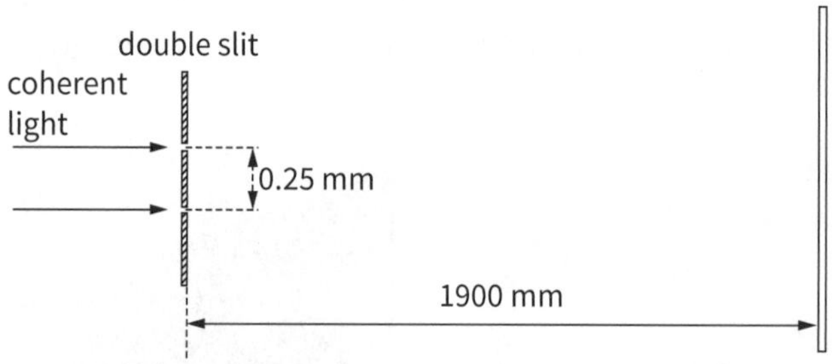

The wavelength of the light is 5.0×10^{-7} m

a Calculate the spacing of the fringes on the screen.

b The pattern on the screen of intensity against distance can be drawn graphically. Copy and complete this graph:

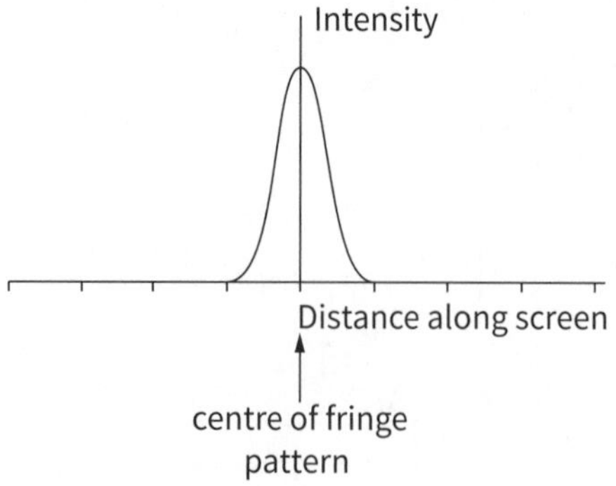

In the following situations, **c** to **g**, state what happens, if anything, to the dark and bright fringes.

c The slits are moved closer together.

d The wavelength of the light is increased.

e The intensity of the light passing through both slits is reduced.

f The intensity of the light passing through only one of the slits is reduced. (Think about what happens in destructive and constructive interference when waves have different amplitude.)

g The coherent light is replaced by light of the same wavelength, but from two different sources that are not coherent. (Consider what happens if the phase of one source suddenly changes.)

2 A double-slit interference experiment uses a source of wavelength 5.86×10^{-7} m. The separation of the two vertical slits is 0.30 mm and the distance from the slits to the screen is 1.7 m.

a Describe the appearance of the fringes.

b Calculate the fringe separation.

c Calculate the distance on the screen between the middle of the central fringe and the middle of the first dark fringe.

3 This diagram shows the central section of the double-slit interference pattern on a screen:

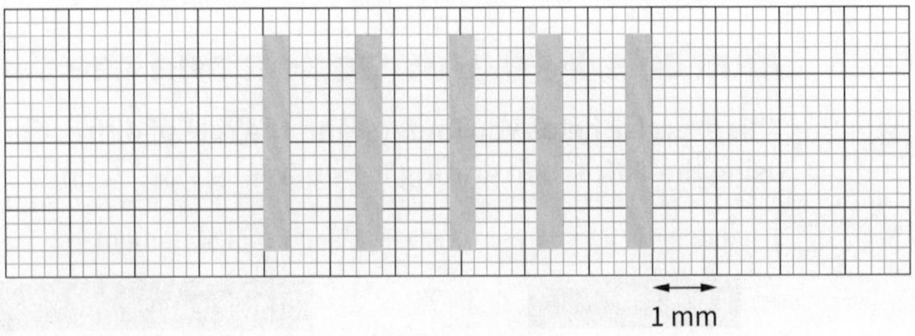

a Determine a value for the separation of the fringes on the screen.

b The screen is 2.0 m from the slits and the separation of the slits is 1.0 mm. Calculate the wavelength of the light.

c Draw the pattern obtained when the separation of the slits is halved. Make sure you include the scale.

d Describe the pattern obtained when a white light source is used. The light from the two slits is still coherent, even though it is now white and contains a mixture of wavelengths.

4 Two coherent light sources are 0.30 mm apart. They each emit light of wavelength 4.95×10^{-7} m. An interference pattern is produced on a screen placed 2.00 m from the sources. Calculate the distance between two neighbouring bright fringes on the screen.

5 In a double-slit interference experiment, the distance from the two sources to the screen is 1.6 m. A pattern of dots is seen on the screen with one central dot and three dots on either side of the central dot.

The distance between the central dot and the third dot on one side is 10.0 mm.

The wavelength of the light from the laser used is 6.0×10^{-7} m.

The third dot away from the central dot is three fringe spacings away.

a Calculate the fringe separation, x.

b Calculate the separation of the slits, a.

6 Two slits in a metal barrier are placed in front of a source of microwave radiation, as shown:

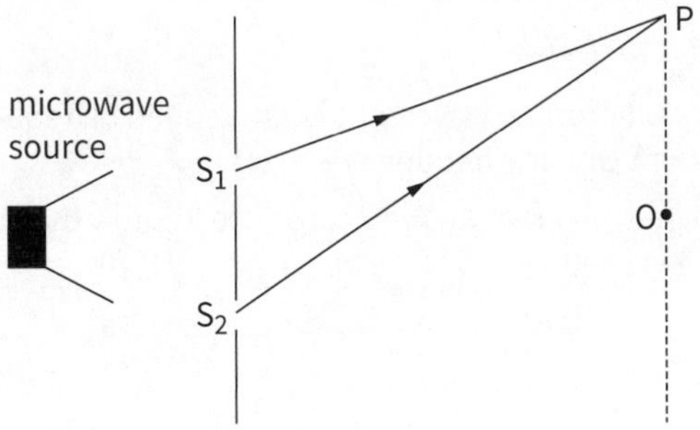

The wavelength of the microwaves is 3.0 cm.

The distance S_1P is 90.0 cm and the distance S_2P is 99.0 cm.

a Calculate the path difference between the two waves, one travelling from S_1 to P and the other travelling from S_2 to P. Give your answer in cm.

b State the phase difference between the two waves arriving at P.

c State the type of interference occurring at P.

d A detector of microwaves is placed at O and moved slowly towards P. Describe what is observed. Use your answer to **b** to see how many maxima and minima there are between O and P.

Exercise 14.4 Diffraction and the diffraction grating

This exercise helps you understand the role of diffraction and gives you practice in using the diffraction grating formula.

1 Match the four wave terms with the correct statement:

Term
diffraction
interference
coherence
superposition

Statement
needs a constant phase difference between two waves
occurs when waves meet and the resultant displacement is the sum of the displacements of each wave
causes a pattern due to cancellation and reinforcement of the waves
causes waves to spread out as they pass through narrow gaps

2 This diagram shows a student's drawing of the diffraction pattern of a water wave as it passes from left to right through a gap which is larger than the wavelength:

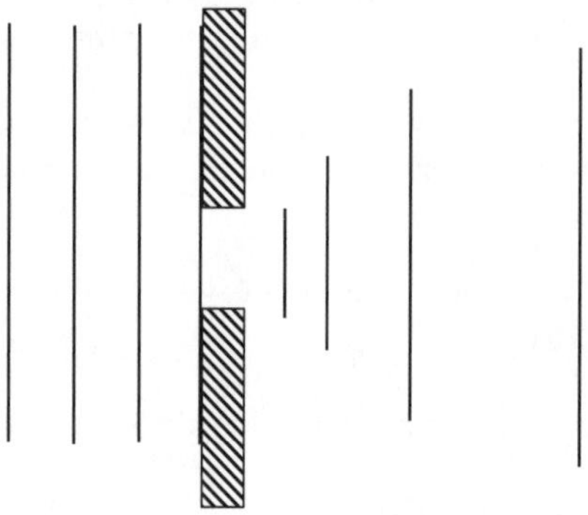

a State two things that are incorrect about the diagram.

b Draw a diagram of the diffraction pattern if the gap is much smaller than the wavelength.

3 The speed of sound is 320 m s^{-1}.

a Calculate a value for the wavelength of the sound of frequency 2.0 kHz. (Take care to use the equation $v = f\lambda$ with the frequency in Hz.)

b Draw a diagram of apparatus you could use to show the diffraction of sound. Suggest the size of the gap used.

4 A diffraction grating has 500 lines per millimetre. Light is incident normally on the grating.

a Calculate the distance, in metres, between one line and the next on the diffraction grating.

b Calculate the wavelength of light that gives a first-order maximum at an angle of 22.0°.

c Calculate the angle of the second-order maximum when light of this wavelength is used.

d State what happens when you try to use the diffraction grating formula for the third-order. This limits the number of orders to only two in this case.

e State the total number of lines seen in the diffraction pattern if only two orders are present in the spectrum of a monochromatic source of light.

5 Light of wavelength 590 nm is incident normally on a diffraction grating of width 30.0 mm which contains 10 000 lines.

a Calculate the spacing of the lines in the grating.

b Calculate the angular positions of the various orders.

6 When red light of wavelength 700 nm is passed normally through a diffraction grating, the first-order maximum is found at an angle of 25° to the zero-order beam.

a Calculate the grating spacing and the number of lines per millimetre in the grating.

b Calculate the angle for the first-order maximum using blue light of wavelength 400 nm.

c Calculate the difference in angle between the blue light and the red light in the first-order spectrum.

7 Light of wavelength 600 nm is incident normally on a diffraction grating, as shown:

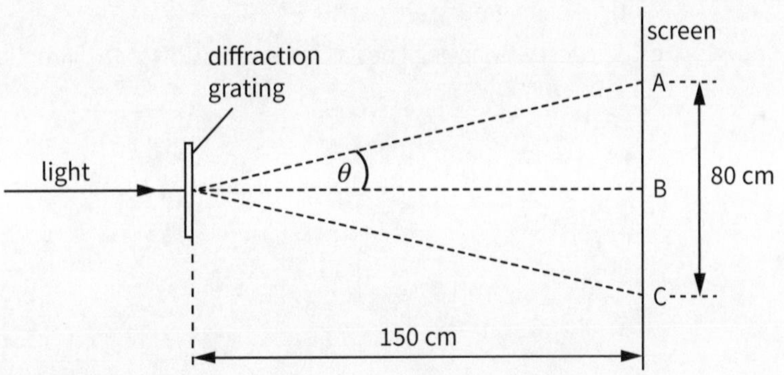

First order maxima are seen at positions A and C on the screen.

a Calculate the angle θ.

b Calculate the grating spacing.

c Calculate the distance on the screen between B and the position of a second-order maximum.

Exam-style questions

> **TIP**
> Be careful not to confuse questions on the double-slit experiment and on the diffraction grating.

1 A vertical screen is placed some metres from a vertical double slit. A single beam of red light from a laser shines on the double slit and a pattern of red dots is seen on the screen.

- **a** Explain how the pattern of red dots is formed on the screen. Use ideas about path difference, phase difference and interference in your answer. [3]
- **b** Explain, using ideas about diffraction why this pattern becomes less bright towards the edge of the screen. [2]

2 Diffraction gratings can be used to find the wavelength of light.

- **a** Describe how you would use a diffraction grating to find the wavelength of light from a laser. [4]
- **b** State an advantage of using a diffraction grating rather than double slits in your experiment. Explain your reasoning. [2]

3 In an experiment using double slits, eight fringe spacings on the screen are found to occupy a distance of 0.40 cm. The screen is 50 cm from the slits. The wavelength of the light is 700 nm.

- **a** Calculate the fringe spacing. [1]
- **b** Calculate the separation of the slits. [2]
- **c** The double slits are replaced with a diffraction grating. The slits in this grating are separated by the same distance as the double slits. Light of the same wavelength (700 nm) is shone through the grating. Calculate the angle of the first-order maximum. [2]
- **d** State two differences between the patterns seen when the double slits and the diffraction grating are used. [2]
- **e** Suggest why having lines as far apart as this for a diffraction grating experiment is not suitable. [2]

Chapter outline

- explain and use the principle of superposition in simple applications of stationary waves
- show an understanding of experiments that demonstrate stationary waves using microwaves, stretched strings and air columns
- explain the formation of a stationary wave using a graphical method, and identify nodes and antinodes
- determine the wavelength of sound using stationary waves

KEY TERMS

stationary wave: a wave pattern produced when two progressive waves of the same frequency travelling in opposite directions combine

progressive wave: a wave that carries energy from one place to another

node: a point on a stationary wave where the amplitude is zero

antinode: a point on a stationary wave where the amplitude is a maximum

superposition: when two waves meet at a point and the resultant displacement is the algebraic sum of the displacement of each wave

Equations: distance from one node to the next (or one antinode to the next) $= \frac{\lambda}{2}$

distance from one node to the nearest antinode $= \frac{\lambda}{4}$

Exercise 15.1 How superposition leads to stationary waves

This exercise gives you practice using graphs of stationary waves and in applying the principle of superposition.

1 This diagram shows a string fixed at both ends vibrating with a stationary wave pattern:

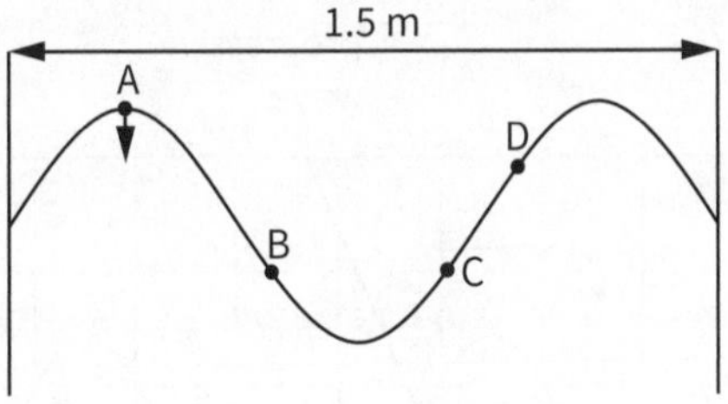

At the time shown, the displacement is a maximum.

a Draw the string vibrating between the same ends a quarter of cycle later than in the diagram.

b Draw the string vibrating between the same ends a half cycle later than in the diagram. Remember the stationary wave is not moving along – some of the points on it are just moving up and down and some points do not move up and down at all, they stay as zero all the time

c Calculate the wavelength of the wave. Use the idea that the distance between successive nodes is $\frac{\lambda}{2}$.

d In the diagram, the arrow on point A shows the direction in which the string at A is about to move. State the directions in which points B, C and D are about to move.

2 This diagram shows the displacement of two waves P and Q at one instant in time:

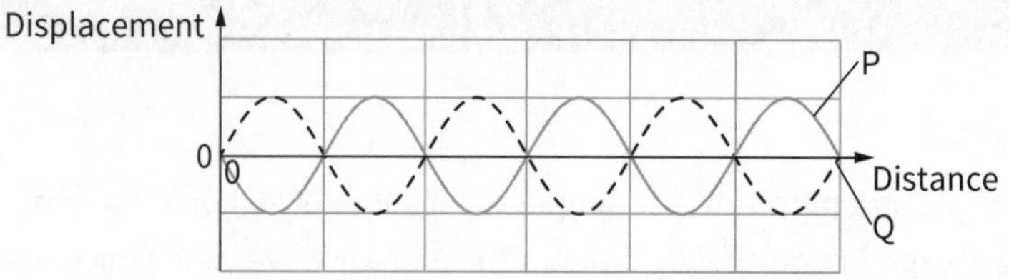

The two waves travel in opposite directions. Wave P moves to the right and wave Q moves to the left. These two waves combine by the principle of superposition to form a stationary wave.

a Copy the diagram onto a piece of graph paper, leaving enough space below for three similar diagrams. Draw and label the resultant of P and Q on your diagram.

A short time *t* later, the waves have moved a quarter of a wavelength in opposite directions, as shown:

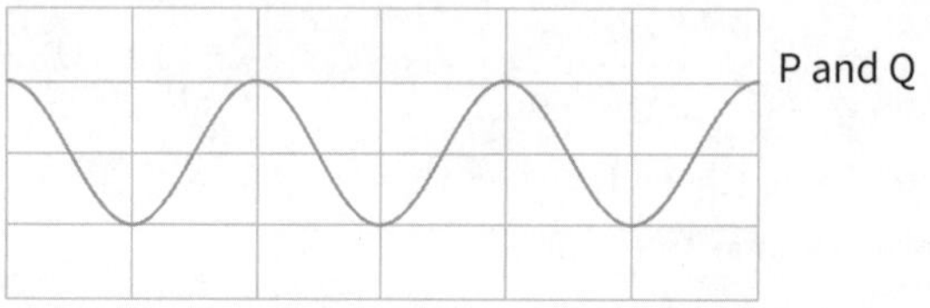

b Copy this diagram underneath part **a**, on the same sheet of paper. Draw the resultant of P and Q.

c Draw the diagram and resultant again, with each wave having moved a further quarter of a wavelength in opposite directions.

A progressive wave moves along. Half the distance between the vertical lines is $\frac{\lambda}{4}$.

d Draw the diagram and resultant again, with each wave having moved a further quarter of a wavelength in opposite directions.

e Mark on your diagram the letter A at all the places where the resultant wave always has a maximum amplitude. Add the letter N at all places where the resultant is always zero.

3 A stationary wave is formed by the superposition of two progressive waves.

This diagram shows a stationary wave and **one** of the two progressive waves at one instant of time. The distance along the *x*-axis is the horizontal distance along the wave:

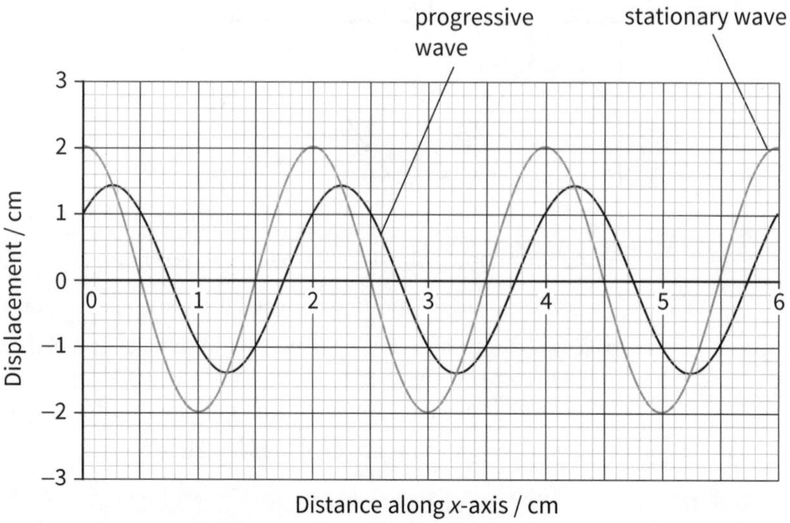

a Complete this table. Show the values of:

- the displacement of the stationary wave
- the displacement of the progressive wave at the distances along the *x*-axis shown in the table
- the displacement of the other progressive wave (the one not shown on the diagram).

One row has been done for you.

Distance along *x*-axis / cm	Displacement of stationary wave / cm	Displacement of progressive wave shown / cm	Displacement of other progressive wave / cm
0	+2.0	+1.0	+1.0
0.50			
1.00			
1.50			
2.00			

b State the values of the distances along the *x*-axis on the diagram where nodes are formed.

c State the values of the distances along the *x*-axis on the diagram where antinodes are formed.

d State the distance in centimetres between a node and the nearest antinode and compare this distance with the wavelength λ of the progressive wave.

Exercise 15.2 Using stationary wave patterns

This exercise helps you to use stationary wave patterns to find wavelengths, frequencies and speed.

1 This diagram shows three stationary wave patterns on the same wire PQ:

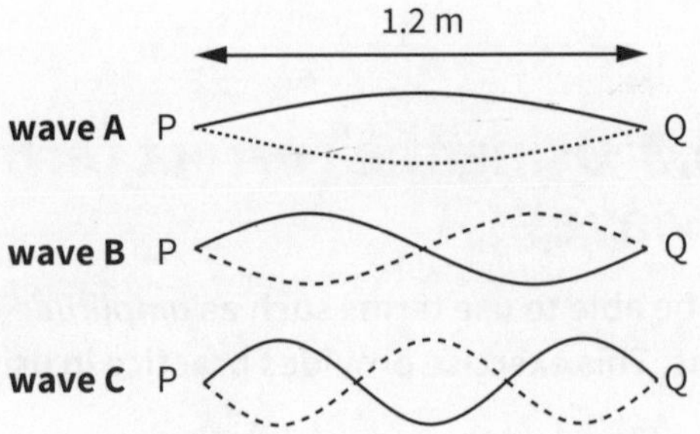

The distance between points P and Q is 1.2 m.

a State the wavelengths of waves A, B and C.

b The frequency of wave A is 240 Hz. State the frequencies of waves B and C.

c State the number of antinodes shown on each of the waves A, B and C.

d Describe the motion of wave A, starting with the wave position shown by the solid line.

2 The length of a string is 60 cm.

a Calculate the longest wavelength of a stationary wave that can be set up on the string.

b The sound heard from the wave in **a** has a frequency of 100 Hz. Calculate the speed of the wave on the string.

3 A wire of length 0.24 m is fixed at both ends. An oscillator makes the wire move up and down as a stationary wave. At certain values of the oscillator frequency, stationary waves are formed; the different stationary waves have different wavelengths.

a State the three largest wavelengths of stationary waves that can form on the wire.

b The speed of the wave along the wire is 100 m s^{-1}. Calculate the three smallest frequencies that produce stationary waves.

4 A loudspeaker creates a stationary wave in a tube. The dust in the tube collects in piles at the nodes. There is also a node at the closed end:

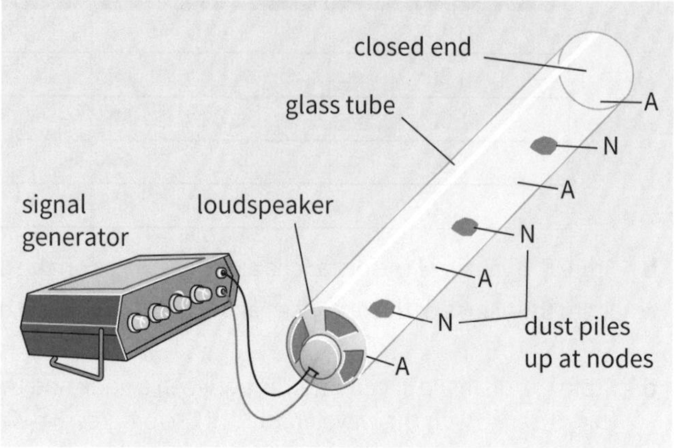

a Explain why the dust collects at the nodes.

b The distance between successive nodes in the pattern is 5.0 cm. The speed of sound in the tube is 320 m s^{-1}. Calculate the wavelength and frequency of the sound from the loudspeaker.

c In the diagram, starting from the open end, there is a sequence ANANANA of antinodes and nodes, where A is an antinode and N is a node. Suggest two other possible sequences within the tube where the distance between successive nodes is larger than 5.0 cm.

Exercise 15.3 Using the correct terms to explain stationary waves

It is important to be able to use terms such as *amplitude* and *phase* correctly and to make comparisons. This exercise provides practice in using these terms and making comparisons.

1 This diagram shows a string carrying a **stationary wave** at the instant when the displacement is a maximum:

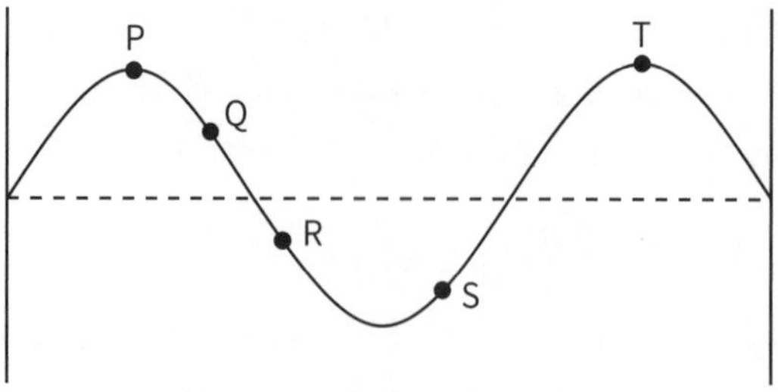

P, Q, R, S and T are points marked on the string.

a The point P is at an antinode. Explain what is meant by an *antinode*.

b Explain what is meant by a *node*.

c State how many nodes there are on the diagram.

d Complete this table to give the phase difference between different points on the stationary wave. Two values have been done for you.

Remember points between nodes on a stationary wave move up and down in phase.

Points	Phase difference between the points
P and Q	0
P and R	180°
P and S	
P and T	
Q and R	
Q and S	
R and S	

e Describe where points with no phase difference will be found on a stationary wave.

f Compare the phase difference between points at different distances along a *stationary wave* with the phase difference between points along a *progressive wave*.

g Point Q vibrates up and down in phase with point P but with a lower amplitude. Place the amplitudes of the oscillations at P, Q, R, S and T in order, from largest to smallest.

h Describe how the amplitude of oscillation of a point on a stationary wave varies along the wave. Compare this with the amplitude of oscillation of different points along a progressive wave.

i Compare the transmission of energy along a stationary wave and along a progressive wave. Explain why there is a difference.

2 This diagram shows the shape of one stationary wave formed on a guitar string when a note is played:

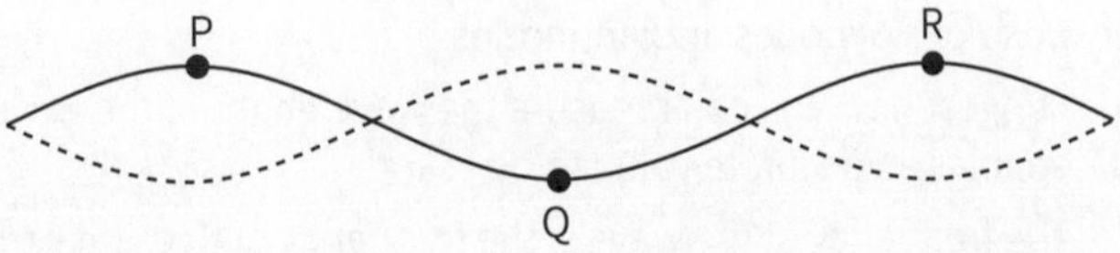

Points P, Q and R are three marks on the string, placed at the antinodes.

a Explain how a stationary wave is formed on the guitar string from a progressive wave travelling along the string.

b Describe the motion of point P.

c Compare the oscillation at the three points. You should describe any similarities and differences in the *amplitude* and in the *phase difference* between the points.

d Draw the shape of another stationary wave that forms on the same length of string but which has a larger wavelength than shown in the diagram. Mark the nodes on your diagram.

3 This diagram shows a mode of vibration of a stationary wave set up in a closed tube:

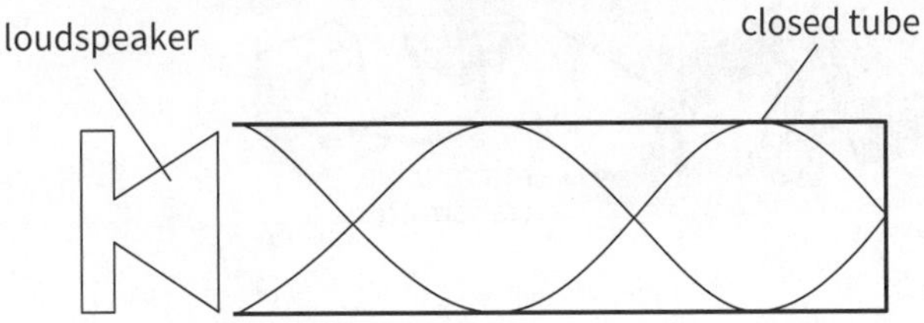

a Describe the motion of a molecule of air at an antinode.

b Explain how waves from the loudspeaker produce stationary waves in the tube.

c The wavelength of sound from the loudspeaker is 8.0 cm. Determine the length of the tube. (Ignore end corrections.)

The frequency of sound from the loudspeaker is gradually increased and the next mode of vibration is found.

d Sketch this mode.

e Determine the wavelength of the wave formed in this mode.

Exercise 15.4 Planning experiments on stationary waves

Being able to describe and plan experiments needs practice and thought. This exercise includes a number of structured approaches to experiments involving stationary waves.

1 This diagram shows apparatus that can be used to show a stationary wave on a string and to measure the wavelength of the wave:

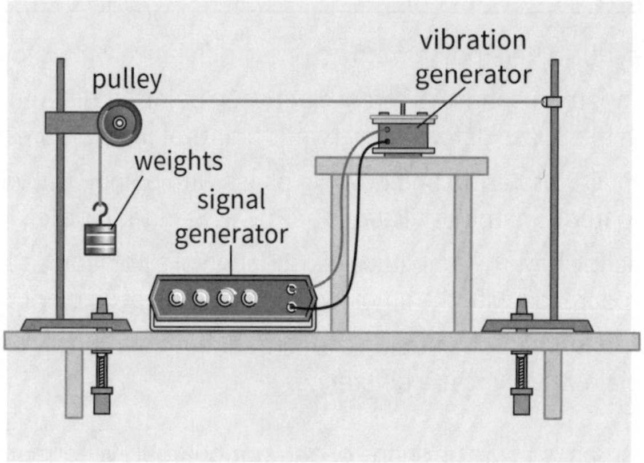

a State how you can obtain a stationary wave on the string and how you would recognise the positions of nodes and antinodes.

b Suggest how you can measure the wavelength of the wave. Include one precaution that enables an accurate value to be found.

c The frequency of the wave is the frequency of the signal from the signal generator. Explain how this frequency can be measured using an oscilloscope.

d Suggest how the experiment can be used to determine how the speed of the wave on the string depends on the tension in the string.

2 This diagram shows apparatus that can be used to produce a stationary microwave:

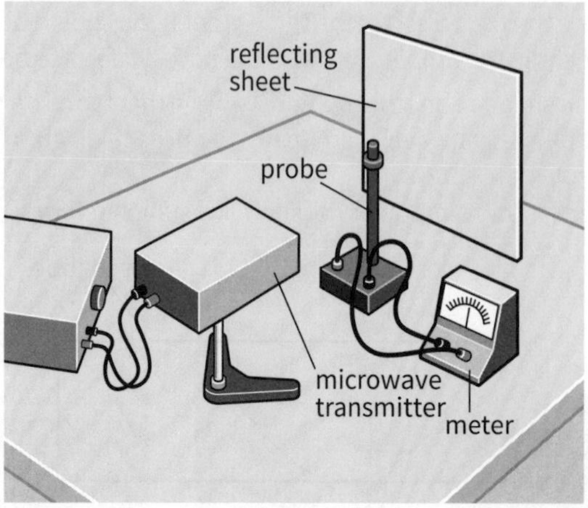

a Describe how you would use the apparatus to demonstrate a stationary wave.

b Explain why a stationary wave is set up.

c Explain how to use the stationary wave to measure the frequency of the microwave from the transmitter.

3 This diagram shows a column of water and a tuning fork:

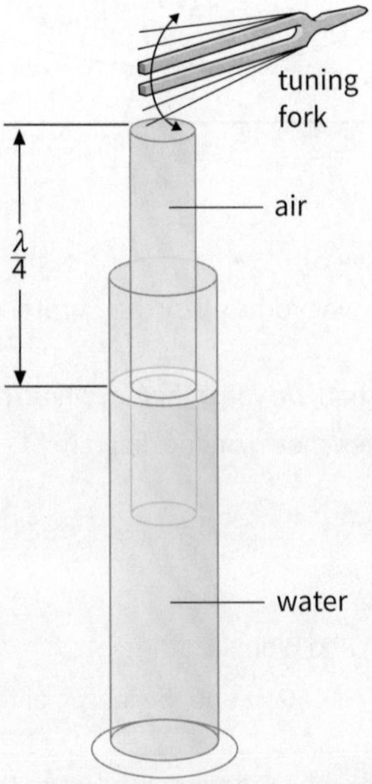

When the length of the air column is $\frac{\lambda}{4}$, a stationary sound wave is produced with one node and one antinode.

a State whether a node or an antinode is found at the top of the air column.

b State whether a node or an antinode is found at the surface between the water and the air.

c State, in terms of λ, what length of air column produces a stationary wave with two nodes and two antinodes.

d Describe how you would use the apparatus to demonstrate that stationary waves can be set up.

e Describe and explain how you would use the apparatus to measure the wavelength of sound. Since the antinode at the open end of the tube is slightly outside the tube, your method should involve the difference in the lengths of two air columns where there is a stationary wave.

f The frequency of a tuning fork is marked on the tuning fork. The experiment is repeated with different tuning forks. Describe the graph obtained when the wavelength λ of the sound wave is plotted against the frequency f of the tuning fork.

g Suggest a graph that may be plotted involving f and λ to give a straight line with a gradient equal to the speed of the sound in the air column.

Exam-style questions

1 A string is fixed at one end and made to vibrate by a vibrator close to that end. The frequency of the vibrator is altered until a stationary wave forms, as shown:

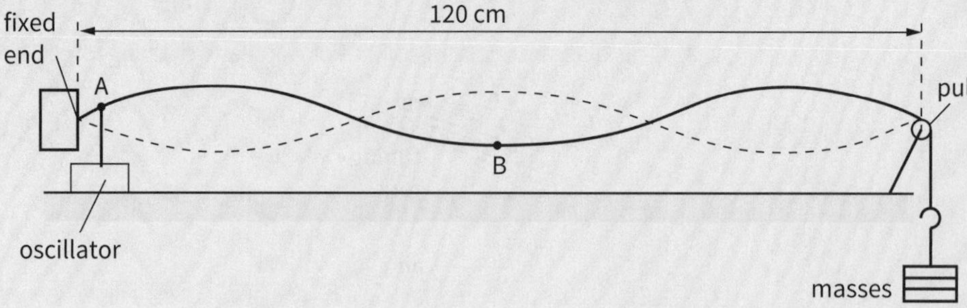

a Explain how a progressive wave produced by the vibrator causes the stationary wave to form. [2]

b Copy the wave pattern and mark on your diagram where nodes are found. [1]

c State the number of antinodes shown on the diagram. [1]

d Compare:

i the phase [1]

ii the amplitude [1]

of the oscillations of points A and B on the string.

e The frequency of the vibrator is 150 Hz and the length of the string between the pulley and the fixed end is 120 cm.

i Calculate the wavelength of the progressive wave on the string. [2]

ii Calculate the speed of the progressive wave along the string. [2]

f Adding more masses to the hook hanging from the string increases the speed of the progressive wave along the string.

A small mass is added and the stationary wave shown disappears.

i Explain why the stationary wave pattern shown disappears. [2]

ii State whether the frequency of the vibrator must be increased or decreased to form the same stationary wave pattern on the string as shown in the diagram. Explain your thinking. [2]

2 This diagram shows a demonstration of a stationary wave on a string:

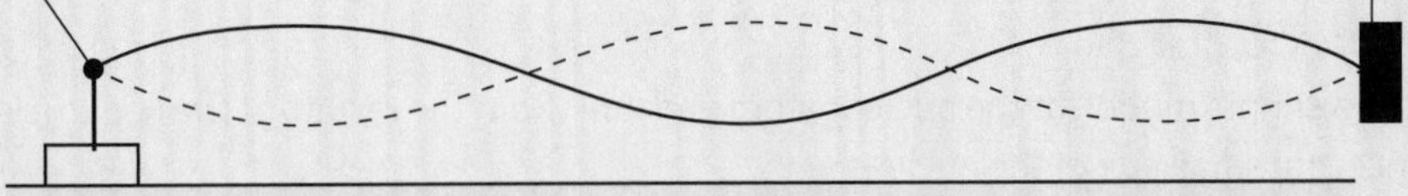

A vibrator is attached near one end of the string and the other end of the string is fixed. The vibrator causes a progressive wave to travel along the string.

a Use the principle of superposition to explain the formation of the stationary wave. [2]

b The speed of the progressive wave is 24 m s^{-1} and the vibrator has a frequency of 50 Hz.

i Calculate the wavelength of the progressive wave on the string. [1]

ii Calculate the distance between the nodes on the string. [1]

c When the frequency of the vibrator is **doubled**, the number of loops on the stationary wave changes from three to six. State whether this change affects the speed of the progressive wave along the string. Explain your thinking. [2]

3 a Describe the difference between a progressive wave and a stationary wave, both on a string. [2]

b Explain what is meant by a displacement node and a displacement antinode on a stationary wave. [2]

c A loudspeaker is placed close to the open end of a long tube which is closed at the other end, as shown. The length of the tube is 30 cm:

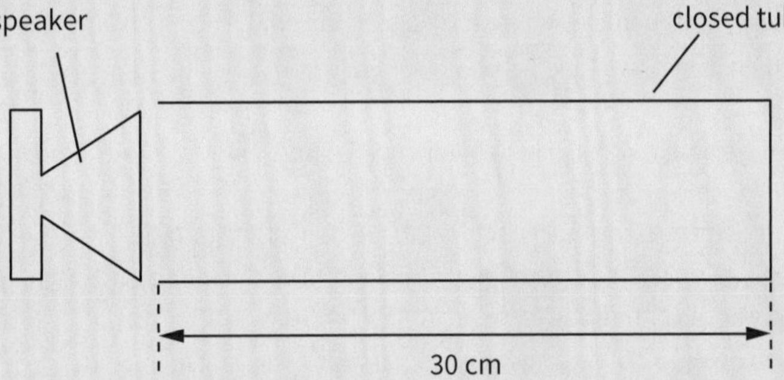

The frequency of the loudspeaker is altered slowly.

i Describe what you would expect to hear. Explain these observations. [3]

ii Sound of wavelength 24 cm from the loudspeaker causes a loud sound. Describe the position of the nodes and antinodes within the tube at this wavelength. [2]

iii The speed of sound in the tube is 320 m s^{-1}. Determine the lowest frequency at which a loud sound is produced in the tube. [3]

Chapter outline

- describe a simple model for the nuclear atom and infer from the results of the α-particle scattering experiment the existence and small size of the nucleus
- distinguish between nucleon number and proton number
- understand that an element can exist in various isotopic forms, each with a different number of neutrons
- represent nuclides with notation, and appreciate that nucleon number, proton number, and mass–energy are all conserved in nuclear processes
- show an understanding of the nature and properties of α-, β^+-, β^-- and γ-radiations
- describe leptons including electrons and neutrinos, including how antineutrinos and (electron) neutrinos are produced during β^-- and β^+-decay
- describe a simple quark model of hadrons, including protons and neutrons
- describe β^-- and β^+- decay in terms of a simple quark model and the weak interaction

KEY TERMS

alpha-particle: two protons and two neutrons ($^4_2\alpha$, the nucleus of a helium atom $^4_2$He) emitted from a nucleus during radioactive decay

beta-particle: an electron (β^--particle $^0_{-1}$e) or a positron (β^+-particle $^0_{+1}$e) emitted from a nucleus. In β^--decay, proton number increases by 1 (a β^--particle and an antineutrino are emitted). In β^+-decay, proton number decreases by 1 (a β^+-particle and a neutrino are emitted)

gamma-radiation: a high frequency (and energy) photon emitted from a nucleus during radioactive decay

isotopes: nuclei of the same element with different number of neutrons but the same number of protons

fundamental particle: an elementary particle that is not made from other particles

antiparticle: a particle with the same mass and opposite charge as another particle, for example the antiparticle of the electron is the positively charged electron, or positron

neutrino: a lepton released during beta-decay having no charge and very small mass

quark: the fundamental particles of which hadrons are made

hadron: any particle which is affected by the strong nuclear force, made from a quark and an antiquark, three quarks or three antiquarks

lepton: a sub atomic particle that is not affected by the strong nuclear force, for example an electron, positron and neutrino

weak interaction: the weak nuclear force, a fundamental force involved in radioactive β-decay

Equations: nucleon number = proton number + number of neutrons in a nucleus

Exercise 16.1 Discovering the structure of the atom

In this exercise you will discover how we know that an atom has a small central, positive nucleus. Remember the α-particle and the nucleus are both positive.

1 This diagram shows three alpha-particles approaching a gold nucleus in a scattering experiment:

All three alpha-particles have the same initial energy.

- **a** State which alpha-particle is deviated through the *smallest* angle. Explain why.
- **b** Copy the diagram and draw the paths of the three α-particles as they approach and leave the nucleus.
- **c** A force acts on each alpha-particle as it approaches the gold nucleus. On your diagram add an arrow to show the direction of this force at the point where α-particle 3 is closest to the nucleus. Explain why it acts in the direction that you have shown.

2 In an experiment, a large number of α-particles are fired at random towards a thin gold foil. The particles pass through the foil. Some are deviated only a little and some are deviated through large angles.

Compare the number of particles that deviate through small and large angles if:

- **a** the gold nuclei are far apart from each other
- **b** the gold nuclei are very close together.

Experiments show that most α-particles pass straight through the foil with only a small deviation.

- **c** Explain what this shows about the amount of empty space in the atom.

3 Link the observation in the α-particle scattering experiment with the best explanation.

Observation
most α-particles pass straight through the gold foil
some α-particles are deflected
a few α-particles are deflected by more than 90°

Explanation
there are electrons outside the nucleus
electrons have a negative charge
most of an atom is empty space
the mass of an atom is concentrated in a small space
the nucleus is positively charged
the nucleus contains neutrons

4 In a scattering experiment, α-particles are fired at a thin gold foil.

- **a** State the direction in which the maximum number of α-particles will be detected after hitting the foil.
- **b** State what this observation suggests about the structure of an atom.
- **c** Some α-particles are scattered through more than 90°. State and explain what this suggests about the structure of a gold atom.

Exercise 16.2 Particles in the atom and some decay equations

This exercise give you practice completing decay equations making the proton number (or charge) and nucleon numbers match on either side of the equation.

1 **a** Complete this table to show the number of protons, the number of neutrons, the number of electrons in a neutral atom, and the nuclide notations:

Nuclide notation	Number of protons	Number of neutrons	Number of electrons in a neutral atom
$^{238}_{92}U$			
He	2	2	
^{63}Cu	29		
^{58}Ni		30	
^{14}N	7		
^{15}O		7	

b State the difference in structure between a neutral *atom* of ^4_2He, a singly charged *ion* of ^4_2He and an α-particle.

c This diagram represents three different nuclei:

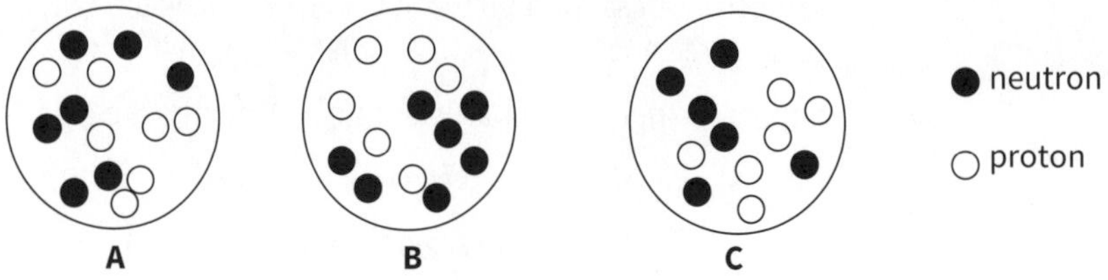

State and explain which of the nuclei are isotopes of the same element. (Think about what isotopes have in common with each other).

2 State three quantities that are conserved in a nuclear process. There are several quantities to choose from – do not just say *mass* or *energy*.

3 An isotope of phosphorus $^{30}_{15}P$ decays by emitting a beta-minus-particle (β^- or $^0_{-1}e$) and an electron antineutrino ($\bar{\nu}$) to form a Si nucleus.

a Copy and complete this equation:

$^{30}_{15}P \rightarrow Si + ^0_{-1}e + \bar{\nu}$

Note: $\bar{\nu}$ is an electron antineutrino; neutrinos have no proton or nucleon number.

b In the reaction, the total rest mass of the products is smaller than the mass of the $^{30}_{15}P$ nucleus. Explain why rest mass does not appear to be conserved.

c Give the nuclide notation of another isotope of phosphorus.

4 Calculate the values of *p*, *q*, *r* and *s* in each of these nuclear reactions:

a $^{241}_{95}Am \rightarrow ^p_qNp + ^r_sHe$

b $^{14}_{6}C \rightarrow ^p_qN + ^0_{-1}e + \bar{\nu}$

c $^{23}_{12}Mg \rightarrow ^p_qNa + ^0_{+1}e + \nu$

Notes:

^r_sHe is an α-particle, which you should know about.

$^0_{-1}e$ is a β^--particle and $\bar{\nu}$ is an electron antineutrino.

$^0_{+1}e$ is a β^+-particle and ν is an electron neutrino.

5 A nucleus of uranium $^{238}_{92}U$ undergoes a series of nuclear decays, as shown by the arrows in this diagram. Each circle represents a nucleus present during the decay series:

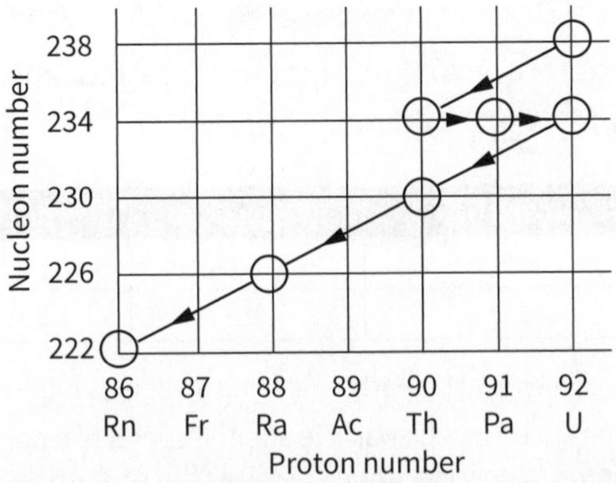

a State the nuclide notation of the final nucleus in the series.

b Write out the decay equation for one example of α-decay in this series.

c Write out the decay equation for one example of β^--decay in this series.

d State how many β^--particles and α-particles are emitted during the series.

e State the nuclide notation of two pairs of isotopes in this series.

f A nucleus emits a beta-plus-particle (β^+). Describe the arrow that needs to be added to the diagram for this decay.

6 An atom of $^{238}_{92}U$ decays progressively into $^{206}_{82}Pb$ by emitting eight α-particles and a number of β^--particles. How many β^--particles are emitted?

Exercise 16.3 The nature and properties of nuclear radiation

This exercise helps you understand that the *nature* of radiation is what it is made of; its *properties* are what it can do. The properties involved in radioactivity are a result of the nature of the particles.

1 A student lists some of the properties of α-particles, β^--particles, β^+-particles and γ-radiation. Link the property to the correct radiation. One of the particles is linked to two properties.

Property
has the most positive charge
passes through paper but not 2 cm lead
is not affected by an electric field
travels at the speed of light
is an antiparticle of a common particle

Radiation
α-particle
β^--particle
β^+-particle
γ-radiation

2 **a** Copy and complete this table to show the mass and charge of the four different types of radiation.

Give values of charge in terms of e where e is 1.60×10^{-19} C.

The rest mass of a proton and a neutron are each 1.7×10^{-27} kg to two significant figures.

The rest mass of an electron is 9.1×10^{-31} kg.

	α-particle	β^--particle	β^+-particle	γ-radiation
mass / kg				
charge		$-1e$		

b The speed of a typical β^--particle leaving a nucleus is 0.9 c, where c is the speed of light.

i State the speed of a β^+-particle and the speed of a particle of γ-radiation, each of which has approximately the same energy as the β^--particle.

ii Calculate the speed of an α-particle which has approximately the same energy as the β^--particle. Give your answer as a fraction of c.

3 Describe and explain what happens to a neutral atom as an α-particle passes near and causes ionisation.

4 State which of the four types of radiation (α, β^-, β^+ or γ):

a produces the most ionisation per mm along its path through air atoms

b has the shortest range in air

c is not affected by a magnetic field

d is attracted by a negatively charged object

e is deflected the opposite way to α-radiation by an electric field

f has the highest speed

g are emitted with a range of speeds (note: consider those emissions that are emitted with a neutrino or antineutrino from a nucleus)

h is the same as a fundamental particle found in the atom

i is an electromagnetic wave

j is made up of protons and neutrons.

5 Explain why each type of radiation that you chose in question 4, parts **a–g**, has the property described. (Think about why ionisation happens in parts **a** and **b**.)

6 A positron (β^+-particle) is an *antiparticle*.

a State the name of the corresponding *particle*.

b State one property of an antiparticle that is the same for its corresponding particle.

c State one property of an antiparticle that is different for its corresponding particle.

7 Outline how you could use the absorption properties of nuclear radiation to show that a radioactive source emits only γ-radiation. Include one precaution you would take to reduce the effect of random errors.

Exercise 16.4 Fundamental particles including quarks

This exercise helps you to learn about some types of quark and where they are found in the nucleus, and which particles are leptons and which particles are hadrons.

1 Copy this table and add ticks to show if a particle is fundamental, whether it is a lepton or a hadron, and if it contains quarks. There may be one or more ticks for each particle.

Particle	Fundamental	Lepton	Hadron	Contains quarks
neutron				
proton				
electron				
neutrino				

2 Leptons include electrons and neutrinos. State two differences between electrons and neutrinos.

3 An up quark is written as u, a down quark as d and a strange quark as s. The charge on an electron is *e*.

a State the quark structure of a neutron.

b An up quark has a charge $+\frac{2}{3}e$. Use your answer to **a** to show that the charge on a down quark is $-\frac{1}{3}e$.

c State the quark structure of a proton.

d Show that your choice of quarks in **c** have a total charge of $+e$.

4 When a neutron decays it produces a β^--particle (an electron ${}^{0}_{-1}e$) and two other particles.

a State the name of the two other particles and complete this decay equation:

${}^{1}_{0}n \rightarrow {}^{0}_{-1}e +$ _____ $+$ _____

b State the name of the interaction that causes β^--decay.

c State what happens to the quarks inside the neutron during the decay.

d State which of the particles in the decay equation in **a** are leptons and which are antiparticles.

5 One step in the fusion process that takes place in the Sun involves the β^+-decay of a proton (p) into a neutron (n) and a neutrino (ν).

The equation for the step is: $p \rightarrow n + \beta^+ + \nu$

a Show that charge is conserved in the equation shown.

b Show that nucleon number is conserved in the equation shown.

c State what happens to the quarks inside the proton during β^+-decay.

6 A neutral carbon atom ${}^{12}_{6}C$ contains quarks, leptons and hadrons.

a State which particles in the carbon atom are leptons and how many leptons in total are found in one neutral atom of carbon.

b State which particles in the carbon atom are hadrons and how many hadrons in total are found in one neutral atom of carbon.

c State how many quarks there are in one neutral atom of carbon.

7 **a** A nuclear decay is written in terms of the quarks in the nucleus as:

d → u + _____ + _____

State the two particles that are not shown on the right-hand side.

b A nuclear decay is written in terms of the quarks in the nucleus as:

u → d + _____ + _____

State the two particles that are not shown on the right-hand side.

8 A nuclear process that does **not** occur is $\nu + p \rightarrow n + \beta^-$.

a Show that this process does not conserve charge.

b Show that the nuclear process $\bar{\nu} + p \rightarrow n + \beta^+$ conserves charge, proton number and nucleon number.

9 Hadrons like the neutron and proton contain either three quarks or three antiquarks. They do **not** contain a mixture of quarks and antiquarks.

a Using only up (u) and down (d) quarks and their antiparticles ($\bar{u}$ and $\bar{d}$) write all the quark combinations of three quarks or three antiquarks.

b Write all the combinations of quarks that contain one strange quark (s) with only up and down quarks to make a combination of three quarks.

c Write all the combinations of three antiquarks that contain two strange antiquarks ($\bar{s}$) with an up or down antiquark.

d Suggest a name for the hadron which contains two $\bar{u}$ quarks and one $\bar{d}$ quark.

Exam-style questions

1 This table shows some of the isotopes of aluminium and their type of nuclear decay:

Isotope	${}^{25}_{13}\text{Al}$	${}^{26}_{13}\text{Al}$	${}^{27}_{13}\text{Al}$	${}^{28}_{13}\text{Al}$	${}^{29}_{13}\text{Al}$
Type of decay	β^+	β^+	stable	β^-	β^-

a Describe the similarities and the differences in the structure of neutral atoms of the isotopes. [3]

b Describe the structure of a nucleus of ${}^{27}_{13}\text{Al}$ in terms of:

i the number of protons and neutrons it contains [2]

ii the number of up (u) and down (d) quarks it contains. [2]

c Describe what happens during beta-minus (β^-) decay using a quark model. [2]

d State two quantities conserved in beta decay. [2]

e By considering the difference between the isotopes in the table, suggest why some isotopes emit β^--radiation and some emit β^+-radiation. [2]

2 **a** Complete this table for the four types of radiation: [8]

Radiation	Nature	Charge	Penetrating ability in air	Affected by magnetic fields
α			6 cm in air	a little
β^-		$-1e$		
β^+	positron		2.0 m of air	
γ				

b **i** A radioactive nucleus decays with the emission of an α-particle and a γ-particle Describe the changes that occur in the proton number and the nucleon number of the nucleus. [2]

ii Describe briefly, with the aid of a sketch diagram, an experiment to distinguish between the α-, β^-- and γ-radiation emitted from a radioactive source using a magnetic field. Explain why the experiment is difficult to perform with α-radiation and how the experiment shows that β^--particles are emitted with a range of speeds. [4]

c About 100 years ago, experiments were performed by firing α-particles at gold foil. A detector was used to see how many particles were scattered at different angles. Summarise the results of these experiments and explain the conclusions that were drawn. [3]

3 Leptons and hadrons are two classes of sub-atomic particles.

a Some classes of particles are fundamental; others are not. State and explain whether leptons and hadrons are fundamental or not fundamental. [3]

b Name the class of particles of which the neutron is a member. [1]

c Give two examples of a lepton. [2]

d In beta-minus (β^-) decay, a nucleus of calcium (Ca) emits a β^--particle as shown in the reaction:

$${}^{45}_{20}\text{Ca} \rightarrow {}^{46}_{21}\text{Sc} + \beta^- + \overline{\nu}_e$$

i State the name of the particle $\overline{\nu}_e$. [1]

ii Explain, in terms of the neutrons and protons involved, how this change occurs. [2]

iii Explain, in terms of the quarks involved, how this change occurs. [2]

e State the quark change that is responsible for beta-plus (β^+) decay. [1]

f Name the interaction responsible for beta-decay. [1]

Chapter outline

- use degrees and radians as measures of angle, including the expression of angular displacement in radians
- explain uniform circular motion in terms of a centripetal force causing a centripetal acceleration
- solve problems involving angular displacement and velocity, including use of the equation $v = r\omega$
- solve problems involving centripetal force and acceleration, including use of the equations $a = r\omega^2 = \frac{v^2}{r}$ and $F = mr\omega^2 = \frac{mv^2}{r}$

KEY TERMS

radian: a unit of angle such that 2π radians = 360°

angular displacement θ: the angle through which an object moves in a circle

angular velocity ω: the rate at which the angular displacement changes

centripetal force: the resultant force acting on an object that is moving in a circle

Equations: angular velocity = $\frac{\text{angular displacement}}{\text{time}}$; $\omega = \frac{\Delta\theta}{\Delta t}$

speed = radius × angular velocity; $v = r\omega$

centripetal acceleration = radius × (angular velocity)^2; $a = r\omega^2 = \frac{v^2}{r}$

centripetal force = mass × centripetal acceleration; $F = mr\omega^2 = \frac{mv^2}{r}$

Exercise 17.1 Angular measure

The radian is a more 'natural' unit of measurement of angles than the degree. Angles in radians can be calculated knowing the length *s* of the arc subtended by the angle and the radius *r* of the circle: $\theta = \frac{s}{r}$. This exercise provides practice in calculating angles in radians and converting between degrees and radians.

1 For each diagram **a–f**, calculate the unknown quantity θ, *s* or *r*, from the other two:

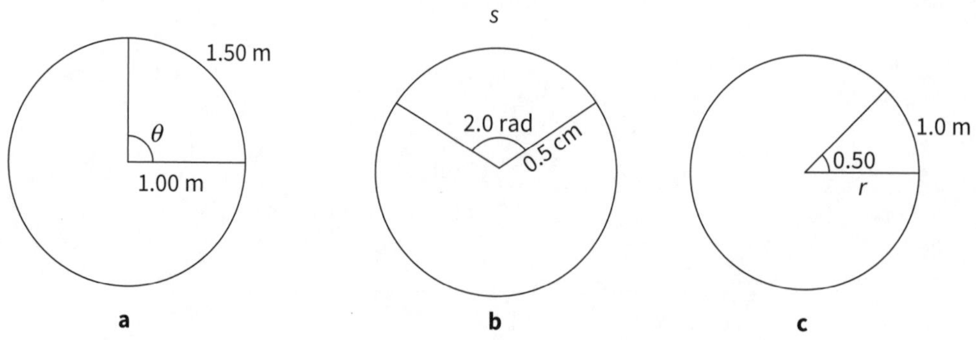

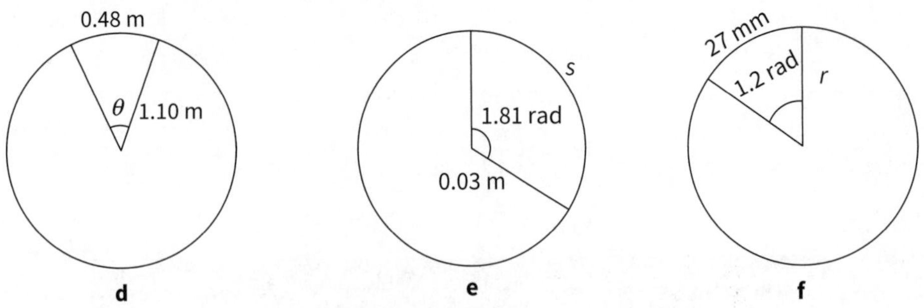

2 When an object moves around a complete circle, its angular displacement is 2π radians or 360°.

- **a** Show that one radian is approximately equal to 57°.
- **b** Convert each of these angles in degrees to radians:
  - **i** 20°
  - **ii** 75°
  - **iii** 175°.
- **c** Convert each of the following angles in radians to degrees:
  - **i** 0.40 rad
  - **ii** 1.35 rad
  - **iii** 2.0 rad.
- **d** Express each of these angles as multiples of π radians:
  - **i** 180°
  - **ii** 90°
  - **iii** 45°.

3 This diagram shows how an angle of one radian is defined – *the arc subtended by the angle is equal in length to the radius of the circle*:

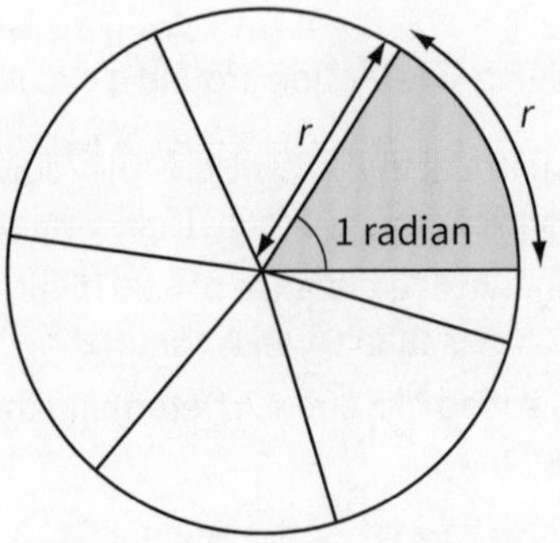

- **a** Draw a similar diagram to show the dimensions of an angle of 2.0 radians.
- **b** Draw a similar diagram to show the dimensions of an angle of $\frac{\pi}{3}$ radians.

TIP

If a question about circular motion seems unclear, draw a diagram of the circle and angles involved to help your understanding.

4 You may need to find the value of a trigonometric function (such as sine or cosine) of an angle whose value is given in radians. Make sure that you know how to set your calculator to work with angles in radians.

- **a** Check that your calculator shows that sin (1.0 rad) = 0.841.
- **b** Calculate the values of the following, where all angles are given in radians; give your answers to three significant figures:

i $\cos 1.0$

ii $\tan 1.0$

iii $\sin 0.10$

iv $\sin\left(\frac{\pi}{4}\right)$

v $\cos\left(\frac{\pi}{3}\right)$

Your calculator is likely to have a π key.

c Determine the following angles; give your answers in radians and to three significant figures:

i $\sin^{-1} 0.50$

ii $\cos^{-1}(-0.65)$.

Exercise 17.2 Uniform circular motion

An object that moves around a circular path at a steady speed is described as having uniform circular motion. This is an exercise to develop understanding of the relationships between velocity, angular velocity, period, angle and radius.

1 A fairground ride consists of several cars travelling around on a vertical wheel of radius $r = 20.0$ m. Each car makes one complete circuit in a time $T = 35$ s.

a During each circuit, a car travels around 360°. This is its angular displacement θ. Give the value of θ in radians.

b Calculate the car's angular velocity ω.

c Calculate the distance travelled by the car during one circuit ($= 2\pi r$).

d Calculate the car's speed v using speed $= \frac{\text{distance}}{\text{time}}$.

e Calculate the car's speed using $v = r\omega$. Check that your answers to **d** and **e** are the same.

2 Two runners, A and B, are jogging side by side around a circular running track.

a Runner A jogs along the centre of the track. Here, the radius of the track is 100.0 m. Calculate the distance travelled in one complete circuit. (Give your answer to one decimal place.)

b Runner B jogs beside runner A, at a distance of 0.80 m further from the centre of the track. How much further does B travel than A when completing a circuit?

c Runner A runs at a steady speed of 5.0 m s^{-1}. Determine the speed at which B must run in order to stay beside runner A.

3 A train moves along a curved section of track at a steady speed of 18.0 m s^{-1}.

a The curved section of track has a length of 900 m. Deduce how long it will take the train to travel this distance.

b The radius of curvature of the track is 3.60 km. Calculate the angle through which the train has moved (its angular displacement). Remember: angle in radians $= \frac{\text{length of arc}}{\text{radius}}$

c Calculate the angular velocity of the train.

d Draw a diagram to show the curved section of the track. Add arrows to show the velocity of the train at the start of the section and at the end.

17.3 Centripetal force and acceleration

An object moving in a circle must be acted on by a resultant force which is not zero. In this exercise, you need to decide whether an object is acted on by a non-zero resultant force. If it is, you can then calculate quantities such as angular velocity and acceleration.

1 **a** Describe the motion of an object which is acted on by balanced forces (resultant force = 0).

b The resultant force acting on an object as it travels around in a circle can be described as a *centripetal* force. State the direction of such a force.

2 This diagram shows an object at several points around its path. It is moving with uniform circular motion in a clockwise direction:

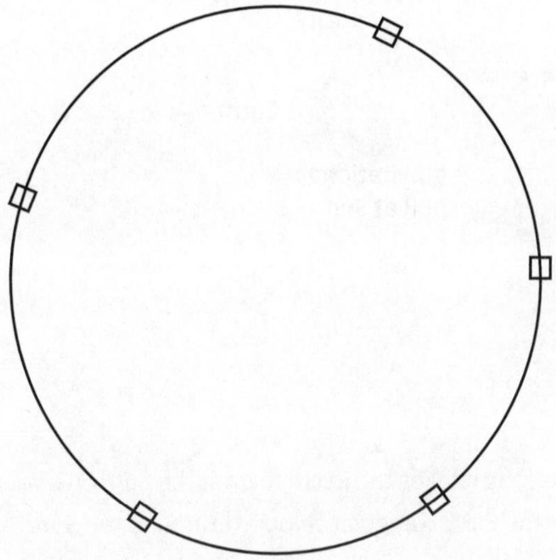

a Explain what the word *uniform* tells you about the object's speed.

b State whether the object's velocity is constant. Explain your answer.

c Copy the diagram and add an arrow (labelled *v*) to each image of the object to represent its velocity. Add a second arrow (labelled *F*) to represent the centripetal force acting on it.

3 This diagram shows a rubber bung being moved around in a circle on the end of a length of string:

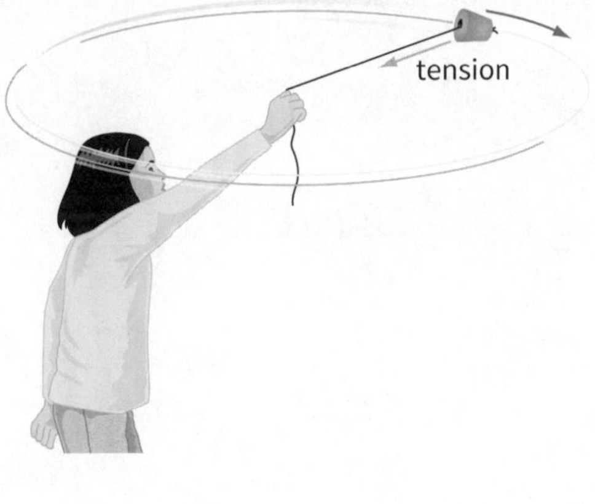

The bung travels around eight complete circuits in 10 s. The radius r of its path is 40.0 cm.

a State the name of the force that provides the centripetal force which causes the bung to travel in a circle.

b Calculate the speed v of the bung.

c Use the equation $a = \frac{v^2}{r}$ to calculate the bung's centripetal acceleration.

d Draw a diagram of the bung and add arrows to show the directions of its velocity and its acceleration.

e State the other quantity you would need to know in order to determine the centripetal force acting on the bung.

f Describe how the bung will move if the girl releases the string.

4 The Earth is kept in its orbit by the gravitational pull of the Sun:

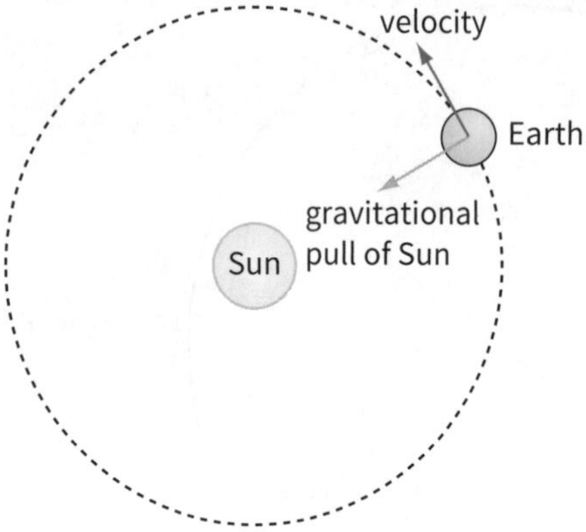

a State how long it takes the Earth to orbit the Sun. Give your answer in seconds.

b Calculate the Earth's angular velocity ω around the Sun.

c The radius of the Earth's orbit is 150×10^6 km. Use the equation $a = r\omega^2$ to calculate the Earth's centripetal acceleration.

d The gravitational acceleration of an object near the Earth's surface is 9.8 m s^{-2}. How many times greater is this than your answer to part **c**?

5 A car is travelling at 28 m s^{-1} along a curved section of road. The radius of curvature of the road is 300 m.

a Calculate the car's centripetal acceleration.

b The car has a mass of 1200 kg. Calculate the centripetal force acting on the car.

The road surface is banked at an angle θ (that is, it slopes across the direction of travel) so that the car can travel around the bend without slipping. This diagram shows the forces acting on the car: its weight mg and the contact force of the road N:

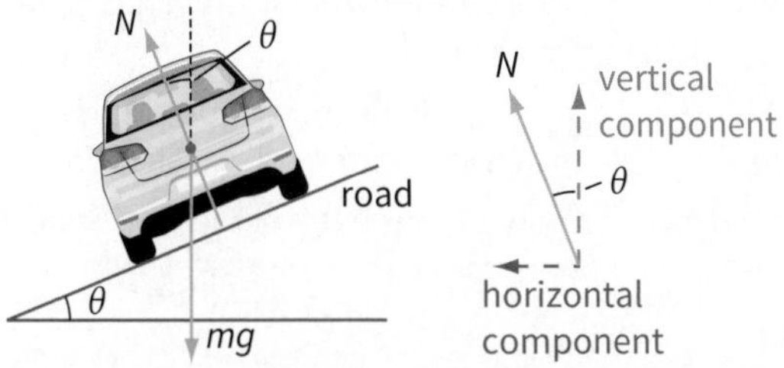

c What force provides the car's centripetal acceleration? State its direction. (Any force that has a component at right angles to an object's velocity will provide a centripetal acceleration.)

d The best angle of banking is given by this equation:

$$\tan\theta = \frac{v^2}{rg}$$

Find the value of θ for vehicles travelling at 28 m s^{-1}.

6 This diagram shows a rubber bung on the end of a length of string:

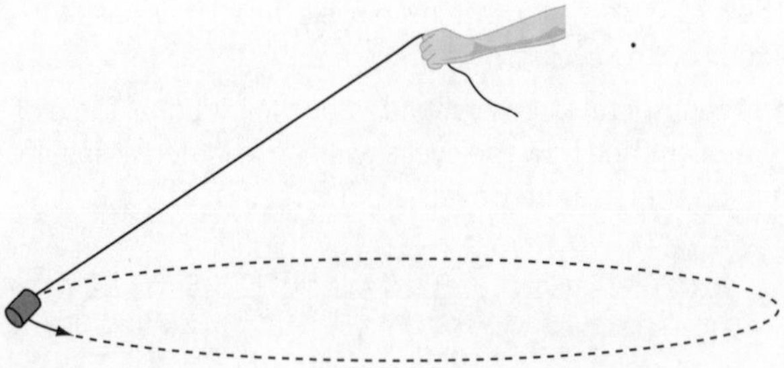

The bung is being swung around in a horizontal circle. The string makes an angle of 60° with the vertical.

a Two forces act on the bung. Name these forces and draw a free body diagram to show their directions.

b The mass of the bung is 150 g. Calculate its weight.

c The weight of the bung is balanced by the vertical component of the tension in the string. Use this fact to calculate the tension in the string.

d The centripetal force acting on the bung is provided by the horizontal component of the tension. Calculate the value of this horizontal component.

e Calculate the bung's acceleration.

f The radius of the bung's path is 60 cm. Calculate its speed.

g Calculate the time taken for one complete revolution of the bung.

Exam-style questions

1 **a** Explain what is meant by the term *angular velocity*. [2]

b A merry-go-round in a children's park completes 10 revolutions in one minute. Calculate its angular velocity. [2]

c A child sitting on the edge of the merry-go-round is at a distance of 1.20 m from the centre. Calculate the child's centripetal acceleration. [2]

d The child moves closer to the centre of the ride. State whether each of these quantities increases, decreases or stays the same:

i angular velocity

ii centripetal acceleration

iii centripetal force. [3]

2 A racing cyclist is practising by cycling around a flat, circular track. The track has a radius of 50.0 m.

a The cyclist travels half way around the track. Show that his angular displacement is π radians. [2]

b The electronic timing system indicates that the cyclist took 11.51 s to complete this ride. Calculate his angular velocity and his speed. [3]

c The cyclist, together with his bicycle, has a mass of 94.2 kg. Calculate the centripetal force acting on the cyclist. [2]

d The centripetal force is provided by the frictional force of the track on the bicycle's tyres. Describe how the cyclist will move if there is insufficient friction to keep him on course as he travels around the track. [2]

Chapter outline

- understand the concept of a gravitational field and define gravitational field strength and gravitational potential
- recall how, in gravitational problems, the mass of a uniform sphere may be considered to be a point mass at its centre
- derive a formula for the gravitational field strength of a point mass
- solve problems involving gravitational field strength and potential
- recall and use Newton's law of gravitation to solve problems
- analyse circular orbits in an inverse square law field, including geostationary orbits
- appreciate that on the surface of the Earth, g is approximately constant

KEY TERMS

gravitational field: a region where an object feels a force because of its mass

gravitational field strength: the gravitational force exerted per unit mass on a small object placed at a point

gravitational potential: the work done per unit mass in bringing a mass from infinity to a point

Newton's law of gravitation: any two point masses attract each other with a force that is directly proportional to the product of their mass and inversely proportional to the square of their separation

Equations: gravitational field strength $= \frac{\text{gravitational force}}{\text{mass}}$; $g = \frac{F}{m}$

gravitational potential $= \frac{\text{work done}}{\text{mass}}$; $\phi = \frac{W}{m}$

Newton's law of gravitation: $F = \frac{Gm_1m_2}{r^2}$

centripetal force = mass × centripetal acceleration; $F = mr\omega^2 = \frac{mv^2}{r}$

Exercise 18.1 Newton's law of gravitation

Isaac Newton discovered the law that describes the gravitational pull of one object on another. This exercise provides practice in drawing and interpreting field diagrams, and using the equation for gravitational force.

1 This diagram shows how we can represent the gravitational field of the Earth:

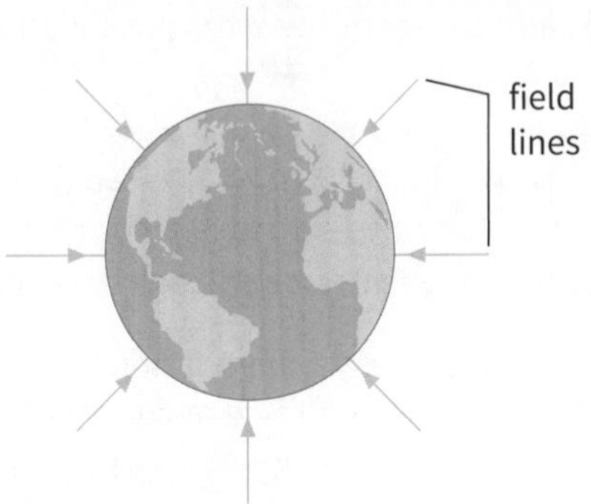

a Explain why the arrows on the field lines are all directed into the Earth.

b At what point would all the field lines meet?

The building you are sitting in is on the surface of the Earth. Here, the Earth's gravitational field is described as *uniform*.

c Draw a diagram to show gravitational field lines in the area around you.

d State how the field lines you have drawn show that the field is uniform.

e Look back at the diagram. Explain how this shows that the Earth's gravitational field is not uniform on this scale.

2 This diagram shows two objects, A and B. The mass of A is greater than the mass of B. A and B attract each other with a gravitational force. These forces are shown as F_1 and F_2:

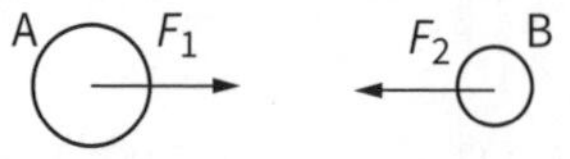

a What can you say about the *directions* of forces F_1 and F_2?

b What can you say about the *magnitudes* of forces F_1 and F_2?

c A and B are initially stationary. The gravitational forces cause them to accelerate towards each other. Which object will have the greater acceleration? Explain your answer. (You will need to think about the masses of the objects.)

3 Newton's law of gravitation is represented by the equation $F = \frac{Gm_1m_2}{r^2}$, where G is the gravitational constant.

a Rearrange the equation to make G its subject.

b Show that the units of G are N m^2 kg^{-2}.

4 This diagram shows an object of mass M on the surface of the Earth:

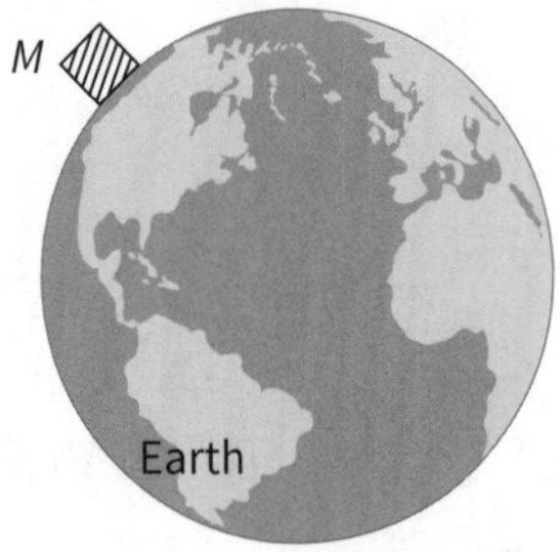

a Copy the diagram and add an arrow to show the direction of the Earth's gravitational force F on the object.

b The object is attracted to all points within the Earth. Which region of the Earth causes the *strongest* gravitational pull on the object? Label this region A. Explain your answer.

c Which region of the Earth causes the *weakest* gravitational pull on the object? Label this region B. Explain your answer.

d We can consider the Earth's gravitational pull as if all of its mass were concentrated at one point, its centre of gravity. Label this point C. Explain your answer.

5 The value of the gravitational constant is $G = 6.67 \times 10^{-11}$ N m^2 kg^{-2}.

a Use Newton's law to calculate the gravitational force of the Earth on a mass of 6.0 kg placed on its surface (mass of Earth = 6.0×10^{24} kg; radius of Earth = 6400 km).

b Calculate the gravitational force of the Sun on the Earth (mass of Sun = 2.0×10^{30} kg; radius of Earth's orbit around Sun = 150×10^6 km).

Exercise 18.2 Gravitational field strength

The idea of gravitational field strength g is familiar because we use the quantity g to calculate the weight W of an object of mass m, using $W = mg$. On the Earth's surface, $g = 9.8\ \mathrm{N\ kg^{-1}}$ approximately. This is an exercise in calculating and using gravitational field strength for different objects in the solar system.

1 Because the Earth is not a perfect sphere, the value of g varies from $9.78\ \mathrm{N\ kg^{-1}}$ at the Equator to $9.83\ \mathrm{N\ kg^{-1}}$ at the poles.

An object of mass 20.0 kg is transported from the Equator to the North Pole.

- **a** Calculate the weight of an object of mass 20.0 kg at a point where the Earth's gravitational field strength $g = 9.80\ \mathrm{N\ kg^{-1}}$.
- **b** Calculate the amount by which the object's weight increases.
- **c** Explain how g will change if you climb to the top of a high mountain.

Remember that the gravitational force of one object on another depends on the distance between their centres of mass.

2 The gravitational force of one mass on another is given by Newton's law, equation $F = \frac{Gm_1m_2}{r^2}$. The definition of gravitational field strength g says that its value is the force acting *per unit mass* acting near a body of mass m.

- **a** Show that this leads to the equation for the gravitational field strength at a distance r from a point mass M: $g = \frac{GM}{r^2}$.
- **b** Calculate the gravitational field strength at the Earth's surface. Give your answer to two significant figures (mass of Earth $= 6.0 \times 10^{24}$ kg; radius of Earth $= 6400$ km; gravitational constant $G = 6.67 \times 10^{-11}\ \mathrm{N\ m^2\ kg^{-2}}$).

3 The Moon has a mass of 7.4×10^{22} kg and its mean radius is 1.74×10^6 m.

- **a** Calculate the gravitational force on a mass of exactly 1 kg on the surface of the Moon (gravitational constant $G = 6.67 \times 10^{-11}\ \mathrm{N\ m^2\ kg^{-2}}$).
- **b** State the value of the gravitational field strength on the surface of the Moon.
- **c** Calculate the weight of an object of mass 20.0 kg on the surface of the Moon.
- **d** Imagine that you dropped an object close to the surface of the Moon. Determine the object's acceleration.

4 The dwarf planet Pluto is orbited by its moon Charon, as shown:

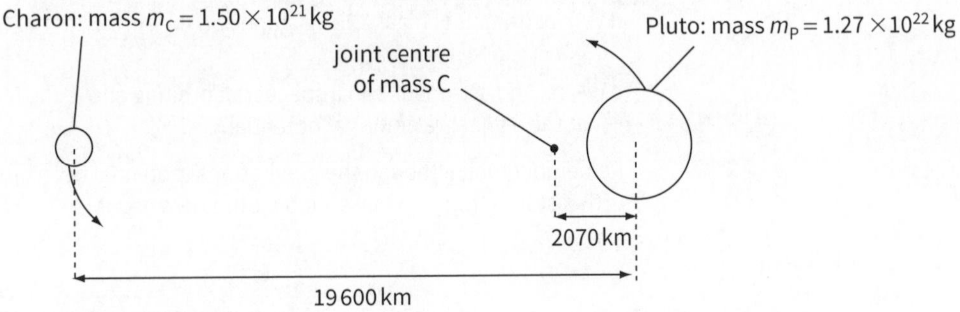

They orbit around their joint centre of mass C.

a Calculate the gravitational field strength at C due to Pluto. Give its direction (gravitational constant $G = 6.67 \times 10^{-11}$ N m^2 kg^{-2}).

b Calculate the gravitational field strength at C due to Charon. Give its direction.

c What is the gravitational force on an object of mass 1.0 kg placed at C? Explain your answer.

Think about the definition of field strength and remember that it is a vector quantity.

Exercise 18.3 Gravitational potential

The gravitational potential at a point is defined in terms of the work done in bringing unit mass from infinity to the point. You can think of it as the gravitational potential energy per unit mass, but remember that its value is zero at infinity and less than zero everywhere else. This is an exercise in understanding and using the equation for calculating gravitational potential.

1 At point P, the gravitational potential $\phi = -60$ J kg^{-1}.

Thinking about the definition of ϕ:

a State the gravitational potential energy of a mass of 1.0 kg at point P.

b Calculate the gravitational potential energy of a mass of 50.0 kg at point P.

c State the work done in moving a mass of 50.0 kg from infinity to point P.

d State the work done in moving a mass of 50.0 kg from point P to infinity.

At point Q, the gravitational potential $\phi = -40$ J kg^{-1}.

e Which point is at a higher potential, P or Q?

f Calculate the work done in moving a mass of 50.0 kg from point P to point Q.

2 You will need this data for this question:

gravitational constant $G = 6.67 \times 10^{-11}$ N m^2 kg^{-2}

Earth: mass = 6.0×10^{24} kg; radius = 6.4×10^6 m

Moon: mass = 7.4×10^{22} kg; mean radius = 1.74×10^6 m

The gravitational potential ϕ in the field of a point mass is given by $\phi = -\frac{GM}{r}$

a State the meaning of each of the symbols G, M and r.

b Use the equation for ϕ to calculate the gravitational potential on the surface of the Earth.

c Calculate the gravitational potential ϕ on the surface of the Moon.

d An astronaut of mass 120 kg stands on the surface of the Moon. Calculate his gravitational energy.

e A second astronaut is in a spacecraft orbiting above the Moon's surface. Which astronaut is at the higher gravitational potential?

Remember that, although the gravitational potential near a mass is always negative, it *increases* with distance from the mass – it becomes *less negative*.

3 When an object of mass m is raised through a height h, its increase in gravitational energy = mgh.

You should be familiar with this equation, but note that it only applies close to the Earth's surface where g is roughly constant. In this question, you can check that you get the same answer using this equation as using the more general relationship $\phi = -\frac{GM}{r}$.

a An object of mass 1.0 kg is placed on the Earth's surface. It is now at a distance of 6.40×10^6 m from the centre of the Earth. Calculate its gravitational energy. Give your answer to eight significant figures. (You will need to use an electronic calculator.)

b The object is now lifted a distance of 100 m vertically upwards. Its distance from the Earth's centre of mass is now $6.400\,100 \times 10^6$ m. Using the equation $\phi = -\frac{GM}{r}$, calculate the new value of its gravitational potential energy.

c Calculate the *increase* in its gravitational potential energy.

d Calculate the same quantity using the equation:

change in gravitational potential energy = mgh

Do you get the same answer as you did for part **c**?

Exercise 18.4 Orbiting under gravity

Gravity is the most important force for astronomical objects such as the planets and moons of the Solar System. It also holds satellites in their orbits around the Earth. This is an exercise that considers spacecraft and satellites in different types of orbits around the Earth.

1 This diagram shows three spacecraft that share a circular orbit around the Earth. Each spacecraft has a mass of 450 kg:

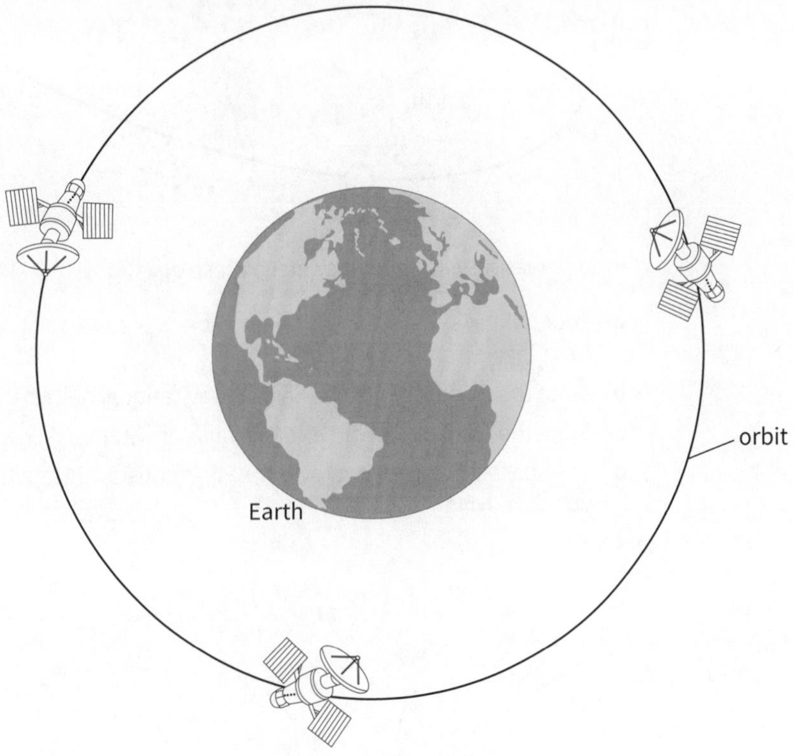

a Copy the diagram and add a force arrow to each spacecraft to show the force of the Earth's gravitational pull on it.

b Each spacecraft orbits at a distance of 2600 km above the Earth's surface. Calculate the distance of each spacecraft from the centre of the Earth and the gravitational force on it (gravitational constant $G = 6.67 \times 10^{-11}$ N m^2 kg^{-2}; Earth: mass $= 6.0 \times 10^{24}$ kg; radius $= 6.4 \times 10^6$ m).
Remember to always calculate a spacecraft's distance from the centre of the Earth, not its distance above the Earth's surface.

c A spacecraft must travel at the correct speed if it is to stay in its orbit. Calculate this speed for the spacecraft, using the circular motion equation $F = \frac{mv^2}{r}$.

d Calculate the time for one of the spacecraft to complete a single orbit of the Earth. Give your answer in minutes.

2 This diagram shows a spacecraft in an elliptical orbit around the Earth. Its distance from the Earth varies as it travels around its orbit:

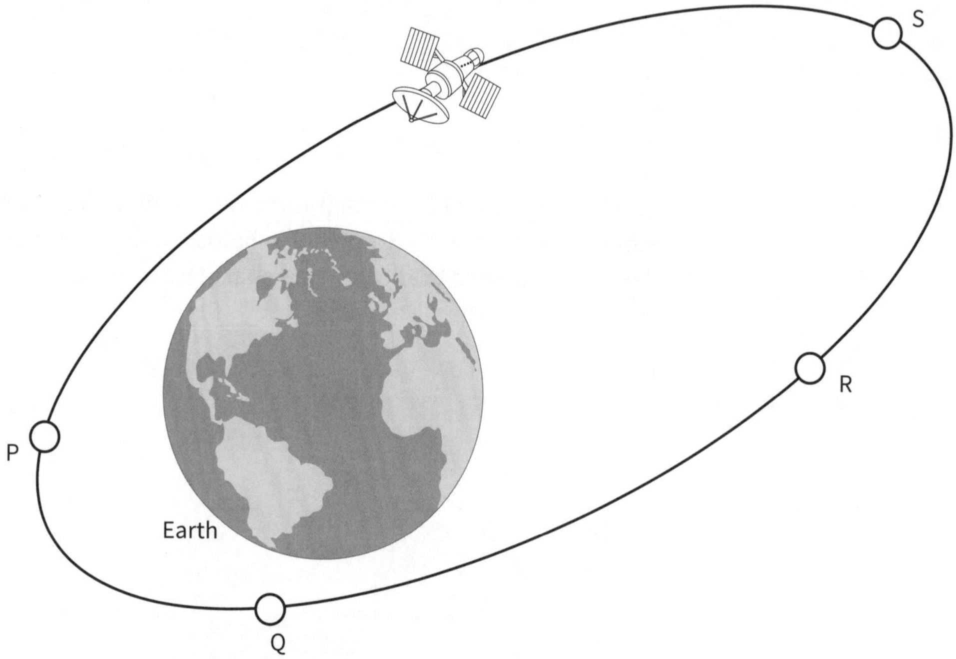

Include reasons with your answers to these questions:

a Four points P–S are marked on the orbit. State the point at which the spacecraft is furthest from the Earth.

b State the point at which the Earth's gravitational pull on the spacecraft is weakest.

c State the point at which the spacecraft's gravitational energy is greatest.

d The spacecraft's total energy (KE + PE) is constant. State the point at which the spacecraft will be moving most slowly.

3 A geostationary spacecraft orbits a planet once each day. It appears to remain at a fixed point in the sky, above the planet's equator.

a Determine the period of orbit of a geostationary spacecraft around the Earth. Give your answer in seconds.

A geostationary spacecraft could be placed in orbit around the planet Mars in order to maintain communication with a lander on the planet's surface. The period *T* of such a spacecraft would be given by the equation:

$$T^2 = \left(\frac{4\pi^2}{GM}\right)r^3$$

b State which quantities are represented by the symbols *M* and *r*.

c Calculate the radius of orbit for a geostationary planet orbiting Mars. Use a reference book or the internet to supply the necessary data.

Exam-style questions

Note: gravitational constant $G = 6.67 \times 10^{-11}$ N m^2 kg^{-2}.

Earth: mass $= 6.0 \times 10^{24}$ kg; radius $= 6.4 \times 10^6$ m.

1 **a** Explain what is meant by the term *gravitational field strength.* [2]

b A spacecraft of mass of 220 kg lands on the surface of Mars. An on-board sensor determines its weight to be 836 N. Calculate the gravitational field strength on the surface of Mars. [2]

c Measurements from Earth show that the diameter of Mars is 6.75×10^6 m. Determine the planet's mass. [3]

d The gravitational field on the surface of Mars is described as *uniform*. Explain what this means. [2]

2 **a** Explain what is meant by the term *gravitational potential.* [2]

A spy spacecraft orbits the Earth in a circular orbit, 500 km above the planet's surface.

b Calculate the gravitational potential at this height. [3]

c State the amount of energy per kilogram that would be required to move the spacecraft entirely out of the Earth's gravitational field. [1]

d Calculate the speed of the spacecraft in its orbit. [2]

e Calculate the time taken for the spacecraft to complete one orbit around the Earth. [2]

Chapter outline

- describe oscillations using appropriate terminology
- express the period of oscillation in terms of both frequency and angular frequency
- analyse graphical representations of simple harmonic motion including changes in displacement, velocity, acceleration and the interchange between kinetic and potential energy
- recall and use the equations of simple harmonic motion, including those for displacement, velocity and acceleration
- describe the effects of damping, including the importance of critical damping
- describe forced oscillations and resonance, including examples of resonance that are useful or that should be avoided

KEY TERMS

simple harmonic motion: motion of an oscillator in which its acceleration is directly proportional to its displacement from its equilibrium position and is directed towards that position

frequency: the number of oscillations per second

period: the time for one oscillation

amplitude: the maximum displacement of an oscillating mass

Equations: frequency $= \frac{1}{\text{period}}$; $f = \frac{1}{T}$

defining s.h.m.: acceleration ∝ – displacement; $a = -\omega^2 x$

sinusoidal displacement in s.h.m.: $x = x_0 \sin 2\pi ft$ or $x = x_0 \sin \omega t$

maximum velocity = amplitude × angular frequency $v_0 = \omega x_0$

Exercise 19.1 Describing oscillations

There are many types of oscillation, but they can all be described in terms of basic quantities: amplitude, frequency and period. This exercise provides practice in using these key terms and calculating these quantities.

1 The *frequency* is the number of oscillations per second; the *period* is the number of seconds per oscillation.

- **a** State the SI units of frequency and period. Give their names and symbols.
- **b** State how the units of frequency and period are related.
- **c** Write down an equation relating frequency *f* and period *T*.
- **d** A mass on the end of a spring oscillates up and down with a period of 0.40 s. Calculate its frequency.
- **e** A pendulum completes 40 swings in one minute. Calculate its period and frequency.
- **f** A loudspeaker can oscillate with frequencies between 20 Hz and 20 kHz. Determine the corresponding periods of oscillation.
- **g** If the frequency of an oscillation increases, state whether its period increases, decreases or stays the same.

2 This graph represents the oscillations of a simple pendulum:

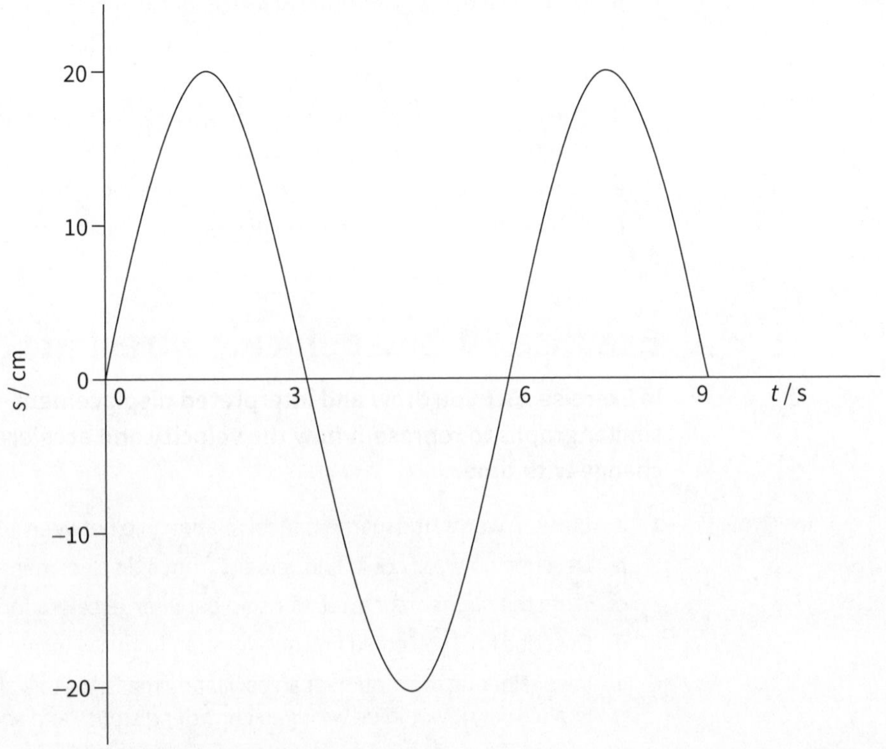

a State the quantity shown on the *y*-axis.

b State the amplitude of the oscillation.

c State the quantity shown on the *x*-axis.

d State the period of the oscillation.

e Determine the frequency of the oscillation.

f Explain the meaning of the term *simple pendulum*.

3 A mass suspended from a spring oscillates up and down.

- The highest point in the oscillation is 0.20 m above the lowest point.
- The mass completes 250 oscillations in 30 s.

a State the amplitude of the oscillation. Give your answer in cm.

b Calculate the period of the oscillation. Give your answer in ms.

c Determine the frequency of the oscillation.

d Draw a graph to represent the oscillation. Your graph should show 1.5 complete oscillations.

4 Two masses A and B are oscillating with the same frequency, but there is a phase difference between them. This graph represents their motion:

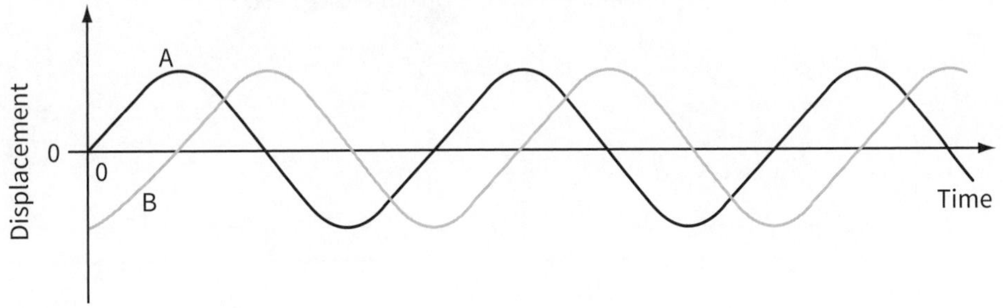

a Determine the displacement of B when A has maximum displacement.

b Determine the displacement of A when B has maximum displacement.

c The graphs start at time $t = 0$. State which oscillation is first to reach its maximum after this time.

d There is a phase difference between A and B. Calculate the fraction of a complete oscillation that this phase difference represents.

e Express the phase difference in radians (one oscillation $= 2\pi$ rad).

f Express the phase difference in degrees (one oscillation $= 360°$).

Exercise 19.2 Graphical representations

In Exercise 13.1 you drew and interpreted displacement–time graphs. We can draw similar graphs to represent how the velocity and acceleration of an oscillating mass change with time.

1 a State, in words, the mathematical relationship between velocity and displacement.

b Describe how you could find velocity from a displacement–time graph.

c Write the mathematical relationship between acceleration and velocity.

d Describe how you could find acceleration from a velocity–time graph.

e In considering the motion of an oscillating mass, we talk about *displacement* and *velocity*. Explain why it would be wrong to consider *distance* and *speed*.

2 This graph is a displacement–time graph for an oscillating mass:

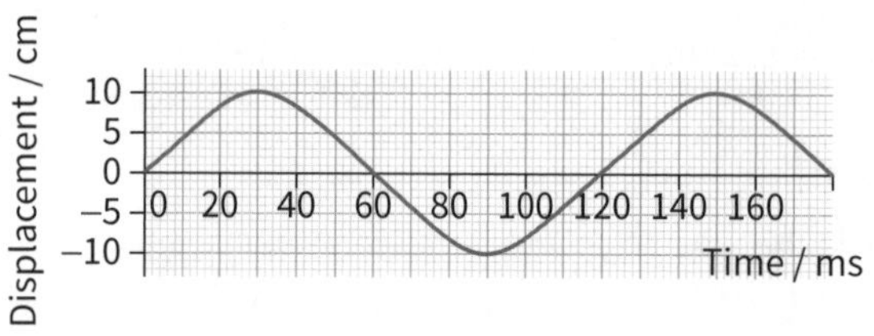

a State two times at which the mass has maximum positive displacement.

b What is the mass's velocity at these times? Explain how you can deduce this from the graph.

c State one time at which the mass has maximum negative displacement. State the velocity at this time.

d State two times at which the mass has maximum positive velocity. Explain how you can deduce this from the graph.

e State two times at which the mass has maximum negative velocity.

f Draw two sets of graph axes, one above the other. On the upper set of axes, sketch the displacement–time graph shown above. On the lower set of axes, sketch the corresponding velocity–time graph using the information you have deduced above. (There is no need to include numbers on either set of axes.)

3 This velocity–time graph represents the motion of an oscillating mass:

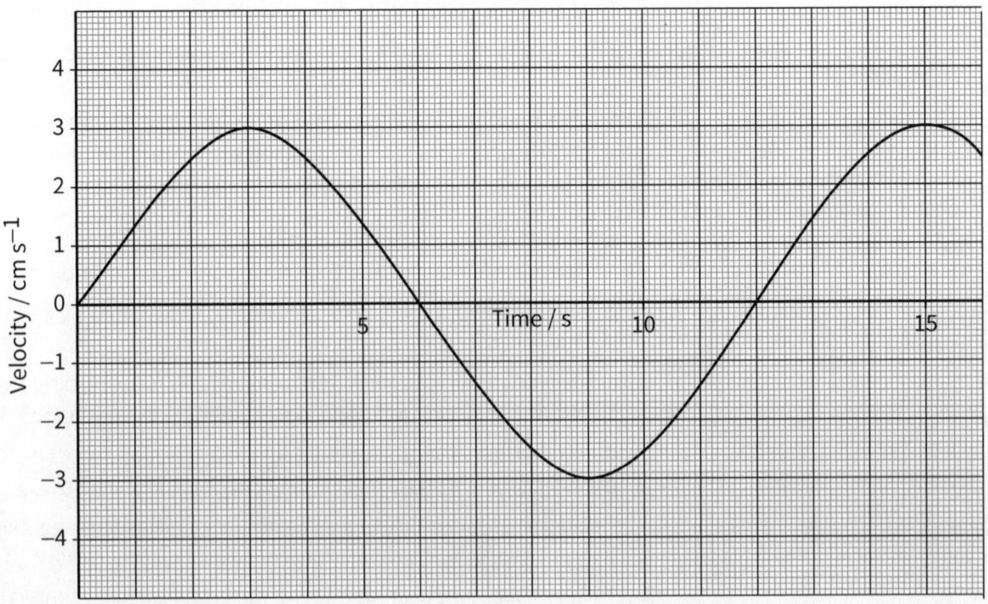

a From the graph, deduce the period and frequency of the oscillations.

b State three times at which the acceleration of the mass is zero. Explain how you can deduce this from the graph.

c The acceleration of the mass has its greatest positive values when time $t = 12$ s. At what time does the acceleration have its maximum negative value?

d You can estimate the maximum acceleration as follows: lay a ruler on the graph so that it lies along the steepest slope of the graph (at $t = 12$ s). Note the points where it crosses the top and bottom of the grid. Use these values to deduce the maximum acceleration.

e You can also estimate the amplitude of the oscillation. This is equal to half of the area under the first 'bump' of the graph (between $t = 0$ s and $t = 6$ s). Each large square on the graph represents 1 cm. Use this idea to estimate the amplitude.

f Draw two sets of graph axes, one above the other. On the upper set of axes, sketch the velocity–time graph shown above. On the lower set of axes, sketch the corresponding acceleration–time graph using the information you have deduced above. Your sketch graphs should indicate maximum and minimum values of the quantities on the *y*-axes.

Exercise 19.3 Equations of s.h.m.

Simple harmonic motion (s.h.m.) is the term used to describe a very specific type of oscillation. The graphs of displacement, velocity and acceleration against time are all sinusoidal. This is an exercise about representing s.h.m. using diagrams, graphs and equations.

1 This diagram shows a mass fixed between two springs:

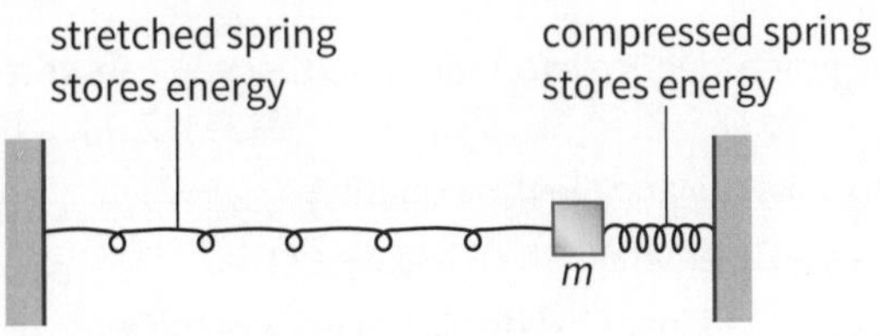

When released, it will oscillate back and forth. Its equilibrium position is half way between the two fixed ends.

a Copy the diagram and mark the equilibrium position of the mass.

b Add an arrow labelled x to show the displacement of the mass.

c Add an arrow labelled F to show the restoring force acting on the mass.

2 Simple harmonic motion is defined as 'the motion of an oscillator in which its acceleration is directly proportional to its displacement from its equilibrium position and is directed towards that position'. It can also be defined simply by the equation $a = -\omega^2 x$.

a In this equation, ω is the angular frequency of the oscillation. State the quantities represented by a and x. Give their names and standard SI units.

b The angular frequency ω is related to the frequency f. Write down the equation that relates them.

c The definition of s.h.m. states that acceleration is directly proportional to displacement. What is the constant of proportionality in the equation?

d Explain why there is a minus sign in the equation.

e For a mass undergoing s.h.m. the acceleration–displacement graph is a straight line. Sketch such a graph. Indicate the maximum positive and negative displacements of the mass ($\pm x_0$).

3 The displacement of an oscillating mass can be represented by an equation of the form $x = x_0 \sin \omega t$, where x_0 is the amplitude of the motion. This can also be written as $x = x_0 \sin 2\pi ft$.

By comparing a specific equation to this 'standard equation', you can deduce a great deal of information about the motion of an oscillating mass.

The displacement (in mm) of an oscillating mass is given $x = 25 \sin 40\pi t$.

It may help you to write down this equation with the 'standard equation' below it, for ease of comparison.

a State the amplitude of the oscillation.

b Show that the frequency $f = 20$ Hz.

c Calculate the period of the oscillation.

d The maximum velocity of the moving mass is given by $v_0 = \omega x_0$. Calculate this quantity. State its units.

e Calculate the maximum acceleration of the mass. (You can find the maximum acceleration using the equation that defines s.h.m.)

4 This graph shows how the velocity of a mass varied as it executed s.h.m:

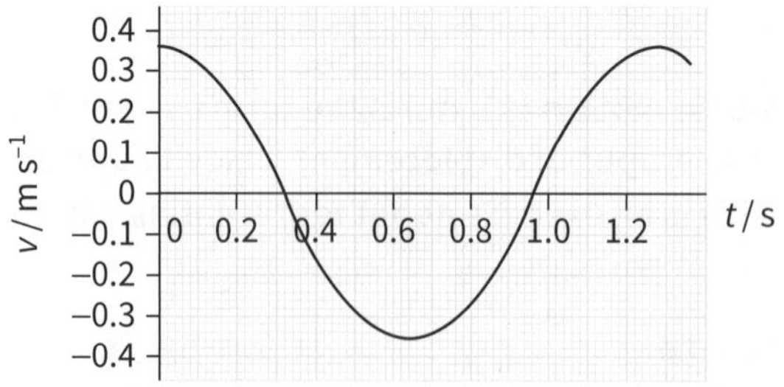

a From the graph, deduce information so that you can write an equation for this motion in the form $v = v_0 \cos \omega t$.

b State the units of v and t in this equation.

c State the displacement of the mass when $t = 0$.

d Deduce an equation for the displacement x of the mass as a function of time. (Think carefully: will the displacement vary as a sine or cosine function?)

e State the unit of x in this equation.

Exercise 19.4 Energy and damping in s.h.m.

As a mass oscillates, there is a constant interchange of energy between kinetic and potential (stored) forms. Damping introduces an extra force that removes energy from the system. This exercise explores damping and resonance.

1 This picture shows how a simple pendulum can be set in motion:

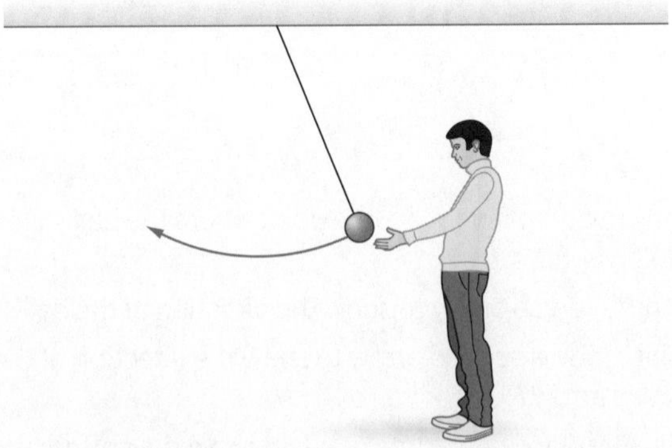

- **a** The student does work against gravity in pulling the mass to one side. State the form of energy that the mass now has.
- **b** Describe how you could calculate the energy stored by the mass in this position. Include a diagram in your answer.
- **c** The student releases the mass. State the point at which the mass is moving fastest.
- **d** Describe how you could calculate the speed of the mass from your answer to part **b**.

A student suggests that an object with a greater mass will swing faster because it has more energy.

- **e** Is the student correct that a greater mass will have greater energy? Explain your answer.
- **f** Is the student correct that a greater mass will move faster? Explain your answer.

2 A mass is fixed between two springs so that it can oscillate horizontally (as shown in Exercise 19.3, question 1).

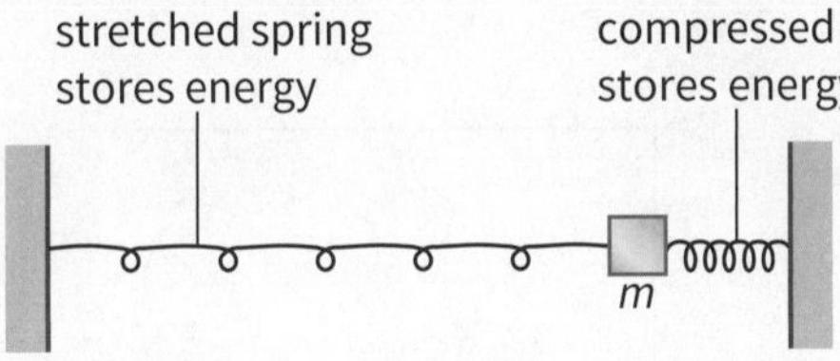

- **a** Name the form of energy stored by a stretched or compressed spring.
- **b** State the equation you would use to calculate the energy stored in a stretched spring. Explain any symbols used in the equation.
- **c** Explain how you would use this equation to calculate the maximum velocity of a mass executing s.h.m. between two springs.
- **d** The period T of a simple pendulum does not depend on the mass that is oscillating. How will the period of oscillation of a mass–spring system change if the mass is increased? Explain your answer.

3 A simple pendulum can be made by attaching a polystyrene (Styrofoam) ball to a length of thread. As the pendulum swings, air resistance causes the amplitude of the oscillations to decrease. This is an example of damping.

This diagram shows how the pendulum swings:

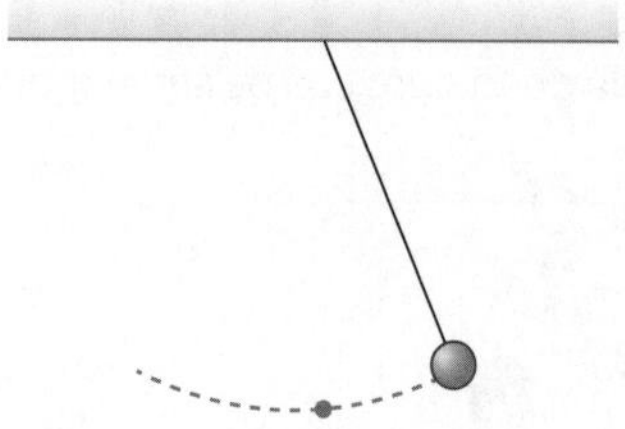

a Copy the diagram and mark the point where the ball will be moving most quickly. Label this point X.

b At point X, add an arrow to show the direction of the ball's velocity. Label this arrow *v*.

c At point X, add a second arrow to show the direction of the force of air resistance on the ball. Label this arrow *F*.

d Sketch a displacement–time graph to show the pattern of the ball's oscillations. Your graph should show the amplitude of oscillation decreasing significantly in the time of about five oscillations.

e Sketch an amplitude–time graph to show how the amplitude decreases towards zero over a longer period of time.

f Imagine that you could gradually increase the density of the air in which the pendulum is swinging. This will increase the damping of the oscillations. How would this affect the rate at which the amplitude of the oscillations would decrease to zero?

g Eventually, the pendulum would be *critically damped*. Explain how you would recognise this condition.

4 This diagram shows two identical masses hanging from strings of equal lengths. The upper ends of the strings are tied to a horizontal string:

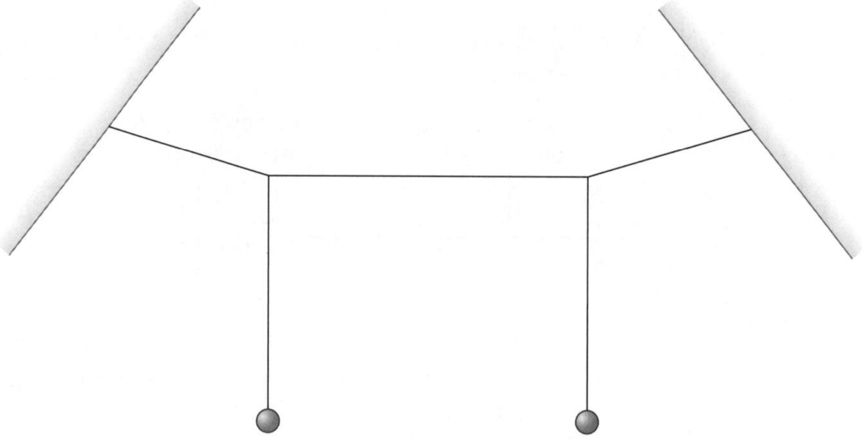

At the start of the experiment, one mass is pulled forwards and released so that it swings back and forth. As time passes, its oscillations become smaller but the second mass starts to swing. After a while, the first mass stops swinging while the second mass has its maximum amplitude. Then the process goes into reverse and the second mass gradually slows down while the first mass starts to swing again.

a What can you say about the natural frequencies of oscillation of the two pendulums?

b The second mass is forced to oscillate by the motion of the first one. Name this phenomenon.

c It is surprising to see one pendulum come to a halt while the other starts moving. Explain whether energy is conserved in this experiment.

d If the second pendulum were 20% longer it would not swing with such great amplitude. Explain why.

Exam-style questions

1 This graph represents the displacement of an oscillating mass:

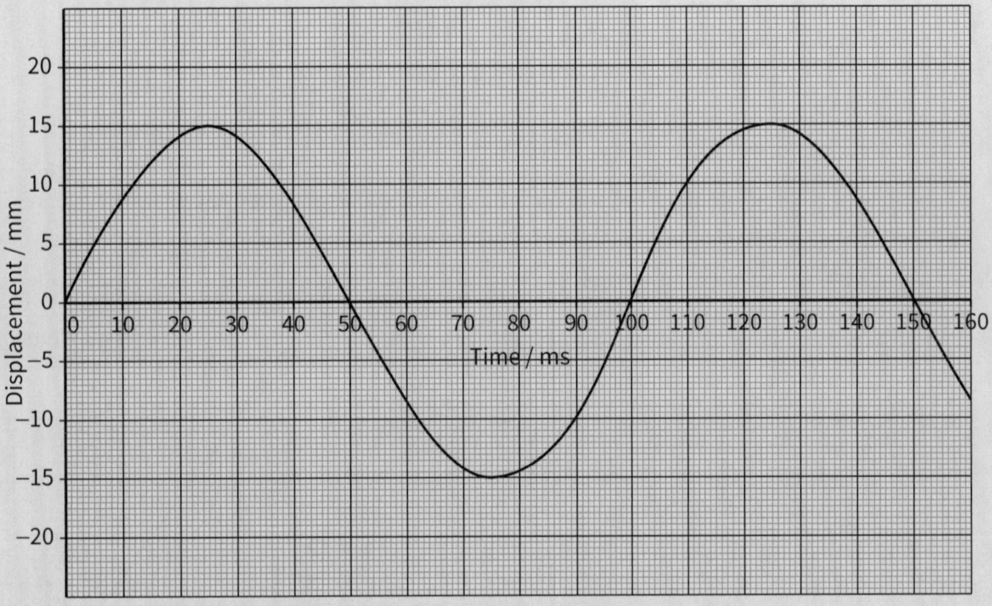

a Deduce the period and frequency of the oscillations. [3]

b Write an equation to represent the oscillations of the form $x = x_0 \sin \omega t$. [2]

c Deduce the maximum velocity of the mass. [2]

d The oscillating object has a mass of 17 kg. Calculate the maximum restoring force acting on the mass as it oscillates. [3]

2 One end of a long ruler is clamped to a bench. A large mass is attached to the other end. The mass is pushed downwards and released. It oscillates up and down, executing simple harmonic motion about its equilibrium position.

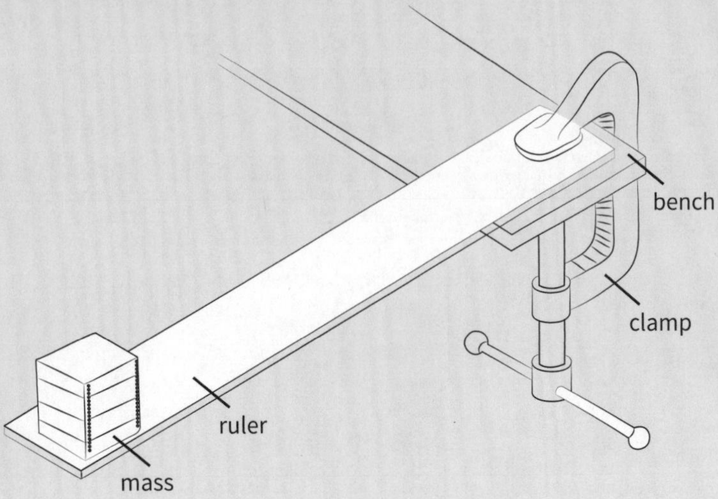

a Explain what is meant by *simple harmonic motion*. [2]

b Describe how you would find the equilibrium position of the mass. [2]

An accelerometer is attached to the mass. This measures and records its acceleration.

c Sketch a graph to show how you would expect the mass's acceleration to vary with time, starting with the mass in its position of maximum negative displacement. [3]

This graph shows how the acceleration of the mass depends on its displacement:

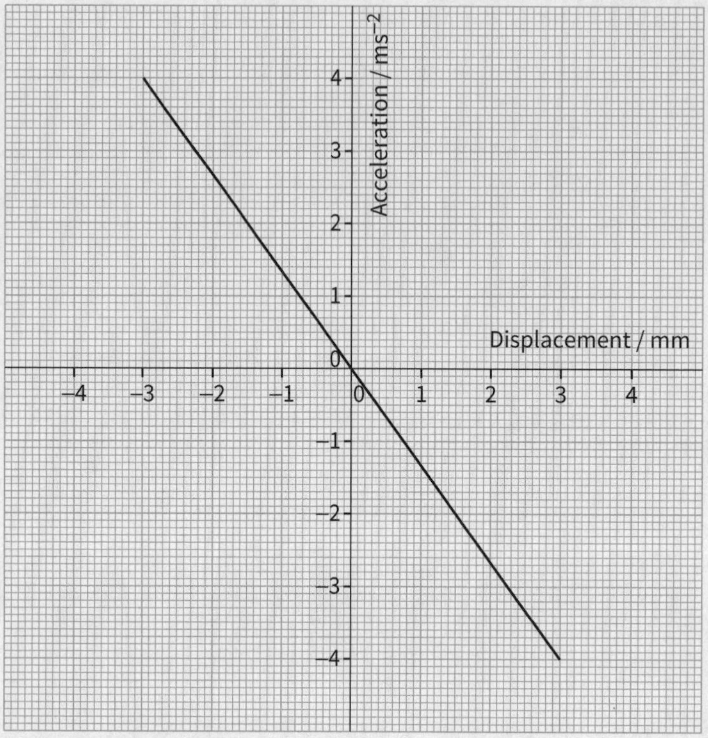

d Explain why the graph has a negative gradient. [1]

e From the graph, deduce the value of the amplitude of the oscillations. [1]

f Deduce the angular frequency of the oscillations. [2]

g Calculate the period of the oscillations. [2]

Chapter outline

- appreciate that information may be carried by a number of different channels and discuss the relative advantages and disadvantages of: wire-pairs, coaxial cables, radio and microwave links, optic fibres, recalling the frequencies and wavelengths used
- understand the terms modulation and bandwidth, and be able to distinguish between amplitude modulation and frequency modulation and state the advantages of each
- recall the meanings of the terms *carrier wave* and *sideband frequencies*
- understand that the digital transmission of data involves analogue-to-digital conversion (ADC) and digital-to-analogue conversion (DAC), and suggest the advantages of transmission of data in digital form
- for digital signals, understand the effects of the sampling rate and the number of bits in each sample recall the relative merits of both geostationary and polar orbiting satellites
- understand and use signal attenuation expressed in dB and dB per unit length
- recall and use the expression number of dB $= 10\lg\left(\frac{P_1}{P_2}\right)$ for the ratio of two powers

KEY TERMS

bandwidth: the difference between the highest-frequency signal and the lowest-frequency signal of a range of frequencies being transmitted

amplitude modulation (AM): the process of using one waveform to alter the amplitude of another waveform

frequency modulation (FM): the process of using one waveform to alter the frequency of another waveform

sampling: the process of taking the value of a continuous signal at regular intervals

bit: a basic unit of information storage stored as a binary digit 0 or 1

attenuation: the gradual loss in strength or intensity of a signal

sideband: a band of frequencies higher than or lower than the carrier frequency, produced as a result of the modulation process

carrier wave: a waveform (usually sinusoidal) that is modulated by an input signal to carry information

Equations: $\text{dB} = 10\lg\left(\frac{P_1}{P_2}\right)$

bandwidth of AM signal = 2 × highest frequency in signal

Exercise 20.1 Modulation

This exercise helps you understand the difference between amplitude modulation (AM) and frequency modulation (FM), and know the meaning of the technical terms used to describe them.

1 **a** Draw a sketch graph of an amplitude modulated (AM) signal.

b Explain how the carrier wave and the signal are used to form the AM wave.

c State whether amplitude or frequency is constant for the AM signal.

2 a Draw a sketch graph of a frequency modulated (FM) signal.
  b Explain how the carrier wave and the signal are used to form the FM wave.
  c State whether amplitude or frequency is constant for the FM signal.

3 State two advantages for each of:
  a FM transmissions when compared with AM transmissions
  b AM transmissions when compared with FM transmissions.

4 An AM waveform is composed of a carrier wave of frequency 50 kHz modulated by a sine wave of frequency 5.0 kHz.
  a Calculate the time period of the carrier wave. (Remember $f = \frac{1}{T}$).
  b Calculate the time period of the sine wave.

  The modulated wave has a frequency spectrum which contains two sidebands.

  c Sketch the frequency spectrum of the AM waveform.

  The *y*-axis of your graph should be labelled 'power' and the *x*-axis should be labelled 'frequency'. Mark values of frequency on the *x*-axis.

  d State what is meant by a *sideband*.
  e State the values of the sideband frequencies in the frequency spectrum.
  f Calculate the bandwidth of the signal.

5 An AM radio wave is used to broadcast music with frequencies between 25 Hz and 4300 Hz. The radio station uses a waveband with frequencies between 3.0×10^4 and 3.0×10^5 Hz.
  a Determine the bandwidth of the broadcast.
  b Determine the maximum possible number of similar radio stations in the same waveband.

6 A sinusoidal carrier wave has frequency 800 kHz and amplitude 6.0 V.

  The carrier wave is frequency modulated by a signal wave of amplitude 1.5 V.

  The frequency deviation is 40 kHz V^{-1}. This means that a signal of 1.0 V causes a change in frequency of 40 kHz in the modulated wave.

  a Determine the amplitude of the modulated wave.
  b Determine the maximum frequency of the modulated wave.
  c Determine the minimum frequency of the modulated wave.
  d The signal wave causes the frequency of the modulated wave to change from the maximum to the minimum and then back to the maximum frequency 20 times a second. State the frequency of the signal wave.

7 A sinusoidal carrier wave has frequency 800 kHz and amplitude 6.0 V.

  The carrier wave is amplitude modulated by a signal wave of frequency 5.0 kHz and amplitude 1.0 V. A signal of 1.0 V causes a change in amplitude of 0.5 V in the modulated wave.

  a Determine the maximum amplitude of the modulated wave.
  b Determine the minimum amplitude of the modulated wave.
  c State the frequency of the modulated wave.
  d State the number of times per second that the modulated wave goes from maximum to minimum amplitude.

Exercise 20.2 Analogue and digital signals

This exercise give you practice converting between digital and analogue signals, and understanding how electronics enables these conversions.

1 a Explain what is meant by a *bit*.
 b Convert the decimal number 11 into a 4-bit digital number.
 c Convert the digital number 0011 into a decimal number.
 d In the digital number 0011, state which is the most significant bit.
 e Determine the smallest number of bits needed to convert the number 17 into a digital number.

2 To record one channel of audio on a DVD, a signal is sampled at a frequency of 48 kHz, and each sample is a 24-bit number.

 a Explain what it means to *sample* a signal.
 b Calculate the total number of bits stored on a DVD if its playing time is 30 minutes.
 c Explain why the sampling frequency is more than twice the maximum frequency in the signal.

3 This diagram shows apparatus used to demonstrate the transmission of an analogue signal using digital technology:

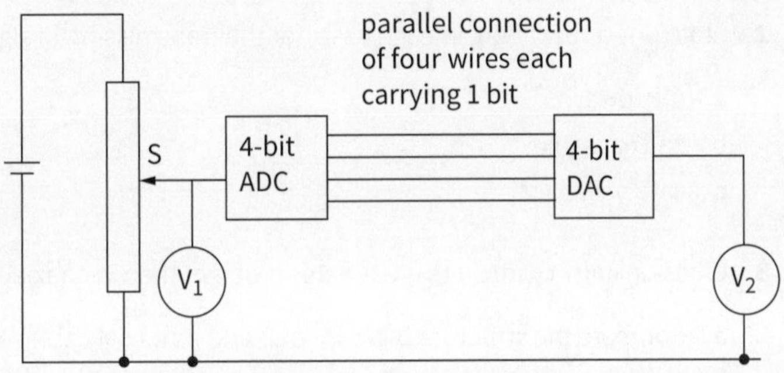

As the slider S moves up and down, voltmeter V_1 shows an analogue signal.

 a Explain what is meant by an *analogue signal*.
 b Draw a possible variation with time of the analogue signal at voltmeter V_1.

The analogue signal is connected to a 4-bit analogue-to-digital converter (ADC).

 c Draw a possible variation of the output of the ADC with time.
 d State what is meant by a *DAC*.

The ADC samples the analogue signal five times a second and converts the signal into a 4-bit number, such as 1001.

 e Explain why the reading on voltmeter V_2 has only 16 different values (which includes 0).
 f S is moved very fast up and down. Explain why the voltmeter V_2 does not respond to all the changes.
 g Suggest two changes to the ADC and DAC that will increase the number of different values on voltmeter V_2 and allow it to respond to fast changes in the signal.
 h To have only one wire connecting the ADC and DAC , a parallel-to-serial converter is used at one end of the wire and a serial-to-parallel converter at the other. Describe what these converters do.

4 Noise affects both analogue and digital signals. Amplifiers have to be used at regular distances for long-distance transmission of data.

- **a** State what is meant by *noise*.
- **b** A regenerator amplifier only recognises highs and lows in a signal. Explain why this removes small amounts of noise in a digital signal.
- **c** Explain how less noise means that it is cheaper to transmit data over long distances.

Exercise 20.3 Channels of communication

This exercise helps develop your understanding of the different ways and frequencies in which data is sent from place to place.

1 There are many satellites orbiting Earth that are used for communications.

- **a** Draw the orbits of a polar-orbiting satellite and a geostationary satellite around the Earth.
- **b** State one other use made for a polar-orbiting satellite.
- **c** State the time taken for a geostationary satellite to make one orbit.
- **d** Explain why a satellite dish on Earth in line-of-sight with a geostationary satellite is fixed in position.
- **e** Suggest which areas of the Earth are not always in line-of-sight with a geostationary satellite.

2 State one application, in each case, for the transmission of signals using:

- **a** microwaves
- **b** coaxial cables
- **c** wire pairs.

3 Cross-linking in wire pairs is a greater problem than in coaxial cables.

- **a** Compare the structure of a wire pair and a coaxial cable.
- **b** Describe *cross-linking* between two wire pairs.
- **c** Suggest how the structure of a coaxial cable reduces cross-linking and noise.

4 In a satellite communication system, a signal of frequency 14 GHz is transmitted from Earth up to a satellite and a frequency of 11 GHz is transmitted back from the satellite down to Earth, as shown:

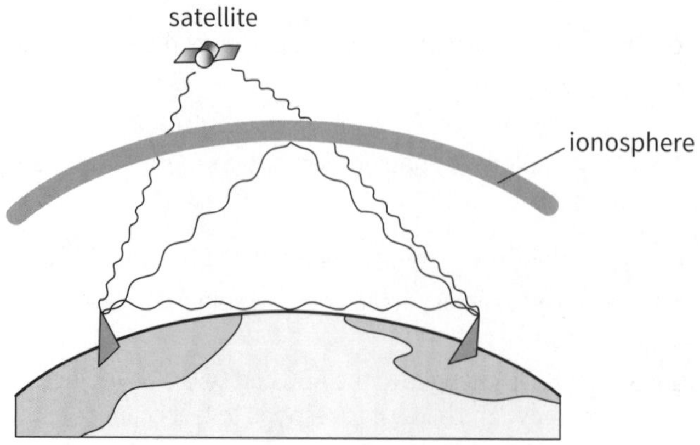

- **a** State why frequencies in the GHz range are used.
- **b** Explain why the two signals have different frequencies.

c Copy the diagram and label the sky wave, the space wave and the surface wave.

d State two reasons why long distance communication using the sky wave is unreliable.

5 Data is transmitted large distances under the oceans using optic fibres. Describe the advantages of optic fibres over coaxial cables for the transmission of data.

Exercise 20.4 Attenuation

This exercise that provides practice in calculations of attenuation. The equations for attenuation can be difficult to use because they involve logarithms and antilogarithms. Remember to use logarithms to base 10, where the logarithm of 20 is written as lg(20). The antilogarithm button on a calculator is often shown as 10^x.

1 a Calculate lg(100).

b Calculate x where $\lg(x) = 1.2$.

2 The power received by a satellite is 10^{19} times less than that transmitted from Earth.

a Calculate the ratio of the two powers in dB.

b Suggest why attenuation of a signal is usually measured on a logarithmic scale rather than on a linear scale.

3 An input signal of power 3.6×10^{-3} W is attenuated and becomes 3.6×10^{-5} W at the other end. Calculate the attenuation.

4 A signal transmitted from Earth to a satellite has a power of 3000 W. The signal received by the satellite is attenuated by 170 dB. Calculate the power received by the satellite. (You have to use an antilogarithm.)

5 A cable has attenuation per unit length of 2.0 dB km^{-1}. The input power to the cable is 600 mW.

a Calculate the output power for a 20 km cable.

b The minimum acceptable signal power in the cable is 7.2×10^{-8} mW. Calculate the maximum length of the cable.

6 The attenuation produced by an optic fibre is 12 dB. The noise power at the receiver is 4.6×10^{-6} W. The minimum permissible signal-to-noise ratio at the receiver is 20 dB.

a Calculate the minimum signal power at the receiver. (Use signal-to-noise ration = $10 \lg(P_1/P_2)$ with P_1 as the signal and P_2 as the noise)

b Calculate the minimum input signal power to the fibre.

7 A signal is transmitted along a cable system of total length 120 km.

The cable has an attenuation of 2.0 dB km^{-1}. Amplifiers, each having a gain of 40 dB, are placed along the cable.

a Calculate the total attenuation in the signal if no amplifiers are used.

b Determine the number of amplifiers necessary along the cable for the final signal to be of the same power as the initial signal.

Exam-style questions

1 A radio station emits an amplitude modulated (AM) signal.

It starts operating by sending out a carrier wave for a few seconds. A person listening to a radio receiver tuned to the station hears silence for those seconds. She then hears a single note for a few minutes and then hears music being broadcast.

This diagram shows the power spectrum of each of the three situations:

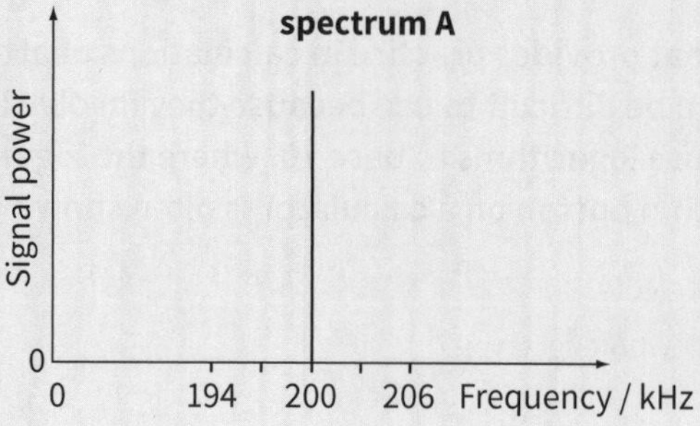

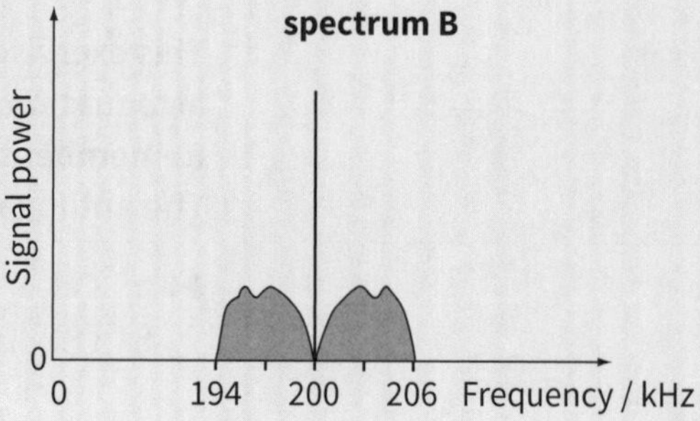

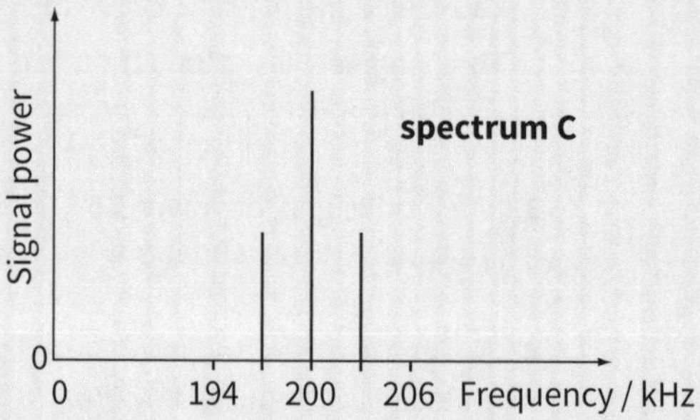

a Explain what is meant by an *amplitude modulated signal*. [2]

b State and explain which spectrum is emitted by the radio station when the person hears:

i silence [2]

ii a single note [2]

iii music. [2]

c Determine:

i the transmission frequency of the radio station [1]

ii the frequency of the single note [2]

iii the bandwidth of the radio station. [2]

d The radio station operates in the LW band using amplitude modulation. State two advantages and two disadvantages of AM transmission when compared with FM transmission. [4]

2 An analogue electrical signal is sent along coaxial cable to a receiver.

The signal is attenuated as it passes along the cable. The maximum length of the coaxial is determined by the minimum acceptable value of the signal-to-noise ratio at the receiver.

a **i** State what is meant by *attenuation* of the signal. [1]

ii Explain what causes attenuation in the coaxial cable. [1]

iii State one cause of noise or electrical interference in the wire. [1]

iv Write an expression for the signal-to-noise ratio expressed in decibels (dB). [2]

v State and explain how the signal-to-noise ratio changes as the length of the coaxial cable increases. [2]

b This data applies to the transmission:

input signal to the coaxial cable	760 mW
noise at the receiver end of the cable	4.8 μW
minimum acceptable signal-to-noise ratio	25 dB
attenuation of coaxial cable	6.0 dB km^{-1}

i Calculate the smallest acceptable signal power at the input to the receiver. [3]

ii Calculate the maximum attenuation that can be caused by the coaxial cable. [3]

iii Calculate the maximum length of the coaxial cable. [2]

c The attenuation caused by an optic fibre is 0.2 dB km^{-1}.

i Explain why the distance between regeneration amplifiers is larger when using fibre optic transmission rather than coaxial cable. [2]

ii State two other advantages of transmission using optic fibre rather than coaxial cable. [2]

Chapter outline

- understand and explain the transfer of thermal energy and the concept of thermal equilibrium
- understand how certain physical properties can be used to measure temperature
- understand the absolute temperature scale and convert between temperatures measured in Kelvin and in degrees Celsius
- compare the advantages and disadvantages of thermistors and thermocouples
- use a simple kinetic model of matter to explain the different states of matter, temperature and energy changes
- understand that the internal energy of a system is determined by the state of the system
- recall and use the first law of thermodynamics
- define and use specific heat capacity and specific latent heat

KEY TERMS

internal energy: the sum of the random distribution of kinetic and potential energies of the atoms or molecules of a system

specific heat capacity of a substance: the energy required per unit mass to raise the temperature by 1 K (or 1°C)

specific latent heat of a substance: the energy required per kilogram to change its state without any change in temperature

Equations: first law of thermodynamics:

increase in internal energy = energy supplied by heating + energy supplied by doing work; $\Delta U = q + w$

$$\text{specific heat capacity} = \frac{\text{energy supplied}}{\text{mass} \times \text{temperature change}}; \; c = \frac{E}{m\Delta\theta}$$

$$\text{specific latent heat} = \frac{\text{energy supplied}}{\text{mass}}; \; L = \frac{E}{m}$$

converting between Celsius and Kelvin scales of temperature:

$T(K) = \theta(°C) + 273.15$

Exercise 21.1 Kinetic model and internal energy

In the kinetic model of matter, we picture matter as being made of many particles (atoms, ions or molecules). The model can be used to explain many phenomena, and this exercise develops an understanding of the model at its simplest.

1 These diagrams show how we can picture the arrangement of particles in a solid, a liquid and a gas:

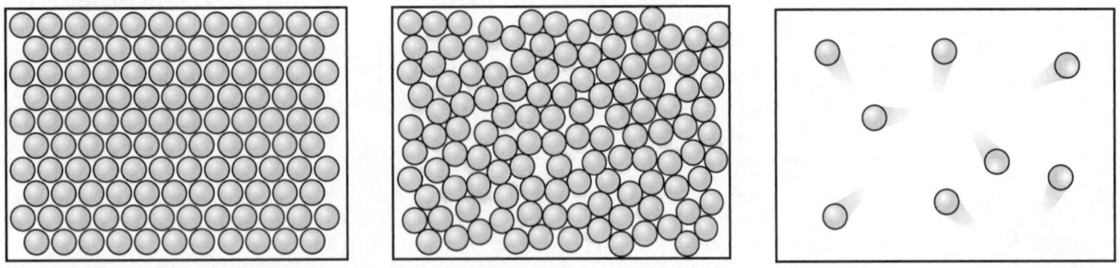

- **a** In which state (or phase) of matter are the particles packed most closely together? In which state are they farthest apart?
- **b** If a solid is heated, its particles gain energy. Describe how the motion of the particles changes.
- **c** In a solid, the particles are closely packed together. State whether the force between neighbouring particles is attractive or repulsive.
- **d** To change a solid to a gas, its particles must be separated. State how the potential energy of the particles changes as they are pulled apart. Is energy being added to the material, or being removed?
- **e** By comparing the diagrams for a solid and a gas, you can see two ways in which the particles of a gas have more energy than the particles of a solid. State the two differences and name the corresponding forms of energy.

2 On a sunny day, a steel railway line absorbs the energy of the sunlight that falls on it. You cannot see any obvious change in the appearance of the rail.

Imagine that you could see the atoms of which the rail is made.

- **a** Describe the difference in the *motion* of the atoms on a hot day.
- **b** Describe the difference in the *separation* of the atoms on a hot day.
- **c** Explain what happens to the energy of the sunlight that has been absorbed by the rail.

3 Two identical beakers, A and B, contain equal amounts of water. The water in A is at a temperature of 20°C while the water in B is at 50°C. The water in each beaker gradually evaporates.

- **a** In which beaker do the water molecules have the greater average energy?
- **b** Explain why the initial rate of evaporation of the water in beaker B is greater than that of the water in beaker A. Refer to your answer to part **a**.
- **c** Explain why the temperature of the water in each beaker decreases as the water evaporates.
- **d** Explain why the temperature of the water in beaker B falls more quickly than that of the water in beaker A.

4 This diagram shows a mass of gas in a cylinder:

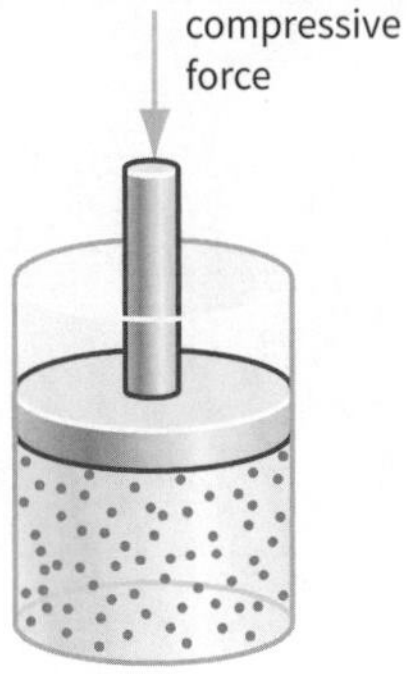

A piston is being pushed downwards to compress the gas.

- **a** In a collision, momentum is transferred from one object to another. The piston and the particles collide with one another. Momentum is transferred from the piston to the particles. Describe the effect this has on the average speed of the particles.
- **b** Describe any changes in the total kinetic energy of the particles.
- **c** Describe any changes in the temperature of the gas.
- **d** State the phrase that describes this way of transferring energy to a gas.

The average force pushing the piston is 20 N and it moves through a distance of 12 cm.

e Calculate the amount of energy transferred to the gas.

In practice, the force needed to compress the gas would increase as the piston is pushed downwards (because the pressure of the gas would increase). This graph shows how the force might increase:

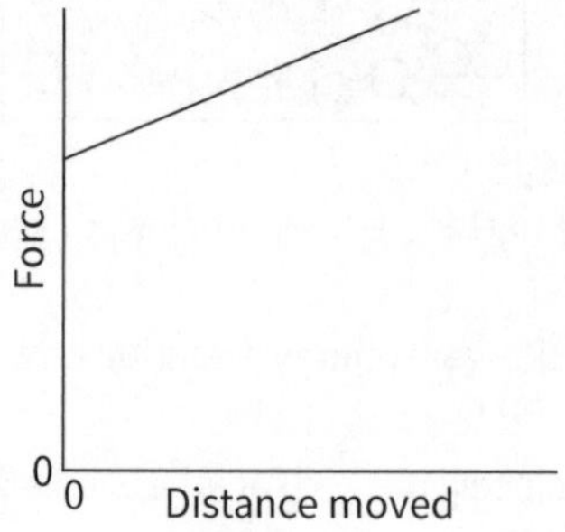

f Describe how you could determine the energy transferred to the gas from such a graph. Include a sketch graph in your answer.

5 The internal energy of a material can be increased in two ways: by heating it and by doing work on it. The first law of thermodynamics tells us how the internal energy changes, and can be represented by this equation:

$\Delta U = q + w$

a State the meaning of each of the symbols in this equation, and their units.

b A gas is heated by transferring 400 kJ to it. At the same time, it is compressed so that 300 kJ of work is done on it. Calculate the increase in its internal energy.

c A cylinder of air is compressed by a force of 240 N moving through a distance of 0.05 m. Because the temperature of the air increases, it loses 4.0 J of energy through the walls of the cylinder to its surroundings. Calculate the increase in the internal energy of the air.

6 If two objects are in contact with each other, energy will transfer from the hotter object to the colder object. A temperature difference leads to the transfer of energy.

This diagram shows three objects in contact with each other. Their temperatures are: A 20 °C; B 30 °C; C 20 °C.

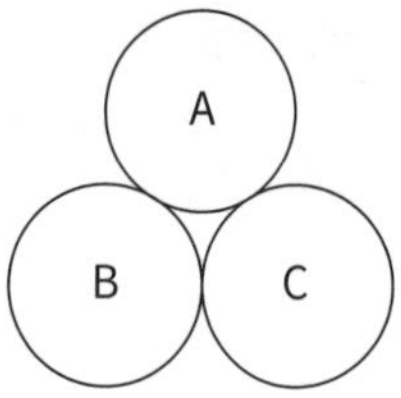

a There will be a net transfer of energy between A and B. State the direction of this transfer.

b Explain why we describe this as a *net* transfer of energy.

c Between which two objects will there be no net transfer of energy? Explain your answer.

d Which two objects are in thermal equilibrium? Explain your answer.

e Eventually all three objects are in thermal equilibrium. What can you say about their temperatures at this time?

Exercise 21.2 Thermometers and temperature scales

There are many different types of thermometer: liquid-in-glass, thermocouple, electrical resistance etc. Each is based on a different physical property which varies with temperature. In this exercise you will answer questions about thermometers and the Celsius and thermodynamic (Kelvin) scales of temperature.

1 In this question, use the approximate relation $T(K) = \theta(°C) + 273.15$.

a Convert each of the following temperatures from °C to K:

i 0
ii 100
iii 523
iv −196.

b Convert each of the following temperatures from K to °C:

i 0
ii 200
iii 350
iv 1000.

c State which temperature is greater, 400 K or 125 °C.

d A block of ice is allowed to warm from −20 °C until it melts at 0 °C. Calculate the increase in its temperature. Give your answer in K.

2 This graph shows how the resistance of a thermistor changes with temperature:

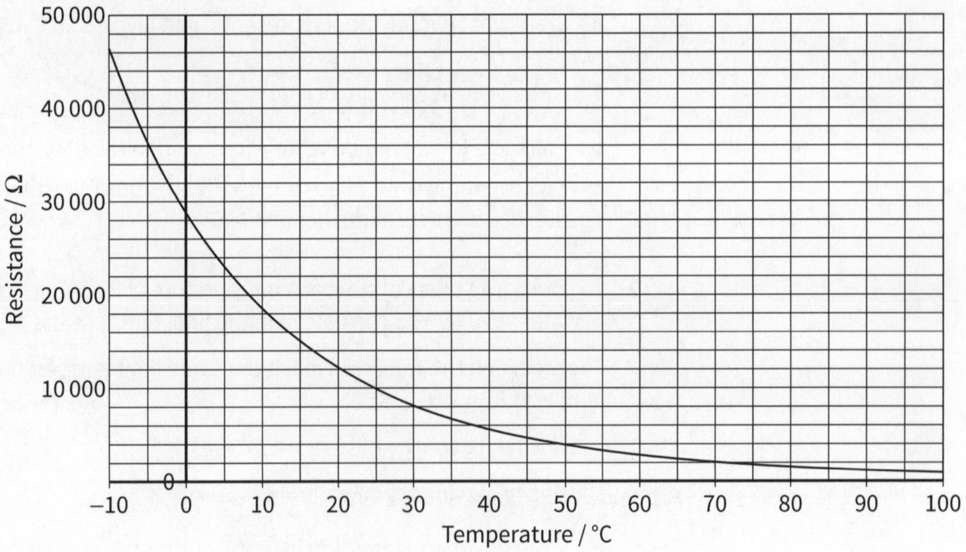

a State the temperature at which the thermistor has a resistance of 10 kΩ.

b State the resistance of the thermistor at 60 °C.

c Explain why the thermistor would be more useful for measuring temperatures close to 0 °C than to 100 °C. Use the word *sensitivity* in your answer.

3 Two important types of electrical thermometer are the **resistance thermometer** and the **thermocouple thermometer**.

a Which of these two thermometers is constructed from wires of two different metals?

b Which of these two thermometers generates a voltage that depends on the temperature difference between two points?

c A resistance thermometer may be based on a resistance wire or a thermistor. State which of these two types of thermometer shows a big change in resistance over a small change in temperature.

d A resistance thermometer is likely to have a greater mass than a thermocouple. Explain why this means that a thermocouple thermometer is likely to respond more quickly to a change in temperature.

e A thermocouple has a non-linear response to temperature and hence will require calibration if it is to be used as a thermometer. Explain the meanings of the terms *non-linear* and *calibration*.

4 The thermodynamic (Kelvin) scale of temperature has two fixed points.

a State the lower fixed point and give its value in K and in °C.

b The upper fixed point is the *triple point of water*. Explain what this means.

c Give the value of the upper fixed point in K and in °C.

Exercise 21.3 Energy change calculations: s.h.c. and s.l.h.

Knowing the values of a material's specific heat capacity and its specific latent heat allows us to calculate energy changes. This is an exercise in calculating and using both of these quantities.

1 The equation $c = \frac{E}{m\Delta\theta}$ defines specific heat capacity.

a State what each symbol represents, and give its SI unit. (Note: $\Delta\theta$ is a single quantity.)

The specific heat capacity of lead is 126 J kg^{-1} K^{-1}.

b Calculate the amount of energy required to raise the temperature of 1 kg of lead by 10 °C.

c 1 kJ of energy is supplied to 1 kg of lead. Determine the amount by which the temperature of the lead will rise, to the nearest 1 °C.

2 To cool a 5 kg block of steel at a temperature of 200 °C, it is plunged into a tank containing 50 kg of water at 20 °C. You can calculate the final temperature of the water like this:

The steel and the water will reach the same final temperature. We can write this as *final temperature* = X °C.

specific heat capacity of steel = 450 J kg^{-1} K^{-1}

specific heat capacity of water = 4200 J kg^{-1} K^{-1}

a Write down an expression in terms of X for the energy *lost* by the steel in cooling from 200 °C to X.

b Write down a similar expression for the energy *gained* by the water in being heated from 20 °C to X.

c These two quantities are equal (assuming no energy is lost to the surroundings). Write an equation in which these quantities are shown to be equal.

d Solve the equation for X.

e You could use a method like this to determine the specific heat capacity of a material. Outline how you would do this. List the quantities you would measure. State one other quantity whose value you would need to know.

3 A block of copper was heated with a 60 W electrical heater. This graph shows how the temperature of the block increased:

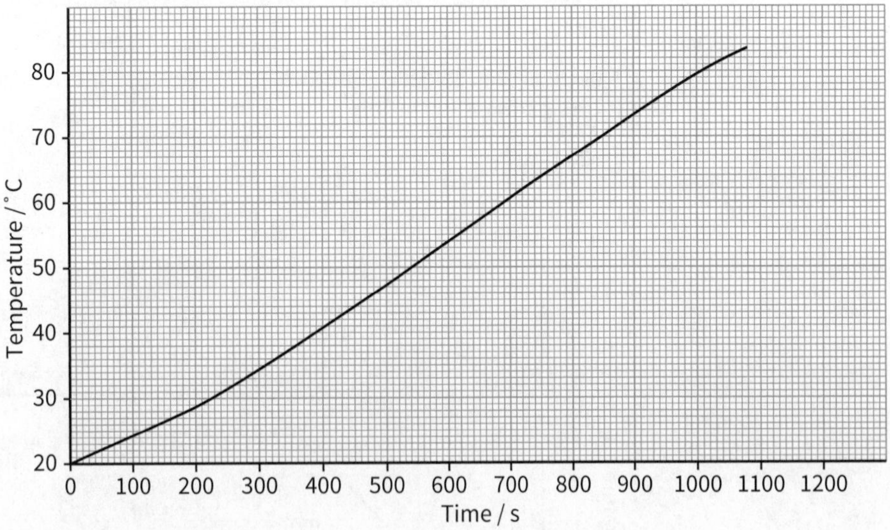

a Choose a suitable section of the graph and deduce by how much the block's temperature increased in 200 s.

b Calculate the energy supplied to the block in this time.

c The mass of the block was 2.00 kg. Calculate the specific heat capacity of copper.

d In this experiment, it is likely that some of the heat supplied to the block was lost to the surroundings. What feature of the graph suggests that this was the case? Explain your answer.

e Is the true value for the specific heat capacity of copper likely to be higher or lower than that calculated in part **c**? Explain your answer.

4 The equation $L = \frac{E}{m}$ defines specific latent heat.

a State what each symbol represents, and give its SI unit.

The specific latent heat of fusion of water $L = 330\,000$ J kg^{-1}.

b Explain the meanings of the words *specific* and *fusion* in this sentence.

c A freezer converts 10 g of water at 0 °C to ice at the same temperature in five minutes. Determine the amount of energy that must be removed from the water to achieve this.

5 These diagrams show the typical arrangements of atoms in a solid, a liquid and a gas:

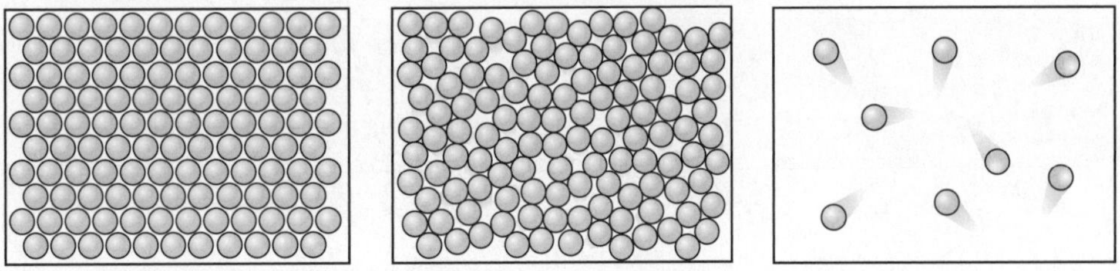

a As represented in the diagram of a solid, each atom is in contact with a number of neighbouring atoms. How many?

b Describe how this number changes when the material is heated so that it changes from a solid to a liquid and then to a gas.

c Use this idea to explain why the specific latent heat of vaporisation is greater than the specific latent heat of melting for a given substance.

Exam-style questions

1 Solder is an alloy of two metals which is used to join wires together. It has a relatively low melting point.

A block of solid solder was heated at a steady rate until it melted. This graph below shows how its temperature increased:

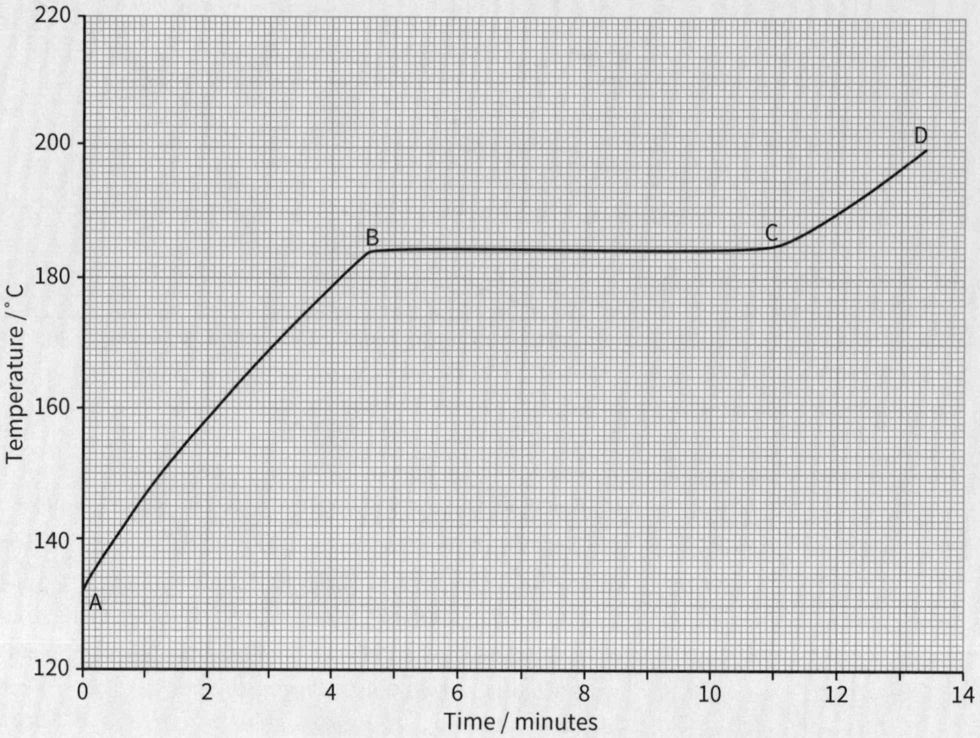

a Deduce the melting point of the solder. [1]

Consider the region BC of the graph. Describe how the following quantities were changing in this part of the heating process:

b the total kinetic energy of the atoms of the solder [1]

c their potential energy [1]

d the internal energy of the solder. [1]

The block had a mass of 25.0 g.

e State the other information you would need in order to deduce the specific heat capacity of the solder. [2]

f Suggest the required physical properties of the two metals that are alloyed to make solder. Explain your thinking. [3]

2 This diagram shows a simple method to estimate the specific latent heat of vaporisation of water, *L*:

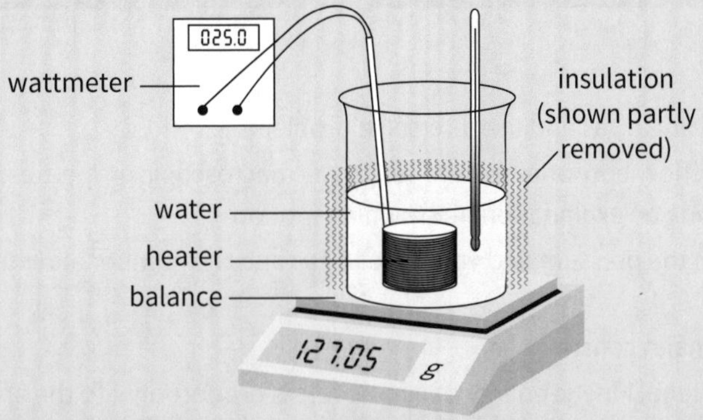

A beaker is filled with hot water and placed on a balance. It is then heated with an electrical heater. The thermometer indicates the temperature of the water.

a Explain what is meant by the *specific latent heat of vaporisation* of a liquid. [2]

b The heater has a power rating of 25 W. Calculate the energy it supplies to the water in 500 s. [1]

The water boils and the mass recorded on the balance gradually decreases. This table shows two measurements of the mass separated by a time interval of 500 s:

Time / s	Mass / g
0	131.36
500	127.05

c Use this data to estimate a value for the specific latent heat of vaporisation of water *L*. [2]

d Most of the energy supplied by the heater results in vaporisation of the water. However, some energy is lost to the surroundings and does not contribute to the vaporisation of the water. Suggest one way in which energy is lost to the surroundings. [1]

e Explain whether energy losses to the surroundings mean that your estimated value for *L* in part **c** above is an under-estimate or an over-estimate. [2]

Chapter outline

- recall the equation of state for an ideal gas and use it to solve problems
- state the assumptions of the kinetic theory and use it to relate the macroscopic properties of a gas to the microscopic properties of its particles, including an explanation of Brownian motion
- deduce the relationship between the pressure and volume of a gas and the number and mean square speed of its particles
- recall the definition of the Boltzmann constant
- deduce that the average translational kinetic energy of a molecule is proportional to the absolute temperature

KEY TERMS

ideal gas: a gas that behaves according to the equation $pV = nRT$

mole: the amount of a substance that contains the same number of particles as there are in 0.012 kg of carbon-12

Boyle's law: The pressure exerted by a fixed mass of gas is inversely proportional to its volume, provided the temperature of the gas remains constant

Equations: the ideal gas equation: $pV = nRT$

$$\text{number of moles} = \frac{\text{mass (g)}}{\text{molar mass (g mol}^{-1}\text{)}}$$

pressure and volume of a gas: $pV = \frac{1}{3}Nm\langle c^2\rangle$; $p = \frac{1}{3}\rho\langle c^2\rangle$

average molecular KE = $\frac{3}{2}$ × Boltzmann constant × thermodynamic temperature;

$\frac{1}{2}m\langle c^2\rangle = \frac{3}{2}kT$

Exercise 22.1 Ideal gases

An ideal gas does not exist! But gases at low pressures behave very much like ideal gases, so the idea of an ideal gas is very useful. This is an exercise in using the ideal gas equation and Boyle's law.

1 This is the ideal gas equation: $pV = nRT$.

- **a** State the quantity represented by each symbol, giving the unit of each.
- **b** Which two quantities are related by Boyle's law? State the two quantities that are constant in Boyle's law. If you are not sure, look back at the ideal gas equation.
- **c** Which quantity in the equation can be used to calculate the mass of gas? Explain how you would carry out such a calculation.

2 To use the ideal gas equation, $pV = nRT$, you need to be able to calculate the number of moles n in a sample of gas.

a Calculate the number of moles in 0.48 g of oxygen (molar mass of oxygen = 32 g mol^{-1}). It may help to recall that *molar mass* means the mass of one mole.

b 26 g of helium contains 6.5 mol of particles. Calculate the molar mass of helium.

c A classroom has dimensions 2.2 m × 6.0 m × 4.8 m. It contains air of density 1.29 kg m^{-3}. Calculate the number of moles of air this classroom contains (molar mass of air = 29 g mol^{-1}).

3 A cylinder of volume 40.0 litres is filled with air to a pressure of 200 × 10^3 Pa. A piston then compresses the air to a volume of 2.5 litres.

a Calculate the pressure of the compressed air, assuming that its temperature remains constant. You can think in proportions or use $p_1V_1 = p_2V_2$.

b Sketch a graph of pressure against volume to show how these quantities will change as the air is compressed.

c The experiment is performed at a temperature of 27 °C. Calculate the number of moles of gas contained in the cylinder (universal molar gas constant $R = 8.31$ J mol^{-1} K^{-1}).

4 If a gas is heated at constant pressure, its volume will change.

The relationship between volume and absolute temperature at constant pressure is known as Charles's law.

a State whether the volume of the gas will increase or decrease as the temperature increases at constant pressure.

b Sketch a graph to show how the volume of an ideal gas depends on its absolute temperature.

c An ideal gas will have zero volume at absolute zero. Describe how you would expect a real gas to behave as its temperature is reduced towards absolute zero.

d 10 mol of nitrogen is heated from 23 °C to 100 °C at a constant pressure of 100 × 10^3 Pa. Calculate the change in volume of the gas.

5 Usually, when a gas expands or contracts, both its pressure and temperature change. We can solve problems like this using the relationship:

$$\frac{pV}{T} = \text{constant}$$

a What is the constant in this equation? Give its unit.

A balloon contains 0.040 m^3 of helium at a pressure of 3.5 × 10^5 Pa and a temperature of 27 °C. It is heated until it bursts. At this point its volume has expanded to 0.044 m^3 and its temperature has reached 190 °C.

b Calculate the value of the quantity $\frac{pV}{T}$ before the balloon is heated.

c Using your answer to part **b**, calculate the pressure at which the balloon bursts.

d Calculate the temperature at which the balloon would have exploded if it had not expanded as it was heated.

Exercise 22.2 The kinetic model of a gas

We can think of a gas as being made of particles moving about in a box. This is the kinetic model of a gas. Because the particles obey the usual laws of physics, we can use the model to deduce equations linking microscopic behaviour of particles to the macroscopic properties of a gas – pressure, temperature, and so on. This exercise tests your understanding of these relationships.

1 This diagram shows one way to observe Brownian motion:

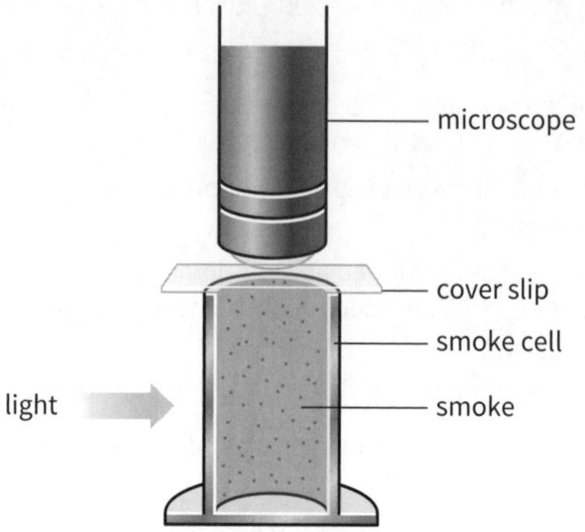

- **a** When you look down the microscope, you cannot see the molecules of the air. Explain why.
- **b** You see tiny specks of light moving about in a random way. Explain what it is that can be seen moving.
- **c** Explain what causes the movement.
- **d** The objects you see are moving quite slowly. How does this compare with the speed of the molecules of the air? Explain your answer.

2 This question relates to the assumptions of the kinetic model of a gas.

This diagram represents the particles of a gas which is contained in a rectangular box:

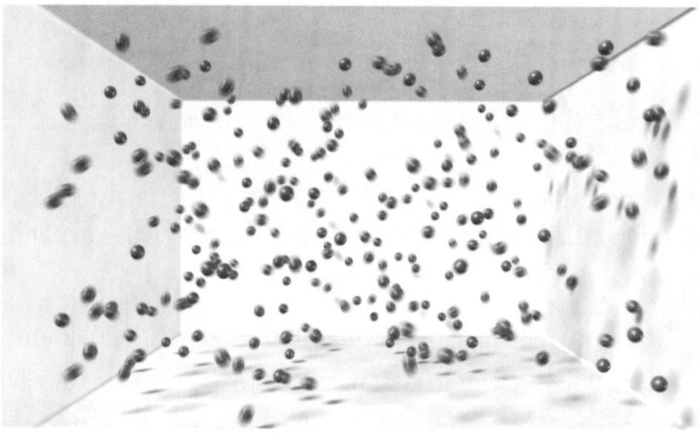

- **a** What can you say about the total volume of the particles compared with the total volume of the box?
- **b** We know that particles attract each other; it is why solids form when matter is cooled. State whether the particles of a gas attract one another.
- **c** Describe the path of an individual particle in between collisions with other particles and with the walls of the box.
- **d** State whether the collisions between particles are elastic or inelastic. Explain what effect this has on the total kinetic energy of the particles.

3 This question relates to the derivation of the relationship between the pressure p of a gas and the motion of its particles. It follows the same steps as the derivation of the relationship:

$p = \frac{1}{3}\rho < c^2 >$

Look at this diagram:

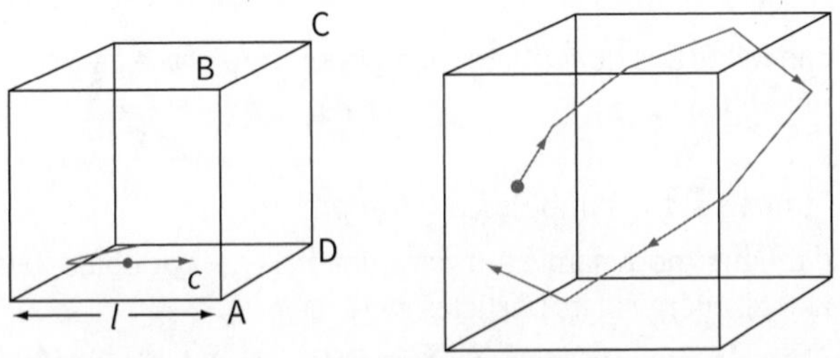

The left-hand side of the diagram shows a single particle in a cube-shaped box. For simplicity, we will suppose its mass is 1 kg and its speed is $c = 500 \text{ m s}^{-1}$:

a Calculate the particle's momentum.

b The particle strikes the cube face ABCD and bounces off it so that its velocity is reversed. Calculate the change in the particle's momentum. Remember that momentum is a vector quantity.

c The particle now bounces off the opposite face and returns to strike face ABCD again. Suppose that the length of each side of the cube is $l = 1.0$ m. Calculate the time interval between collisions on face ABCD. How many times will the particle strike ABCD each second?

d Calculate the force on ABCD due to this one particle. Use the relationship:

$$\text{force} = \frac{\text{change in momentum}}{\text{time}}$$

e Calculate the pressure on ABCD.

f What will be the pressure on the face opposite ABCD?

g In practice, a typical particle will be moving around so that it bounces off all six faces of the cube, rather than just two, as shown in the right-hand part of the diagram above. By what fraction will this reduce the pressure on cube face ABCD? Calculate the new value of the pressure.

h The volume of the cube is 1 m^3.

The density of the 'gas' is 1 kg m^{-3}.

The density of air is about 1.29 kg m^{-3} at 0 °C.

State whether the pressure of the air would be greater or less than the value you have calculated in part **g**.

i State whether the collisions between the particle and the walls of the cube are elastic or inelastic. Justify your answer.

4 We can write the following equation for the average kinetic energy of a particle (atom or molecule) of a gas:

average kinetic energy $= \frac{1}{2}m\langle c^2\rangle$

a State what the symbols m and $\langle c^2\rangle$ represent.

We can relate this quantity to the temperature of the gas:

$\frac{1}{2}m\langle c^2\rangle = \frac{3}{2}kT$

b State what the symbols k and T represent.

c If the thermodynamic temperature of a gas is doubled, by what factor does the average kinetic energy of its particles increase?

d Sketch a graph to show how the mean kinetic energy of the particles of a gas changes as its temperature increases.

Exam-style questions

1 a Explain what is meant by an *ideal gas*. [2]

A container holds 120 g of hydrogen gas at a temperature of 27 °C and a pressure of 100 kPa.

b Determine the volume of the container (molar mass of hydrogen = 2.0 g; universal molar gas constant $R = 8.31\ \text{J mol}^{-1}\ \text{K}^{-1}$). [2]

c The container is heated to 100 °C at fixed volume. Determine the pressure of the gas at this temperature. [2]

d Determine the density of the hydrogen and hence deduce the root mean square (rms) speed of the hydrogen molecules at 100 °C. [3]

2 A rigid container holds a mass of gas.

a Use the kinetic model of matter to explain why the gas exerts a pressure on the walls of the container. [2]

b The mass of gas in the container is doubled. Explain why the pressure of the gas doubles. [2]

c Explain why the pressure of the gas increases when the temperature of the gas increases. [2]

d Calculate the mean kinetic energy of the molecules of a gas at 27 °C (Boltzmann constant $k = 1.38 \times 10^{-23}\ \text{J K}^{-1}$). [2]

e The principal constituents of air are nitrogen (molar mass 28 g) and oxygen (molar mass 32 g). The root mean square speed of the nitrogen molecules is greater than that of the oxygen molecules. Explain this. [2]

Chapter outline

- understand that the charge on a spherical conductor may be considered to act as a point charge at its centre
- recall and use Coulomb's law to solve problems
- recall and use the formula for the field strength of a point charge
- define the electric potential at a point and use the equation for the potential of a point charge
- relate field strength and potential due to a point charge
- compare electric fields and gravitational fields

KEY TERMS

Coulomb's law: any two point charges exert an electrical force on each other that is proportional to the product of their charges and inversely proportional to the square of the distance between them

the electric potential at a point: the work done in bringing a unit positive charge from infinity to that point

Equations: Coulomb's law: $F = \frac{kQ_1Q_2}{r^2}$ where $k = \frac{1}{4\pi\varepsilon_0}$

electric potential $= \frac{\text{work done}}{\text{charge}}$; $V = \frac{W}{Q}$

electric potential: $V = \frac{kQ}{r}$ where $k = \frac{1}{4\pi\varepsilon_0}$

field strength = potential gradient; $E = \frac{\Delta V}{\Delta d}$

Exercise 23.1 Electric field around a point charge

You have already studied general ideas about electric fields (Chapter 8). You have also studied gravitational fields (Chapter 18). This exercise extends these ideas to consider electric fields around point electric charges.

Note: permittivity of free space, $\varepsilon_0 = 8.85 \times 10^{-12}$ F m^{-1}.

1 This question revises the idea of an electric field.

a State what is meant by an *electric field.*

b Write the equation that defines *electric field strength.* Give the equation in words and also in symbols. State the unit of each quantity in the equation.

This diagram shows an electron placed in an electric field of strength 5000 N C^{-1}:

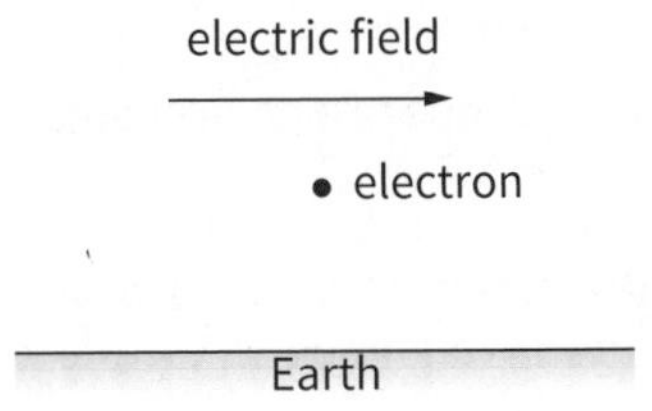

The electron is close to the Earth's surface where the gravitational field strength $g = 9.81$ N kg^{-1}.

c Calculate the electric force on the electron and state its direction. (electron charge = -1.6×10^{-19} C)

d Calculate the gravitational force on the electron and state its direction. (electron mass = 9.11×10^{-31} kg)

2 As with any electric field, we can draw field lines to represent the field around a point charge. This diagram shows the electric field around a positively charged metal sphere:

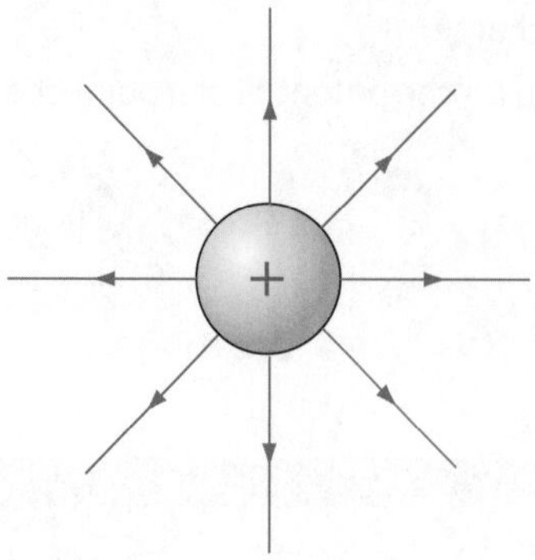

A charged sphere can be considered to behave like a point charge where all of the charge is concentrated at the centre of the sphere.

a Draw a similar diagram to represent the electric field around a metal sphere with a negative electric charge.

b Two charged metal spheres, each of diameter 10.0 cm, are placed so that there is a gap of 20 cm between them. They can be considered to act as two point charges separated by distance *d*. Deduce the value of *d*.

3 Coulomb's law describes the electric force between two point charges.

This diagram shows two point charges, each of +10 C, separated by a distance of 1.0 cm:

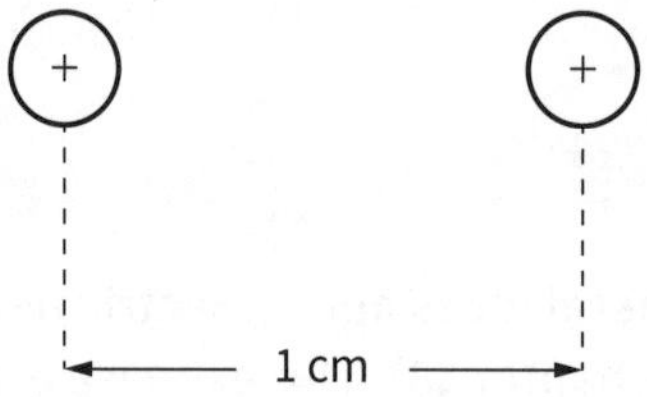

a Copy the diagram and add arrows to represent the force each charge exerts on the other.

b Explain how the sizes and magnitudes of the forces are an example of Newton's third law of motion.

c Describe how the forces will change if one of the charges is changed to −10 C.

d If the two charges are each increased to +20 C, by what factor will the force change?

e If the separation of the charges is increased to 2.0 cm, by what factor will the force change?

f If the separation of the charges is decreased to 0.5 cm, by what factor will the force change?

g Calculate the electric force between the two +10 C charges when they are separated by 1.0 cm ($\varepsilon_0 = 8.85 \times 10^{-12}$ F m^{-1}).

4 To calculate the electric field strength due to a point charge, we need to consider a charge of +1 C placed in the field.

a A charge of +1 C is placed at some distance from a positive charge +*Q*. The electric force on it is 24 N. Calculate the field strength at this point. Give its magnitude and direction.

b Calculate the force on a charge of −5 C placed at the same point.

5 Consider a +5 C point charge which is far from other charges.

- **a** Sketch a diagram to show the field lines around the charge.
- **b** State whether the field due to the charge is uniform. Explain your answer by referring to your diagram.
- **c** Calculate the field strength at a distance of 4.0 cm from the charge.
- **d** Sketch a graph to show how the field strength E depends on the distance r from the charge. (There is no need to include values on the graph axes.)

6 When there are two or more charges present, we can calculate the electric force (or the field strength) by working out the forces due to each charge separately and adding them together.

Remember, force and field strength are vector quantities so it is necessary to take account of their directions.

This diagram shows two point charges, +4 C and +1 C, separated by 3.0 cm:

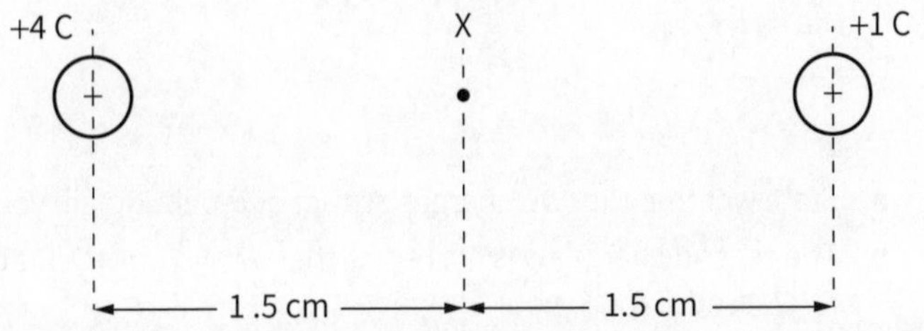

- **a** Consider a charge of +1 C placed at point X. It will be repelled by both charges. Which of the two charges will exert a greater force on it? Explain your answer.
- **b** State the direction in which the electric force on the charge placed at X will act.
- **c** Suggest a point at which the charge could be placed so that the resultant electric force on it would be zero. Justify your answer.

Exercise 23.2 Electric potential

Work must be done to push an electric charge to a higher potential. This energy can be changed to other forms when the charge is moved back to its starting point – that is what happens in an electric circuit when charges move around from the positive terminal to the negative. This exercise will give you practice in calculating electrical forces, work done and electric potential.

1 This question compares movement in gravitational and electric fields.

Look at these diagrams:

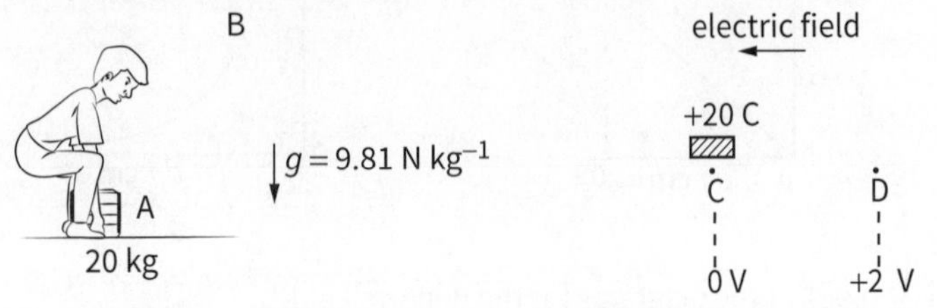

- **a** In the left-hand diagram, a heavy load is being lifted up from the ground at point A. If its mass is 20 kg, by how much has its gravitational potential energy increased when it is lifted to point B, 2.0 m above the ground? State the difference in gravitational potential between A and B. ($g = 9.81$ N kg^{-1})
- **b** In the right-hand diagram, a positive charge of +20 C is being pushed from C to D through a potential difference of 2.0 V. Describe how you can tell from the diagram that work must be done to achieve this.

c Calculate the increase in electrical potential energy when the +20 C charge is pushed from C to D. State the difference in electric potential between C and D.

d If a negative charge of –20 C moves from C to D, deduce the change in its electrical potential energy. Explain your answer.

2 This question is about the electric potential near a point charge.

This diagram shows the electric field around a point charge $+Q$. A second point charge $-q$ is placed near it:

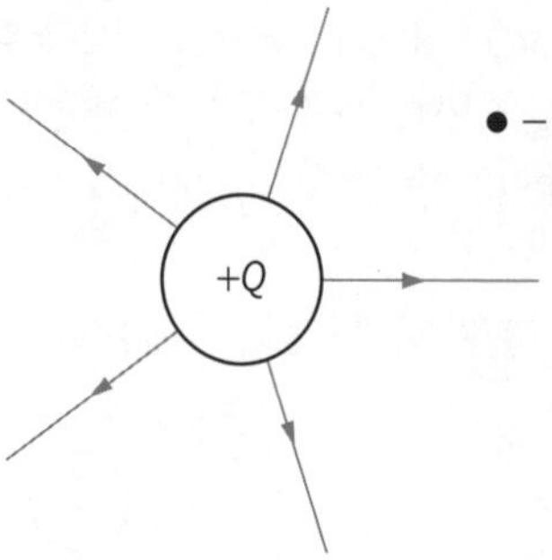

a State whether the two charges attract or repel. Explain your answer.

b The second charge $-q$ is moved further away from $+Q$. State whether work is done or energy is released. Explain your answer.

c State whether the charge $-q$ is now at a higher or lower potential than before.

d If charge $+Q = 0.01$ C, calculate the electric potential at a distance of 0.01 m from it.

e If charge $-q = -0.005$ C, calculate its electric potential energy at a distance of 0.01 m from $+Q$.

3 The electric field strength is equal to the potential gradient. We can write this as $E = \frac{V}{d}$ for a uniform field, and more generally as $E = \frac{\Delta V}{\Delta d}$.

These diagrams show field lines together with graphs of potential V against distance d for a uniform field and for a spherical field (the field around a point charge):

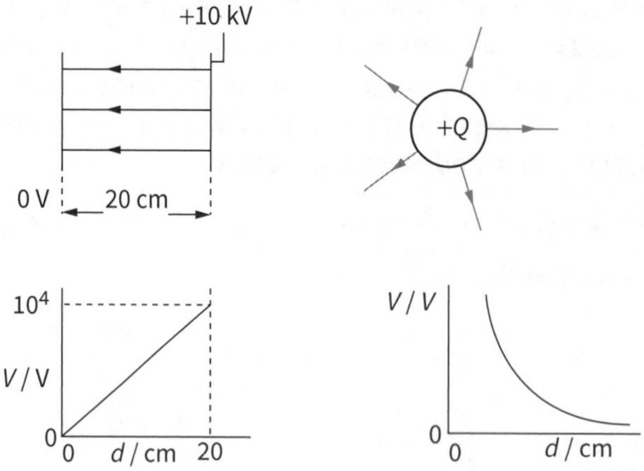

Look at the diagrams for the uniform field.

a Explain how you can tell from the pattern of field lines that this is a uniform field.

b Calculate the field strength in the space between the two plates using $E = \frac{V}{d}$.

c Look at the graph of V against d. Describe the shape of the graph.

d Explain how can you tell from this graph that the field is uniform.

Now look at the diagrams for the spherical field.

e Explain how you can tell from the pattern of field lines that this is *not* a uniform field.

f Look at the graph of *V* against *d*. State where the gradient is greatest (steepest).

g State where the field is strongest.

h Where is the field weakest? Explain your answer.

i Think about the gravitational field around the Earth. Where is the field strongest? Describe how an object could be moved to reach a place where the field is weaker.

j Sketch a graph to show how the Earth's gravitational potential ϕ varies as an object is moved away from its surface.

4 This graph shows how the potential *V* varies with distance *d* close to a positive charge:

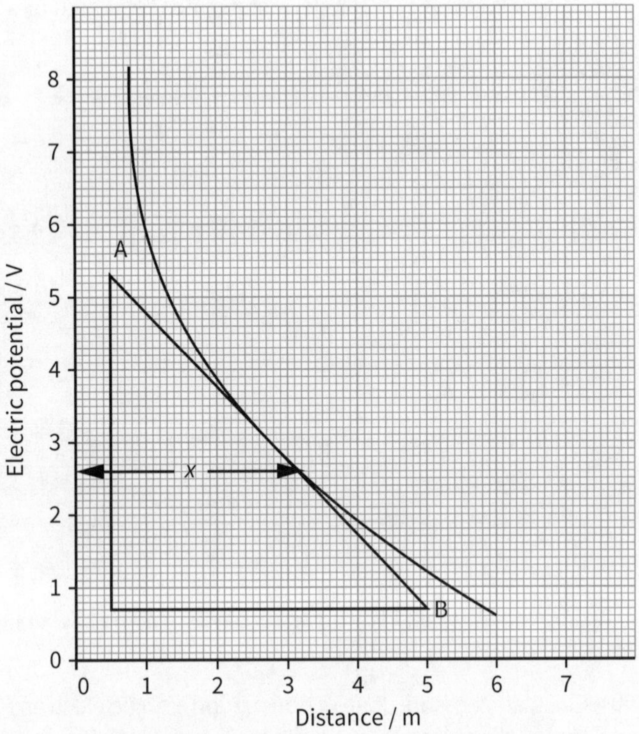

The triangle is used to find the field strength at a point in the field.

The line AB is a tangent to the curve. It touches the curve at the point where we want to know the field strength.

a State the distance *x* at which AB touches the curve.

b Find the gradient of AB. This is the value of the field strength at *x*. Include the appropriate units in your answer.

c State whether the gradient is positive or negative. Explain what this tells you about the force – is it attractive or repulsive?

Exam-style questions

1 a State Coulomb's law. [2]

In a carbon atom, an electron (charge $-e$) orbits the nucleus (charge $+6e$). The diameter of its orbit is 1.4×10^{-10} m. ($e = 1.6 \times 10^{-19}$ C)

b Calculate the electric force on the electron due to the nucleus. [2]

c State the value of the electric force exerted by the electron on the nucleus. [1]

d The electron moves to an orbit with a greater diameter. Explain whether its electric potential energy has increased or decreased. [2]

2 a State what is meant by the *electric potential* at a point. [2]

This diagram shows two parallel metal plates separated by a distance of 8.0 cm:

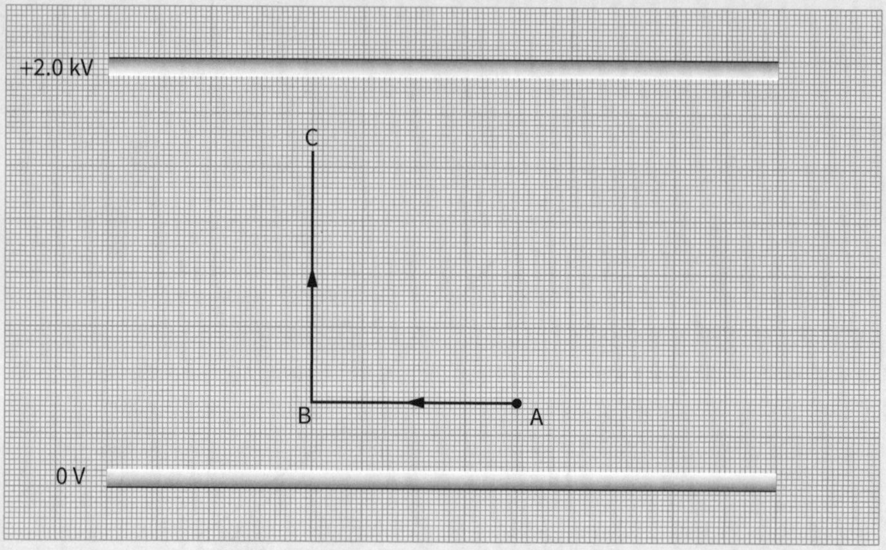

The upper plate is held at a potential of +2.0 kV. The lower plate is connected to earth so that its potential is 0 V.

b Calculate the work done in transferring a single electron from the upper plate to the lower plate. ($e = 1.6 \times 10^{-19}$ C) [2]

c Draw a graph to show how the electric potential varies with distance between the plates. [2]

d Calculate the electric field strength between the plates. [2]

e A charge of +1 C is moved along the path ABC shown in the diagram. Determine the electrical work done in moving the charge. [3]

Chapter outline

- define capacitance and the farad, and use the formula for capacitance
- show an understanding of the functions of capacitors in simple circuits
- solve problems involving charge, voltage and capacitance
- derive and use formulae for the energy stored in a capacitor
- derive and use formulae for the total capacitance of capacitors in series and in parallel

KEY TERMS

capacitance of a capacitor: the charge stored on one plate per unit potential difference between the plates

Equations: $\text{capacitance} = \dfrac{\text{charge}}{\text{potential difference}}$; $C = \dfrac{Q}{V}$

work done = charge × potential difference; $W = QV$

energy stored = $\frac{1}{2}$ charge × potential difference; $W = \frac{1}{2}QV = \frac{1}{2}CV^2$

capacitors in series: $\dfrac{1}{C_{total}} = \dfrac{1}{C_1} + \dfrac{1}{C_2} + \dfrac{1}{C_3} + \ldots$

capacitors in parallel: $C_{total} = C_1 + C_2 + C_3 + \ldots$

Exercise 24.1 Charge, voltage and capacitance

This exercise helps you understand the basic ideas of capacitance.

1 This question is about the definitions of capacitance and the farad. The equation that defines capacitance is $C = \frac{Q}{V}$.

a State the quantities represented by each symbol and give their units (name and symbol).

b Write down an equation relating the farad, coulomb and volt.

You can think of capacitance as telling you how many coulombs of charge are on each plate per volt of potential difference between them.

c A capacitor is marked with the value 10 000 μF. State this in F.

d Determine the charge on a plate of the capacitor when the p.d. across it is 1 V.

e Determine the charge on a plate of the capacitor when the p.d. across it is 50 V.

2 Capacitors are usually labelled with their capacitance either in μF or pF.

a What does the prefix 'p' stand for in the SI system? State the power of 10 that it represents.

b Write these capacitance values in standard form (in other words, in scientific notation, using powers of 10):

i 20 μF

ii 10 000 μF

iii 20 pF

iv 5000 pF.

3 This question is about how capacitors work.

This circuit diagram shows a capacitor that has been connected into a circuit with a cell and a resistor:

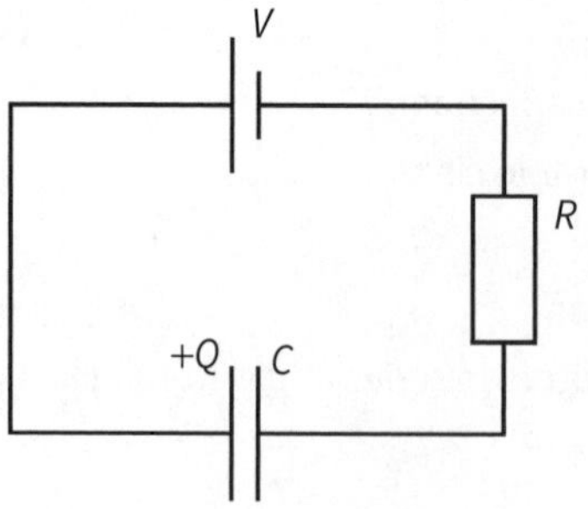

At first there is a current in the circuit, but eventually the capacitor is fully charged.

a When the capacitor is fully charged, state what happens to the current in the circuit.

b State the potential difference across the capacitor. State the p.d. across the resistor.

c The diagram shows that there is charge +*Q* on one plate of the capacitor. State the charge on the other plate.

d Determine how much charge has passed around the circuit during the charging process.

e State the name of the material used between the plates of the capacitor.

f Name the type of field found between the plates of the capacitor.

Now think about the circuit at the start of the charging process, when the capacitor was connected to the cell and the resistor.

g The plates of the capacitor were uncharged. State the p.d. across the capacitor at this time.

h State the p.d. across the resistor at this time.

i Describe how you could calculate the initial current in the circuit. Include the equation you would use.

4 If a capacitor is charged and then connected across a resistor, a current will be established in the circuit. This diagram shows one way in which this can be investigated:

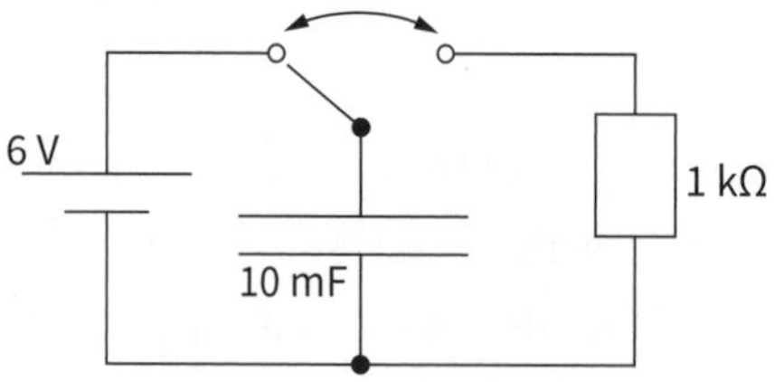

With the switch to the left, the plates of the capacitor become charged. There is no resistance in the circuit, so this will happen instantly.

a Determine the p.d. across the capacitor when it is charged.

b Calculate the charge on each plate of the capacitor.

Now the switch is moved to the right. The circuit consists of the capacitor and a resistor.

c State the initial potential difference across the resistor.

d Determine the current that will be established in the circuit.

e How much charge will leave the capacitor in 1.0 s? Calculate the new charge stored.

f Calculate the p.d. across the capacitor after 1.0 s.

g Calculate the current present in the circuit after 1.0 s.

h Explain why the current has decreased.

5 It can help to think of a capacitor as being similar to a rechargeable battery. Once it has been charged up, a capacitor can provide a source of voltage in a circuit, releasing charge to form a current. However, there is a very important difference between a capacitor and a rechargeable battery.

These graphs show how the voltage across a capacitor and a rechargeable battery change with time when they are connected across a resistor. But which is which?

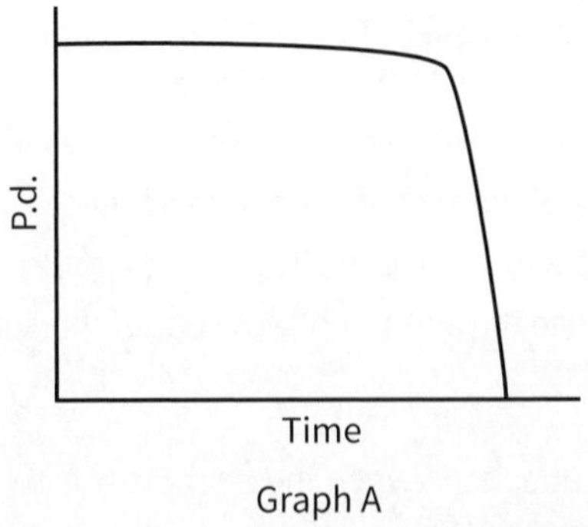

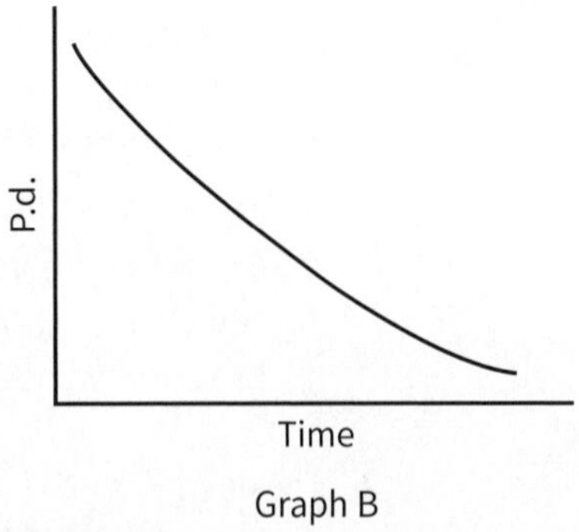

a State which graph, A or B, represents the behaviour of a capacitor. Explain your answer.

b If a capacitor is connected across a large resistor, will it discharge more or less slowly? Explain your answer.

Exercise 24.2 Energy stored by a charged capacitor

Work must be done to charge up a capacitor. This means that the capacitor is a store of energy, which can be recovered when the capacitor discharges. This exercise provides practice in calculating charge, potential difference and the energy stored by a capacitor.

1 This graph shows how the p.d. *V* across a 0.5 mF capacitor increases as the charge *Q* on each of its plates increases:

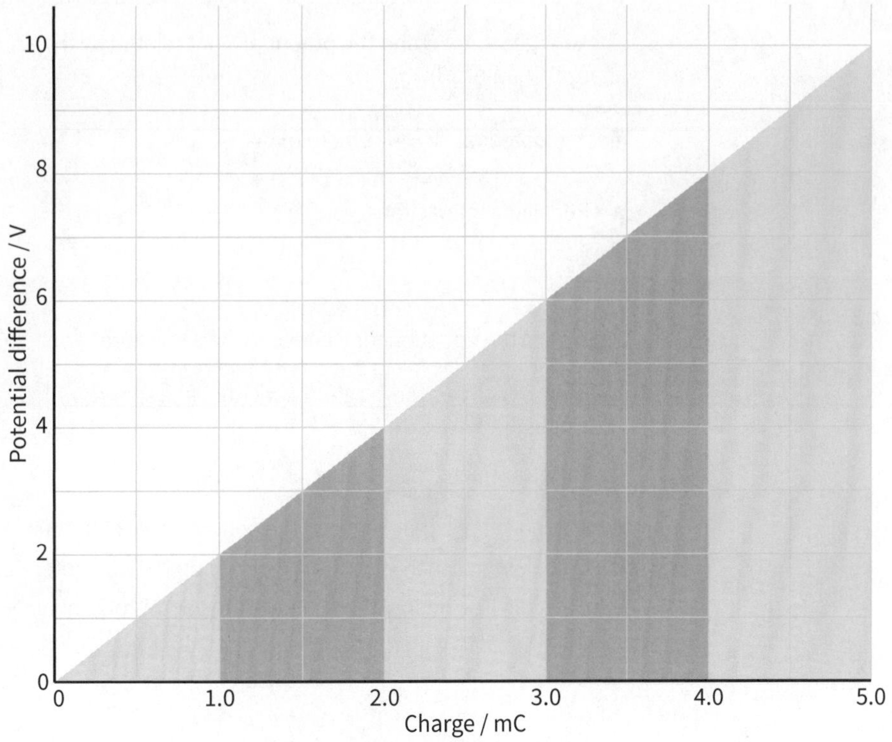

a The graph is a straight line. Think about the equation:

$$C = \frac{Q}{V}$$

State which quantity is represented by the gradient of the graph.

b The graph is divided into strips. The area of each strip represents the work done in transferring 1 mC of charge to the capacitor. The first 'strip' is a triangle. Its area tells us the work done in transferring the first 1 mC to the capacitor. Calculate the area of this strip. (Note: the answer will be in mJ since Q is in mC.)

c Calculate the area of the second strip. How many times bigger is this strip than the first strip?

d Explain what the area of the second strip represents.

e Explain why more work must be done in pushing the second 1 mC on to the capacitor?

f From the graph, deduce the amount of work done in charging the capacitor to a p.d. of 8.0 V. Explain your method.

2 The energy stored by a capacitor C when the p.d. across it is V is given by $W = \frac{1}{2}QV$. (This is the area under the graph of V against Q.)

a A capacitor is charged to a p.d. of 6.0 V. The charge stored on each of its plates is 300 μC. Calculate the capacitance of the capacitor and the energy it stores.

b The equation that defines capacitance is:

$$C = \frac{Q}{V}$$

Use this to show that we can write:

$$W = \frac{1}{2}CV^2$$

c A 20 μF capacitor is charged to 240 V. Calculate the energy stored.

d 200 mJ of work is done in charging a capacitor to a p.d. of 120 V. Calculate its capacitance.

3 A metal sphere can be charged – the dome of a Van de Graaff generator is an example of this. Because it can be charged, we can say that it has a capacitance.

The charge stored Q and the potential V are related by the equation for the potential near a point charge (Chapter 23):

$$\text{electric potential: } V = \frac{kQ}{r} \text{ where } k = \frac{1}{4\pi\varepsilon_0}$$

a Recall that capacitance is:

$$C = \frac{Q}{V}$$

Rearrange the equation for V above to find an expression for C in terms of r and k.

b State which has the greater capacitance: a sphere with a larger radius or a sphere with a smaller radius.

A metal sphere has a diameter of 40 cm.

c Calculate the capacitance of the sphere. ($\varepsilon_0 = 8.85 \times 10^{-12}$ F m^{-1})

d Calculate the charge on the sphere when it is at a potential of 20 kV relative to earth.

e Calculate the energy the sphere stores at this potential.

Exercise 24.3 Capacitors in series and in parallel

Two capacitors may be connected together, so it is useful to be able to calculate their combined capacitance. Alternatively, you may wish to connect two or more capacitors together to give a combined capacitance of a desired value. This is an exercise in combining capacitances in different ways.

1 Here are some calculations that make use of the formulae for combined capacitance:

capacitors in series: $\frac{1}{C_{total}} = \frac{1}{C_1} + \frac{1}{C_2} + \frac{1}{C_3} + ...$

capacitors in parallel: $C_{total} = C_1 + C_2 + C_3 + ...$

Don't forget that the equations work in the opposite way to those for resistors: you use the reciprocal formula for resistors in parallel but for capacitors in series.

a State the total capacitance of two 10 pF capacitors connected together in parallel.

b Calculate the total capacitance of two 10 pF capacitors connected together in series.

c Determine the number of 10 pF capacitors that must be connected in parallel to give a total capacitance of 50 pF.

d Now calculate the total capacitance of the number of 10 pF capacitors from part **c** if they were connected in series.

e Capacitors of values 10 pF, 50 pF and 200 pF are connected in parallel. Calculate their total capacitance.

Check that your answer is greater than the value of the largest of the three capacitances being connected in series.

f The capacitors from part **e** are connected in series..Calculate their total capacitance.

Check that your answer is less than the value of the smallest of the three capacitances being connected in series.

2 Each of these diagrams shows three capacitors connected together. You have to find the total capacitance between A and B.

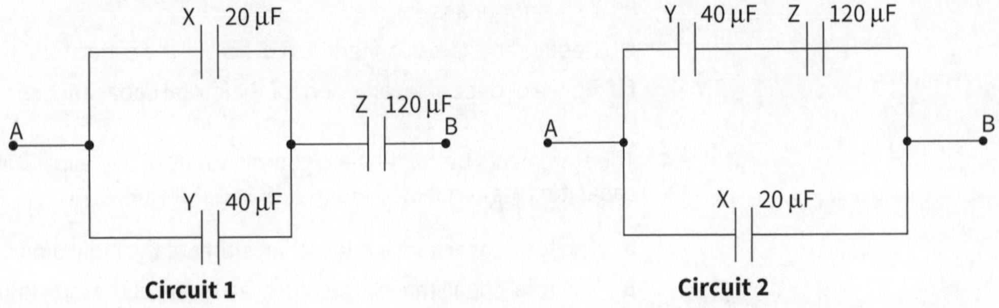

a For Circuit 1, you must first calculate the combined capacitance of X and Y. Notice whether they are connected in series or parallel and deduce their total capacitance.

b Now decide whether the pair of X and Y is in series or parallel with Z and calculate the total capacitance between A and B.

Now look at Circuit 2. The same three capacitors have been connected together, but in a different way.

c Deduce the total capacitance between A and B.
Follow the same logic as in parts **a** and **b**.

3 This question is related to the way in which the equations for capacitors in series and parallel are derived.

These diagrams show two capacitors, C_1 and C_2, connected in series and in parallel.

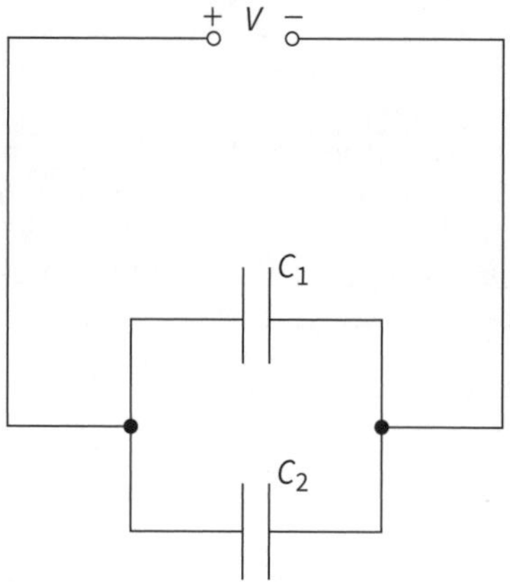

in parallel

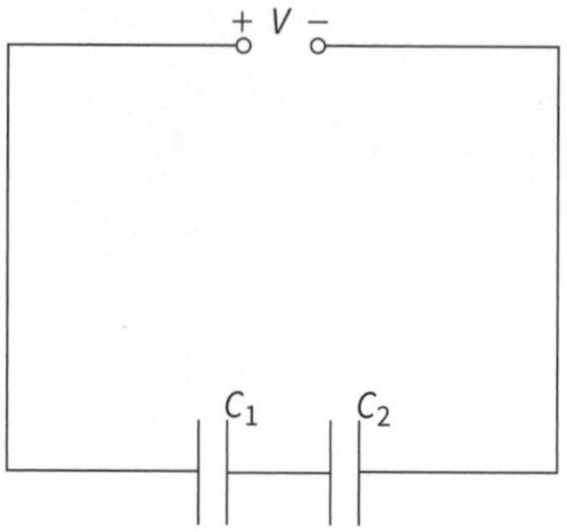

in series

For the capacitors in parallel:

a Which is the same for the two capacitors, the p.d. *V* across them or the charge *Q* on their plates? Explain your answer.

b Deduce an expression for the total charge on the capacitors.

c Hence deduce an expression for their total capacitance.

For the capacitors in series:

d Which is the same for the two capacitors, the p.d. *V* across them or the charge *Q* on them? Explain your answer.

e Deduce an expression for the p.d. across the capacitors.

f Hence deduce an expression for their total capacitance.

4 The statements below relate to combinations of two capacitors. For each, state whether the capacitors are connected in series or in parallel:

a The total capacitance is less than either of the individual capacitances.

b The total capacitance is greater than either of the individual capacitances.

c The p.d. of the supply is shared between them.

d The p.d. across one capacitor is greater than the p.d. across the other.

e One capacitor has less charge on its plates than the other.

Exam-style questions

1 **a** Define *capacitance*. [1]

A 200 μF capacitor is connected in series with a 4 kΩ resistor and a 240 V power supply.

b Determine the initial current in the circuit. [2]

c Calculate the charge on each plate of the capacitor when the current in the circuit has fallen to 0 A. [2]

d Calculate the work done in charging the capacitor. [2]

e Explain the energy transfers involved as a capacitor charges. How does this follow the principle of the conservation of energy? [3]

2 This diagram shows a metal sphere mounted on an insulating stand:

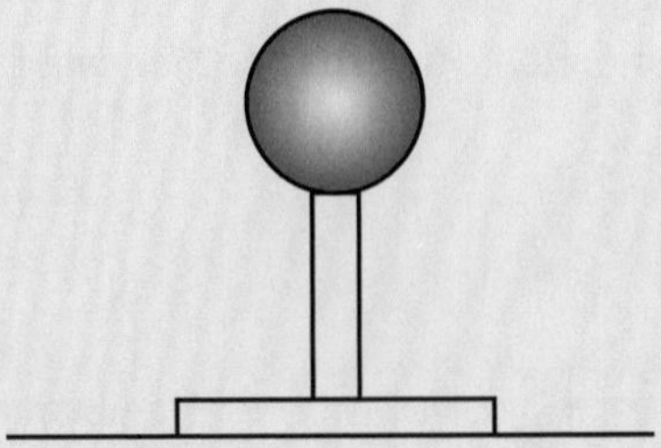

The sphere has a diameter of 40 cm. A positive charge is gradually added to the sphere.

a Sketch a graph to show how the potential changes as the charge on the sphere increases. [2]

b Determine the potential at the surface of the sphere when it carries a positive charge of 200×10^{-6} C. ($\varepsilon_0 = 8.85 \times 10^{-12}$ F m^{-1}) [3]

c Calculate the work done in charging the sphere. [2]

3 This circuit diagram shows two capacitors, C_1 and C_2, connected to a power supply:

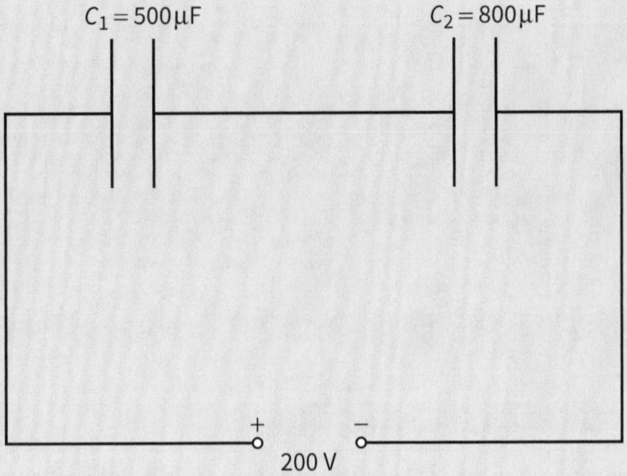

Calculate:

a the total capacitance of C_1 and C_2 when connected in this way [3]

b the charge on each plate of each capacitor. [3]

Chapter outline

- show an understanding of the operation and use of a light-dependent resistor (LDR), a negative temperature coefficient (NTC) thermistor, a piezo-electric transducer, a light-emitting diode (LED) and a relay
- describe the structure and function of a metal-wire strain gauge
- recall the main properties of the ideal operational amplifier (op-amp) and deduce how it may be used as a comparator
- recall the circuit diagrams for both the inverting and the non-inverting amplifier and recall and use expressions for their voltage gain
- for an operational amplifier, understand the virtual earth approximation, how an expression for gain is derived, and the effects of negative feedback on the gain
- understand how the output of an op-amp circuit can be monitored and the need for calibration where digital or analogue meters are used as output devices

KEY TERMS

negative feedback: the output of a system is used to oppose the changes in the input of the system; a fraction of the output is added to the input, out-of-phase to the input by 180°

gain: the voltage gain is the ratio of the output voltage to the input voltage

open loop voltage gain: the ratio of the output voltage to the p.d. between the inverting and non-inverting inputs

virtual earth: an approximation in which the two inputs of an op-amp are nearly at the same potential, that of the 0 V rail or earth.

bandwidth: a range of frequencies; the difference between the highest-frequency signal and the lowest-frequency signal

saturated: an op-amp is saturated if it is providing the maximum or minimum output voltage and is unresponsive to further increases of input signal

Equations: $\text{gain} = \frac{V_{out}}{V_{in}}$

$\text{gain} = -\frac{R_f}{R_{in}}$ for an inverting amplifier, or

$1 + \left(\frac{R_1}{R_2}\right)$ for a non-inverting amplifier

Exercise 25.1 Sensing

This exercise explores the different types and uses of sensing devices.

1 State suitable sensing devices that can be used to detect:

a a change in temperature

b the intensity of a sound wave

c a change in light intensity

d a change in the width of a crack in a wall.

2 Draw a diagram of a metal wire strain gauge and explain how it works.

3 Suggest approximate values for the resistance of a light-dependent resistor (LDR):

a in daylight

b in darkness.

4 A student designs a potential divider circuit to use as a sensing unit to detect temperature change. A 10 V supply, a voltmeter, a fixed resistor and a thermistor are used. The voltage output decreases as the temperature of the sensor increases.

a Draw the circuit diagram, labelling the output voltage.

b Explain the operation of the sensor.

c Explain why the output voltage does not change linearly with temperature.

d State one change to your apparatus that will cause the output voltage to increase as temperature increases.

The thermistor is placed in a water bath at various known temperatures.

e Describe how the reading on an analogue voltmeter can be adapted to find a temperature.

f Describe how the reading on a digital voltmeter can be used to quickly find a temperature.

5 A strain gauge has an initial resistance of 100.0 Ω and, after being stretched, the resistance is 105.0 Ω. The change in the area of cross-section of the strain gauge wire is negligible.

Calculate the percentage increase in the length of the strain gauge.

6 A microphone contains a piezo-electric transducer. Explain the action of the piezo-electric effect in the microphone.

Exercise 25.2 Properties of an op-amp and its use as a comparator

Although the principles behind the operation of an op-amp are reasonably simple, it can be made to work in different ways for different uses. This exercise explores the principles of the op-amp and some of its more straightforward uses. You need to understand these before moving on to consider more complicated uses.

1 This diagram shows an op-amp:

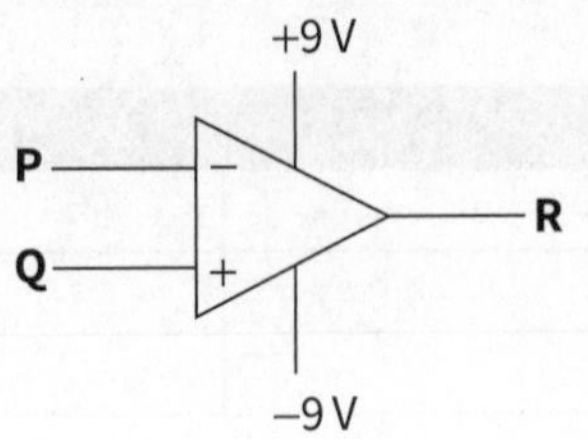

a State which of the terminals, labelled **P**, **Q** and **R**, are the output, the non-inverting input and the inverting input.

b Use the potentials at terminals **P**, **Q** and **R** to explain how the op-amp works.

c Explain the purpose of the potentials shown as + 9 V and –9 V.

2 Match each property of an ideal operational amplifier (op-amp) with the correct explanation:

Property
infinite input resistance
zero output resistance
infinite open loop gain
infinite bandwidth
infinite slew rate

Explanation
output voltage does not fall when connected to an output device
no time delay between applying a voltage and the output changing
draws little current from any input device
small signal can be amplified a large amount
all frequencies are amplified the same amount

3 A sensing unit is connected to the input of an op-amp. The op-amp is the main part of a processing unit. Describe the function of a processing unit.

4 The two input voltages to an op-amp are V_+ and V_-. The op-amp is used to make a comparator circuit. Describe what happens in a comparator circuit in terms of V_+ and V_-.

5 This diagram shows an ideal op-amp:

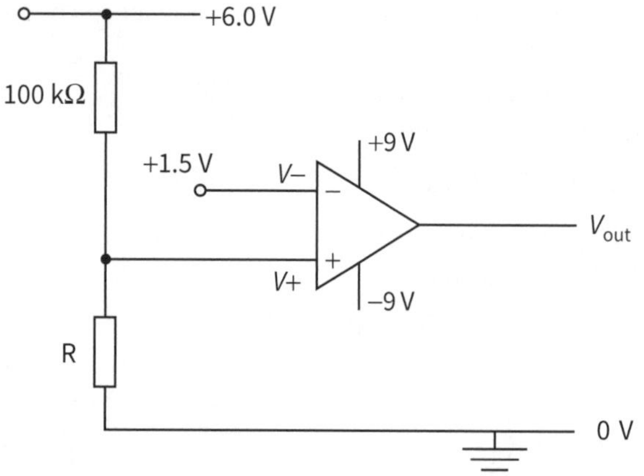

V_+ and V_- are the potentials of the two inputs of the op-amp.

a State the maximum and minimum values of the output voltage V_{out}.

b State the range of values of V_+ when V_{out} has the maximum value.

c State the range of values of V_+ when V_{out} has the minimum value.

d Complete this table to show values of V_+ and V_{out} for different values of the resistance of R. One row has been done for you:

Resistance of R / kΩ	V_+ / V	V / V_{out}
400		
200	+4.0	+9
100		
80		
50		
0		

The resistor R is replaced by a light-dependent resistor (LDR).

e Explain why V_{out} has a high value in the dark.

f State one change to the circuit so that V_{out} has a low value in the dark and a high value in the light.

Exercise 25.3 Inverting and non-inverting amplifiers

This exercise helps develop your understanding of op-amps when used in more complicated circuits, in particular to make use of feedback and gain.

1 An operational amplifier (op-amp) uses negative feedback in practical amplifier circuits.

- **a** State what is meant by *negative feedback*.
- **b** State two effects on the operation of the amplifier of using negative feedback.

2 This circuit shows an inverting amplifier:

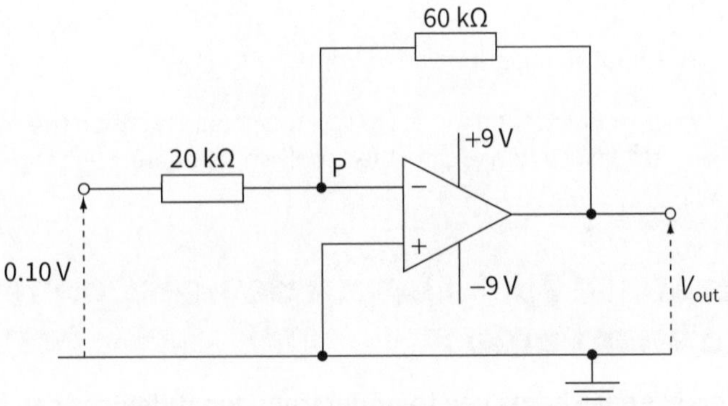

The open loop voltage gain of the amplifier is very high.

- **a** State what is meant by the *open loop voltage gain*.
- **b** Explain why a high gain means that P can be taken as almost at earth potential (0 V).
- **c** Calculate the current in the 20 kΩ input resistor.
- **d** Explain why the currents in the 20 kΩ input resistor and the 60 kΩ resistor are equal.
- **e** Calculate V_{out}.
- **f** Calculate the gain of the amplifier.
- **g** State the effective input resistance of the amplifier.
- **h** Describe what happens to V_{out} if the input voltage 0.10 V is removed and, instead, a voltage is applied that changes from −2 V to +2 V.
- **i** State the value of V_{out} if the input voltage is +6 V.

3 This circuit shows a non-inverting amplifier:

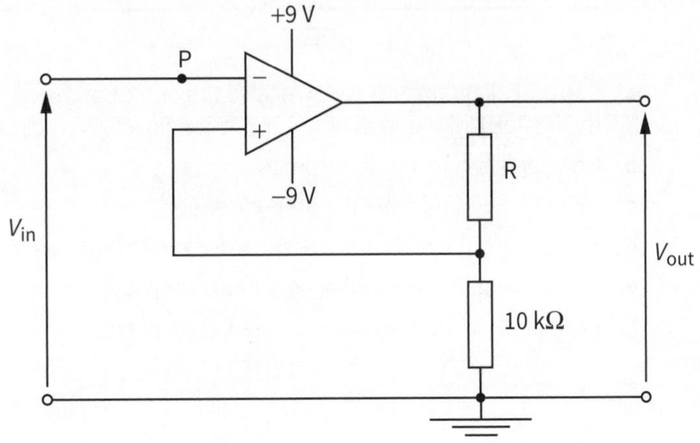

The voltage gain of the amplifier is +15.

a State the formula for the gain of a non-inverting amplifier.

b Calculate the resistance of the resistor R.

c Suggest why there is little current at point P.

The output voltage V_{out} is +3.0 V.

d Calculate the input voltage V_{in}.

e Determine the potential difference across the 10 kΩ resistor.

f State the potential at point P.

The input voltage V_{in} is varied from –1 V to +1 V.

g Describe what happens to V_{out}. You should mention the value of V_{in} when important changes take place. (Take care: the supply voltages are ± 9 V).

Exercise 25.4 Output devices connected to an op-amp

This exercise helps you to understand what devices can be connected to the output of an op-amp and why they are needed.

1 Suggest two reasons why a relay is sometimes connected to the output of an op-amp. (Think about dangerous electrical situations or where the output of an op-amp is not enough.)

2 This diagram shows part of a circuit to control a mains heater:

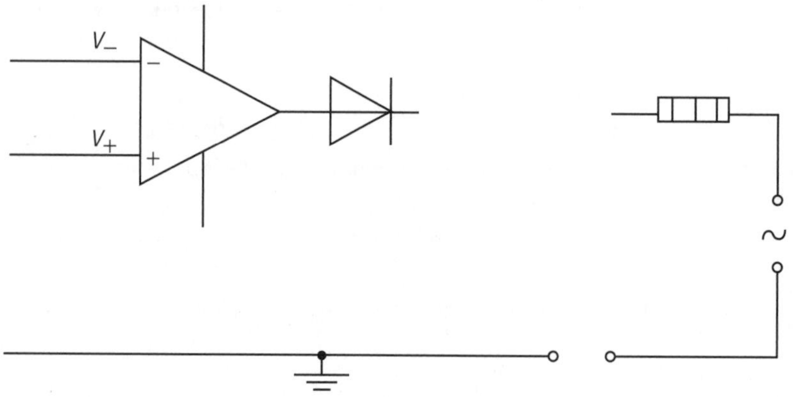

a Copy the diagram and add a relay to the output of the op-amp so that the relay switches on the heater. Make sure that no current can flow from the mains to the op-amp.

b On your diagram, mark the processing unit.

c On your diagram, mark the output device.

d Explain why the relay is needed in this circuit.

e Explain what happens when V_+ is larger than V_-.

f Explain what happens when V_- is larger than V_+.

3 A red light-emitting diode (LED) is used to indicate when the output of an op-amp is positive and a green LED is used to indicate when the output is negative.

The two LEDs are connected to the output of an op-amp. Each LED has a safety resistor in series to reduce the current in the LED.

a Draw a diagram showing the two LEDs connected to the output of the op-amp. Label the colours on the two LEDs.

The maximum output voltage of the op-amp is +9 V. The red LED is marked as 3.0 V, 10 mA.

b Calculate the p.d. across the safety resistor.

c Calculate the resistance of the safety resistor.

Exam-style questions

1 An operational amplifier (op-amp) is run using ± 12 V supplies. The input voltage to the op-amp is 480 mV and the output voltage is 9.6 V.

a State the maximum output voltage of the op-amp. [1]

b Draw a circuit diagram to show the op-amp used to make a non-inverting amplifier. [3]

c Calculate the voltage gain of the amplifier and suggest suitable values for the resistance of the resistors in your amplifier. [4]

d An inverting amplifier uses negative feedback.

i State what is meant by *negative feedback*. [2]

ii Negative feedback reduces the gain of the amplifier. Explain why this is useful. [2]

2 This diagram shows an LED and an LDR in a circuit with an op-amp:

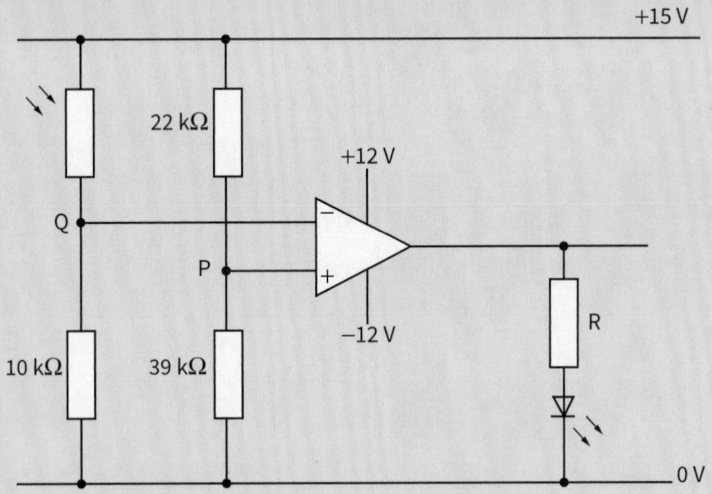

a Copy the symbols for the LED and the LDR and label them. [2]

b The potential at **P** is constant. Describe and explain how the output of the op-amp changes as the potential at **Q** changes. [3]

c Calculate the potential at **P**. [3]

d At one level of light, the LDR has a resistance of 5.0 kΩ.

i Calculate the potential at **Q**. [3]

ii Determine the output voltage of the op-amp. [1]

e Explain why the resistor R is required on the output of the op-amp. [2]

3 This diagram shows an op-amp connected to a signal generator:

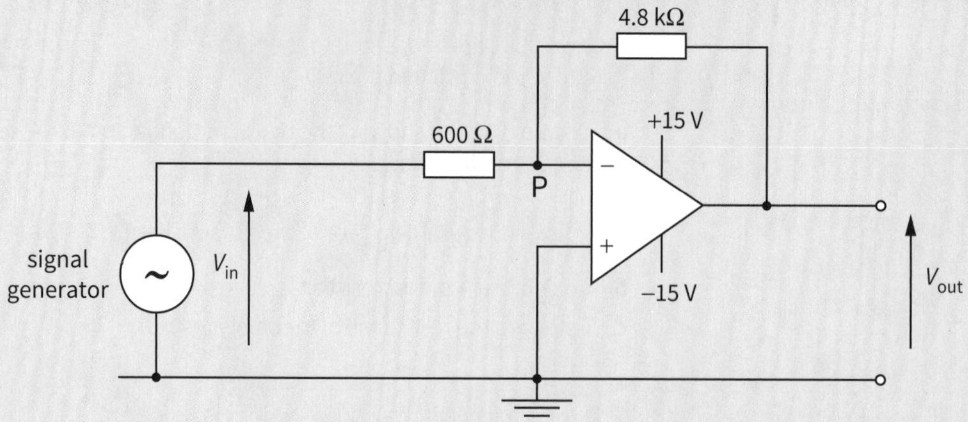

The output of the signal generator is a sinusoidal waveform.

a A student investigates the phase relationship between the input voltage V_{in} to the op-amp and the output voltage V_{out}.

i State the name of the measuring instrument needed to show the phase relationship and describe how the instrument is connected to the circuit. [2]

ii Describe what the student should observe as the phase relationship between the two voltages. You may draw a diagram if you wish. [2]

iii At large values of V_{in}, the output voltage V_{out} becomes almost constant. Explain why. [2]

b State three properties of an ideal op-amp. [3]

c At one instant in time, the value of V_{out} is +6.0 V.

i Explain why the potential at **P** is known as a *virtual earth*. [2]

ii Calculate the current in the 4.8 kΩ resistor. [2]

iii Calculate the value of V_{in}. [2]

Chapter outline

- use the idea of a magnetic field as a field of force, represented by field lines
- sketch the magnetic field patterns due to a long straight wire, a flat circular coil and a long solenoid
- determine the size and direction of the force on a current-carrying conductor in a magnetic field, including the magnetic field produced by another current-carrying conductor
- define magnetic flux and the tesla
- describe how the force on a current-carrying conductor in a magnetic field can be measured using a current balance
- describe the effect of a ferrous core on the magnetic field due to a solenoid

KEY TERMS

magnetic flux density: the force experienced per unit length by a long straight conductor carrying unit current and placed at a point in a magnetic field at right angles to the field

Equations: $\text{flux density} = \dfrac{\text{force}}{(\text{current} \times \text{length})}$; $B = \dfrac{F}{Il}$

Exercise 26.1 Magnetic field lines

We use magnetic field lines to represent the strength and direction of a magnetic field. This is an exercise in drawing and interpreting magnetic field lines.

1 Any wire carrying an electric current is surrounded by a magnetic field. This diagram shows a long straight wire carrying a current upwards from B to A:

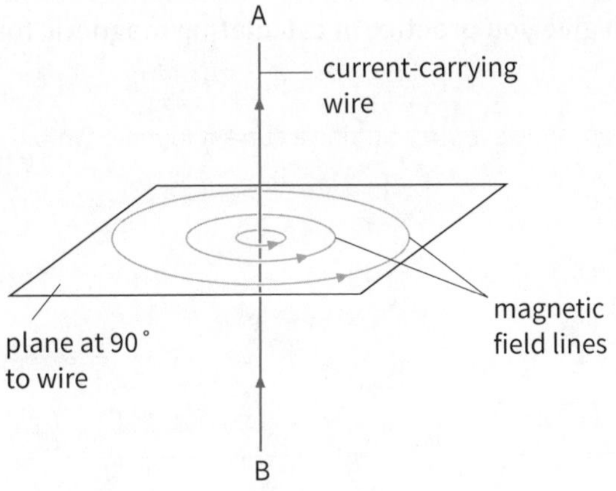

a Describe the shape of the magnetic field lines.

b State whether the field lines, as viewed from A, go around clockwise or anticlockwise.

c Where is the field strongest? Describe how this is represented in the diagram.

d Describe how the diagram would change if the direction of the current was reversed.

e Describe how the diagram would change if the strength of the current was increased.

2 The direction of the magnetic field lines around a current-carrying conductor can be determined as follows:

- Grip the wire, curling four fingers around the wire.
- Point the thumb along the wire.

a State which hand must be used for this.

b State what the direction of the thumb indicates.

c State what the direction of the curled fingers indicates.

3 A stronger magnetic field can be created by winding a wire to form a solenoid. This diagram shows how to find the direction of the magnetic field lines:

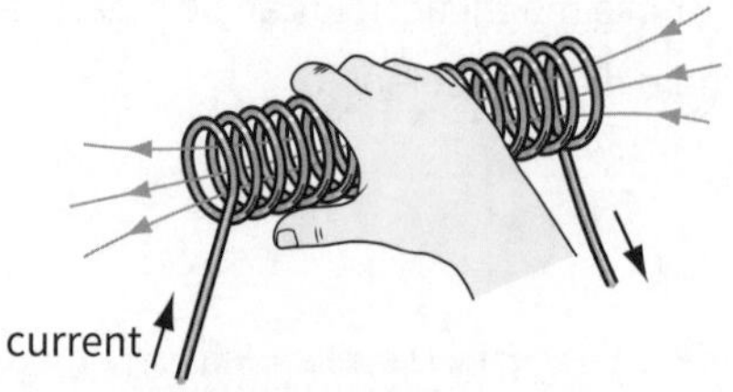

a State which hand must be used for this.

b State what the direction of the thumb indicates.

c State what the direction of the curled fingers indicates.

d State three ways in which you could increase the strength of the magnetic field.

e If a second, identical solenoid is placed immediately to the left of the one shown above, will the two solenoids attract or repel each other? Explain your answer.

f Explain how you could reverse the force that acts between the two solenoids.

Exercise 26.2 Force on a current-carrying conductor

There is a magnetic field around an electric current. When the direction of a current is across a magnetic field, the two fields interact to produce a force on the current. This exercise will give you practice in calculating magnetic forces and determining their directions.

1 This diagram shows a wire carrying a current (directed into the page):

The wire is in a magnetic field due to the two magnets.

a Copy the diagram and add the field lines between the two magnets.

b Add the field lines around the current.

c Add an arrow to show the direction of the force on the conductor.

d Use your diagram to explain why the force acts in the direction you have shown.

2 To find the direction of the force, it is simpler to use Fleming's left-hand rule.

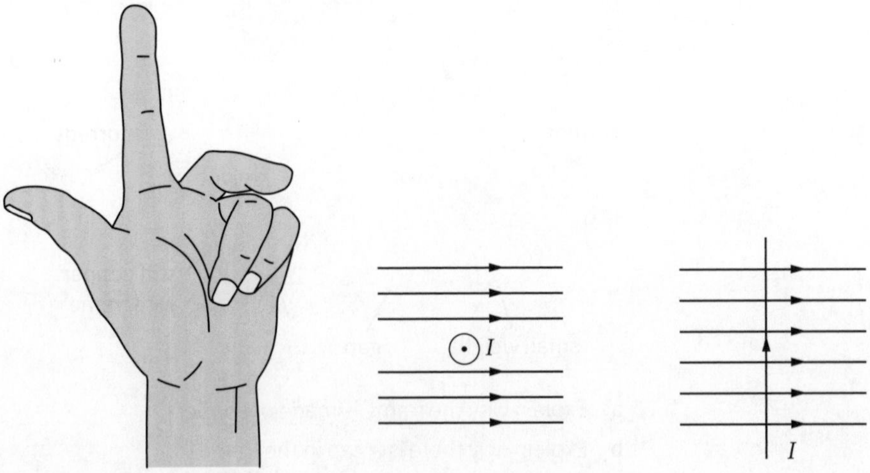

a State what the thumb and first two fingers represent in this rule.

b Look at the two diagrams on the right above. For each, decide whether there will be a force on the current-carrying conductor and state its direction.

3 The magnetic force on a current-carrying conductor is calculated using:

$F = BIl$

a State the quantity represented by each symbol in this equation. For each, state the SI unit (name and symbol).

b The equation is used to define the tesla. Rearrange the equation and use it to express the tesla in SI base units.

c State which quantities in this equation are vector quantities.

d Show how the equation must be modified if there is an angle θ between the current and the magnetic flux.

e Calculate the force on a wire of length 0.40 m carrying a current of 0.30 A which is at right angles to a magnetic field of flux density 250 mT.

f Draw a diagram to show how the wire could be positioned in the magnetic field so that the resultant force on it was zero.

4 The flux density of a magnetic field can be determined by measuring the force on a current-carrying conductor placed in the field.

a A 10 cm length of copper wire carries a current of 200 mA and is directed at right angles to a magnetic field. The force on the conductor is found to be 8.0×10^{-3} N. Calculate the flux density of the field.

The flux density of the Earth's magnetic field is about 32 μT.

b Calculate the force on a wire of length 1.0 m carrying a current of 5.0 A placed in the Earth's field.

c The wire has a mass of 20 g. Explain why the magnetic force on the wire is unlikely to be noticed in normal circumstances.

5 The current balance is a device used to determine the flux density of a magnetic field. An example is shown below:

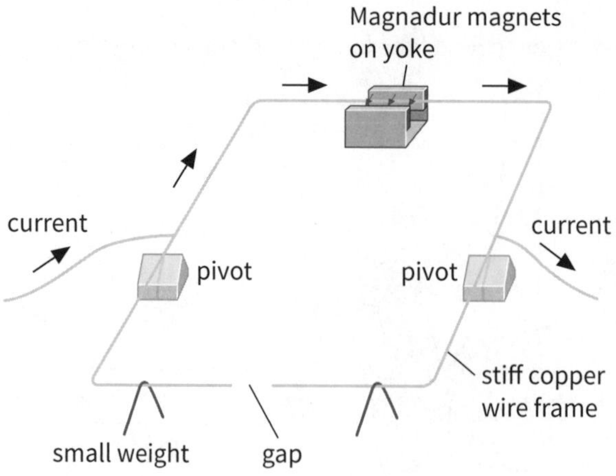

a Explain why the frame is made of copper.

b Explain why there is a gap in the frame.

c State which instrument you could use to measure the current.

d Explain how you could determine l, the length of the conductor in the magnetic field.

e Explain the purpose of the small weights placed on one end of the frame.

f Explain how you would find B with this apparatus.

g Describe how you would use this apparatus to show that the magnetic force F is proportional to the current I.

Exam-style questions

1 a Define *magnetic flux density.* [1]

This diagram shows two identical solenoids, with a current present in each, placed side by side:

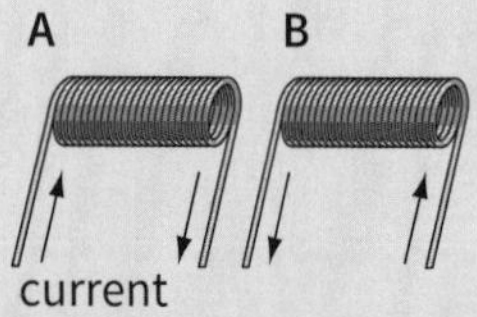

b Consider solenoid A. State the type of magnetic pole that it will have at its left-hand end. [1]

c Each solenoid exerts a magnetic force on the other. State whether they will attract or repel each other. Justify your answer. [2]

d The current in A is 2 A; the current in B is 1 A. What can you say about the magnitudes of the forces the magnets exert on each other? Explain your answer. [2]

2 This diagram shows a triangle ABC formed of copper wire, placed in a magnetic field of flux density 2.8×10^{-4} T:

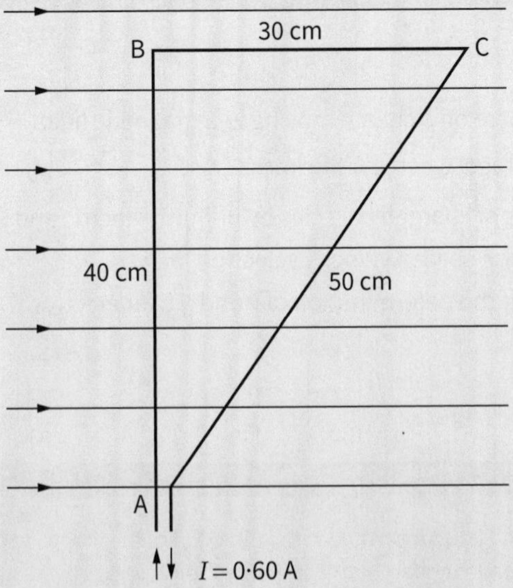

There is a current of 0.60 A in the wire.

a Calculate the force on side AB and state its direction. [3]

b Calculate the force on side CA and state its direction. [2]

c Explain why there is no force on side BC. [2]

Chapter outline

- determine the size and the direction of the force on a charge moving in a magnetic field
- derive the expression $V_H = \frac{BI}{ntq}$ for the Hall voltage, where t = thickness
- describe and analyse the deflection of beams of charged particles by uniform electric and uniform magnetic fields
- explain how electric and magnetic fields can be used in velocity selection
- explain the main principles of one method for the determination of v and $\frac{e}{m_e}$ for electrons

KEY TERMS

Fleming's left-hand rule: if the first finger of the left hand is pointed in the direction of the magnetic field and the second finger in the direction of the conventional current, then the thumb points in the direction of the force or motion produced

Equations: $F = BQv \sin\theta$

$F = qE$

$E = \frac{V}{d}$

acceleration in a circle $a = \frac{v^2}{r} = \omega^2 r$

$v = r\omega$

$F = ma$

$V_H = \frac{BI}{ntq}$

$I = Anvq$

Exercise 27.1 Magnetic forces on particles

In this exercise, you need to equate the formula for the magnetic force to the centripetal force. You also need to understand the various directions of fields and movement for particles of positive and negative charge.

charge on an electron = -1.6×10^{-19} C

mass of an electron = 9.1×10^{-31} kg

mass of a proton = 1.7×10^{-27} kg

1 Look at this formula for the force F acting on a charged particle in a magnetic field of flux density B:

$F = BQv \sin\theta$

a State the meaning of the symbols Q, v and θ.

b Describe what a charged particle must do to experience a force in a magnetic field.

c State two situations in which there is **no** magnetic force on a charged particle, even though it is in a magnetic field.

2 A particle with charge q and mass m moves in a circular path with velocity v at right angles to a magnetic field B.

a Show that the radius R of the path is given by: $R = \frac{mv}{Bq}$.

b Show that the time T for one revolution of the particle is given by: $T = \frac{2\pi m}{Bq}$.

(Remember, the particle is travelling in a circle of circumference $2\pi r$ with speed v.)

c Derive an expression for the angular speed ω of the charged particle in terms of B, q and m.

3 This diagram shows the circular path of an electron moving in a uniform magnetic field that is at right angles to the circle:

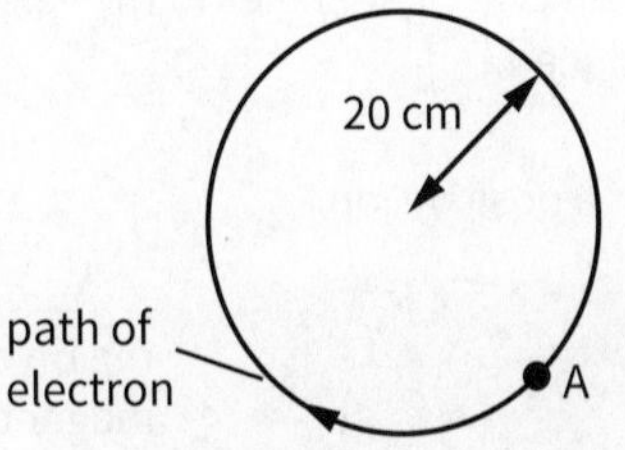

a State the direction of the force acting on the electron when it is at point A.

b Use Fleming's left-hand rule to find the direction of the magnetic field. (Remember, an electron is negative and so conventional current is opposite to its motion.)

c Explain why the force on the electron does no work on the electron.

The speed of the electron is 1.5×10^6 m s^{-1}.

d Calculate the size of the force acting on the electron.

e Calculate the magnetic flux density of the field.

f Calculate the time taken for the electron to travel once around the circle.

4 This diagram shows a proton entering and leaving a magnetic field:

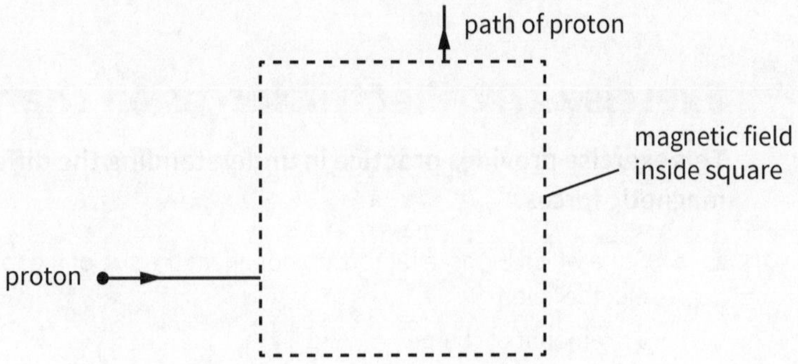

The field is at right angles to the page and is uniform inside the square shown and zero outside it.

a Describe the path of the proton through the magnetic field.

b State the direction of the magnetic force on the proton just after the proton enters the square.

c State the direction of the magnetic force on the proton just before the proton leaves the square.

d Use Fleming's left-hand rule to find the direction of the magnetic field.

e The speed of the proton is 2.5×10^6 m s^{-1} and the magnetic flux density is 0.40 T. Calculate the size of the magnetic force on the proton. (the charge on a proton = −charge on an electron)

An electron with the same velocity as the proton is used instead of the proton.

f State **two** differences in the paths taken by the proton and the electron.

g State **two** changes that need to be made to the magnetic field for the electron to follow the same path as the proton.

5 A proton, travelling at a speed of 4.0×10^6 m s^{-1} enters a region of uniform magnetic field, of flux density 0.15 T. The magnetic field is at right angles to the velocity of the proton. Calculate the radius of the circular track produced.

6 This diagram shows the path of a positive ion:

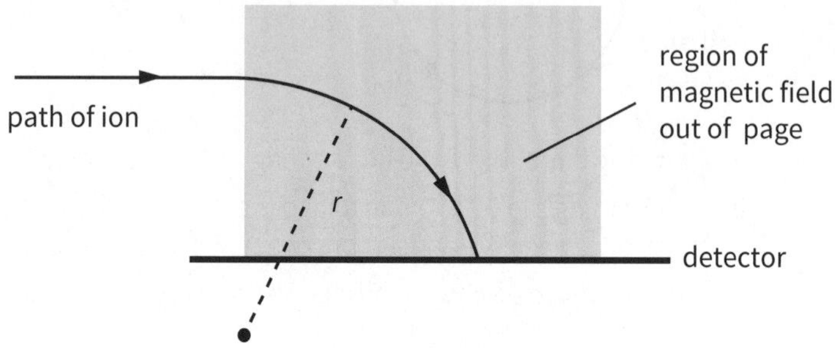

The ion enters the field with a speed of 4.0×10^6 m s^{-1}. When the ion is within the magnetic field of flux density 0.15 T, the force on the ion is 1.9×10^{-13} N. The mass of the ion is 2.0×10^{-26} kg.

a Calculate the charge on the ion.

b Calculate the radius *r* of the circular path.

c Another ion, with the same speed as the original ion, describes a circular arc with a larger value of *r*. Explain how this is possible.

Exercise 27.2 Electric forces on charged particles

This exercise provides practice in understanding the difference between electric and magnetic forces.

1 a State which of these factors do not affect the size of the force on a charged particle in an electric field:

- amount of charge
- speed of movement
- direction of movement
- strength of electric field.

b A positively charged particle, travelling horizontally, enters a region with a horizontal magnetic field and then a region with a horizontal electric field. Compare the direction of the force on the particle and its path in the two fields.

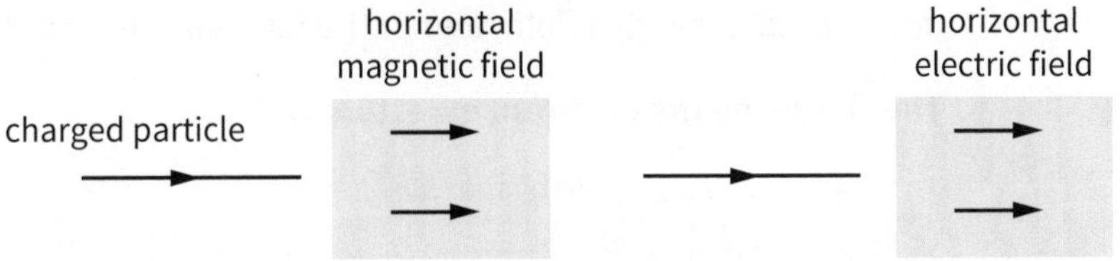

c A charged particle, travelling horizontally, enters a vertical magnetic field and then a vertical electric field. Compare the direction of the force on the particle and its path in the two fields.

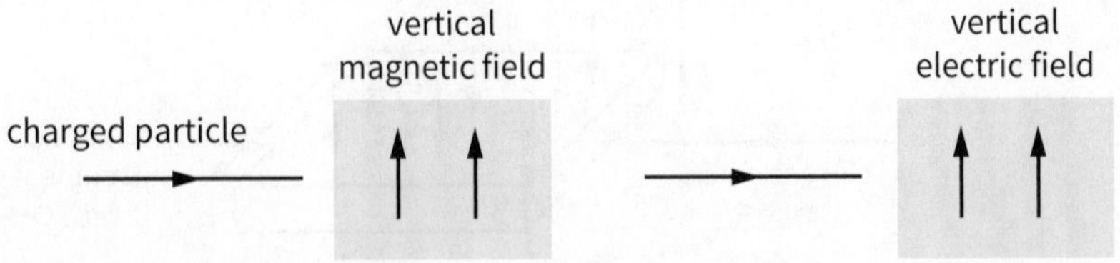

2 A charged particle of mass 6.6×10^{-27} kg and charge $+3.2 \times 10^{-19}$ C enters the uniform electric field between two parallel plates in a vacuum, as shown:

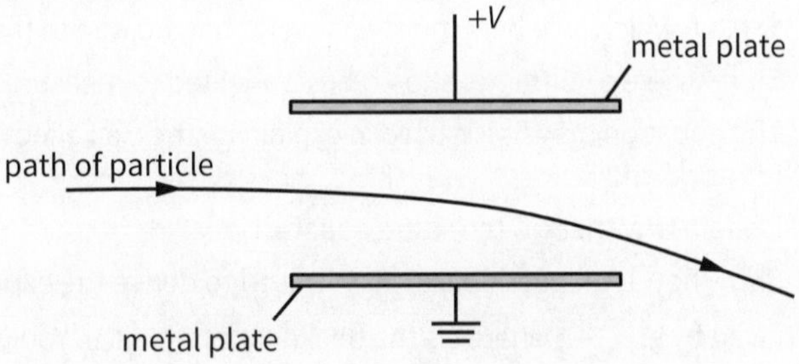

The electric field between the plates has magnitude 2.0×10^4 V m^{-1} and is zero outside the plates.

a Describe what happens to the horizontal speed of the particle as it moves between the plates.

b Describe what happens to the vertical speed of the particle as it moves between the plates.

c Describe what happens to the direction of the acceleration of the particle as it moves between the plates.

d Explain why the path of the particle in the electric field is not circular.

e Calculate the vertical acceleration of the particle due to the electric field.

f Suggest why gravity has little effect on the particle in the experiment.

Another particle with the same charge but with twice the mass enters the parallel plates with the same speed as the original particle.

g Describe the path taken by the new particle.

h State two ways in which the apparatus can be modified so that the new particle has the same track as the original particle.

i Explain how your modifications in **h** produce the same acceleration for the more massive particle.

Exercise 27.3 The Hall effect

This exercise develops your understanding of the idea of an electron passing undeviated through a field, and of the formula that involves mean drift velocity.

The charge on the electron, $e = -1.6 \times 10^{-19}$ C.

1 Describe what is meant by the *Hall effect*.

2 A conventional current enters face P of a thin slice of a semiconductor. Only electrons flow in the thin slice. A magnetic field *B* acts downwards.

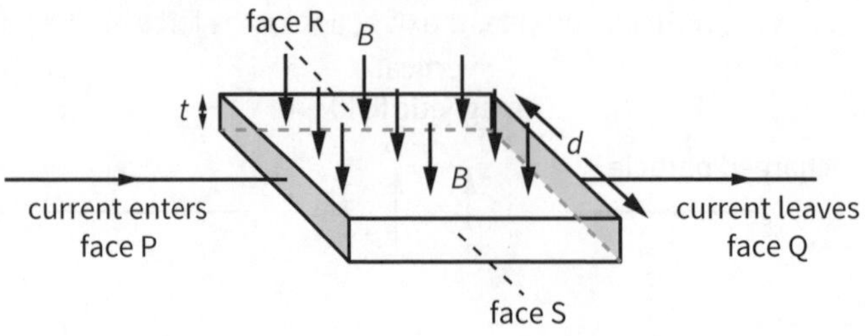

a State the direction of movement of the electrons as the current enters face P.

b Use Fleming's left-hand rule to find the direction of the magnetic force on the electrons.

c Explain which face becomes negatively charged due to the Hall effect.

d State where a voltmeter should be connected to measure the Hall voltage.

e The equation $qE = Bqv$ is used in explaining the Hall effect. State the meaning of the two terms qE and Bqv.

f Explain why the two terms are equal.

g Show how the equation $qE = Bqv$ is used to derive the expression for V_H the Hall voltage, given by $V_H = \frac{BI}{ntq}$, where *t* is the thickness of the slice. You will need to use the electric field formula for parallel plates and the formula for current in terms of the mean drift velocity of the electrons, as well as recognising that the area $A = dt$.

h The current in the film is 0.042 A, $t = 0.9$ mm, $d = 10$ mm, the Hall voltage is 2.0×10^{-4} V and the concentration of free electrons in the semiconductor is 1.5×10^{23} m^{-3}. Calculate the magnetic field strength, *B*.

i Calculate the electric field strength in the slice due to the Hall effect voltage.

j Calculate the mean drift velocity of the electrons.

3 This diagram shows a Hall probe placed near a wire carrying a direct current:

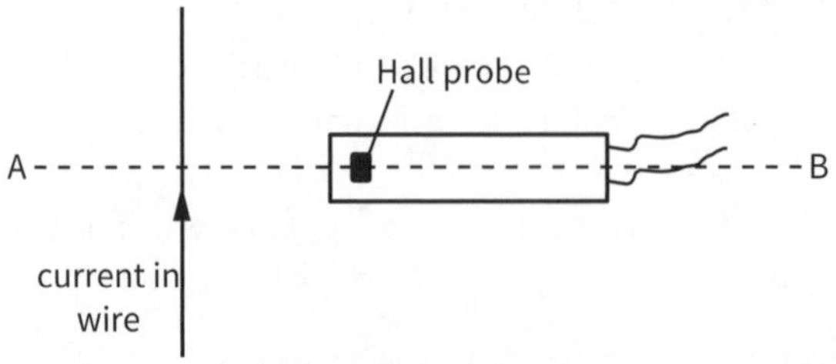

The Hall voltage is +1.6 mV.

a State the cause of the magnetic field that produces the Hall voltage in the probe.

b Explain why the Hall voltage is zero when the coil rotates 90° about the axis AB from the position shown.

c Explain why the Hall voltage is −1.6 mV when the coil rotates 180° about the axis AB from the position shown.

d Explain why the Hall voltage decreases when the probe is moved towards B along the line AB.

Other measurements made with the probe were:

- current in the Hall probe = 100 mA
- thickness, t = 1.0 mm
- width, d = 6.0 mm
- flux density of magnetic field = 0.080 T. (Remember, 1 mm = 10^{-3} m and 1 mA = 10^{-3} A).

e Calculate the number density of free electrons in the Hall slice. Remember to give the unit.

f Calculate the mean drift velocity of the free electrons in the Hall slice.

g Calculate the mean value of the magnetic force on a free electron at it moves through the slice.

h Calculate the value of the electric force on each free electron at it moves through the slice.

4 The Hall effect can be shown with a thin strip of metal. A copper strip of thickness 1.0 mm carries a current of 25 A at right angles to a magnetic field of 2.5 T. The Hall effect voltage is 6.0×10^{-6} V.

a Calculate the number density of free electrons in copper.

b Explain why Hall voltages obtained with metals are smaller than with semiconductors of the same dimensions and with the same current. Use ideas about the number density of free electrons and the velocity of the charge carriers.

Exercise 27.4 The velocity selector

The questions in this exercise about the velocity selector always involve an electric field and a magnetic field, both at right angles to a particle's velocity. Think carefully about the directions of the forces of the fields on the charged particle.

1 This diagram shows a source of ions. The ions accelerate and pass through a velocity selector:

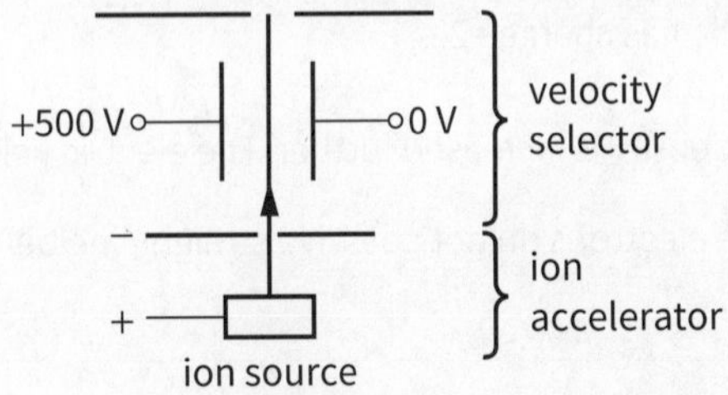

Within the parallel plates, both the magnetic field and the electric field are uniform. The magnetic flux density is 0.12 T and the electric field strength is 2.4×10^4 V m^{-1}.

Positive ions flow upwards. The deflection of the ions due to the electric field between the plates is cancelled by the deflection caused by the magnetic field in the same region.

a State the direction of the magnetic force on the ions in the magnetic field.

b State the direction of the magnetic field within the plates.

c Calculate the velocity selected.

d Write down an equation relating the speed of the electrons v to the electric field E between the plates and the magnetic flux density B when the ions are not deflected within the plates.

e Calculate the separation of the plates. The p.d. across the plates is shown on the diagram.

f Explain, in terms of the magnetic force and the electric force on the ion, what happens when an ion of larger speed than the value in **d** passes into the velocity selector.

2 Electrons with speed *v* and charge *e* travel in a vacuum between two narrow slits S_1 and S_2.

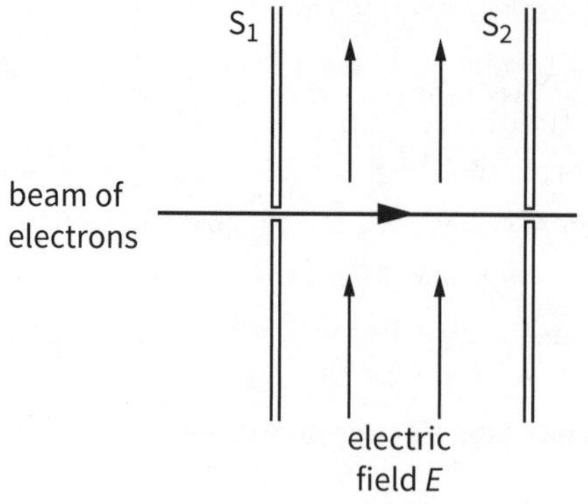

Between the slits, there is a magnetic field *B* and an electric field *E*, both of which are uniform. Only the electric field direction is shown in the diagram. The electron passes in a straight line between the slits.

a State the expression for the force *F* acting on a charged particle due to the electric field.

b State the expression for the force *F* acting on a charged particle due to the magnetic field.

The electric field acts upwards in the plane of the paper, as shown in the diagram. The electrons pass undeflected through the region between the slits.

c State the direction of the electric force on the electron.

d State the direction of the magnetic field.

e Explain how it is possible for the electron to be undeflected.

An alpha-particle with speed *v* passes along the same path as the electron.

f Explain, in terms of the forces acting why the alpha-particle is also undeflected. Remember, an alpha-particle has charge +2*e*.

The magnetic flux density is increased further. The electric field strength is unchanged.

g Explain why the electrons do not pass in a straight line between the slits.

Exercise 27.5 The charge-to-mass ratio of a particle

The specific charge of a particle is the ratio *q/m* of the charge to the mass of the particle. This exercise shows how this ratio can be found in a number of ways, either by finding the speed of a charged particle or by using the kinetic energy of the particle.

charge on an electron = -1.6×10^{-19} C

mass of an electron = 9.1×10^{-31} kg

mass of a proton = 1.7×10^{-27} kg

1 Calculate the charge-to-mass ratio of:

a an electron

b a proton

c an alpha-particle (remember this is two protons and two neutrons).

2 A proton and an electron with the same speed enter a magnetic field. Explain in terms of the forces and accelerations why the deflection of the proton is less.

3 Show that the specific charge of a particle moving in a circular path of radius *r* with speed *v* at right angles to a magnetic field of flux density *B* is v/rB.

4 A charged particle has a circular path of radius 20 cm in magnetic field of flux density 0.85 T. If the speed of the particle is 8.0×10^6 m s^{-1}, calculate the specific charge of the particle.

5 Outline how a velocity selector and another magnetic field can be used to find the specific charge on an electron.

6 A charged particle of charge *q* and mass *m* is accelerated from rest through a potential difference *V*. The final speed is *v*.

a Explain why $qV = \frac{1}{2}mv^2$

b Show that:

$$v = \sqrt{\frac{2Vq}{m}}$$

c The circular path of the particle in a magnetic field of flux density *B* has radius *r*. Show that:

$$v = \frac{qrB}{m}$$

d Combining the equations in **b** and **c**, derive an expression for q/m, the ratio of charge to mass in terms of *V*, *r* and *B*.

e Outline how the formula obtained in **d** can be used to find the ratio of charge to mass for an electron.

7 A particle is accelerated from rest through a potential difference of 800 V. The specific charge of the particle is 4.7×10^7 C kg^{-1}. Calculate the final velocity of the particle.

Exam-style questions

1 A charged particle of mass *m* and charge *q* travels in a vacuum at constant speed *v*. It enters a magnetic field of flux density *B*. The initial angle between the direction of the magnetic field and the motion of the particle is 90°.

a Explain why the path of the particle is a circle in the magnetic field. [2]

b The radius of the circular path is *r*. Show that the ratio $\frac{q}{m}$ is given by the expression $\frac{q}{m} = \frac{v}{Br}$. [3]

c A beam of electrons enters a uniform electric field produced by a p.d. of 800 V applied across two parallel plates 40 mm apart. The beam is deflected by the electric field until a uniform magnetic field of 0.80 mT perpendicular to the beam is applied, which cancels the deflection and the beam then passes in a straight line. Calculate the speed of the electrons. [2]

2 When a gamma-ray photon passes close to a nucleus, a positron and an electron can be formed. This diagram shows the tracks of the electron and positron in a magnetic field at right angles to the plane that contains their movement:

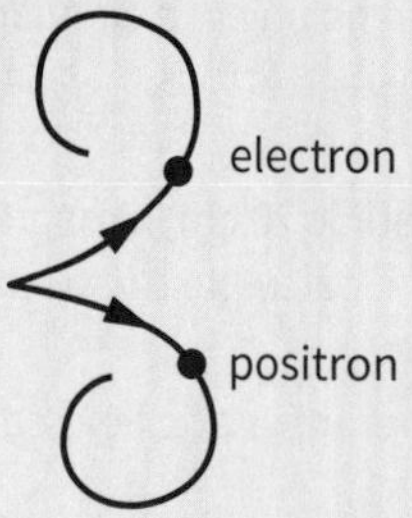

The speed of the electron is known to be equal to the speed of the positron. The tracks start as circles but become spirals.

a Explain how the diagram shows that the charge on the positron is positive. [2]

b Explain how the diagram shows that the specific charge (the ratio of charge to mass) of the two particles is equal. [2]

c Suggest what is happening to the speed of the particles to cause the paths to be spirals rather than circles. Give a reason for your answer. [2]

3 In a Hall effect experiment, a current of 15 A passes through a thin strip of copper of thickness 0.10 mm, as shown:

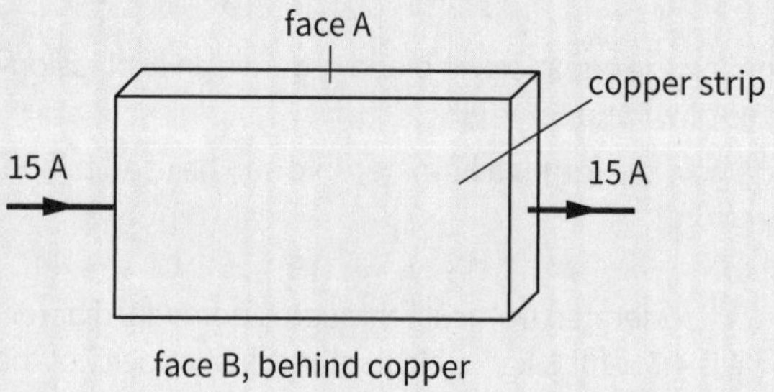

A Hall voltage of 8.8 μV occurs between the two smaller faces, A and B, at the top and bottom of the strip. This is produced by a magnetic field of flux density 0.80 T acting on the strip. Face B is more positive than face A.

a State the direction of the magnetic field acting on the copper strip. Explain your answer. [2]

b Explain why:

i electrons pass in a straight line through the strip, even though there is a magnetic force acting on them [1]

ii increasing the current increases the Hall voltage. [2]

c Calculate the number density of free electrons in the copper. [2]

Chapter outline

- define magnetic flux, magnetic flux linkage and the weber
- recall and use $\Phi = BA$
- infer from appropriate experiments on electromagnetic induction:
  - that a changing magnetic flux can induce an e.m.f. in a circuit
  - that the direction of the induced e.m.f. opposes the change producing it
  - the factors affecting the magnitude of the induced e.m.f.
- recall and solve problems using Faraday's law of electromagnetic induction and Lenz's law
- explain simple applications of electromagnetic induction

KEY TERMS

Faraday's law of electromagnetic induction: the induced e.m.f. is proportional to the rate of change of magnetic flux linkage

Lenz's law: an induced current or e.m.f. acts in such a direction so as to produce effects which oppose the change producing it

magnetic flux: the product of the magnetic flux density perpendicular to a circuit and the cross-sectional area of the circuit

magnetic flux linkage: the product of magnetic flux through a coil and the number of turns in a coil

weber: the flux that passes through an area of 1 m^2 when the magnetic flux density is 1 T. It is also the flux change per second linking a 1 turn coil which produces 1 V in the coil

Equations: flux $\Phi = BA$

flux linkage $= N\Phi = NBA$

induced e.m.f. $V = \dfrac{\Delta(N\Phi)}{\Delta t}$

Exercise 28.1 Flux, flux density and flux linkage

This exercise explores the meanings of the terms *flux*, *flux density* and *flux linkage*, and some of their applications. You will need to think clearly about the angle between a coil and a magnetic field. This angle may be the angle between the plane of the coil and the field or between the normal to the plane of the coil (the axis of the coil) and the field. These angles are not the same.

1 Match the terms with the correct definitions:

Term	Definition
magnetic flux	the magnetic flux that passes through an area of 1 m^2 when the magnetic flux density is 1 T
magnetic flux linkage	magnetic flux through a circuit times the number of turns
magnetic flux density	the magnetic flux density perpendicular to a circuit multiplied by the cross-sectional area of the circuit
the weber	the strength of a field equal to the force per unit length on a wire carrying unit current at right angles to the field

2 Magnetic fields are drawn with magnetic field lines that pass through coils. The field lines are sometimes close together and sometimes far apart.

a Describe briefly the difference between *magnetic flux density*, *magnetic flux* and *magnetic flux linkage* in terms of magnetic field lines.

b State the units of magnetic flux, magnetic flux density and magnetic flux linkage.

c The primary coil of an ideal transformer carries a direct current. Suggest why the magnetic flux through the primary and secondary coils is the same but the magnetic flux linkage is different.

3 A physicist has a ring of area 1.8×10^{-4} m^2. The Earth's magnetic field is 5.0×10^{-5} T.

a Describe how she places the ring so that the magnetic flux through the ring is as large as possible.

b Calculate the maximum value of the magnetic flux through the ring.

c Explain why the magnetic flux linkage and the magnetic flux through the ring are the same.

4 A flat coil of *N* turns has area A. The coil is placed so that the plane of the coil is at an angle θ to a magnetic field of magnetic flux density *B*:

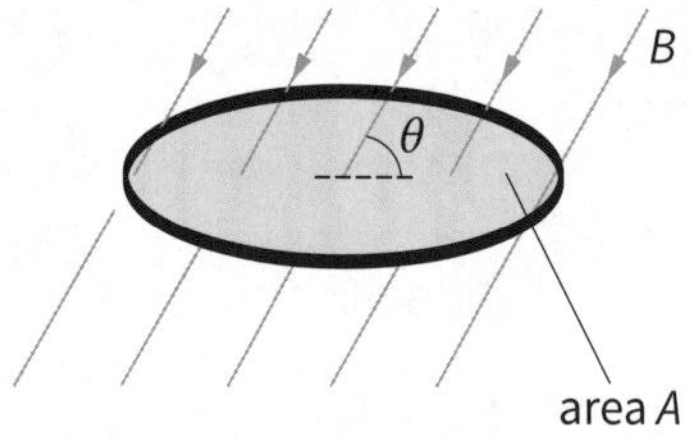

Use the definition of magnetic flux and magnetic flux linkage to show that the magnetic flux linkage through the coil is $NBA \sin \theta$.

5 A coil of cross-sectional area 2.5×10^{-4} m^2 is placed in a magnetic field of magnetic flux density 0.028 T. Calculate the magnetic flux through the coil when the plane of the coil is:

a perpendicular to the field

b at 0° to the field

c at 30° to the field.

6 A square coil of side 2.0 cm has 50 turns. It is placed in a magnetic field of magnetic flux density 2.8×10^{-2} T. Calculate the flux linkage through the coil when the angle between the plane of the coil and the field is 35°. (Take care: the units of area have to be in m^2).

7 A coil of cross-sectional area 2.0×10^{-4} m^2 is placed in a field of magnetic flux density 0.010 T. The magnetic flux linkage through the coil is 3.0×10^{-5} T. Calculate:

a the magnetic flux through the coil

b the number of turns in the coil.

Exercise 28.2 Faraday's and Lenz's laws

1 Describe an experiment in which Faraday's law of electromagnetic induction is demonstrated. You should include:

- **a** a labelled diagram of the apparatus
- **b** an explanation as to how the results or observations demonstrate Faraday's law.

2 A magnet is dropped vertically through a coil of wire. This diagram shows the current induced in the coil with time:

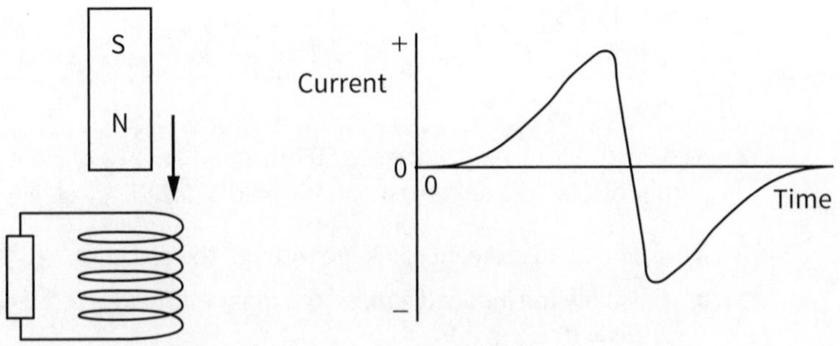

The current in the coil makes the coil into an electromagnet.

- **a** State why there is an induced current in the coil.
- **b** As the N-pole approaches the top of the coil, state whether the top of the coil is a N-pole or a S-pole. Explain your idea using Lenz's law.
- **c** As the S-pole leaves the bottom of the coil, state whether the bottom of the coil is a N-pole or a S-pole. Explain your idea using Lenz's law.
- **d** Use Faraday's law to explain why the negative peak is larger in value than the positive peak.
- **e** State two changes that could be made to the experiment to increase the induced current.

3 A generator contains a coil rotating in a magnetic field, as shown:

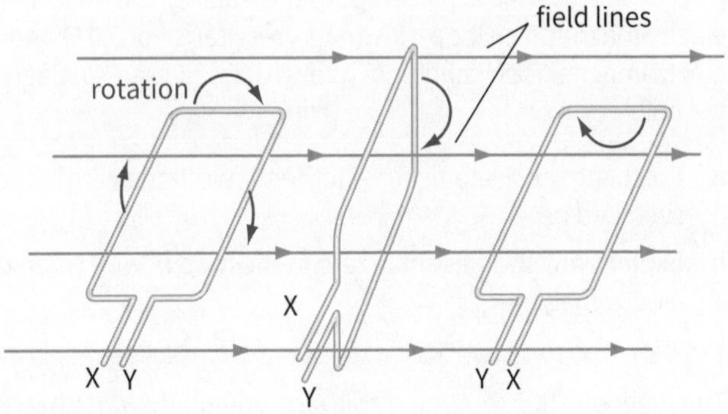

- **a** Use ideas about the magnetic flux through the coil to explain why there is an induced e.m.f. in the coil.
- **b** Use Faraday's law to explain why the induced e.m.f. is a maximum when the coils are horizontal in the diagram.
- **c** State two ways in which the size of the induced e.m.f. can be increased. Explain your answer using ideas about flux linkage and Faraday's law.

Exercise 28.3 Faraday's law in more detail

This exercise provides more practice in performing calculations using Faraday's law.

1 Which three of these units are equivalent to $Wb\ s^{-1}$, the rate of change of flux linkage?

- $J\ s^{-1}$
- $J\ C^{-1}$
- $V\ s^{-1}$
- V
- $T\ m^2\ s^{-1}$
- $T\ m^2$

2 A coil with a total resistance has 50 turns and an area of $8.0 \times 10^{-4}\ m^2$. The coil is placed perpendicular to a uniform magnetic field of 0.20 T.

a Calculate the total flux linkage through the coil.

b Calculate the induced e.m.f. if the magnetic field is reduced to zero in 50 ms. ($1\ ms = 10^{-3}\ s$)

c Calculate the induced e.m.f. if the magnetic field is *reversed* in 50 ms.

3 A coil has 3000 turns and a cross-sectional area of $2.0 \times 10^{-4}\ m^2$. Calculate the change in magnetic flux density every second that causes an induced e.m.f. of 12 V in the coil.

4 A coil with 200 turns and cross-sectional area $1.6 \times 10^{-3}\ m^2$ is placed in a uniform magnetic field of flux density 0.090 T. When the coil is pulled out of the magnetic field, the average e.m.f. induced in the coil is 15 V. Estimate the time taken to pull the coil out of the magnetic field.

5 A single loop of wire is placed perpendicular to the uniform magnetic field produced by an electromagnet. The loop of wire has resistance of 3.6 Ω and area of $6.0 \times 10^{-4}\ m^2$. When the electromagnet is switched on, it takes 0.6 s to reach a magnetic flux density of 5.0×10^{-4} T within the coil.

a Calculate the average current that flows in the wire in the 0.6 s after the electromagnet is switched on.

b Explain why the current is zero in the loop of wire when there is a steady current in the electromagnet.

6 The magnetic flux through a coil varies regularly with time as a sine wave. The maximum value of the flux through the coil is $+\theta_0$. Explain why:

a The induced e.m.f. in the coil is zero when the flux has the value $+\theta_0$.

b The induced e.m.f has the largest value when the flux is zero.

7 This diagram shows how the magnetic flux linkage through a coil varies with time:

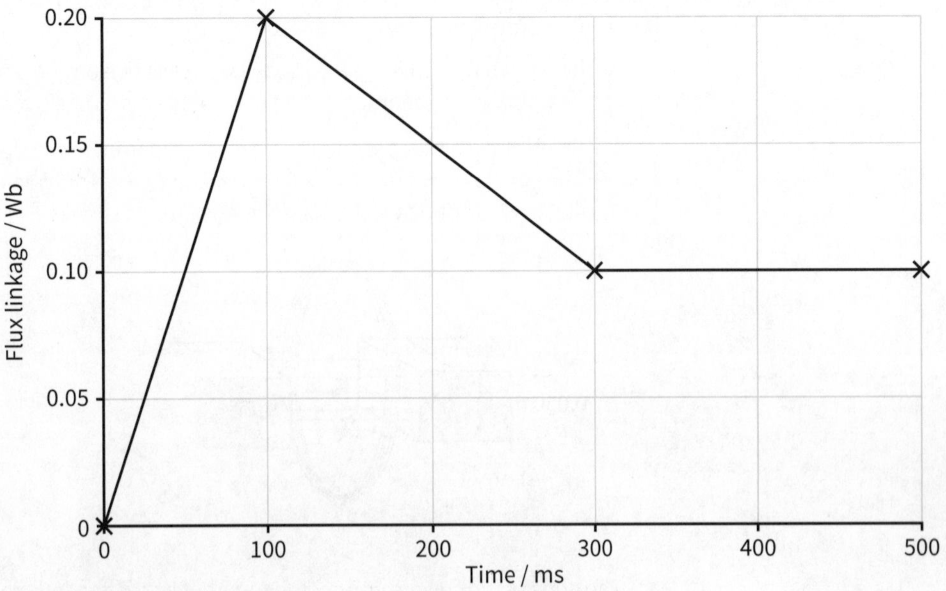

Calculate the induced e.m.f. between:

a 0 and 100 ms

b 100 and 300 ms

c 300 and 500 ms.

8 This graph shows the variation of flux linkage through a coil with time:

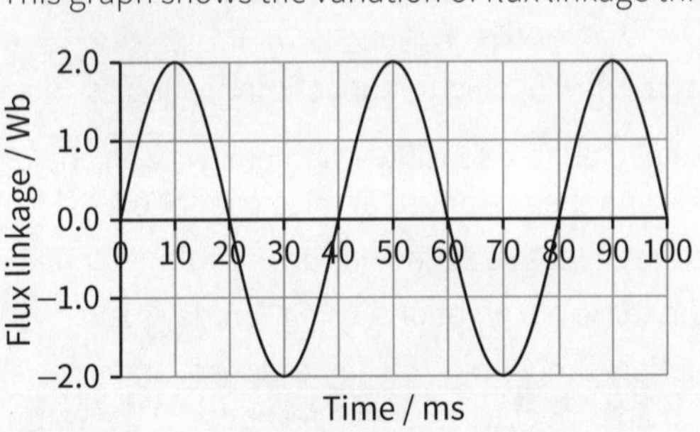

a State a time at which the e.m.f. induced in the coil has a maximum value.

b State a time at which the e.m.f. induced in the coil is zero.

c State the physical quantity that is equal to the gradient of the graph.

d Take readings from the graph to estimate the maximum value of the e.m.f. induced in the coil.
(You can place a ruler along the curve at the point where the e.m.f. is largest.)

e If the cross-sectional area of the coil is 1.6×10^{-2} m^2 and it contains 500 turns, calculate the maximum value of the magnetic flux density.

Exam-style questions

1 a i State Lenz's law. [2]

ii You have available a coil of wire, a sensitive ammeter and a bar magnet. Describe a simple experiment using this apparatus to illustrate Lenz's law. [2]

b An electromagnet produces a uniform field from left to right in the gap between its poles. The gap has sides 0.050 m × 0.080 m and there is no field outside the gap. A circular coil of 40 turns surrounds all of the magnetic flux, as shown:

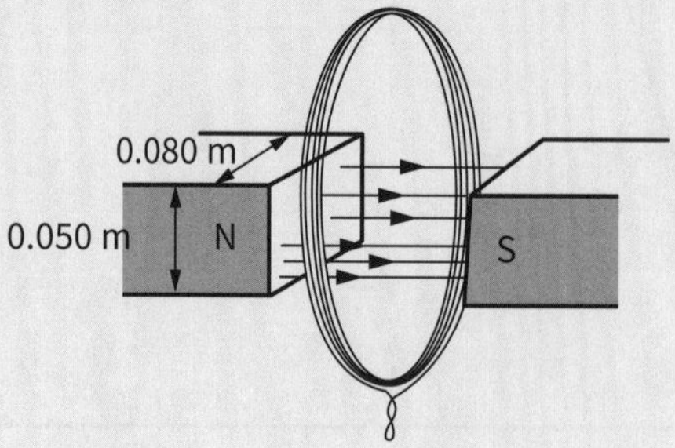

The ends of the coil are connected together so that an induced e.m.f. in the coil produces a current in the coil.

The magnetic field of the electromagnet falls linearly from 0.15 T to zero in a time of 3.0 s.

i Calculate the initial flux linkage through the coil. [2]

ii Calculate the induced e.m.f. in the coil as the magnet field decreases. [2]

iii State and explain the direction of the magnetic field created by the current in the coil when the field of the electromagnet decreases. [2]

2 a State Faraday's law of electromagnetic induction. [2]

b A coil is connected to a sensitive voltmeter with an analogue display. A bar magnet is pushed into the coil and then removed at the same speed.

i State the effect this action has on the voltmeter reading. [2]

ii Explain these observations, using Faraday's law. [2]

iii The action is repeated at a higher speed. State and explain what difference you would expect to see in the response of the voltmeter. [2]

c A rectangular coil is rotating at constant angular speed with its axle perpendicular to a uniform magnetic field of 0.15 T:

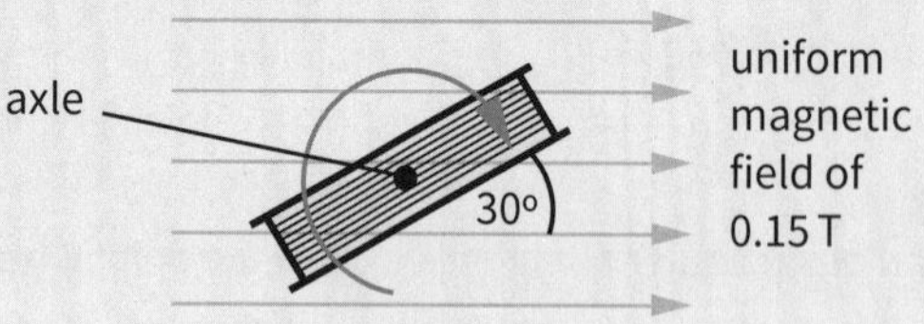

At the instant shown, the angle between the plane of the coil and the magnetic field is 30°.

The coil has 50 turns and has a cross-sectional area of 4.0×10^{-4} m^2.

i Calculate the flux through the coil in the position shown. [2]

ii The coil moves from the position shown to a position where the flux through the coil is zero. The change takes a time of 0.25 s. Calculate the average value of the induced e.m.f. in the coil. [2]

iii Explain why the induced e.m.f. is not constant even though the coil is turning at a constant angular speed. [2]

Chapter outline

- understand and use the terms period, frequency, peak value and root-mean-square value
- deduce that the mean power in a resistive load is half the maximum power
- represent a sinusoidally alternating current or voltage by an equation of the form $x = x_0 \sin\omega t$
- recall the relationship $I = \frac{I_0}{\sqrt{2}}$ and use it to solve problems
- describe the operation of a transformer and the sources of energy loss
- recall and solve problems using $\frac{N_s}{N_p} = \frac{V_s}{V_p} = \frac{I_p}{I_s}$ for an ideal transformer
- describe the advantages of alternating current and high voltage for the transmission of electrical energy
- explain and distinguish between half-wave rectification and full-wave rectification, and describe the use of a capacitor in smoothing

KEY TERMS

root-mean-square (r.m.s.) current or voltage: the square root of the average value of the square of the current or voltage; numerically equal to the steady d.c. current or voltage that produces the same heating effect in a pure resistance

half-wave rectification: the conversion of one half of a cycle of an alternating current into a direct current, in only one direction

full-wave rectification: the conversion of both halves of a cycle of an alternating current into a direct current, in only one direction

Equations: $I_{rms} = \frac{I_0}{\sqrt{2}}$

$x = x_0 \sin\omega t$

$\frac{N_s}{N_p} = \frac{V_s}{V_p} = \frac{I_p}{I_s}$

$P = VI = I^2R$

Exercise 29.1 Understanding the terms used for alternating current and power

This exercise gives you practice in using the terms used to describe alternating current and in understanding the difference between alternating and direct current.

1 Distinguish between *direct current* and *alternating current*.

2 An alternating voltage is connected to a resistor. Explain how heat is produced in the resistor, even though the average current is zero and there is a current in both directions.

3 Explain what is meant by the r.m.s. value of an alternating current. Include in your ideas the heating effect of the alternating current.

4 Using the formula $I_{rms} = \frac{I_0}{\sqrt{2}}$, show that:

for a.c., $\frac{\text{maximum power converted in resistor}}{\text{average power converted in resistor}} = 2$

5 This graph shows the alternating p.d. (voltage) across a resistor:

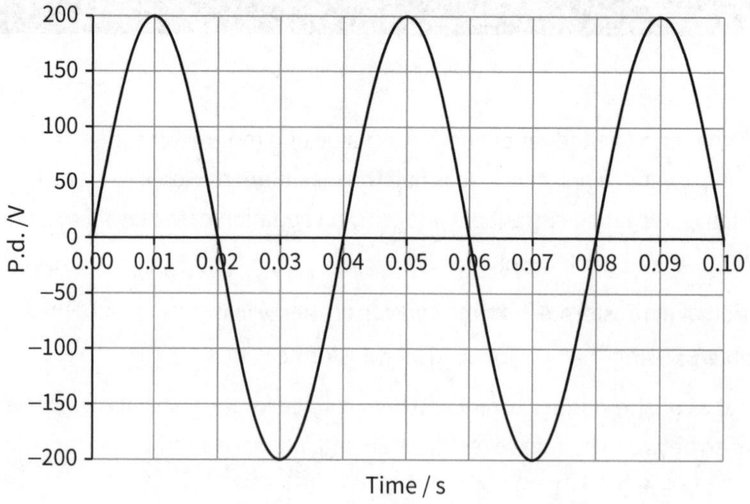

The resistance of the resistor is 50 Ω.

Use the graph to calculate:

- **a** the period of the alternating voltage
- **b** the frequency of the supply
- **c** the peak voltage
- **d** the r.m.s. voltage
- **e** the average voltage
- **f** the peak current
- **g** the r.m.s. current
- **h** the peak power
- **i** the average power.

6 Unless stated otherwise, electrical ratings are r.m.s. values.

An electrical device is rated at 250 V, 1000 W.

Calculate:

- **a** the peak voltage
- **b** the r.m.s. current
- **c** the peak current
- **d** the peak power.

7 An alternating current, I is defined by the equation:

$I = I_0 \sin \omega t$

where I_0 is the peak current and ω is the angular frequency of the supply.

For a particular circuit, $I = 4 \sin 200t$ where I is measured in A and t in s.

Calculate:

- **a** the peak value of the current
- **b** the r.m.s. value of the current
- **c** the frequency of the supply.

Exercise 29.2 The transformer

This exercise gives you practice in describing how a transformer works and with the equations that are used with an ideal transformer.

1 This diagram shows a simple transformer:

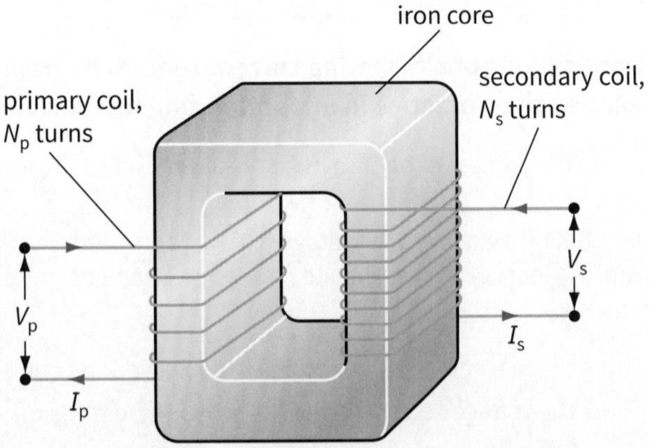

a Explain how an e.m.f. is induced in the secondary coil.

b State why the transformer does not work if a d.c. voltage is applied to the primary coil.

c State what is meant by an *ideal* transformer.

d Explain how induction causes the production of heat in the core.

e Explain why the core is laminated (made out of thin sheets).

f Apart from heat produced in the core by induction, state one other source of energy loss.

g Suggest why thicker wire is used for the coil with the larger current.

2 An ideal transformer has 6000 turns on its primary coil. It is to be used to convert 230 V to 9.0 V. Calculate the number of turns on the secondary coil.

3 An ideal transformer has 200 turns on the primary coil and 6000 turns on the secondary coil. It is connected to a resistor. The root-mean-square input voltage to the primary coil is 6.0 V. Calculate the peak voltage across the secondary coil. (Hint: find the r.m.s. voltage first.)

4 An ideal transformer steps down voltage from 240 V to 16 V. The r.m.s. current in the secondary coil is 3.3 A. Calculate the r.m.s. current in the primary coil.

5 Electrical power is transmitted over a long distance from a generator to some equipment. The cables have a total resistance of 0.20 Ω and the current is 0.50 A.

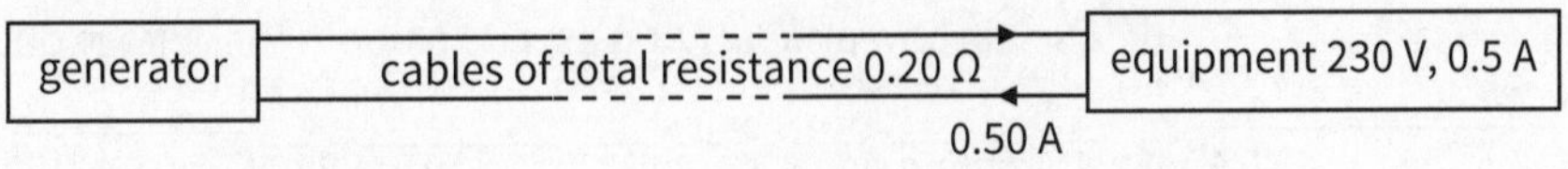

a Calculate the power loss in the cables. (Take care: the p.d. across the 0.20 Ω is not 230 V).

Ideal transformers are used at either end. There is a p.d. of 2300 V at one end of the cables between points P and Q. A transformer steps this voltage down to 230 V for the equipment, which still draws 0.50 A.

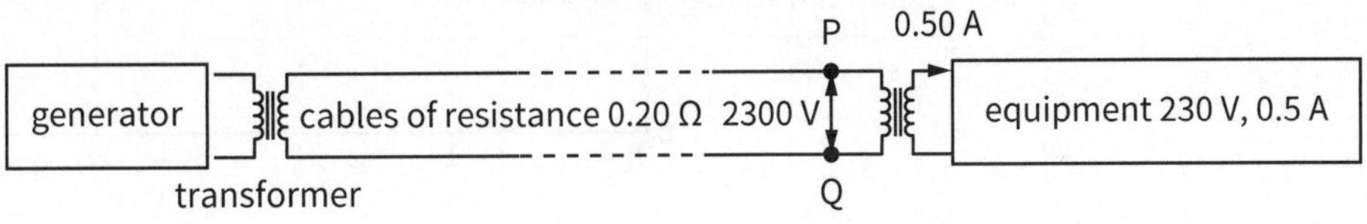

b Calculate the current in the cables.

c Calculate the power provided to the equipment.

d Calculate the power lost in the cables.

e Explain in words how this example shows why electrical power is transmitted at very high voltages.

Exercise 29.3 Rectification

Many applications of alternating current require its transformation to direct current. This exercise gives practice in understanding full-wave and half-wave rectification.

1 Describe the process of half-wave rectification using a single diode.

2 An alternating signal of peak voltage 6.0 V is connected in series to an ideal diode and a pure resistor. An ideal diode has infinite resistance when not conducting and no p.d. across it when conducting.

a State the maximum voltage across the diode during one cycle.

b State the voltage across the resistor when there is the maximum voltage across the diode.

3 This diagram shows a full-wave bridge rectifier:

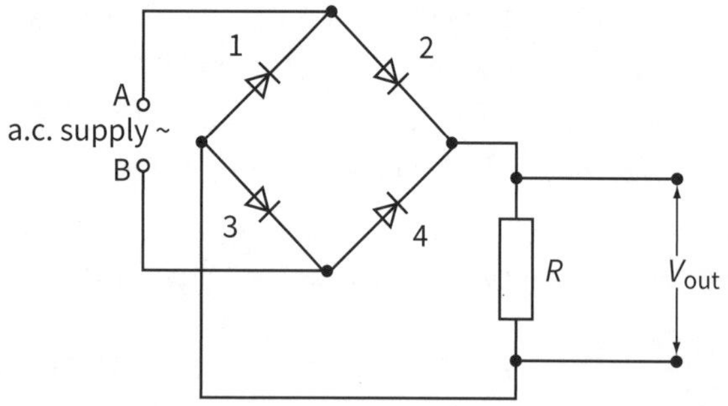

Complete these sentences to explain which diodes the current passes through:

a When the AC supply makes A positive and B negative, the current flows in diodes __ and __

b When the AC input makes B positive and A negative, the current flows in diodes __ and __

c The current from the supply is __________ but the current in *R* is __________

4 a Describe the difference between the voltage obtained after half-wave rectification and after full-wave rectification

b State one advantage of full-wave rectification when compared to half-wave rectification.

c Explain what is meant by *smoothing* the voltage obtained after rectification.

d Explain how a capacitor is used to smooth the voltage obtained after rectification.

5 An alternating signal is connected to an ideal full-wave rectifier. This diagram shows the voltage across a load resistor connected to the output:

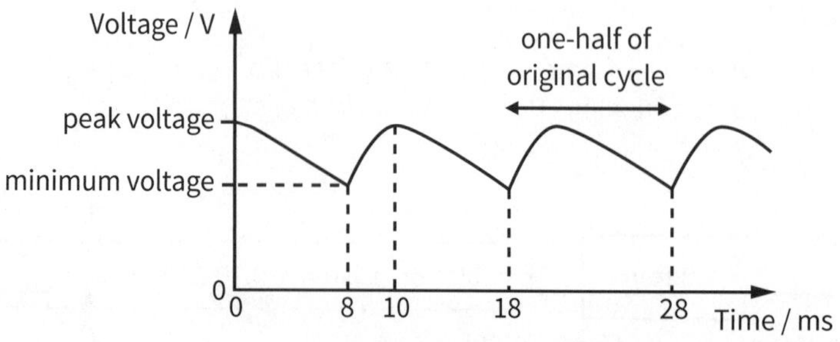

The voltage is partially smoothed by a capacitor across the resistor.

Remember 1 ms = 0.001 s.

a Determine the length of time in each half-cycle during which the capacitor is charging.

b Determine the length of time in each half-cycle during which the capacitor is discharging.

c Calculate the frequency of the original alternating supply. As the original waveform is full-wave rectified, you need to work out the time for the whole of an original cycle and then calculate frequency.

The resistance of the resistor is increased and the output is smoother.

d State what happens to the peak voltage reached.

e State what happens to the minimum voltage during one cycle.

f State what happens to the time taken to charge the capacitor in each half-cycle.

g State what happens to the time taken to discharge the capacitor in each half-cycle.

h State what change in the capacitor would produce the same change as increasing the resistance of the resistor.

Exam-style questions

1 The alternating mains electricity supplied to a house has a root mean square voltage V_{rms} of 230 V and a frequency of 50 Hz.

a **i** State what is meant by *root mean square voltage*. [1]

ii Calculate the peak value of the supply voltage V_0. [2]

iii Calculate the mean voltage V. [1]

b The alternating supply is connected in series with a resistor of resistance 5.9 kΩ. Calculate the peak power dissipated in the resistor. [2]

c Sketch the graph of the supply voltage against time for two complete periods. Label the axes with appropriate values. [2]

2 This diagram shows a transformer used to provide power to a lamp:

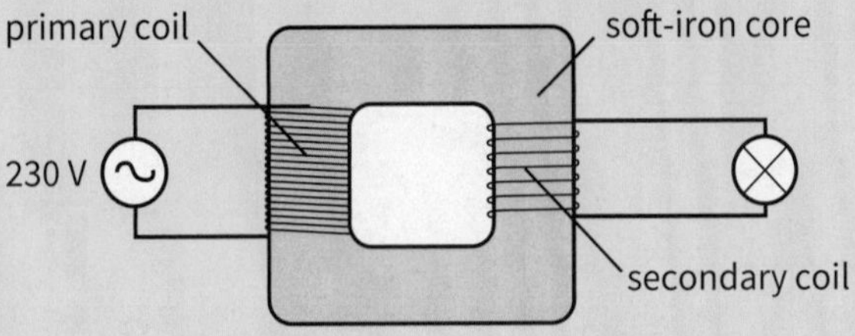

a Use Faraday's law of electromagnetic induction to explain how the transformer works. [3]

b Suggest why:

i there is a soft-iron core [1]

ii the core is laminated. [1]

c The transformer has 1600 turns in the primary coil and is connected to the mains supply which has an r.m.s. value of 230 V. The peak voltage across the secondary coil is 13 V. The electrical power supplied to the transformer is 15 W. Assuming the transformer is ideal, calculate:

i the number of turns in the secondary coil [2]

ii the r.m.s. current in the primary coil [2]

iii the r.m.s. current in the secondary coil. [2]

d State two advantages of the use of alternating voltage for the transmission of electrical power. [2]

3 The diagram shows how the output voltage *V* across a load resistor, connected to a power supply, varies with time. Inside the power supply, an alternating voltage is connected to a rectifier and a capacitor. The capacitor is connected in parallel to the load resistor.

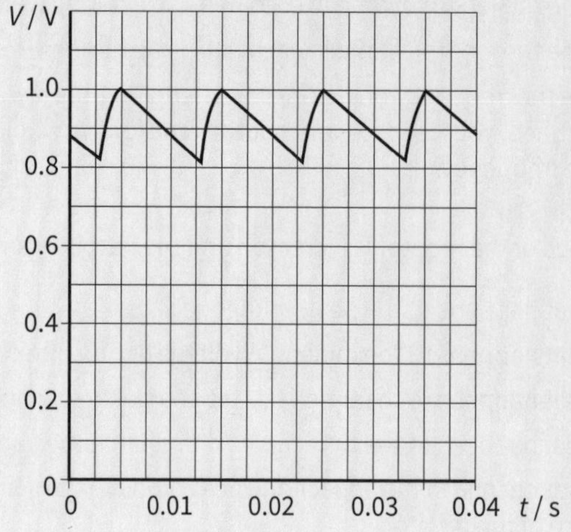

a State:

i how the diagram shows that the current in the load resistor is direct current [1]

ii the type of rectifier used. [1]

b The diodes used in the rectifier are ideal diodes. Determine the original alternating supply's:

i peak voltage [1]

ii root-mean-square voltage [2]

iii frequency. [2]

c Explain why the output voltage rises and falls, and suggest how the smoothing can be increased using the same load resistor. [4]

Chapter outline

- describe evidence for the particulate and wave nature of electromagnetic radiation
- recall and use $E = hf$
- explain the photoelectric effect in terms of photon energy, work function energy and the threshold frequency, and recall use and explain the significance of $hf = \phi + \frac{1}{2}mv^2_{max}$
- explain why the maximum photoelectric energy is independent of intensity, whereas the photoelectric current is proportional to intensity
- explain how discrete electron energy levels in isolated atoms produce spectral lines
- distinguish between emission and absorption line spectra
- recall and solve problems using the relation $hf = E_1 - E_2$
- describe band theory using the terms valence band, conduction band and forbidden band (band gap), and use it to explain the temperature dependence or light dependence of resistance in some materials
- describe and interpret the evidence provided by electron diffraction for the wave nature of particles
- recall and use the relation for the de Broglie wavelength $\lambda = \frac{h}{p}$

KEY TERMS

photoelectric effect: the emission of an electron from the surface of a metal when light shines on the surface

threshold frequency: the minimum frequency of electromagnetic radiation that will eject electrons from the surface of a metal

photon: a particle of electromagnetic radiation containing a discrete amount of energy

quantum: the smallest amount of a quantity that exists independently, particularly the smallest amount of electromagnetic radiation that can be emitted or absorbed

work function: the minimum energy required by a single electron to escape from a metal surface

emission line spectrum: a pattern of bright lines or discrete wavelengths emitted by atoms

absorption line spectrum: a pattern of dark lines or discrete wavelengths caused by the absorption of electromagnetic radiation

valence band: a range of electron energies in a solid in which electrons are bound to individual atoms

conduction band: a range of electron energies in a solid in which electrons are free to move throughout the material

forbidden band (band gap): a range of energy values which an electron in a solid cannot have

de Broglie wavelength: the wavelength associated with a moving particle

Equations: $c = f\lambda$

$$E = hf$$

$$hf = \phi + \frac{1}{2}mv^2_{max}$$

$$hf = E_1 - E_2$$

$$\lambda = \frac{h}{p}$$

Exercise 30.1 Light: wave or particle?

You can imagine the wave properties of light by thinking of light as an oscillating electric and magnetic field moving through space, just as a boat on the surface of water oscillates as a water wave moves through water. You can imagine the particle properties of light by thinking of light as many cars all moving at the same, fast speed along a road, carrying energy. This exercise is about these ideas.

The Planck constant, $h = 6.63 \times 10^{-34}$ J s.

1 Light shows wave properties such as reflection, refraction, diffraction and interference.

- **a** State which two of these properties best suggest that light is a wave rather than a particle.
- **b** Describe how the dark positions in Young's double-slits pattern can be explained if light is a wave, but cannot be explained if light is a series of particles.

2 a Describe what happens in *photoelectric emission*.

- **b** Describe an experiment that demonstrates photoelectric emission.

3 The wave theory tries to explain photoelectric emission as the slow absorption of energy by electrons from the wave, eventually giving them enough energy to escape. However, various observations in photoelectric emission suggest that light has particle properties, one of which is that there is a threshold frequency.

- **a** State what is meant by *threshold frequency*.
- **b** Explain how it is difficult to explain a threshold frequency using wave theory.
- **c** Explain how threshold frequency is explained in the particle theory, if the energy of the photon depends on frequency.
- **d** State two other observations about photoelectric emission that suggest light has particle properties.

4 The light from a lamp is made brighter but the colour is kept the same.

- **a** Use wave theory to state what happens to the amplitude, frequency and speed of the light.
- **b** Use particle theory to state what happens to the energy of a photon and the number of photons emitted per second.

The light causes photoelectric emission. The light intensity is steadily increased.

- **c** State what happens to the maximum energy of the emitted electrons.
- **d** State what happens to the number of electrons emitted per second.

5 Light from a source does not cause photoelectric emission when it hits a metal surface. A student suggests making the light brighter will then allow photoelectric emission to occur.

- **a** Use the particle theory to explain why this is wrong.
- **b** Suggest two changes that may allow photoelectric emission to occur.

6 a Calculate the energy of a photon with a frequency of 6.0×10^{14} Hz.

- **b** Calculate the energy of a photon with a wavelength of 4.0×10^{-7} m.

7 A lamp emits 10 J of energy each second as light of frequency 5.0×10^{14} Hz.

- **a** Calculate the energy of one photon of this light.
- **b** Calculate the number of photons emitted per second.

8 Light is incident on a metal surface, and causes photoelectric emission. The frequency of the light is increased, but the total amount of light energy incident on the surface each second is constant.

a State what happens to the energy of each photon.

b State what happens to the number of photons per second in the incident light.

c State what happens to the rate of emission of the electrons from the surface.

d State what happens to the maximum kinetic energy of an electron emitted from the surface.

Exercise 30.2 The photoelectric equation

This exercise provides practice in understanding and using the photoelectric equation.

energy of photon = work function energy + maximum kinetic energy of electron emitted

speed of electromagnetic radiation, $c = 3.0 \times 10^{8}$ m s^{-1}

The Planck constant, $h = 6.63 \times 10^{-34}$ J s

1 a Explain the term *photon*.

b State what is meant by *work function energy*.

c Explain why the equation gives a maximum value for the energy of the emitted electron.

d Suggest why only a few electrons are emitted with the maximum kinetic energy.

2 Photons with energy 1.2×10^{-18} J are incident on a metal surface. The maximum energy of electrons emitted from the surface is 5.0×10^{-19} J. Calculate the work function of the metal.

3 Radiation of wavelength 3.0×10^{-7} m falls on a sodium surface. Sodium has a work function of 3.6×10^{-19} J. Calculate the maximum kinetic energy of the electrons emitted.

4 In a photoelectric experiment, electrons of maximum kinetic energy 1.5×10^{-19} J are emitted from a metal surface of work function 3.2×10^{-19} J. Calculate the frequency of the incident radiation.

5 When light of frequency 5.3×10^{14} Hz is incident on a metal surface, electrons are emitted with almost zero kinetic energy.

a State the threshold frequency of the material of the surface.

b Calculate the work function of the surface.

c Calculate the maximum kinetic energy of electrons emitted when light of frequency 6.0×10^{14} Hz is used.

6 When electromagnetic radiation of wavelength 400 nm strikes a metal surface, the maximum kinetic energy of the emitted electrons is 1.2×10^{-19} J. Calculate the work function of the metal.

7 The work functions of sodium and zinc are 3.6×10^{-19} J and 6.9×10^{-19} J respectively. Explain why only one metal emits electrons when light of frequency 6.0×10^{14} Hz is incident on the surface.

8 This graph shows the variation with frequency f of the maximum kinetic energy E_K of the electrons emitted from the surface of a metal:

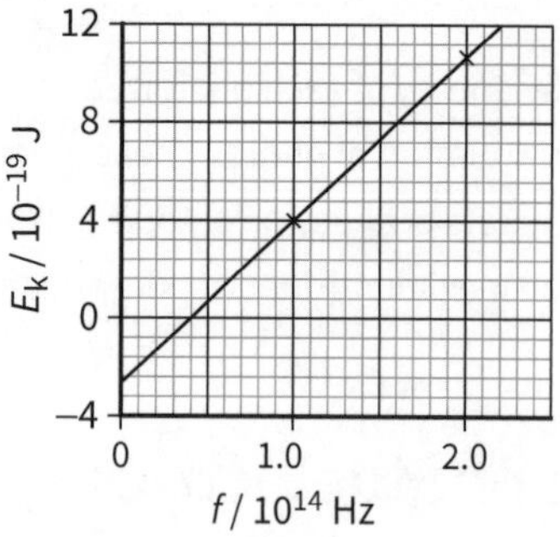

a Use the photoelectric equation to show that the gradient of the graph is equal to Planck's constant.

b Obtain a value for Planck's constant from the graph.

c State how the work function energy ϕ can be obtained from the graph.

d Obtain a value for the work function energy.

Imagine that the graph is redrawn for a metal with a smaller work function.

e State how the gradient and intercept of the new graph compare with the old graph.

Exercise 30.3 Line spectra and band theory

This exercise tests your understanding and interpretation of line spectra, and gives you practice calculating energies including band gaps.

1 This diagram shows energy levels of the hydrogen atom:

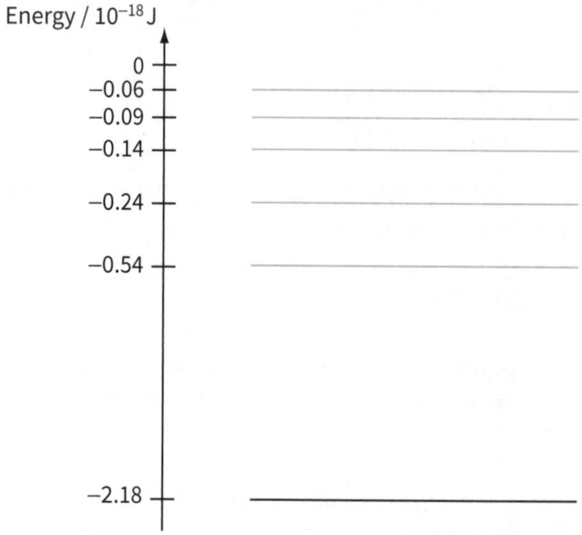

An electron is on the energy level at -0.24×10^{-18} J. The electron can emit or absorb a photon to change levels.

a Complete this table to show the energy of the photon, and state whether the electron emits or absorbs a photon to move to the new level:

Energy of new level	Energy of photon emitted or absorbed	Does the electron emit or absorb a photon to move to the new level?
-0.54×10^{-18} J		
-0.14×10^{-18} J		
-2.18×10^{-18} J		
-0.09×10^{-18} J		

b Apart from absorbing a photon, suggest two other ways in which the electron can be made to move to a higher level.

2 **a** Describe the difference between an *emission* line spectrum and an *absorption* line spectrum.

b Explain why the lines in an emission line spectrum of a gas occur at the same wavelengths as the lines in the absorption line spectrum of the same gas.

c Describe how to show an emission line spectrum of a gas.

d Describe how to show an absorption line spectrum of a gas.

3 This diagram shows four energy levels of the helium atom:

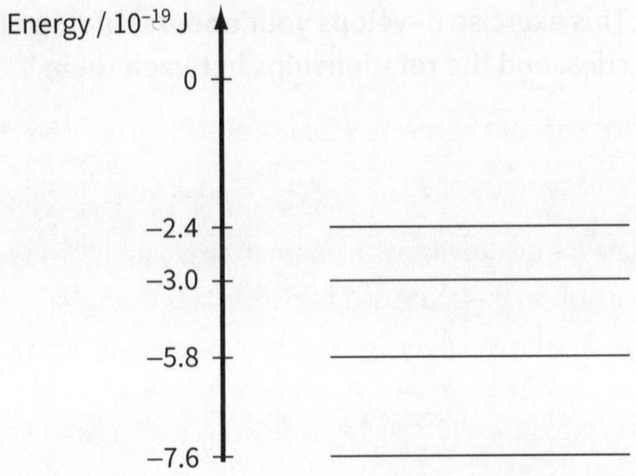

An emission line spectrum is formed when electrons move between these levels.

a Show how six different lines are found in the spectrum involving these levels.

b State the two levels associated with the line in the spectrum with the highest frequency.

c For the line in the spectrum with the highest frequency, calculate the energy of the photon emitted.

d State the two levels associated with the line in the spectrum with the highest wavelength.

4 Red light of frequency 5.0×10^{14} Hz is incident on a light-dependent resistor (LDR).

The forbidden band (band gap) between the valence and conduction bands of the LDR is 1.5 eV.

a Explain what is meant by the *forbidden band*.

b Show that the energy of a photon of the red light is greater than the band gap energy.

c Explain, using band theory, what happens when the light is incident on the LDR and why the resistance of the LDR decreases as the intensity of the red light increases.

d Calculate the minimum frequency of radiation that causes electrons to move across the forbidden band.

5 This diagram shows the valence and conduction bands in silicon, an intrinsic semiconductor:

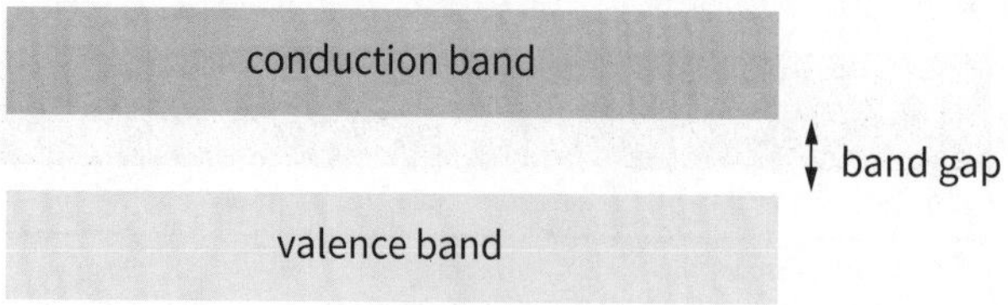

The energy band gap in silicon is 1.1 eV.

a State what is meant by the *conduction band*.

b Calculate the maximum wavelength of electromagnetic radiation that allows an electron to cross the band gap.

c The average thermal kinetic energy of an electron at room temperature is 0.04 eV. A student suggests that an increase in temperature produces more electrons in the conduction band and decreases resistance. Explain why the student is wrong for normal temperatures.

d Suggest why the resistance of a resistor increases with temperature.

Exercise 30.4 De Broglie

Electrons can be shown to have wave properties, even though they have particle properties. This exercise develops your understanding of the different particle and wave properties, and the relationships between them.

1 Explain what is meant by the *de Broglie wavelength* of an electron.

2 An electron has a mass of 9.11×10^{-31} kg. Planck's constant h is 6.63×10^{-34} J s.

a Calculate the de Broglie wavelength of an electron if its speed is 1.6×10^{6} m/s.

b Calculate the momentum of an electron if its kinetic energy is 4.0×10^{-16} J.

c Calculate the de Broglie wavelength of the electron if its kinetic energy is 4.0×10^{-16} J.

3 A neutron of mass 1.7×10^{-27} kg has a de Broglie wavelength of 5.0×10^{-12} m.

a Calculate its momentum.

b Calculate its speed.

4 Electron energies are often given in *electronvolts* (eV). 1 eV = 1.6×10^{-19} J.

An electron is accelerated from rest through a potential difference of 1000 V.

a Calculate the final kinetic energy of the electron in J.

b Determine the final speed of the electron.

c Calculate the final momentum of the electron.

d Calculate the de Broglie wavelength of the electron.

5 Sometimes electrons behave like particles and sometimes they behave like waves.

a State an example of a wave behaviour of an electron.

b State which term in the de Broglie equation $\lambda = \frac{h}{p}$ refers to wave behaviour and which term refers to particle behaviour.

c Show that the de Broglie equation has the same units on each side of the equation.

6 A person of mass 50 kg walks at a speed of 0.20 m s^{-1}.

a Calculate his de Broglie wavelength.

b Suggest why it is difficult to show diffraction with a wave of this wavelength but it is possible to show diffraction with a wave of the wavelength you calculated in question 4.

Exam-style questions

1 In the photoelectric effect, when electromagnetic radiation strikes the surface of a metal, electrons leave the metal surface. However, when radiation of less than a certain frequency strikes the surface, it is observed that there is no emission of electrons.

a Explain why there is no emission of an electron if the frequency is too low. [2]

b State two other pieces of evidence provided by the photoelectric effect which suggest that electromagnetic radiation has particle properties. [2]

c The work function of the metal is 3.8 eV. Calculate the minimum frequency of electromagnetic radiation that causes photoelectric emission. [2]

d An electron at the surface of the metal is emitted with a kinetic energy of 4.5×10^{-19} J. Calculate the energy of the incident photon in eV. [2]

2 Electrons are known to show wave properties, with a wavelength given by the de Broglie equation.

a State the de Broglie equation in words. [1]

b Show that the wavelength of an electron of kinetic energy *E* is given by the equation:

$$\lambda = \frac{h}{\sqrt{(2mE)}}$$

where *m* is the mass of the electron. [2]

c Calculate the de Broglie wavelength of an electron accelerated through a p.d. of 2.0 kV. [2]

d The electrons in part **c** are passed through a crystal structure and diffract. Explain why the electrons are diffracted. [1]

3 a Explain how an emission line spectrum provides evidence for the existence of discrete electron energy levels in atoms. [3]

b Electron transitions between three levels **A**, **B**, and **C** in this energy diagram produce electromagnetic radiation of wavelengths 557 nm and 358 nm:

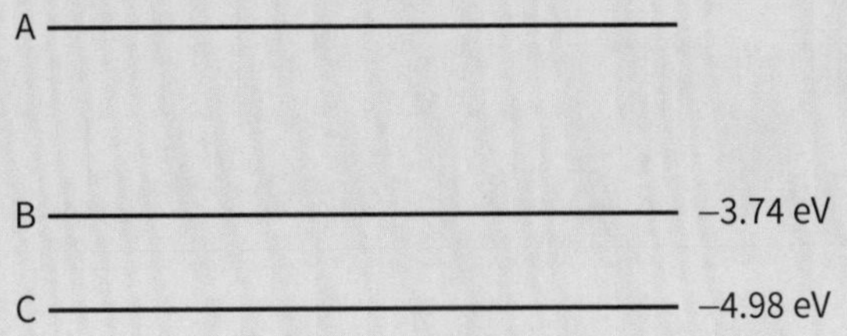

i Calculate the energy of photons of these two wavelengths. [2]

ii Describe the transitions that give rise to each of these two wavelengths. [2]

iii Calculate the value of the energy level **A**. [2]

iv Calculate the wavelength of another line produced by transition between these three levels. [2]

Chapter outline

- recall and use the relationship $E = mc^2$
- define and understand the terms mass defect, mass excess, binding energy, activity, half-life and decay constant
- represent simple nuclear reactions by nuclear equations of the form:
  $^{14}_{7}N + ^{4}_{2}He \rightarrow ^{17}_{8}O + ^{1}_{1}H$
- sketch the variation of binding energy per nucleon with nucleon number
- explain what is meant by nuclear fusion and nuclear fission, and the relevance of binding energy
- describe the spontaneous and random nature of nuclear decay
- recall $A = -\lambda N$ and use it to solve problems
- use the relationship $x = x_0 e^{-\lambda t}$, including sketching exponential decay graphs
- solve problems using the relation $\lambda = \frac{0.693}{t_{1/2}}$

KEY TERMS

mass defect: the difference between the total mass of the individual, separate nucleons and the mass of the nucleus

mass excess: the difference between the mass of a nuclide (in u) and its nucleon number

binding energy: the minimum external energy required to separate all the nucleons in a nucleus to infinity (the neutrons and protons completely separate)

nuclear fusion: a nuclear reaction in which two light nuclei join together to form a heavier nucleus

nuclear fission: the splitting of a nucleus

spontaneous decay: the decay of a nucleus that is not affected by outside factors and occurs because of factors within itself

random decay: the decay of a nucleus that cannot be predicted, producing slightly different counts, above or below a mean value, in the same time interval

half life: the time taken for half the number of active nuclei in a radioactive sample to decay

activity: the number of nuclei that decay per unit time interval in a sample

radioactive decay constant: the probability that an individual nucleus will decay per unit time interval

Equations: $E = mc^2$

$A = -\lambda N$

$x = x_0 e^{-\lambda t}$

$\lambda = \frac{0.693}{t_{1/2}}$

Exercise 31.1 Balancing equations

This exercise provides practice in balancing equations, as well as recognising particles and types of reaction.

1 Determine the particle X in the nuclear reaction:

$^{14}_{7}N + ^{1}_{0}n \rightarrow ^{14}_{6}C + X$

2 A nuclear reaction is:

$$^{235}_{92}U + ^{1}_{0}n \rightarrow ^{90}_{38}Sr + ^{144}_{54}Xe + 2^{x}_{y}X$$

a Determine the value of *x*.

b Determine the value of *y*.

c State the name of the particle $^{x}_{y}X$

d State the name of this type of nuclear reaction.

3 A nuclear reaction is written as $4^{1}_{1}H \rightarrow ^{4}_{2}He + x^{0}_{1}e + 2\nu$ where ν is a neutrino

a Determine the value of *x*.

b State the name of the particle $^{0}_{1}e$.

c State the name of this type of nuclear reaction.

d Explain why high temperatures are needed in order for the $^{1}_{1}H$ particles to come together.

4 A nuclear reaction is written as:

$$^{238}_{92}U \rightarrow ^{x}_{90}Th + ^{4}_{2}He$$

a Determine the value of *x*.

b State the name of the particle $^{4}_{2}He$.

c State the name of this type of nuclear reaction.

5 Helium-3 (proton number 2) absorbs a neutron to become another isotope of helium. Write down the nuclear reaction.

6 A boron-10 nucleus ($^{10}_{5}B$) absorbs a neutron and emits a nucleus of lithium-3 ($^{7}_{3}Li$) and an alpha-particle. Write down the nuclear reaction.

Exercise 31.2 Mass defect, mass excess and binding energy

Mass defect, mass excess, binding energy, nucleon number and proton number are all different quantities for a particular nucleus. This exercise develops your understanding of these terms. You also need to understand that masses can be measured in kg or in terms of the unified atomic mass unit u, and that energy can be measured in joules or electronvolts.

1 Match each quantity with its definition:

Quantity
binding energy
nucleon number
mass excess
mass defect

Definition
the difference between the total mass of the individual, separate nucleons and the mass of the nucleus
the difference between the mass of a nuclide (in u) and its nucleon number
the minimum external energy required to separate all the nucleons in a nucleus to infinity
the total number of protons and neutrons in one nucleus

2 **a** Calculate the energy equivalence of 1.0 g of matter.

(Remember: $E = mc^2$ uses mass in kg).

b Show that 1.0 u has an energy equivalence of 930 MeV. (You will need to look up the mass of 1 u in kg, then use $E = mc^2$. This gives the energy in joules. It is quite easy to remember that the conversion factor between energies in J and in eV is the charge on the electron, $1\,\text{eV} = 1.6 \times 10^{-19}\,\text{J}$).

c Explain why a neutron has no nuclear binding energy.

3 A thorium atom contains 90 electrons outside the nucleus.

- mass of a thorium-228 atom = 228.0278 u
- mass of a bismuth-199 atom = 198.9785 u
- rest mass of electron = 0.000549 u

a Calculate the mass excess of thorium-228, in u.

b Calculate the mass excess of bismuth-199, in u. (Mass excess can be positive or negative).

c Calculate the mass of a thorium-228 *nucleus*, in u.

4 The mass of a thorium-228 nucleus = 3.7857×10^{-25} kg

The rest mass of a proton = 1.6726×10^{-27} kg

The rest mass of a neutron = 1.6749×10^{-27} kg

a Calculate the number of protons and the number of neutrons in one $^{228}_{90}\text{Th}$ nucleus.

b Calculate the total mass, in kg, of all the nucleons when they are separated from the nucleus. Give your answer for **b** to as many significant figures as you can so that the mass defect in **c** is accurate.

c Calculate the mass defect of $^{228}_{90}\text{Th}$, in kg.

d Calculate the binding energy of $^{228}_{90}\text{Th}$, in J.

e Calculate the binding energy of $^{228}_{90}\text{Th}$, in eV.

5 The masses of three particles are:

- helium-4 nucleus = 4.0015 u
- proton = 1.0073 u
- neutron = 1.0087 u.

a Calculate the mass defect of a helium-4 nucleus, in u.

b Calculate the mass defect of a helium-4 nucleus, in kg.

c Calculate the binding energy of a helium-4 nucleus, in J.

d Calculate the binding energy of a helium-4 nucleus, in eV.

6 The binding energy of a $^{2}_{1}\text{H}$ nucleus is 2.24 MeV. A nucleus contains one proton and one neutron.

- rest mass of proton = $1.672\,62 \times 10^{-27}$ kg
- rest mass of neutron = $1.674\,93 \times 10^{-27}$ kg

a Calculate the binding energy of the nucleus, in J.

b Calculate the mass defect of the nucleus, in kg.

c Calculate the total mass of the proton and neutron when separated to infinity, in kg. Keep all significant figures.

d Calculate the mass of the nucleus, in kg.

7 One possible reaction when a neutron strikes a uranium nucleus is:

$^{1}_{0}n + ^{235}_{92}U \rightarrow ^{90}_{36}Kr + ^{144}_{56}Ba + 2^{1}_{0}n$

- mass of $^{1}_{0}n = 1.009$ u
- mass of $^{235}_{92}U = 235.124$ u
- mass of $^{90}_{36}Kr = 89.920$ u
- mass of $^{144}_{56}Ba = 143.923$ u

a Calculate the mass defect of the whole reaction, in u.

b Calculate the energy released, in joules, by one such reaction.

Exercise 31.3 Binding energy per nucleon, fusion and fission

In this exercise you will develop your understanding of the difference between binding energy and binding energy per nucleon and how they are used to calculate the energy released in an nuclear reaction.

1 **a** Complete this table:

Nuclide	Number of nucleons	Binding energy / MeV	Binding energy per nucleon / MeV
$^{235}_{92}U$			7.6
$^{56}_{26}Fe$		492	
$^{87}_{35}Br$			8.6

b State which of the three nuclides in the table is most stable. Explain how the table shows this.

2 A simple nuclear fusion reaction is:

$^{2}_{1}H + ^{2}_{1}H \rightarrow ^{4}_{2}He$

The binding energy per nucleon is $^{4}_{2}He$ is 7.1 and for $^{2}_{1}H$ is 1.1 MeV.

a Calculate the binding energy of $^{2}_{1}H$. (This is for the whole nucleus, not the binding energy per nucleon).

b Calculate the binding energy of $^{4}_{2}He$.

c Calculate the energy released in the nuclear reaction. (If the total binding energy on the left of the equation is different from the total binding energy on the right, then energy must be released – the difference in the totals).

3 This graph shows the binding energy per nucleon plotted against nucleon number:

Binding energy per nucleon / 10^{-13} J per nucleon

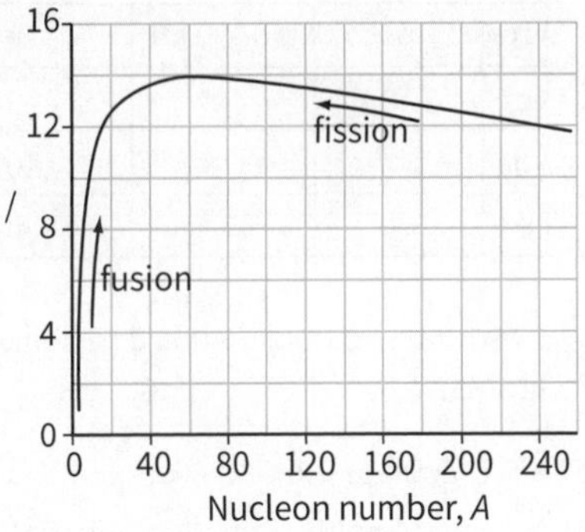

Fission and fusion are nuclear processes that give out energy.

a Use the graph to estimate the nucleon number of the most stable isotope.
b State the difference between fission and fusion in terms of the nuclei involved.
c Use the graph to explain how nuclear fission and nuclear fusion both liberate energy.
d Explain why the energy given out per nucleon from fusion is greater than the energy given out per nucleon from fission.
e Explain why two nuclei of $^{110}_{48}$Cd cannot produce energy by fusing together.
f Use the graph to estimate the binding energy of a U-238 nucleus.
g Use the graph to estimate the binding energy of a nucleus with nucleon number 119.
h In fission, a nucleus of U-238 splits into two nuclei of nucleon number of about 119. Use your answers to **f** and **g** to estimate the energy emitted.
i Use your answer to **h** to calculate the energy released in the fission of 1 g of uranium-238. Remember, 6.02×10^{23} atoms (Avogadro's constant) is contained in one mole of material; in this case, 238 g.

Exercise 31.4 Half-life and the decay constant

This exercise provides practice in determining and using half-lives and decay constants.

The problem is recognising which equation to use.

Use $\lambda = \frac{0.693}{t_{1/2}}$ **to find half-life from the decay constant or vice versa.**

Use $A = -\lambda N$ **to relate activity and number of nuclei** ***at one instant of time.***

Use $x = x_0 e^{-\lambda t}$**, to relate** ***the same quantity*** **at** ***different times; x*** **can be activity or the number of undecayed nuclei.**

Watch out for the units of time. If half-life is measured in ***hours*** **then the decay constant is in** ***hours***$^{-1}$ **and if you then use** $A = -\lambda N$**, the activity** ***A*** **is in number of decays per hour.**

1 Complete this table. Include the units of your answers. You can use the formula $x = x_0 e^{-\lambda t}$ to calculate the last two columns but you may be able to use simple ideas about halving in one half life, particularly in **a** and **e**:

	Half-life	Decay constant	Initial number of nuclei	Initial activity	Number of undecayed nuclei left after 10 s	Activity after 10 s
a	5.0 s		1000			
b		0.0020 s^{-1}		10 Bq		
c	100 s		100			
d			10000	1000 Bq		
e			4000		1000	

2 A radioactive nuclide has a half-life of 300 minutes. It initially contains 1.8×10^6 radioactive atoms.

a Calculate the decay constant of the nuclide in min^{-1}.
b Calculate the initial activity of the nuclide in min^{-1}.
c Calculate the initial activity in Bq.

3 The half-life of potassium-42 is 12 hours.

a Calculate the decay constant in h^{-1}.

b Calculate the decay constant in s^{-1}.

c Calculate the percentage of the original radioactive potassium present after 12 hours.

d Calculate the percentage of the original radioactive potassium present after 20 hours.

4 A sample of bone contains 5.0×10^{-14} g of carbon-14 and has an activity of 30 Bq.

a Use the Avogadro constant to find the number of carbon-14 atoms in the sample. (Remember N_A is the number of atoms in one mole which is the nucleon number in grams; in this case, 14 g.)

b Calculate the decay constant.

c Calculate the half-life.

d Calculate the time before the activity falls to 6.0 Bq.

Exam-style questions

1 A small number of the atoms in the atmosphere are those of the isotope tritium ^3_1H. These atoms are unstable and their radioactive decay is both random and spontaneous.

a **i** Explain what is meant by *spontaneous decay*. [1]

ii Explain what is meant by *random decay*. [1]

iii State an experimental observation that suggests that radioactive decay is random. [1]

b A nucleus of tritium ^3_1H decays by the emission of a beta-minus-particle and an antineutrino to form an isotope of helium (He).

The rest masses of a tritium nucleus, the helium nucleus formed, a beta-particle, a proton and a neutron are shown in this table. The antineutrino has negligible mass:

	Mass / u
tritium nucleus	3.016050
helium nucleus	3.014932
beta-particle	0.000549
proton	1.007277
neutron	1.008665

i Write down the nuclear equation that represents the decay of tritium. [2]

ii Calculate the mass defect of a tritium nucleus. [2]

iii Explain the term *binding energy* of a nucleus. [2]

iv Calculate the binding energy, in joules, of a tritium nucleus. [3]

v Calculate the energy released in the decay of a tritium nucleus. [2]

2 The isotope sodium-22 ($^{22}_{11}Na$) undergoes β^+-decay to form neon-22, which is stable.

The half-life of sodium-22 is 2.60 years.

a Write down the nuclear equation for the decay. [2]

b **i** Define *radioactive decay constant*. [1]

ii Calculate the decay constant of sodium-22. [2]

iii Explain, in words, why a nucleus with a small decay constant has a long half-life. [2]

c A pure sample of sodium-22 has an initial activity of 1.7×10^3 Bq.

i Calculate the initial number of sodium-22 nuclei in the sample. [2]

ii Calculate the number of sodium-22 nuclei that remain in the sample after 5.0 years. [3]

iii After 5.0 years, the sample contains only sodium-22 and neon-22 nuclei. Use your answers to parts **i** and **ii** to calculate the ratio: [2]

$$\frac{\text{number of sodium-22 nuclei after 5.0 years}}{\text{number of neon-22 nuclei after 5.0 years}}$$

3 a Explain what is meant by the phrase *radioactivity is random*. [1]

b Uranium-235 was present during the formation of the Earth. Of an original sample of uranium-235, only 1.1% of the original amount is present in rocks today. The half-life of uranium-235 is 7.0×10^8 years. Calculate the age of the Earth suggested by this data. [3]

c i Sketch a graph of binding energy per nucleon against nucleon number for naturally occurring nuclides. [2]

ii Use your graph to explain how energy is released when some nuclides undergo fission and when other nuclides undergo fusion. [3]

Chapter outline

- explain the principles of medical imaging of internal body structures using X-rays, ultrasound and magnetic resonance (MRI)
- describe the main features of a modern X-ray tube
- solve problems concerning the attenuation of X-rays and ultrasound in matter
- understand the principles and purpose of CT scanning
- understand and use the terms specific acoustic impedance and intensity in relation to ultrasound
- understand the function of the non-uniform magnetic field in MRI

KEY TERMS

ultrasound: sound waves of frequencies higher than 20 kHz

Equations: acoustic impedance = density × speed of sound; $Z = \rho c$

fraction of ultrasound reflected; $\frac{I_r}{I_0} = \frac{(Z_2 - Z_1)^2}{(Z_2 + Z_1)^2}$

Larmor frequency = gyromagnetic ratio × flux density; $\omega_0 = \gamma B_0$

Exercise 32.1 Producing X-rays

X-rays have been used to make images of the insides of human beings for 120 years. This exercise is about the nature of X-rays and how they are produced.

1 X-rays are produced for medical imaging. This diagram shows the construction of a typical X-ray tube:

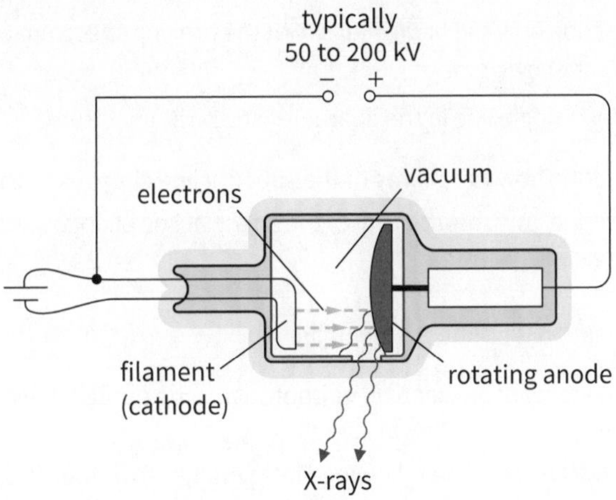

a State the names of the positive and negative electrodes.

b Explain why there is a high voltage between the two electrodes.

c Describe the type of field that exists between the two electrodes.

d Explain why there is a vacuum in the tube.

e X-rays are emitted over a large angle. Only those emerging from the tube are shown. State the name of the thin-walled section of the tube through which they emerge.

f Describe the energy changes which occur as electrons emerge from one electrode and strike the other.

g Explain why the anode rotates.

h State the word which describes a beam of X-rays which is roughly parallel-sided.

2 This diagram shows typical X-ray spectra produced using electrons of different energies:

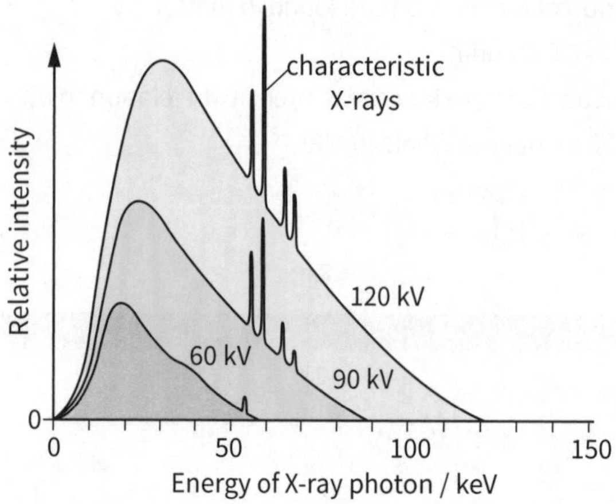

a State the greatest accelerating voltage used to produce these spectra.

b Determine the greatest X-ray photon energy produced using an accelerating voltage of 100 kV.

Each of the three spectral curves consists of two parts: *braking radiation* and *characteristic X-rays*.

c Which of these has a continuous spectrum?

d State the word that describes the other spectrum.

e State the minimum X-ray energy in the braking radiation spectrum.

f Describe how the *peak energy* of the braking spectrum changes as the accelerating voltage is increased.

g Describe how the *peak intensity* of the braking spectrum changes as the accelerating voltage is increased.

Consider a single line in the characteristic X-ray spectrum.

h Describe how the *energy* of the spectral line changes as the accelerating voltage is increased.

i Describe how the *intensity* of the spectral line changes as the accelerating voltage is increased.

3 This question is about energy units.

a The energy of an electron or photon may be quoted in eV. State the full name of this unit. State the value of 1 eV in J.

b Convert each of the following energy values to J: 100 eV, 500 keV, 2.2 MeV.

c Convert each of the following energy values to eV: 8.0×10^{-19} J, 8.0×10^{-16} J, 2.56×10^{-14} J.

The energy E of a photon is related to its frequency f by $E = hf$ where Planck's constant $h = 6.63 \times 10^{-34}$ J s.

d Calculate the energy of an X-ray photon of frequency 4.0×10^{18} Hz.

e Calculate the frequency of an X-ray photon of energy 60 keV.

An electron is accelerated through a p.d. of 80 kV. Its energy is converted into a single X-ray photon.

f Calculate the frequency of the photon.

g Calculate the wavelength of the X-ray in free space.
Remember, the speed of electromagnetic radiation in free space is: $c = f\lambda$ where $c = 3.0 \times 10^8$ m s^{-1}.

Exercise 32.2 X-rays and matter

This exercise is about how X-rays interact with matter and how high-quality X-ray images can be produced.

1 X-ray photons carry energy. If a beam of X-rays is spread over a large area, its *intensity* I will be low. This is represented by the equation:

$$I = \frac{P}{A}$$

a What quantities are represented by the symbols P and A in this equation? Give their names and their SI units.

b Calculate the intensity of an X-ray beam of power 150 W passing through an area of 60 cm^2. Take care when converting cm^2 to m^2.

When a beam of X-rays enters a patient's body, its intensity is *attenuated*. This graph shows how the intensity changes as the beam passes through flesh and bone:

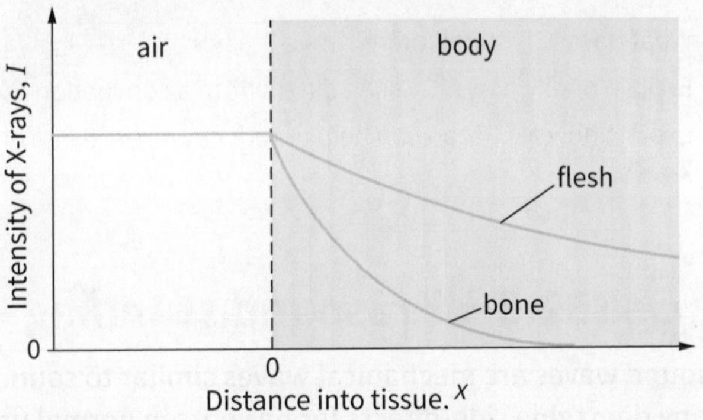

c Explain how you can tell from the graph that the beam is collimated (parallel-sided) as it passes through the air.

d Of the three materials represented (air, flesh, bone), which absorbs X-rays most strongly? Explain how you can tell.

e Which material is the least absorbing? Explain how you can tell.

The intensity of the X-rays decreases exponentially as it passes through flesh and bone. This can be characterised by the *half-thickness* of the material.

f Explain what is meant by half-thickness. Include a sketch graph of intensity against distance in your answer.

g Which has a greater half-thickness: flesh or bone?

2 The intensity of an X-ray beam decreases as it passes through biological material according to the equation $I = I_0 e^{-\mu x}$, where μ is the attenuation coefficient of the material.

- **a** The quantity $\frac{I}{I_0}$ is the fraction of the initial intensity that remains after the beam has passed through a thickness x of the material. Rearrange the equation for I to make $\frac{I}{I_0}$ its subject.
- **b** Calculate the fraction of the intensity of a 250 keV X-ray beam that remains after it has passed through 4.0 cm of bone whose attenuation coefficient $\mu = 0.32\ \text{cm}^{-1}$. (Remember to calculate the value of the exponent first.)
- **c** Determine the fraction that has been absorbed by the bone.
- **d** Calculate the value of $\frac{I}{I_0}$ when x = the half-thickness of the absorbing material.
- **e** Use this idea to calculate the half-thickness of bone for 250 keV X-rays.

3 Medical physicists try to produce the best possible X-ray images while causing as little damage as possible to the patient.

They want to produce images which are as sharp as possible, and with as much contrast as possible.

- **a** Explain why it is important to keep the radiation dose to the patient as low as possible.
- **b** Explain how an image intensifier helps to keep the radiation dose low.
- **c** A narrow X-ray beam can be produced by reducing the size of the window of the X-ray tube. Explain how this helps to improve the X-ray image.
- **d** Explain what is meant by the term *contrast* in connection with X-ray images.
- **e** Explain how a barium meal helps to improve the contrast of an X-ray image.

4 A CT scan is a technique that can be used to produce images of a patient's organs.

- **a** What does 'CT' stand for?
- **b** Explain briefly how a CT scan differs from a conventional X-ray image.
- **c** Explain how a CT scan can help to reduce the exposure of healthy organs to damaging X-rays.

Exercise 32.3 Ultrasound scanning

Ultrasound waves are mechanical waves similar to sound waves and are not thought to have any damaging side-effects for patients in normal use. This exercise looks at how they are produced and used in medicine.

1 Ultrasound waves travel at about 330 m s^{-1} in air, 1500 m s^{-1} in water and 1590 m s^{-1} in tissue such as muscle.

- **a** Explain the term *ultrasound*.
- **b** Calculate the wavelength of ultrasound waves of frequency 40 kHz in water and in muscle tissue.
- **c** The speed of ultrasound waves changes as they pass from air into tissue. State whether the frequency increases, decreases or stays the same, and whether the wavelength increases, decreases or stays the same.
- **d** To resolve small objects, it is necessary to use ultrasound with a wavelength comparable to the size of the objects. Suggest a suitable frequency of ultrasound if you wish to observe kidney stones of diameter 2 mm.

2 This diagram shows an ultrasound *transducer* – this means that it both produces and detects ultrasound waves:

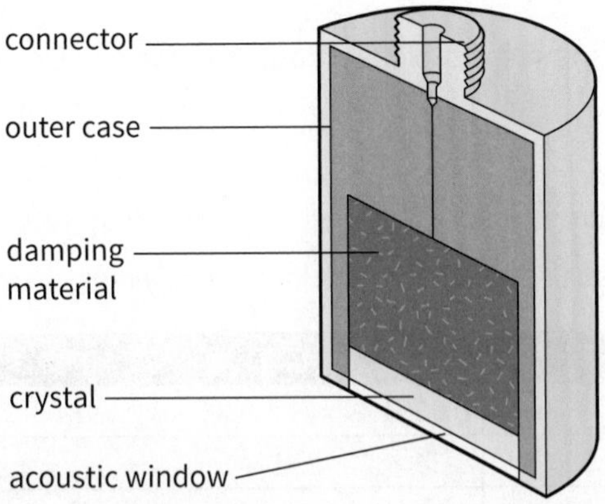

a The piezo-electric crystal is the part which generates ultrasound waves. Describe how it is caused to vibrate.

b Explain the function of the acoustic window.

The transducer sends pulses of ultrasound into the patient's body. It also detects ultrasound waves reflected from inside the body.

c Describe how the crystal behaves when the reflected waves reach it.

d Explain why the ultrasound waves are sent out in pulses.

e Explain the function of the damping material.

The crystal is usually made of polyvinylidene difluoride. The speed of sound in this material is 2200 m s^{-1}.

f Calculate the wavelength of ultrasound waves of frequency 2.2 MHz in this material.

g The thickness of the crystal is usually one half-wavelength. Calculate this value.

3 This diagram shows what happens when an ultrasound wave strikes the boundary between two different materials. Only part of the wave is transmitted.

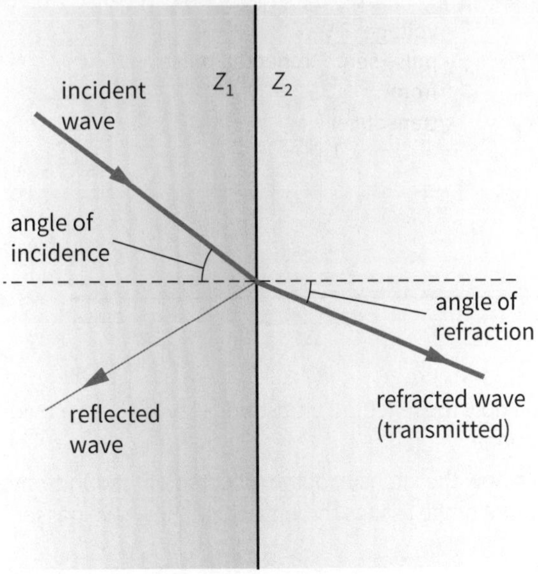

a Explain what happens to the rest of the ultrasound.

b Explain what causes the wave to change direction. (Think about the refraction of light).

The fraction of the intensity of the ultrasound wave reflected is given by:

$$\frac{I_r}{I_0} = \frac{(Z_2 - Z_1)^2}{(Z_2 + Z_1)^2}$$

where Z represents the acoustic impedance of the material.

This table gives values of Z for air and for three different tissues:

Material	Acoustic impedance Z / 10^6 kg m^{-2} s^{-1}
air	0.0004
fat	1.34
muscle	1.71
bone	6.40

c Fat and muscle have similar values for Z. Calculate the fraction of an ultrasound beam transmitted when passing from muscle to fat. Take care! The equation tells you the fraction *reflected.*

d Using data from the table, explain why a boundary between bone and muscle will give a strong reflected signal.

e Air has a very low acoustic impedance. This means that very little of an ultrasound wave will pass from air into tissue. Explain how this problem may be overcome when a patient is given an ultrasound scan.

4 This diagram shows how ultrasound could be used to investigate a patient's bone:

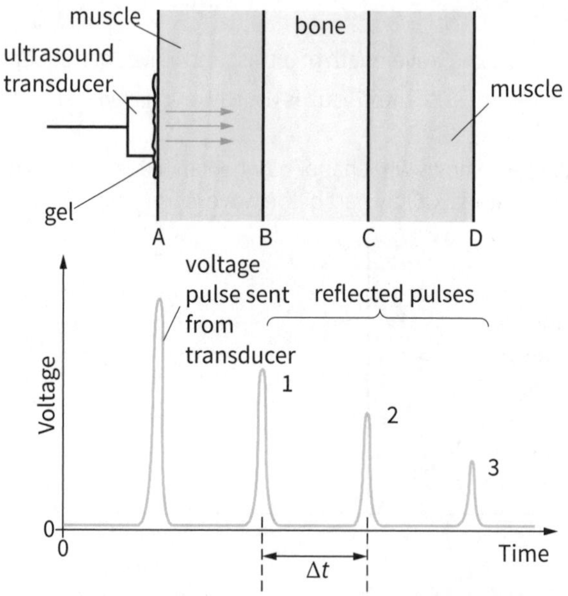

a Explain how the reflected ultrasound waves could provide information about the *thickness* of the bone.

b Explain how the intensity of the reflected ultrasound waves could provide information about the nature of the tissues through which they have passed.

Exercise 32.4 Magnetic resonance imaging (MRI)

MRI is another imaging technique. It relies on the fact that protons behave like little magnets in a magnetic field. This exercise looks at how MRI works and how it is used.

1 This diagram shows a proton in an external magnetic field:

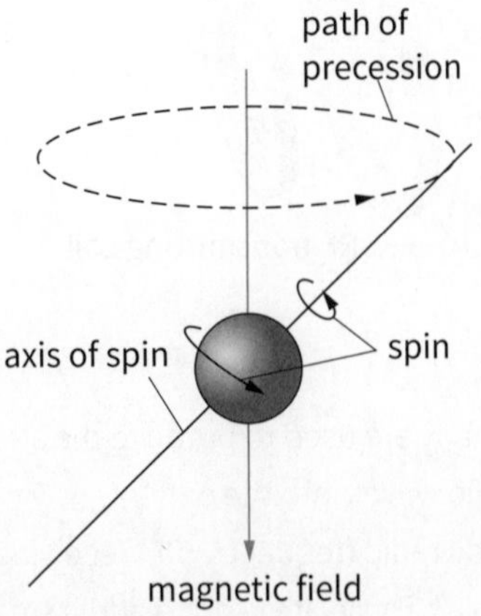

a Describe where protons are usually found.

b State the electrical charge of a proton.

The proton spins so that it behaves like a tiny magnet. A proton lines up in a magnetic field. Its axis precesses about the field.

c Explain what the word *precesses* means.

The angular frequency of precession (the Larmor frequency) is given by $\omega_0 = \gamma B_0$ where γ is the gyromagnetic ratio. For a proton, $\gamma = 2.68 \times 10^8$ rad s^{-1} T^{-1}.

d Calculate the Larmor frequency of protons in a magnetic field of flux density 2.25 T.
In magnetic resonance imaging, radio waves are directed into tissue. If the waves have the correct frequency, their energy will be absorbed by protons. This is an example of resonance.

e From your answer to part **d**, calculate the frequency of radio waves that will cause protons to resonate in a magnetic field of flux density 2.25 T.

When the protons have absorbed energy, they are in a higher energy state. They gradually lose their extra energy and return ('relax') to their lower energy state.

f Sketch a graph to show the pattern of relaxation of protons with time.

g State the mathematical term that describes the shape of this graph.

2 MRI imaging relies on the fact that protons relax at different rates according to their surroundings. In other words, their relaxation times depend on the tissue they are in.

Here are three types of tissue: watery, cancerous and fatty.

a Name the type of tissue in which proton relaxation times are longest.

b Name the type of tissue in which proton relaxation times are shortest.

c Explain why the radio waves are sent into the patient's tissues in pulses.

3 This diagram shows the arrangement of coils in an MRI scanner:

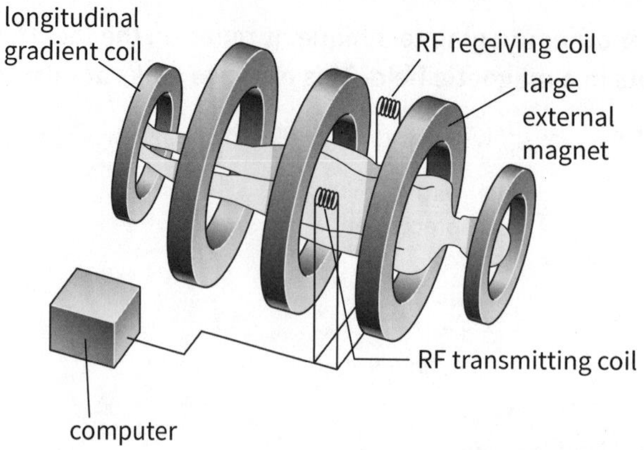

a Of the coils shown, how many are used to produce the strong external field?

b State which coil sends radio waves into the patient.

c Describe the function of the radio frequency (RF) receiving coil.

d There are two 'gradient coils'. These are used to add a small additional field that is stronger at one end of the patient than the other. Explain how changing this gradient field allows the patient's body to be scanned gradually.

e Explain the functions of the computer.

Exam-style questions

electron charge $e = -1.60 \times 10^{-19}$ C

Planck's constant $h = 6.63 \times 10^{-34}$ J s

1 Ultrasound waves travel at 1590 m s^{-1} in muscle tissue. The density of muscle tissue is 1075 kg m^{-3}.

a Explain what is meant by *ultrasound*. [1]

b Calculate the acoustic impedance of muscle. [2]

The acoustic impedances of two other tissue types are:

- fat: $Z = 1.34 \times 10^6$ kg m^{-2} s^{-1}
- bone: $Z = 6.40 \times 10^6$ kg m^{-2} s^{-1}.

c Use this data to explain why an ultrasound scan will give clearer images of muscle-bone boundaries than muscle-fat boundaries. [3]

2 X-rays are produced for medical use in an X-ray tube.

An X-ray tube has a p.d. between the anode and cathode of 115 kV.

a Calculate the maximum energy (in J) of X-ray photons produced in such a tube. [2]

b Calculate the maximum frequency of these X-rays. [2]

X-rays can be used to produce images of bones that are embedded in muscle tissue. The attenuation coefficient for bone: $\mu = 600$ m^{-1}.

c A beam of X-rays of intensity 15 W m^{-2} is directed on to a patient's arm. Calculate the intensity of the beam after it has passed through 3.0 mm of bone. [3]

d Muscle tissue has a lower attenuation coefficient than bone. Explain how this allows X-rays to be used to produce a 'shadow image' of bone embedded in tissue. [2]

MRI scanning can be used as an alternative to CT scanning (which uses X-rays).

e State and explain one way in which MRI scanning is safer for the patient than CT scanning. [2]

f State one way in which MRI scanning can give a clearer image than CT scanning. [2]

Chapter outline

You should be able to:

- use appropriate techniques for the measurement of length, volume, angle, mass, time, temperature and electrical quantities
- understand and explain the effects of systematic errors and random errors
- understand the distinction between precision and accuracy
- assess the uncertainty in a calculated quantity by addition of absolute, fractional or percentage uncertainties

KEY TERMS

analogue display: a continuous display which represents the quantity being measured on a dial or scale

digital display: a display that gives the information in the form of characters (numbers or letters)

calibration curve: a graphical or mathematical relationship between the readings obtained from an instrument and the true or reference values

systematic error: an error of measurement that differs from the true value by the same amount in each measurement

random error: an error in a measurement that is unpredictable and which may vary from one measurement to the next

uncertainty: an estimate of the spread of values around a measured quantity within which the true value will be found

precision: the smallest change in value that can be measured by an instrument or operator or that is shown in a measurement; a precise measurement is one that, when made several times, gives the same or very similar values

accuracy: an accurate value of a measured quantity is close to the true value of the quantity

zero error: the measurement of a quantity when the true value is zero

range: the difference between the largest value and the smallest value of a measurement

independent variable: a physical quantities whose value is controlled or selected by the person performing an experiment

dependent variable: a physical quantities whose value changes as a result of the change in another quantity

Equations: $\text{uncertainty} = \frac{1}{2}(\text{maximum reading} - \text{minimum reading})$

$$\text{percentage uncertainty} = \frac{\text{uncertainty}}{\text{mean value}} \times 100\%$$

when $A = B \pm C$ absolute uncertainty in A = sum of absolute uncertainties in B and C

when $A = \frac{B}{C}$ or BC percentage uncertainty in A = sum of percentage uncertainties in B and C

Exercise P1.1 Scales and uncertainties

This exercise gives you practice reading the scales of a number of different instruments, and estimating the uncertainties in measurements.

The number of significant figures given in a reading should be decided by looking at the measuring instrument used. For example, it is not sensible to record a distance measured on a ruler with a millimetre scale as 3 cm or 3.00 cm; it should be recorded as 3.0 cm.

1 **a** Record the position of the left-hand and right-hand edge of the coin placed on this metre rule:

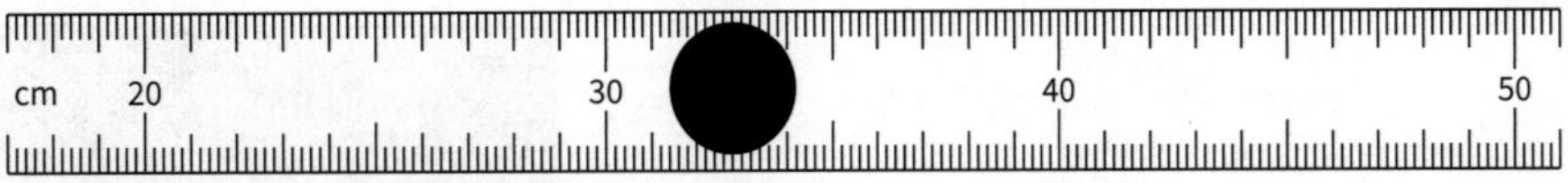

b Read the temperature shown on this thermometer:

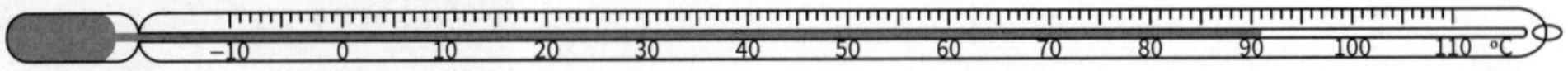

c Read the current shown on this meter:

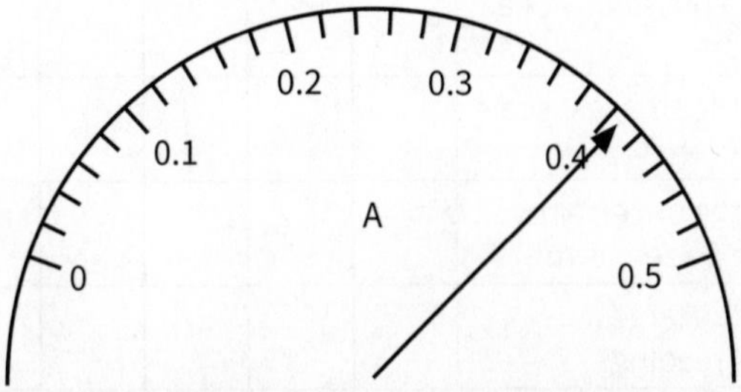

d Read the volume shown on measuring cylinder A:

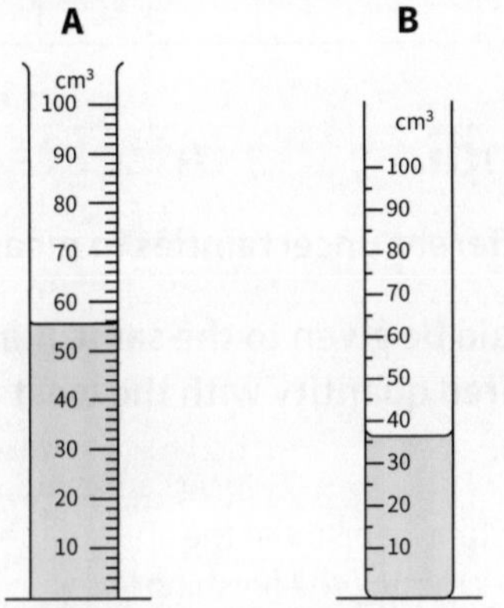

e State whether cylinder A or B has the *lower precision*. Explain why.

f A small volume, 6 cm³, of glue has become solid at the bottom of cylinder A. Unless taken into account, this causes a zero error when the cylinder is used to measure the volume of a liquid, and makes cylinder A less accurate. Explain what is meant by a *zero error* and how cylinder B is likely to be more accurate.

TIP

To decide the uncertainty you will have to think about whether it is possible to read the scale within the divisions on the instrument. Some of the instruments are shown in question 1. For example, can you read a thermometer marked with each °C to say half a °C or is it to the nearest °C? If you have the instrument, you can try to take the same reading several times, perhaps with someone else taking the reading as well – see whether the result is the same. If you cannot read within a division then the smallest division is the uncertainty.

2 Copy and complete this table, giving units for any values. Include columns for all instruments that you have available or for which there is a diagram in your textbook.

	Metre rule	30 cm ruler	Callipers	Micrometer	Analogue thermometer	Analogue voltmeter	Measuring cylinder A	Protractor	Top pan balance	Stopwatch
Is there a possibility of a zero error?										
What is the smallest scale division?										
What is the uncertainty (assume no zero error)?										
What is the largest possible reading?										
What is the percentage uncertainty in the largest possible reading?										

Exercise P1.2 Finding the uncertainty in a reading

This exercise considers different uncertainties in measurements and how they arise.

Calculated quantities should be given to the same number of significant figures as (or one more than) the measured quantity with the least accuracy, except when produced by addition or subtraction.

1 When a student hears the starting pistol at the start of the race, he starts his stopwatch and stops it as he sees a runner crossing the finishing line.

The reading on the stopwatch is 26.02 s.

a Suggest the value that the student should write down as his best estimate for the time and for the uncertainty in the time, based on only one reading.

b Three other students also record the same time and the readings on their stopwatches are:

- 25.90 s
- 26.34 s
- 26.14 s.

Calculate the mean value of all four readings and an estimate of the uncertainty of the time.

c The true value of the time is 26.40 s. Explain how this value shows that the students' readings have a systematic error.

d Suggest one cause of a systematic error and one cause of a random error in the readings.

2 A student times a number of oscillations of a ball along a track.

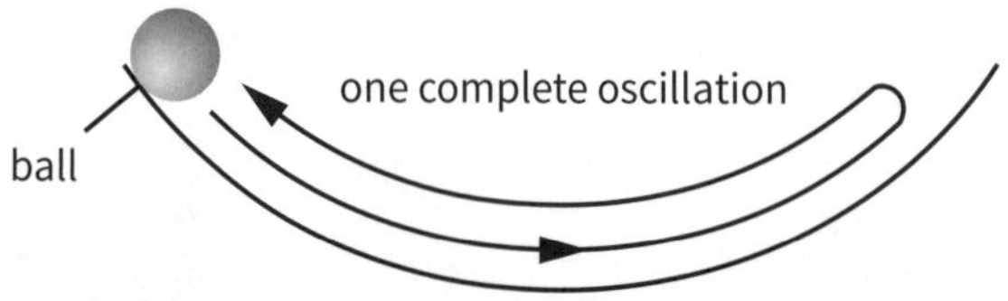

Timing one complete oscillation, her readings were:

- 2.12 s
- 2.32 s.

Timing ten complete oscillations, her readings were:

- 21.20 s
- 21.32 s.

The time for one complete oscillation is T.

a Use the first set of readings to determine the value and uncertainty for T.

b Use the second set of readings to determine the value and uncertainty for T.

c Calculate the percentage uncertainty in the two values of T that you have determined. Note: you should find that the percentage uncertainty in T found using ten complete oscillations is the smaller. Using more oscillations gives a smaller percentage uncertainty.

d Suggest one reason why timing a large number of oscillations – 200, for example – is not possible.

Exercise P1.3 Combining uncertainties

This exercise helps you understand percentages and absolute uncertainties.

There are two simple rules:

- **When quantities are added or subtracted, you add *absolute uncertainties* to find the total absolute uncertainty.**
- **When quantities are multiplied or divided, you add *percentage uncertainties* to find the total percentage uncertainty.**

1 a State the number of significant digits in 0.0254.

b Write $T = 1.25578 \pm 0.1247$ s, keeping two significant digits in the uncertainty.

c Calculate the percentage error for $v = 12.25$ m/s $\pm$ 0.25 m/s.

d Calculate the absolute error if the accepted value is 120 s and the percentage error is 5%.

2 a Each of these measurements was taken several times.
The uncertainty is half the range of the readings:

- $T = 7.5$ s $\pm$ 0.2 s
- $L = 10.0$ m $\pm$ 0.2 m
- $D = 5.6$ cm $\pm$ 4%

Determine which measurement has the smallest percentage uncertainty.

b Two sides of a piece of paper are measured as $A = 29.5 \pm 0.1$ cm and $B = 21.0 \pm 0.1$ cm. The circumference of the paper is $2A + 2B$. Calculate the absolute error in C.

c A pressure P is calculated using the formula $P = \frac{F}{\pi R^2}$. The percentage possible uncertainties are $\pm$2% in F and $\pm$1% in R. Calculate the percentage uncertainty in P.

3 The area A of a circle of radius r is given by $A = \pi r^2$.

If r measures 10.0 ± 0.2 cm, calculate:

a the percentage uncertainty in r

b the percentage uncertainty in A (r is squared and so is multiplied by itself; there is no error in π)

c the absolute uncertainty in A (changing from percentage to absolute uncertainty, you will need the value of $A = 314$ cm^2).

4 These readings were obtained in an experiment to measure the density of a ball bearing:

- mass = 7.0 ± 0.1 g
- volume = 1.20 ± 0.05 cm^3.

A student obtains the density as 5.8333 g cm^{-3}.

a Calculate the percentage uncertainty of each reading.
b Calculate the percentage uncertainty in the density value.
c Calculate the absolute uncertainty in the density.
d Write down the density and uncertainty to a reasonable number of significant figures.

5 Measurements taken as a ball falls a distance *D* in a time *T* are:

- *D* = 1.215 ± 0.004 m
- *T* = 0.495, 0.498, 0.503, 0.496, 0.501 s.

The mean average value of *T* is 0.499 s and the acceleration due to gravity *g* is 9.77 m s^{-2} (calculated using the formula $g = \frac{2D}{T^2}$).

Calculate the:

a percentage uncertainty in *D*
b range in the measurements of *T*
c absolute uncertainty in the average value of *T*
d percentage uncertainty in the average value of *T*
e percentage uncertainty in *g* (remember, as $g = \frac{2D}{T \times T}$ you add the percentage uncertainty in *T* twice to the percentage uncertainty in *D*)
f absolute uncertainty in *g*.

Exercise P1.4 Tables, graphs and gradients

This exercise gives you practice tabulating results, drawing graphs and finding gradients.

1 A student investigates the speed of water waves in a shallow tray:

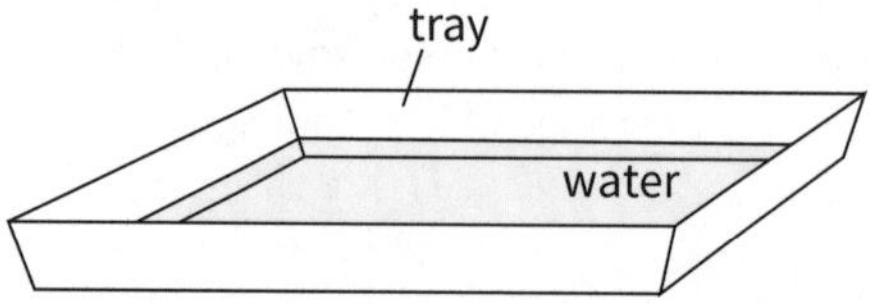

One end of the tray is lifted and then lowered quickly. A wave moves backwards and forwards across the tray several times before it dies away.

The student measures the depth *d* of the water and the time *T* taken by the wave to travel from one end of the tray to the other and back again. She repeats the reading of *T*. The distance travelled by the wave in time *T* is 5.00 m.

The student's measurements for different values of *d* are shown in this table:

d / m	*T* / s 1st value	*T* / s 2nd value
0.005	22.2	22.3
0.010	15.9	16.0
0.015	12.9	13.1
0.020	11.3	11.4
0.025	10.1	10.1
0.030	9.2	9.3
0.035	8.5	8.4

The speed v of the water wave is found using the formula:

$$v = \frac{5.00}{t}$$

where t is the average value of the two values of T.

When T is measured in s, the formula gives a value for v in m s^{-1}.

a Produce a table for the readings showing the depth d in m, the average time t and the speed v. Also include values of v^2 in your table. Give appropriate units for all quantities.

b Plot a graph of v^2 on the y-axis against d on the x-axis.

c Draw a straight line of best fit.

d Determine the gradient and y-intercept of this line.

e The quantities v and d are related by the formula:

$v^2 = A\,d + B$

where A and B are constants.

Use your answer to part **d** to determine the values of A and B. Give appropriate units.

2 During half of an oscillation of a simple pendulum, the string holding this pendulum bob hits against a stationary horizontal rod:

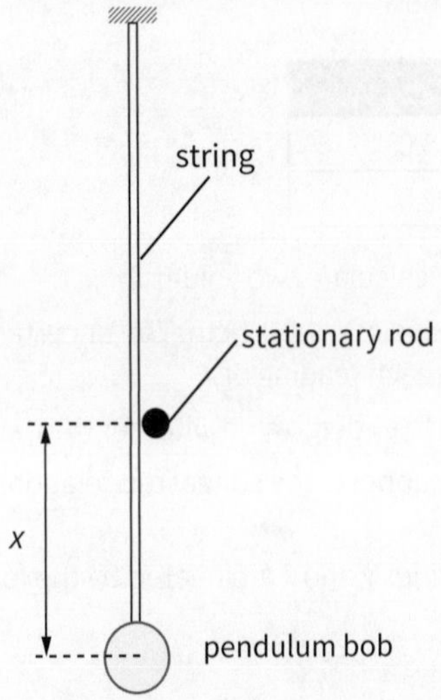

The distance between the pendulum bob and the rod is the distance x. The total length of the string is kept constant.

The distance x as well as the time T_{10} for ten complete oscillations is measured by a student.

This is part of a student's notebook showing the readings:

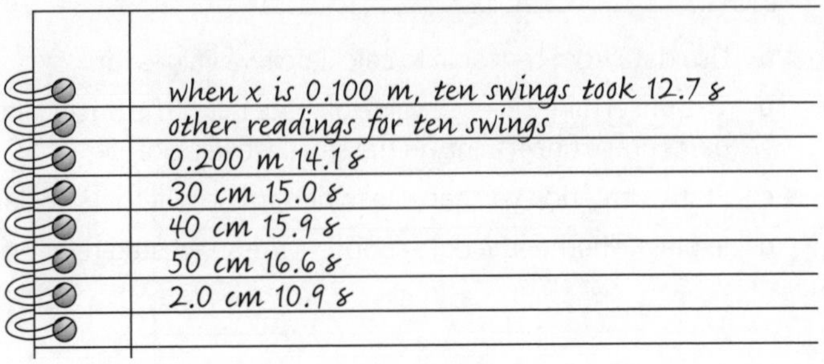

when x is 0.100 m, ten swings took 12.7 s
other readings for ten swings
0.200 m 14.1 s
30 cm 15.0 s
40 cm 15.9 s
50 cm 16.6 s
2.0 cm 10.9 s

a Produce a table for the readings showing the distance x in metres, T_{10} and the time t for one oscillation. Include $\sqrt{x}$ in your table. Give units for all quantities.

b Plot a graph of t on the y-axis against $\sqrt{x}$ on the x-axis.

c Draw the straight line of best fit.

d Determine the gradient and *y*-intercept of this line.

e The quantities *t* and $\sqrt{x}$ are related by the formula:

$t = A\sqrt{x} + B$

where *A* and *B* are constants.

Use your answer to part **d** to determine the values of *A* and *B*. Give appropriate units.

Exercise P1.5 Mathematical relationships and sources of uncertainty

This exercise allows you to test mathematical relationships, suggest sources of uncertainty, and suggest improvements to reduce uncertainty.

1 It is suggested that two quantities *F* and *x* are related by the formula:

$F = kx$

where *k* is a constant.

This table shows values of *F* and *x*:

F / N	*x* / cm
20	18.0
4.2	2.0

a Use data from the table to calculate two values for *k*.

b The uncertainty in each value of *x* is ±0.1 cm. The uncertainty in *F* is very small. Calculate the percentage uncertainty in each reading of *x*.

c State a criterion you can use to determine whether the data supports the relationship.

d Explain whether the data supports the suggested relationship.

2 It is suggested that two quantities *y* and *x* are related by the formula:

$y = kx^2$

where *k* is a constant.

This table shows values of *y* and *x*:

y / cm	*x* / cm
18	6.00
32	7.83

a Use data from the table to calculate two values for *k*.

b The uncertainty in each value of *y* is ±1 cm. The uncertainty in *x* is very small. Calculate the percentage uncertainty in the smallest value of *y*.

c State a criterion you can use to determine whether the data supports the relationship.

d Explain whether the data supports the suggested relationship.

3 It is suggested that two quantities T and x are related by the formula:

$T^2 = kx$

where k is a constant.

This table shows values of T and x:

T / s	x / cm
2.0	4.00
6.3	41.3

a Use data from the table to calculate two values for k.

b The uncertainty in each value of T is ± 0.1 s. The uncertainty in x is very small. Calculate the percentage uncertainty in the smallest value of T.

c State a criterion you can use to determine whether the data supports the relationship.

d Explain whether the data supports the suggested relationship.

4 In this question you will need to describe sources of uncertainty and improvements in a basic experiment. Many such sources of uncertainty or limitations in the procedure will depend on the actual apparatus used. You may have to look up the apparatus in your textbook.

For each situation described:

- imagine that you have taken two sets of readings of two quantities that are related; you have used your readings to see whether a suggested relationship is supported by these readings (remember that in any formula, k represents a constant)
- suggest sources of error or limitations and then suggest improvements to reduce the errors or limitations.

a A metre rule is balanced on a pivot and two masses, one either side of the pivot. You check the relationship clockwise moment = anticlockwise moment.

b You check that resistance R of a wire of constant length is related to the area of cross-section A using the relationship $R = k/A$.

c A hacksaw blade is clamped at one end. You check that the period of oscillation t is related to the length l of the hacksaw blade that is free to vibrate, using the relationship $t^2 = k\,l^3$.

d You check that the width w of a piece of paper tape is related to the maximum force F needed to break the tape when it is pulled by a newtonmeter, using the relationship $F = kw$.

Exam-style questions

1 A student connects a resistor of resistance R to a cell, as shown in this circuit diagram:

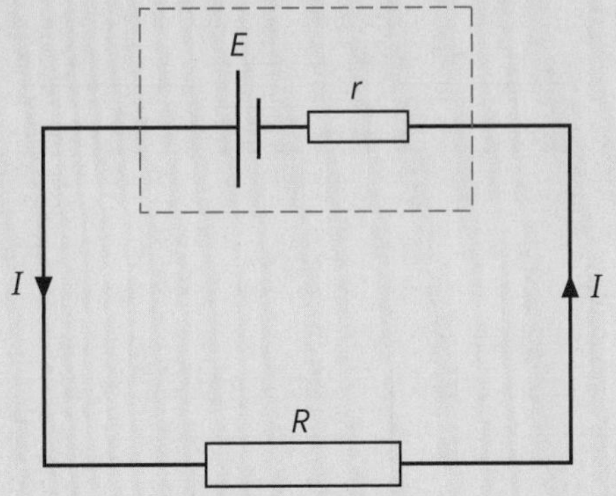

The e.m.f. of the cell is E and its internal resistance is r. The current I is measured by an ammeter, which is not shown.

The student uses a number of different resistances. She records the current and the value of R each time. The cell is only switched on for a short time to take the readings.

The readings the student obtained are shown in this table:

R/Ω	10	20	5	2	15	25	30
I/A	0.118	0.068	0.186	0.286	0.086	0.056	0.048

a Copy the table, placing the readings in order of increasing current. Include values of $\frac{1}{I}$ in your table. [1]

b Plot a graph of $\frac{1}{I}$ on the y-axis against R on the x-axis. [3]

c Draw the straight line of best fit. [1]

d Determine the gradient and y-intercept of this line. [2]

e The quantities I and R are related by the formula:

$$\frac{1}{I} = \frac{1}{E}(R + r)$$

where E is the e.m.f. of the cell and r is the internal resistance of the cell.

Use your answers to part **d** to determine the values of E and r. Give appropriate units. [2]

2 A mass M hanging on the end of a spring was twisted slightly. The time T for one complete oscillation was measured accurately by recording the time T_5 for five complete oscillations.

The results obtained for T_5 were 2.46 s and 2.64 s when $M = 100$ g.

a Determine the value of T when $M = 100$ g. [1]

b Estimate the percentage uncertainty in the average value of T_5. [1]

The measurement of T_5 was repeated using a mass of 300 g.

The results obtained for T_5 were 4.26 and 4.32 s.

c Determine the new value of T when $M = 300$ g. [1]

It is suggested that the quantities T and M are related by the equation:

$T^2 = kM$

where k is a constant.

d Use your answers to parts **a** and **c** to calculate two values of k. [2]

e Explain whether the results support the suggested relationship. [1]

f Describe four sources of uncertainty or limitations of the procedure for this experiment. [4]

g Describe four improvements that could be made to this experiment. You may suggest the use of other apparatus or different procedures. [4]

Chapter outline

You should be able to:

- identify the variables in an experiment and how they are controlled or measured, including the independent variable, dependent variables and variables to be kept constant
- describe and draw the arrangement of apparatus and the procedures for experiments, assess risk and suggest precautions
- describe the use of oscilloscopes, light gates, data loggers and other sensors
- rearrange expressions into the forms $y = mx + c$, $y = ax^n$ and $y = ae^{kx}$, and plot graphs to find the constants from the gradient and y-intercept of a straight-line graph or tangent
- draw graphs including lines of best fit, worst acceptable lines and tangents to curves
- convert absolute into fractional or percentage uncertainty estimates and vice versa
- determine uncertainty estimates through calculation, and from the gradient and y-intercept of a graph
- express a quantity as a value, an uncertainty estimate and a unit, using an appropriate number of significant figures

KEY TERMS

uncertainty: an estimate of the spread of values around a measured quantity within which the true value will be found

independent variable: a physical quantity whose value is controlled or selected by the person performing an experiment

dependent variable: a physical quantity whose value changes as a result of the change in another quantity

Equations: absolute uncertainty = gradient of line of best fit − gradient of worst acceptable line

absolute uncertainty = y-intercept of line of best fit − y-intercept of worst acceptable line

Exercise P2.1 Graphs

This exercise involves the use of error bars on graphs and finding the uncertainty in a gradient, including logarithms.

1 Two quantities x and y are related by the equation $y = kx^n$ where k and n are constants.

a By taking logarithms find an expression for ln y in terms of ln x.

This graph shows ln y plotted against ln x, for two points with error bars shown:

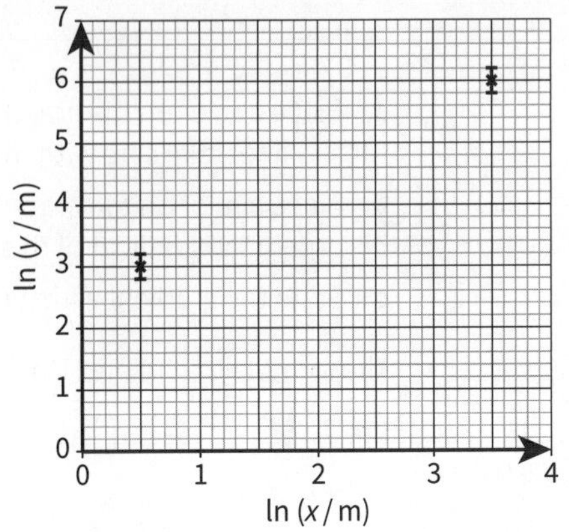

b Calculate the gradient of the best line.

c Calculate the gradient of the worst acceptable line.

d Note down the intercept of the best line on the *y*-axis.

e Note down the intercept of the worst acceptable line on the *x*-axis.

f Using your answers for the gradients state the value of n and its uncertainty.

g Using your answers for **d**, calculate the best value of k. (You will have to use the inverse of a logarithm as the intercept is ln k.)

2 In an experiment, imagine that you have measured the current I and the voltage V across a lamp and obtained the values:

$V = 1.65 \pm 0.07$ V and $I = 0.25 \pm 0.03$ A

A point is plotted at (0.25, 1.65) on a graph with voltage on the *y*-axis and current on the *x*-axis. The error bars now need to be drawn.

a Describe how to plot the vertical error bar, showing the uncertainty in the voltage.

b Describe how to plot the horizontal error bar, showing the uncertainty in the current.

3 Imagine that you have measured a current as 3.6 ± 0.2 A.

a Calculate:

i ln (3.6)

ii ln (3.8)

iii ln (3.4).

b State the length of the error bar required above the point and below the point, when you plot a point with a *y*-value of ln(3.6).

c State the label that should be written on the *y*-axis if you were to plot the point ln(3.6).

4 This graph shows values of ln (V/V) plotted against R^{-1} / 10^{-6} Ω^{-1}:

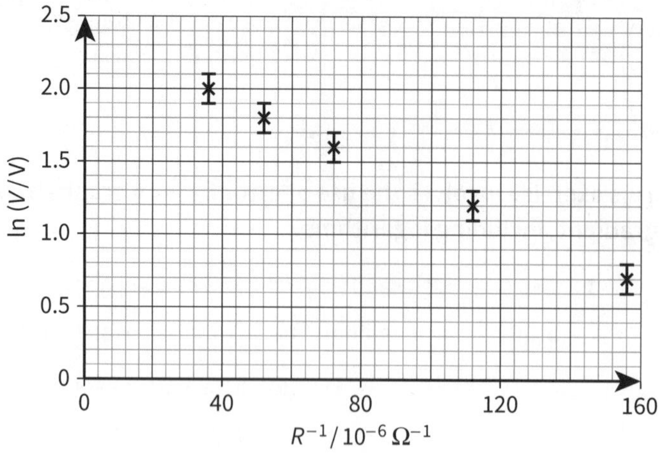

a Place a ruler on the graph along the line of best fit. Read off values and obtain the gradient of this line. Take care with the 10^{-6} on the *x*-axis (120 really means 1.2×10^{-4}, for example).

b Place a ruler on the graph along the worst acceptable straight line. Read off values and obtain the gradient of this line.

c State the gradient with its uncertainty.

The formula that relates V and R is:

$V = V_0 e^{-t/RC}$

where *C* is a capacitance and *t* the time for the reading (in this case, 10 s).

d Express the gradient of the graph in terms of *C* and *t*.

e Using your value for the gradient, determine the value of *C*. Include the unit.

f Determine the percentage uncertainty in your value for *C*.

Exercise P2.2 Uncertainty and using an oscilloscope

This exercise provides more practice estimating uncertainty and in using an oscilloscope.

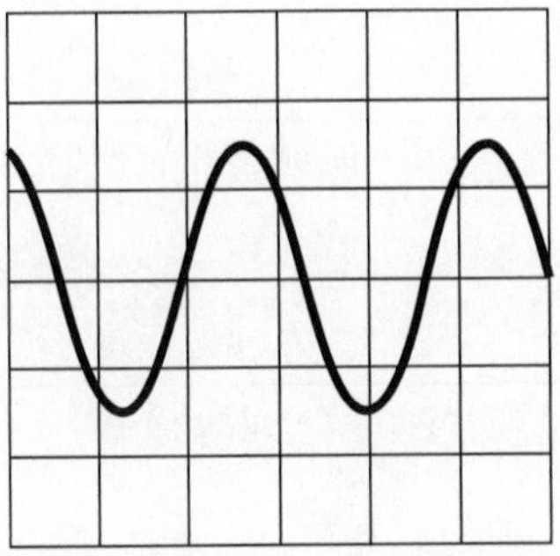

The black grid lines on the trace are one division apart on the screen.

1 This diagram shows the trace of an alternating voltage obtained on an oscilloscope screen:

a Determine the amplitude of the trace. Give your answer as a multiple of one division. Estimate the uncertainty in your answer.

b The Y-gain control is set at 2.0 V/division. Use your answers to **a** to determine the peak voltage and its uncertainty.

c The time base (X-gain) on the oscilloscope is set at 0.5 ms/division. Determine the time for one oscillation and the uncertainty in this value.

d Use your answer to **c** to calculate the frequency of the a.c. and the uncertainty in this value. Since your calculation involves a division, you need to use percentage uncertainties. You can assume that the oscilloscope is calibrated and that there is no uncertainty in the time base value.

2 Light gates are placed on a slope and used to time a ball rolling from rest down a slope. The time measured is 1.26 ± 0.01 s and the distance travelled is 0.245 ± 0.002 m.

a Calculate the average speed of the ball. Give your answer as a value, an absolute uncertainty estimate and a unit. You will need to use the formula:

$$\text{speed} = \frac{\text{distance}}{\text{time}}$$

(To find the uncertainty, remember to add percentage uncertainties to find the percentage uncertainty in the speed).

b Calculate the average acceleration of the ball. Give your answer as a value, an absolute uncertainty estimate and a unit. You will need to use the formula:

$$s = \frac{1}{2}at^2$$

(Remember when finding the total percentage uncertainty that the quantity *t* appears twice).

Exercise P2.3 Experimental methods

Writing a method can be difficult unless you are organised and cover each aspect logically and carefully. This exercise gives you practice thinking about the different aspects.

Read through the descriptions of experiments **A–I** and then, for each experiment:

1 State which is the dependent variable, which is the independent variable and any quantities that should be controlled.

2 Draw a diagram of the apparatus and describe how the variables are measured or how they are calculated from the readings taken.

3 Describe how the independent variable is changed.

4 Give one additional detail, e.g. how to ensure there is a large change in the dependent variable.

5 State one safety precaution.

6 State what graph you would draw and how it is used to find any constants mentioned.

Experiment	Description
A	A student uses light gates to test the relationship between the distance s that a ball rolls down a slope and the time taken t, according to the formula: $s = \frac{1}{2}at^2$ where a is a constant.
B	A student tests that the resistance R of a thermistor varies with the temperature T, (measured in K) according to the formula: $R = e^{-kT}$ where k is a constant.
C	A student tests the relationship between V_s the output voltage from a transformer and V_p, the input voltage. He uses the formula: $V_s = V_p \times \left(\frac{N_s}{N_p} \right)$ where N_s and N_p are the number of turns on the output and input coils respectively.
D	A student tests the relationship between the magnetic flux density B at the centre of a circular coil and the current I in the coil. She uses the formula: $B = \frac{\mu_0 NI}{R}$ where N is the number of turns in the coil, R is the radius of the coil and μ_0 is the permeability of free space.
E	A student tests the relationship between the peak alternating current I_0 and the frequency f of the applied alternating voltage. She finds the formula: $\left(\frac{V_0}{I_0} \right)^2 = R^2 + \left(\frac{1}{4} \pi^2 f^2 C^2 \right)$ where V_0 is the peak value of the alternating voltage, R is the resistance of the circuit and C is the capacitance.
F	A student tests that, when a burette tap is opened, the volume V of liquid changes with time t according to the formula: $V = V_0 e^{-\lambda t}$ where V_0 is the initial volume and λ is a constant.
G	A student tests that the terminal velocity v of a steel ball falling through oil depends upon the radius R of the ball according to the formula: $v = AR^2$ where A is a constant.
H	One end of a metre rule is clamped horizontally and the other end has a mass attached. The distance between the clamp and the centre of the mass is l. A student tests that the period T, when the rule oscillates up and down, depends upon l according to the formula: $T^2 = kl^3$ where k is a constant for the rule.
I	A student has two small coils and notices that an alternating p.d. applied to one coil produces an alternating e.m.f. V in the other, even though they are not connected. There is a distance l between the two coils. He suggests that V is inversely proportional to l.

Exam-style questions

1 A nail is placed vertically with its sharp end in contact with a piece of wood. When a mass falls a height h onto the flat end of the nail, the nail is driven into the wood. It is suggested that the distance d that the nail is driven into the wood depends on h according to the formula:

$$d = kh^n$$

where k and n are constants.

Design a laboratory experiment to investigate the relationship between d and h in order to find a value for n. You should draw a diagram showing the arrangement of your equipment. In your account you should pay particular attention to the:

a procedure to be followed [2]

b measurements to be taken [4]

c control of variables [2]

d analysis of the data [2]

e safety precautions to be taken. [1]

Remember also to give additional detail, state the graph you would plot and how it should be used.

2 A mass M is suspended vertically from a spring with spring constant k. When the mass is displaced downwards it oscillates up and down. The time for ten complete oscillations T is measured.

It is suggested that I, M and k are related by the equation:

$$I = 20\pi\sqrt{\frac{M}{k}}$$

a A graph is plotted of T^2 on the y-axis against M on the x-axis. Determine an expression for the gradient in terms of k. [2]

b Values of T and M are given in this table:

M / kg	T / s	T^2 / s^2
0.075	10.8 ± 0.3	
0.125	13.7 ± 0.3	
0.175	16.8 ± 0.3	
0.225	19.0 ± 0.3	
0.275	20.6 ± 0.3	
0.325	22.5 ± 0.3	

Calculate and record values of T^2 / s^2. Include the absolute uncertainties in T^2. [2]

c **i** Plot a graph of T^2 / s^2 against M / kg. Include error bars for T^2. [2]

ii Draw the straight line of best fit and a worst acceptable straight line on your graph. [2]

iii Determine the gradient of the line of best fit. Include the uncertainty in your answer. [2]

d **i** Determine a value for k. Include an appropriate unit in your answer. [1]

ii Determine the percentage uncertainty in your value of k. [1]

e The experiment is repeated with $M = 0.200$ kg. Determine the value of T. Include the percentage uncertainty in your answer. [2]

Glossary

absolute scale of temperature; *see* thermodynamic scale.

absolute zero The temperature at which a system has minimum internal energy; equivalent to −273.15 °C.

absorption line spectrum A dark line of a unique wavelength seen in a continuous spectrum.

acceleration The rate of change of an object's velocity:

$$a = \frac{\Delta v}{\Delta t}$$

Unit: $m\,s^{-2}$.

accuracy An accurate value of a measured quantity is one which is close to the true value of the quantity.

acoustic impedance Acoustic impedance Z is the product of the density ρ of a substance and the speed c of sound in that substance ($Z = \rho c$). Unit: $kg\,m^{-2}\,s^{-1}$.

activity The rate of decay or disintegration of nuclei in a radioactive sample.

ampere The SI unit of electric current (abbreviated A).

amplitude The maximum displacement of a particle from its equilibrium position.

amplitude modulation A form of modulation in which the signal causes variations in the amplitude of a carrier wave.

analogue signal A signal that is continuously variable, having a continuum of possible values.

analogue-to-digital conversion (ADC) Conversion of a continuous analogue signal to discrete digital numbers.

angular displacement The angle through which an object moves in a circle.

angular frequency The frequency of a sinusoidal oscillation expressed in radians per second:

$$\text{angular frequency } \omega = \frac{2\pi}{T}$$

angular velocity The rate of change of the angular position of an object as it moves along a curved path.

antinode A point on a stationary wave with maximum amplitude.

atomic mass unit A unit of mass (symbol u) approximately equal to 1.661×10^{-27} kg. The mass of an atom of ${}^{12}_{6}C = 12.000$ u exactly.

attenuation The gradual loss in strength or intensity of a signal.

average speed The total distance travelled by an object divided by the total time taken.

Avogadro constant The number of particles in one mole of any substance (approximately $6.02 \times 10^{23}\,mol^{-1}$), denoted N_A.

band theory The idea that electrons in a solid or liquid can have energies within certain ranges or bands, between which are forbidden values.

bandwidth (communications) A measure of the width of a range of frequencies being transmitted.

base units Defined units of the SI system from which all other units are derived.

best fit line A straight line drawn as closely as possible to the points of a graph so that similar numbers of points lie above and below the line.

binding energy The minimum external energy required to separate all the neutrons and protons of a nucleus.

bit A basic unit of information storage, the amount of information stored by a device that exists in only two distinct states, usually given as the binary digits 0 and 1.

Boltzmann constant A fundamental constant given by $k = \frac{R}{N_A}$, where R is the ideal gas constant and N_A is the Avogadro constant.

Boyle's law The pressure exerted by a fixed mass of gas is inversely proportional to its volume, provided the temperature of the gas remains constant.

braking radiation X-rays produced when electrons are decelerated (also called Bremsstrahlung radiation).

capacitance The ratio of charge stored by a capacitor to the potential difference across it.

carrier wave A waveform (usually sinusoidal) which is modulated by an input signal to carry information.

centre of gravity The point where the entire weight of an object appears to act.

centripetal force The resultant force acting on an object moving in a circle; it is always directed towards the centre of the circle.

characteristic radiation Very intense X-rays produced in an X-ray tube, having specific wavelengths that depend on the target metal.

charge carrier Any charged particle, such as an electron, responsible for a current.

Charles's law The volume occupied by a gas at constant pressure is directly proportional to its thermodynamic (absolute) temperature.

closed system A system of interacting objects in which there are no external forces.

coaxial cable An electrical cable with an inner conductor surrounded by a tubular insulating layer and an outside conducting layer.

coherent Two sources are coherent when they emit waves with a constant phase difference.

collimated beam A parallel-sided beam of radiation.

components (of a vector) The magnitudes of a vector quantity in two perpendicular directions.

compression A region in a sound wave where the air pressure is greater than its mean value.

compressive Describes a force that squeezes an object.

computerised axial tomography A technique in which X-rays are used to image the human body in order to produce a computerised 3-D image.

conduction band A range of electron energies in a solid; electrons in the conduction band are free to move throughout the material.

conservation of momentum In a closed system, when bodies interact, the total momentum in any specified direction remains constant.

constructive interference When two waves reinforce to give increased amplitude.

contact force The force an object exerts on another with which it is in contact.

contrast In a high-contrast image, there is a big difference in brightness between bright and dark areas.

contrast media Materials such as barium that easily absorb X-rays. A contrast medium is used to reveal the outlines or edges of soft tissues in an X-ray image.

coulomb The SI unit of electrical charge (abbreviated C). A charge of 1 C passes a point when a current of 1 A flows for 1 s. 1 C = 1 A s.

Coulomb's law Any two point charges exert an electrical force on each other that is proportional to the product of their charges and inversely proportional to the square of the distance between them.

count rate The number of particles (beta or alpha) or gamma-ray photons detected per unit time by a Geiger–Müller tube. Count rate is always a fraction of the activity of a sample.

couple A pair of equal and antiparallel forces having a turning effect but no resultant force.

damped Describes an oscillatory motion in which the amplitude decreases with time due to energy losses.

de Broglie wavelength The wavelength associated with a moving particle, given by the equation:

$$\lambda = \frac{h}{mv}$$

decay constant The constant λ for an isotope that appears in the equation $A = -\lambda N$. It is the probability of an individual nucleus decaying per unit time interval.

decibel A logarithmic unit of measurement that expresses the relative sizes of two powers using the formula $10\lg(\frac{P_1}{P_2})$.

density The mass per unit volume of a material:

$$\rho = \frac{m}{V}$$

Unit: $kg\,m^{-3}$.

dependent variable The variable in an experiment with a value that changes as the independent variable is altered by the experimenter.

derived units Units which are combinations of the base units of the SI system.

destructive interference When two waves cancel to give reduced amplitude.

diffraction The spreading of a wave when it passes through a gap or past the edge of an object.

digital signal A signal that has only a few possible values, often only two.

digital-to-analogue conversion (DAC) Conversion of a series of digital numbers into a continuous analogue signal.

dispersion The splitting of light into its different wavelengths.

displacement The distance moved by an object in a particular direction (measured from a fixed starting point).

Doppler effect The change in frequency or wavelength of a wave observed when the source of the wave is moving towards or away from the observer (or the observer is moving relative to the source).

drag A force that resists the movement of a body through a fluid.

drift velocity, mean The average speed of a collection of charged particles when a current flows.

dynamics The study of motion using quantities such as force and mass.

e.m.f. The total work done when unit charge is moved round a complete circuit. Unit: $J\,C^{-1}$ or volt (V).

efficiency The ratio of useful output energy to the total input energy for a device, expressed as a percentage:

$$\text{efficiency} = \frac{\text{useful output energy}}{\text{total input energy}} \times 100\%$$

Einstein relation This refers to the equation for the energy of a photon:

$$E = hf \quad \text{or} \quad E = \frac{hc}{\lambda}$$

elastic limit The value of stress beyond which an object will not return to its original dimensions.

elastic potential energy Energy stored in a stretched or compressed material.

electric charge A property of a body that gives rise to a force on the body when it is within an electric field.

electric field A region in which a charged body experiences a force.

electric field strength The force per unit positive charge at a point. Unit: $V\,m^{-1}$ or $N\,C^{-1}$.

electric potential The energy per unit charge due to a charged body's position in an electric field.

electrical resistance The ratio of potential difference to current. Unit: ohm (Ω).

electrolyte An electrically conducting solution. The conduction is due to positive and negative ions in the solution.

electromagnetic spectrum The family of waves that travel through a vacuum at a speed of $3.00 \times 10^8\,m\,s^{-1}$.

electronvolt The energy gained by an electron travelling through a p.d. of 1 volt. $1\,eV = 1.60 \times 10^{-19}\,J$.

elementary charge The smallest unit of charge that a particle or an object can have. It has a magnitude of $1.60 \times 10^{-19}\,C$.

emission line spectrum A sharp and bright line of a unique wavelength seen in a spectrum.

energy A calculated quantity which is conserved during any change; that which is transferred when a force does work.

energy band A range of permitted electron energies in a solid.

energy level A quantised energy state of an electron in an atom.

equation of state for an ideal gas:

$$pV = nRT \quad \text{or} \quad pV = NkT$$

(Also known as the ideal gas equation.)

equations of motion Four interrelated equations that can be used to determine the displacement, initial velocity, final velocity and acceleration of a body moving with constant acceleration.

equilibrium An object in equilibrium is either at rest or travelling with a constant velocity because the resultant force on it is zero.

errors Inaccuracies when taking measurements.

evaporation The process by which a liquid becomes a gas at a temperature below its boiling point.

exponential decay Describes the decrease of a quantity where the rate of decrease is proportional to the value of the quantity.

extension The change in the length of a material from its original length.

farad The unit of capacitance (abbreviated F). $1\,F = 1\,C\,V^{-1}$.

Faraday's law of electromagnetic induction The induced e.m.f. is proportional to the rate of change of magnetic flux linkage.

field lines Lines drawn to represent the strength and direction of a field of force.

field of force A region of space where an object feels a force; the force may be gravitational, electric, magnetic, etc.

First law of thermodynamics The increase in internal energy of a body is equal to the thermal energy transferred to it by heating plus the mechanical work done on it.

Fleming's left-hand (motor) rule This rule is used to predict the force experienced by a current-carrying conductor placed in an external magnetic field:
thu<u>m</u>b → <u>m</u>otion, <u>f</u>irst finger → magnetic <u>f</u>ield and
se<u>c</u>ond finger → conventional <u>c</u>urrent.

Fleming's right-hand (generator) rule This rule is used to predict the direction of the induced current or e.m.f. in a conductor moved at right angles to a magnetic field: thu<u>m</u>b → <u>m</u>otion, <u>f</u>irst finger → magnetic <u>f</u>ield and se<u>c</u>ond finger → induced conventional <u>c</u>urrent.

forbidden gap A range of energy values which an electron in a solid cannot have.

force constant The ratio of force to extension for a spring or a wire. Unit: $\mathrm{N\,m^{-1}}$.

forced oscillation An oscillation caused by an external driving force; the frequency is determined by the driving force, and is not the natural frequency of the oscillator.

free-body force diagram A diagram showing all the forces acting on an object (but not the forces it exerts on other objects).

free oscillation An oscillation at is the natural frequency of the oscillator.

frequency The number of oscillations per unit time. Unit: hertz (Hz).

frequency modulation A form of modulation in which the signal causes variations in the frequency of a carrier wave.

fundamental frequency The lowest-frequency stationary wave for a particular system.

gain The voltage gain of an amplifier is the ratio of the output voltage to the input voltage.

geostationary orbit The orbit of an artificial satellite which has a period equal to one day so that the satellite remains above the same point on the Earth's equator. From Earth the satellite appears to be stationary.

gravitational field A region where any object with mass experiences a force.

gravitational field strength The gravitational force experienced by an object per unit mass:

$$g=\frac{F}{m}$$

gravitational potential The gravitational potential energy per unit mass at a point in a gravitational field.

gravitational potential energy The energy a body has due to its position in a gravitational field.

ground state The lowest energy state that can be occupied by an electron in an atom.

hadron Any particle which is affected by the strong nuclear force, made from two or three quarks or anti-quarks.

half-life The mean time taken for half the number of active nuclei in a radioactive sample to decay.

half-thickness The mean thickness of an absorbing material required to reduce the intensity of radiation by half.

Hall effect The production of a voltage across a conductor when a current flows through the conductor at right angles to a magnetic field.

Hall voltage The voltage produced across a conductor when a current flows through the conductor at right angles to a magnetic field; used in a Hall probe to measure B since $V_H \propto B$.

harmonic A wave of frequency n times the fundamental frequency, where n is an integer.

Hooke's law The extension produced in an object is proportional to the force producing it.

ideal gas A gas that behaves according to the equation $pV=nRT$ or $pV=NkT$.

ideal gas equation for an ideal gas:

$$pV=nRT \quad \text{or} \quad pV=NkT$$

(Also known as the ideal gas equation.)

image intensifier A device used to change a low-intensity X-ray image into a bright visual image.

impedance matching The reduction in intensity of ultrasound reflected at the boundary between two substances, achieved when the two substances have similar acoustic impedances.

independent variable The variable in an experiment with a value that is altered by the experimenter.

inelastic A collision is inelastic when kinetic energy is not conserved; some is transferred to other forms such as heat. Momentum and total energy are always conserved.

inertia A measure of the mass of an object. A massive object has large inertia.

instantaneous speed The speed of an object measured over a very short period of time.

intensity The power transmitted normally through a surface per unit area:

$$\text{intensity}=\frac{\text{power}}{\text{cross-sectional area}}$$

Unit: $\mathrm{W\,m^{-2}}$.

interference The formation of points of cancellation and reinforcement where two coherent waves pass through each other.

internal energy The sum of the random distribution of kinetic and potential energies of the atoms or molecules in a system.

internal resistance The resistance of an e.m.f. source.
The internal resistance of a battery is due to the chemicals within it.

intrinsic semiconductor A pure substance whose resistivity is intermediate between that of a conductor and an insulator.

inverting amplifier A circuit, involving the use of an amplifier, where the output is 180° out of phase with the input.

ion An atom with a net positive or negative charge.

isotopes Nuclei of the same element with a different number of neutrons but the same number of protons.

***I–V* characteristic** A graph of current against voltage for a particular component of an electrical circuit.

kinematics The study of motion using quantities such as time, distance, displacement, speed, velocity and acceleration.

kinetic energy Energy of an object due to its motion.

kinetic theory of gases A model based on the microscopic motion of atoms or molecules of a gas.

Kirchhoff's first law The sum of the currents entering any point (or junction) in a circuit is equal to the sum of the currents leaving that same point. This law represents the conservation of charge.

Kirchhoff's second law The sum of the e.m.f.s round a closed loop in a circuit is equal to the sum of the p.d.s in that same loop.

Larmor frequency The frequency of precession of a nucleus in an external magnetic field.

Lenz's law An induced current or e.m.f. is in a direction so as to produce effects which oppose the change producing it.

lepton A sub-atomic particle which is not affected by the strong nuclear force.

light-dependent resistor (LDR) A resistor whose resistance decreases as the intensity of light falling on it increases.

light-emitting diode (LED) A semiconductor component that emits light when it conducts electricity.

linear momentum The product of an object's mass and its velocity, $p=mv$. Momentum is a vector quantity.

longitudinal wave A wave in which the particles of the medium oscillate along the direction in which the wave travels.

lost volts The difference between the e.m.f. and the terminal p.d. in a circuit. It is equal to the voltage across the internal resistance.

magnetic field A force field in which a magnet, a wire carrying a current, or a moving charge experiences a force.

magnetic flux The product of magnetic flux density normal to a circuit and the cross-sectional area of the circuit. Unit: weber (Wb).

magnetic flux density The strength of a magnetic field. Magnetic flux density B is defined as:

$$B=\frac{F}{IL}$$

where F is the force experienced by a conductor in the magnetic field, I is the current in the conductor and L is the length of the conductor in the magnetic field. (The conductor is at right angles to the field.)

magnetic flux linkage The product of magnetic flux and the number of turns. Unit: weber (Wb).

magnetic resonance imaging (MRI) A medical imaging technique which uses nuclear magnetic resonance.

mass A measure of the amount of matter within an object. Unit: kilogram (kg).

mass defect The difference between the total mass of the individual, separate nucleons and the mass of the nucleus.

mass excess the difference between the mass of a nuclide (in u) and its mass number.

mean drift velocity The average speed of a collection of charged particles when a current flows.

microwave link A communications system that uses a beam of radio waves in the microwave frequency range to transmit audio, data or video information.

modulation The process of using one waveform to alter the frequency, amplitude or phase of another waveform.

mole The amount of matter which contains 6.02×10^{23} particles.

moment The moment of a force about a point is the magnitude of the force, multiplied by the perpendicular distance of the point from the line of the force. Unit: N m.

monochromatic Describes light of a single frequency.

natural frequency The unforced frequency of oscillation of a freely oscillating object.

negative feedback The output of a system is used to oppose changes to the input of the system, with the result that the changes are reduced.

neutrino A lepton, released during beta-decay.

neutron number The number of neutrons in the nucleus of an atom.

newton The force that will give a 1 kg mass an acceleration of $1\,m\,s^{-2}$ in the direction of the force. $1\,N=1\,kg\,m\,s^{-2}$.

Newton's first law of motion An object will remain at rest or keep travelling at constant velocity unless it is acted on by a resultant force.

Newton's law of gravitation Any two point masses attract each other with a force that is directly proportional to the product of their masses and inversely proportional to the square of their separation.

Newton's second law of motion The resultant force acting on an object is equal to the rate of change of its momentum. The resultant force and the change in momentum are in the same direction.

Newton's third law of motion When two bodies interact, the forces they exert on each other are equal and opposite.

node A point on a stationary wave with zero amplitude.

noise An unwanted random addition to a transmitted signal.

non-inverting amplifier A circuit, involving the use of an amplifier, in which the output is in phase with the input.

nuclear fission The splitting of a nucleus (e.g. $^{235}_{92}U$) into two large fragments and a small number of neutrons.

nuclear fusion A nuclear reaction in which two light nuclei (e.g. $^{2}_{1}H$) join together to form a heavier but more stable nucleus.

nuclear magnetic resonance A process in which radio waves are absorbed or emitted by nuclei spinning in a magnetic field.

nuclear model of the atom A model of the atom in which negative charges (electrons) are distributed outside a tiny nucleus of positive charge.

nucleon number The number of neutrons and protons in the nucleus of an atom (also called mass number).

nucleon A particle found in an atomic nucleus, i.e. a neutron or a proton.

nucleus The tiny central region of the atom that contains most of the mass of the atom and all of its positive charge.

nuclide A specific combination of protons and neutrons in a nucleus.

number density The number of particles, such as free electrons, per unit volume in a material.

Ohm's law The current in a metallic conductor is directly proportional to the potential difference across its ends, provided its temperature remains constant.

operational amplifier (op-amp) A high-gain electronic d.c. voltage amplifier with differential inputs and, usually, a single output.

optic fibre A glass or plastic fibre that carries light along its length.

oscillation A repetitive back-and-forth or up-and-down motion.

parallel Describes components connected side-by-side in a circuit.

path difference The difference in the distances travelled by two waves from coherent sources at a particular point.

perfectly elastic A collision is perfectly elastic when kinetic energy is conserved. Momentum and total energy are always conserved.

period The time taken by an object (e.g. a planet) to complete one cycle (e.g. an orbit). The period is also the time taken for one complete oscillation of a vibrating object. Unit: second (s).

phase Refers to the point that an oscillating mass has reached in a complete cycle.

phase difference The difference in the phases of two oscillating particles, expressed in degrees or radians.

photoelectric effect An interaction between a photon and an electron in an atom, in which the electron is removed from the atom.

photon A particle of electromagnetic radiation.

piezo-electric crystal A material that produces an e.m.f. when it is stressed, causing its shape to change. Also, when a voltage is applied across it in one direction, it changes its dimensions slightly.

piezo-electric effect The production of an e.m.f. between the faces of a crystal when the crystal is compressed.

Planck constant The constant which links the energy of a photon and its frequency, in the equation:

$$E=hf$$

plum-pudding model A model of the atom in which negative charges are distributed throughout a sphere of positive charge.

positron An anti-electron.

potential difference (p.d.) The energy lost per unit charge by charges passing through a component. Unit: $\mathrm{J\,C^{-1}}$ or volt (V).

potential divider A circuit in which two or more components are connected in series to a supply. The output voltage from the circuit is taken across one of the components.

potentiometer A circuit which allows the measurement of an e.m.f. by comparison with a known e.m.f.

power The rate at which energy is transferred or the rate at which work is done. Unit: watt (W).

precession The movement of the axis of a spinning object (proton) around another axis.

precision The smallest change in value that can be measured by an instrument or an operator. A precise measurement is one made several times, giving the same, or very similar, values.

pressure The force acting normally per unit area of a surface:

$$p=\frac{F}{A}$$

Unit: $\mathrm{N\,m^{-2}}$ or pascal (Pa).

principle of conservation of energy The idea that, within a closed system, the total amount of energy in all its forms is unchanged during any change.

principle of moments For an object in equilibrium, the sum of clockwise moments about a point is equal to the sum of anticlockwise moments about the same point.

principle of superposition When two or more waves meet at a point, the resultant displacement is the sum of the displacements of the individual waves.

progressive wave A wave that carries energy from one place to another.

projectile Any object thrown in the Earth's gravitational field.

proton number The number of protons in the nucleus of an atom (also called atomic number).

quarks The fundamental particles of which hadrons are made.

radian A unit for measuring angles. 2π radians $=360°$ or π radians $=180°$.

range The horizontal distance covered by an object.

rarefaction A region in a sound wave where the air pressure is less than its mean value.

rectification The process of converting alternating current (a.c.) into direct current (d.c.).

red shift the change in frequency or wavelength of a spectral line observed when the source of light is moving away from the observer; *see* Doppler effect.

reflection The bouncing back of a wave from a surface.

refraction The change in direction of a wave as it crosses an interface between two materials where its speed changes.

regeneration Restoration of a signal to its original form, usually by removing or reducing noise and increasing signal strength.

relative speed The magnitude of the difference in velocities between two objects.

relaxation time The time taken for a nucleus or other excited system to fall back to a lower energy state.

relay An electrically operated switch, caused to open and close by current in a coil.

repeater An electronic device that receives a signal and retransmits it.

resistivity A property of a material, a measure of its electrical resistance, defined by:

$$\rho=\frac{RA}{L}$$

Unit: $\Omega\,\mathrm{m}$.

resistor An electrical component whose resistance in a circuit remains constant, is independent of current or potential difference.

resonance The forced motion of an oscillator characterised by maximum amplitude when the forcing frequency matches the oscillator's natural frequency. A system absorbs maximum energy from a source when the source frequency is equal to the natural frequency of the system.

rest mass The mass of a an isolated stationary particle.

resultant force The single force that has the same effect as all of the forces acting on an object.

right-hand grip rule A rule for finding the direction of the magnetic field inside a solenoid. If the right hand grips the solenoid with the fingers following the direction of the conventional current around the solenoid, then the thumb points in the direction of the magnetic field.

sampling Taking the value of a continuous signal at regular intervals.

scalar quantity A scalar quantity has magnitude but no direction.

semiconductor diode An electrical component made from a semiconductor material (e.g. silicon) that only conducts in one direction. A diode in 'reverse bias' has an infinite resistance.

sensor A device that produces an output (usually a voltage) in response to an input.

series A term used when components are connected end-to-end in a circuit.

sharpness The degree of resolution in an image, which determines the smallest item that can be identified.

simple harmonic motion Motion of an oscillator in which its acceleration is directly proportional to its displacement from its equilibrium position and is directed towards that position.

solenoid A long current-carrying coil used to generate a uniform magnetic field within its core.

specific heat capacity The energy required per unit mass of a substance to raise its temperature by 1 K (or 1 °C). Unit: $\text{J kg}^{-1}\text{ K}^{-1}$.

specific latent heat of fusion The energy required per unit mass of a substance to change it from solid to liquid without a change in temperature. Unit: J kg^{-1}.

specific latent heat of vaporisation The energy required per unit mass of a substance to change it from liquid to gas without a change in temperature. Unit: J kg^{-1}.

speed The rate of change of the distance moved by an object:

$$\text{speed} = \frac{\text{distance}}{\text{time}}$$

Unit: m s^{-1}.

spin A fundamental property of subatomic particles which is conserved during atomic and nuclear reactions.

stationary wave A wave pattern produced when two progressive waves of the same frequency travelling in opposite directions combine. It is characterised by nodes and antinodes. Also known as a standing wave.

strain The extension per unit length produced by tensile or compressive forces:

$$\text{strain} = \frac{\text{extension}}{\text{original length}}$$

strain energy The potential energy stored in an object when it is deformed elastically.

strain gauge A device that contains a fine wire sealed in plastic. Its electrical resistance changes when the object to which it is attached changes shape.

stress The force acting per unit cross-sectional area:

$$\text{stress} = \frac{\text{force}}{\text{cross-sectional area}}$$

strong nuclear force A fundamental force which acts between hadrons.

systematic error An error in readings which is repeated throughout an experiment, producing a constant absolute error or a constant percentage error.

tensile Associated with tension or pulling, e.g. a tensile force.

terminal p.d. The potential difference across an external resistor connected to an e.m.f. source.

terminal velocity The maximum velocity of an object travelling through a fluid. The resultant force on the object is zero.

tesla The SI unit of magnetic flux density (abbreviated T). $1\text{ T} = 1\text{ N A}^{-1}\text{ m}^{-1}$.

thermal energy Energy transferred from one object to another because of a temperature difference; another term for heat energy.

thermal equilibrium A condition when two or more objects in contact have the same temperature so that there is no net flow of energy between them.

thermistor A device whose electrical resistance changes when its temperature changes.

thermocouple A device consisting of wires of two different metals across which an e.m.f. is produced when the two junctions of the wires are at different temperatures.

thermodynamic scale A temperature scale in which temperature is measured in kelvin (K).

threshold frequency The minimum frequency of electromagnetic radiation that will eject electrons from the surface of a metal.

threshold voltage The minimum forward bias voltage across a light-emitting diode (LED) when it starts to conduct and emit light.

time constant The time taken for the current, stored charge or p.d. to fall to 1/e (about 37%) of its original value when a capacitor discharges through a resistor. It is also equal to the product of capacitance and resistance.

torque of a couple The product of one of the forces of a couple and the perpendicular distance between them.
Unit: N m.

tracers Radioactive substances used to investigate the function of organs of the body.

transducer A general term used for any device that changes one form of energy into another.

transition When an electron makes a 'jump' between two energy levels.

transverse wave A wave in which the particles of the medium oscillate at right angles to the direction in which the wave travels.

triangle of forces A closed triangle drawn for an object in equilibrium. The sides of the triangle represent the forces in both magnitude and direction.

turns-ratio equation An equation relating the ratio of voltages to the ratio of numbers of turns on the two coils of a transformer:

$$\frac{V_s}{V_p} = \frac{N_s}{N_p}$$

unified atomic mass unit A convenient unit used for the mass of atomic and nuclear particles (1 u is equal to the mass of a ${}^{12}_{6}\text{C}$ carbon atom).

$1\text{ u} = 1.66 \times 10^{-27}\text{ kg}$

uniform acceleration Acceleration that remains constant.

uniform motion Motion of an object travelling with a constant velocity.

upthrust The upward force that a liquid exerts on a body floating or immersed in a liquid.

valence band a range of electron energies in a solid; electrons in the valence band are bound to individual atoms.

vector addition Using a drawing, often to scale, to find the resultant of two or more vectors.

vector quantity A quantity which has both magnitude and direction.

vector triangle A triangle drawn to determine the resultant of two vectors.

velocity The rate of change of the displacement of an object:

$$\text{velocity} = \frac{\text{change in displacement}}{\text{time taken}}$$

Unit: m s^{-1}.

You can think of velocity as 'speed in a certain direction'.

virtual earth approximation An approximation in which the two inputs of an op-amp are nearly at the same potential.

viscous forces Forces that act on a body moving through a fluid that are caused by the resistance of the fluid.

voxel A small cube in a three-dimensional image, the equivalent of a pixel in a two-dimensional image.

wave A periodic disturbance travelling through space, characterised by a vibrating medium.

wavelength The distance between two adjacent peaks or troughs in a wave.

weak nuclear force A fundamental force, involved in radioactive β-decay.

weight The force on an object caused by a gravitational field acting on its mass:

$$\text{weight} = \text{mass} \times \text{acceleration of free fall}$$

Unit: newton (N).

wire-pair A type of electrical wiring in which the two conductors needed to carry a signal are placed close together.

work done The product of the force and the distance moved in the direction of the force.

work function The minimum energy required by a single electron to escape a metal surface.

X-ray tube A device that produces X-rays when accelerated electrons hit a target metal.

Young modulus The ratio of stress to strain for a given material, resulting from tensile forces, provided Hooke's law is obeyed:

$$\text{Young modulus} = \frac{\text{stress}}{\text{strain}}$$

Unit: pascal (Pa; or MPa, GPa).

zero error A systematic error in an instrument that gives a non-zero reading when the true value of a quantity is zero.

This is a legal agreement between 'You' (which for individual purchasers means the individual customer and, for network purchasers, means the Educational Institution and its authorised users) and Cambridge University Press ('the Licensor') for Cambridge International AS and A Level Physics Workbook with CD-ROM. By placing this CD in the CD-ROM drive of your computer You agree to the terms of this licence.

1. Limited licence

(a) You are purchasing only the right to use the CD-ROM and are acquiring no rights, express or implied to it or to the software ('Software' being the CD-ROM software, as installed on your computer terminals or server), other than those rights granted in this limited licence for not-for-profit educational use only.
(b) Cambridge University Press grants the customer the licence to use one copy of this CD-ROM either (i) on a single computer for use by one or more people at different times, or (ii) by a single person on one or more computers (provided the CD-ROM is only used on one computer at any one time and is only used by the customer), but not both.
(c) You shall not: (i) copy or authorise copying of the CD-ROM, (ii) translate the CD-ROM, (iii) reverse-engineer, alter, adapt, disassemble or decompile the CD-ROM, (iv) transfer, sell, lease, lend, profit from, assign or otherwise convey all or any portion of the CD-ROM or (v) operate the CD-ROM from a mainframe system, except as provided in these terms and conditions.

2. Copyright

(a) All original content is provided as part of the CD-ROM (including text, images and ancillary material) and is the copyright of, or licensed by a third party to, the Licensor, protected by copyright and all other applicable intellectual property laws and international treaties.
(b) You may not copy the CD-ROM except for making one copy of the CD-ROM solely for backup or archival purposes. You may not alter, remove or destroy any copyright notice or other material placed on or with this CD-ROM.
(c) The CD-ROM contains Adobe® Flash® Player.
Adobe® Flash® Player Copyright © 1996–2010 Adobe Systems Incorporated. All Rights Reserved.
Protected by U.S. Patent 6,879,327; Patents Pending in the United States and other countries. Adobe and Flash are either trademarks or registered trademarks in the United States and/or other countries.

3. Liability and Indemnification

(a) The CD-ROM is supplied 'as-is' with no express guarantee as to its suitability. To the extent permitted by applicable law, the Licensor is not liable for costs of procurement of substitute products, damages or losses of any kind whatsoever resulting from the use of this product, or errors or faults in the CD-ROM, and in every case the Licensor's liability shall be limited to the suggested list price or the amount actually paid by You for the product, whichever is lower.
(b) You accept that the Licensor is not responsible for the persistency, accuracy or availability of any urls of external or third party internet websites referred to on the CD-ROM and does not guarantee that any content on such websites is, or will remain, accurate, appropriate or available. The Licensor shall not be liable for any content made available from any websites and urls outside the Software.
(c) Where, through use of the CD-ROM and content you infringe the copyright of the Licensor you undertake to indemnify and keep indemnified the Licensor from and against any loss, cost, damage or expense (including without limitation damages paid to a third party and any reasonable legal costs) incurred by the Licensor as a result of such infringement.

4. Termination

Without prejudice to any other rights, the Licensor may terminate this licence if You fail to comply with the terms and conditions of the licence. In such event, You must destroy all copies of the CD-ROM.

5. Governing law

This agreement is governed by the laws of England, without regard to its conflict of laws provision, and each party irrevocably submits to the exclusive jurisdiction of the English courts.